Garden Perennials for the Coastal South

W9-DDJ-721

Garden Perennials for the Coastal South

BARBARA J. SULLIVAN

The University of North Carolina Press

Chapel Hill and London

© 2003

The University of North Carolina Press

All rights reserved

Design by Richard Hendel and
Eric M. Brooks

Set in Minion, Meta, and Bickham types
by Eric M. Brooks

Manufactured in China

The paper in this book meets the guidelines for
permanence and durability of the Committee on
Production Guidelines for Book Longevity of the
Council on Library Resources.

Frontispiece: one of the evergreen glorybowers,
*Clerodendrum thomsoniae; plate opposite table of
contents:* the canna lily Canna 'Bengal Tiger' with
wine sage (*Salvia vanhouttii*). All photographs by
Barbara J. Sullivan.

Library of Congress
Cataloging-in-Publication Data

Sullivan, Barbara J.

Garden perennials for the coastal South /
by Barbara J. Sullivan.

p. cm.

ISBN 0-8078-2795-9 (cloth: alk. paper) —
ISBN 0-8078-5473-5 (pbk.: alk. paper)

1. Perennials — Southern States. 2. Perennials —
Atlantic Coast (U.S.) 3. Perennials — Gulf Coast
(U.S.) I. Title.

SB34 .S86   2003

635.9'32'0975 — dc21   2002155089

cloth   07 06 05 04 03   5 4 3 2 1
paper   07 06 05 04 03   5 4 3 2 1

To the memory of my mother,

JANET SULLIVAN, *who made*

gardening look easy, and to the

memory of my father,

BOB SULLIVAN, *who taught me*

all I know about mowing the lawn.

Contents

Preface

A few years ago I drove from my home in Wilmington, North Carolina, to attend a garden seminar in Charleston, South Carolina, the venerable home of many famous gardens and gardeners and a city with a climate not too dissimilar from Wilmington's. Some of the most preeminent plant experts and garden writers of this country and Great Britain spoke to an appreciative audience. They showed mouthwatering slides of gardens from Dublin, Ireland, to Denver, Colorado. It was truly a feast. But on the drive home I realized that although many of the plants they featured would survive in Wilmington and Charleston, just as many would die miserable, unlovely deaths in our part of the world. Plants are treacherous the way some people are. They lure you with promises of ease and beauty and a possible grab at paradise and then leave you overnight, with just a bare spot to remind you of what might have been.

That was when I decided to sit down and write about the beauties that would survive in our climate—from Tidewater Virginia to Jacksonville, Florida, and from the Florida panhandle to Houston, Texas. I wanted to write about perennials we can show off to the rest of the world; the plants that can help us create the dream gardens we want in the reality of the Southern Atlantic and Gulf Coast environments.

Whether you're new to gardening or have been at it for years, you've probably formed ideas about the gardens you like and don't like, based on your own personal taste. There are people who find drama and beauty in the stark outline of cactus and yucca against the desert sky, and there are those who want the lush, overflowing look of an English cottage garden. There are infinite variations between these two ends of the spectrum, including the natural, almost wild look. If you live and garden in the southern coastal region of the United States, however, you're not going to be blessed with the cool summers of the Cotswolds or challenged by the arid, nearly constant drought conditions of New Mexico. Regardless of whether you prefer the look of clipped boxwood hedges or a tropical panorama, to have a successful garden, you have to know what plants will survive and, better yet, thrive in our area. We have an enormous palette of perennials to choose from to create a variety of effects in the garden. And even the most low-maintenance or formal garden can use perennials to transform it from ho-hum to outstanding.

There should be something in this book for just about every taste and for every kind of garden your imagination can devise. I hope you will discover both new plants and tried-and-true friends from which you can create the garden of your dreams. Happy gardening!

B.J.S.

Acknowledgments

Writing this book has been an education. There is a lot of botanical information available, some of it contradictory. And then there are the personal experiences of real gardeners who often know more about plants than is contained in a reference book. To see for myself what gardening conditions are like along the Southern Atlantic and Gulf Coasts, I traveled from Tidewater Virginia down through North Carolina, South Carolina, Georgia, Florida, Alabama, Mississippi, Louisiana, and Texas. I would like to extend my thanks to the following people who gave me encouragement, hospitality, and invaluable information all along the route:

In Gloucester, Virginia—Brent and Becky Heath, George McLellan, and Cam Williams

In Seaford, Virginia—Pamela Harper

In Wilmington, North Carolina—Barbara Johansen, Jane Farley, Meg Shelton, Frank Galloway, and Jim Lanier

In Myrtle Beach, South Carolina—Chris Todd, Jeff Wolverton, and Nan Wicker

In Charleston, South Carolina—Caroline Madsen, Alan Romanczuk, Peggy Wingard, and Mary Martha Blalock

In Savannah, Georgia—Celia Dunn, Catherine Webster, Ashby Angell, Porter Carswell, Ed Poenicke, Linda Pou, Kathleen Fields, and Jeff Fulton

In Jacksonville, Florida—Mrs. William (Bobbie) Arnold

In Atlantic Beach, Florida—Shep and Maryann Bryan

In Seagrove, Florida—Randy Harelson

In Semmes, Alabama—Thayer Dodd

In Picayune, Mississippi—Bob Brzuszek

In New Orleans, Louisiana—Catherine and Peter Freeman, Ann Donnelly, and Mrs. Lawrence (Judy) Freeman

In Baton Rouge, Louisiana—Peggy Cox

In Lake Charles, Louisiana—David Lanier

In Humble, Texas—Linda Gay

In Houston, Texas—George and Cindy Craft

In Galveston, Texas—Gary Outenreath

(Although I didn't visit Jackson, Mississippi, I thank Felder Rushing there for steering me on the right path on my Gulf Coast excursion.)

I would also like to extend appreciation to my editors, Elaine Maisner and Kathy Malin, and all the hard-working professionals at the University of North Carolina Press at Chapel Hill for making this book possible.

And finally for moral support, love, and encouragement, I thank my husband Michael, my children Rachel and Charles, and the rest of my family and friends.

Garden Perennials

for the

Coastal South

Introduction *Garden Where You're Planted*

The cliché has it that people want what they can't have. This is true in gardening as in life. What Vermont gardener wouldn't be thrilled to wander out in his bathrobe one fine spring morning to discover that an 'Apple Blossom' amaryllis had survived single-digit temperatures and returned to present its rich cream-and-pink striped trumpets for his inspection?

On the other hand, the jaded Savannah gardener might very well take for granted an entire colony of perfectly turned out amaryllis and instead lust after the heady scent of lilacs by the kitchen door. Those whose winters are too warm for peonies have palm trees. Those whose summers are too hot for delphiniums have Cape plumbago. But, generally speaking, you can't have it both ways. There's a saying, "Grow where you're planted." Roughly translated into garden terms, it's still good advice. Grow what does best wherever you happen to garden.

The gardening world is coming to see more than ever before that people need to plant according to where they live. This saves money, time, effort, water, and disappointment. Plants that are suited to the local area will need less care to survive and multiply and will prove more rewarding in the long run than finicky outsiders. In the case of the coastal South the choice of perennials, shrubs, and trees is very large indeed. From stately magnolias, winter-blooming camellias, and heat-loving crape myrtles and oleanders to the workhorses of the perennial garden, like the sages, hibiscus, and various subtropicals, we can

Spanish bayonet (Yucca filamentosa) is one of the plants best adapted to the coastal South.

create our own brand of garden with a particular coastal southern flavor. In place of the delicate wands of blue flax, we can grow the charming purple bells of Mexican petunia. Instead of the dramatic crimson and black of oriental poppies, we can enliven the spring garden with stunning poppy anemones. All that's needed is to understand the particular climatic conditions we are dealing with and to work with them.

Just how and why is the coastal South different from, say, Connecticut? Or its southern mountain neighbors further inland? Or California and Arizona, which also have plenty of heat in the summer? We're different from New England because our ground doesn't freeze and we don't have extended periods of extreme cold that affect plant viability. Some plants, such as peonies, lilacs, and many of the spring-blooming bulbs, require a good, cold winter to stimulate flower production. We're unlike the southern mountain areas of the Great Smokies and the Blue Ridge because our summer nights don't provide the cool resting period many plants need to repair and regenerate. Cool nights are when many plants use the food they've produced during the day to put on new growth. Plants such as English primrose and monkshood, which prefer cool, dappled shade, cannot survive without this nighttime cooling-off period.

Our intense summer humidity distinguishes us from the hot, dry areas of the country such as the Southwest, where plants that require low ground moisture and dry air have staked out their territory. Winter rains, although fairly evenly distributed in our area, can be a problem unless we take precautions. Soggy ground means death for plants such as bearded iris, lavender, and a host of bulbs that require perfect drainage in order to survive.

One other factor that makes gardening in the coastal South a somewhat tricky proposition is the changeability of our weather. We never know if we will have a mild winter, a cold winter, rain or drought. As a result, routine garden chores like fertilizing and cutting back become a toss of the dice. From one year to the next the same garden may experience weather more typical of climates much farther south or, conversely, much farther north. For example, New Orleans may be frost-free three out of five years, but can't count on this the other two. So it is not a truly tropical climate.

Basically, to do well in the coastal South, a plant must be able to withstand punishing summer heat with no promise of a nighttime recovery period, must be able to tolerate a sudden hard freeze, and must stave off the constant threat of fungal disease encouraged by high humidity. The plant must have no need of a sustained winter freeze and must be able to withstand the occasional summer drought and frequent winter saturation. If you think about it, the plants we grow deserve a lot of respect.

One way of finding plants that are suited to the local area is by relying on the revised zone classification map produced by the United States Department of Agriculture (USDA). This map is based on a cold-hardiness paradigm. The assumption is that gardeners need to know whether a particular plant can sur-

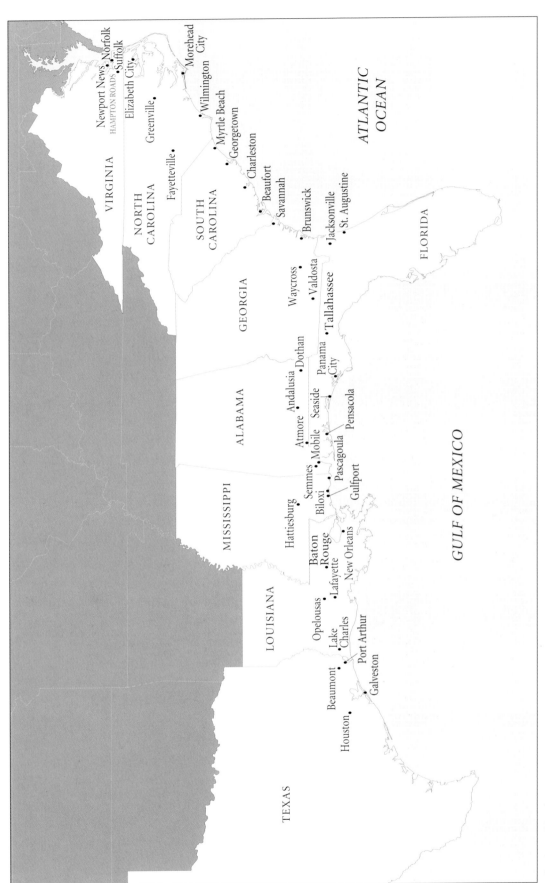

Newport News
HAMPTON ROADS
Norfolk
Suffolk
Elizabeth City
Morehead City
Wilmington
Greenville
Myrtle Beach
Georgetown
Fayetteville
Charleston
Beaufort
Savannah
Brunswick
Jacksonville
St. Augustine
Waycross
Valdosta
Tallahassee
Dothan
Andalusia
Panama City
Seaside
Atmore
Mobile
Pensacola
Semmes
Biloxi
Pascagoula
Gulfport
Hattiesburg
Baton Rouge
New Orleans
Lafayette
Opelousas
Lake Charles
Port Arthur
Beaumont
Galveston
Houston

VIRGINIA
NORTH CAROLINA
SOUTH CAROLINA
GEORGIA
ALABAMA
MISSISSIPPI
LOUISIANA
TEXAS
FLORIDA

ATLANTIC OCEAN
GULF OF MEXICO

The Coastal South

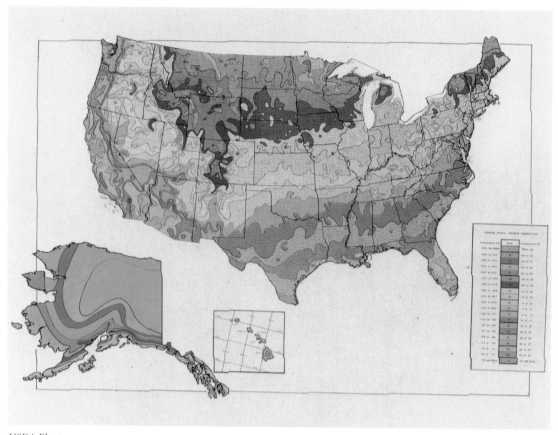

USDA Plant Hardiness Zone Map. Photo courtesy Agricultural Research Service, USDA.

vive winter in a particular location. Under this classification system, most of the coastal South falls into Zones 7b through 10—that is, the average annual minimum winter temperature falls between 5 and 30 degrees Fahrenheit. These are averages figured over a period of years on a historical basis. For example, based on these average minimum winter temperatures, much of coastal North Carolina is classified Zone 8, as is much of coastal Oregon. However, growing conditions in these two locations are not truly comparable, which is the inherent limitation in the USDA zone classification system.

Most plants available from catalogs and nurseries are able to survive well to the north of USDA cold-hardiness Zone 7b—often as far north as Zones 3 and 4. This would lead the unsuspecting gardener to believe that all of those plants could be easily and successfully grown in the coastal South. Not so!

Cold winter temperatures are not usually the real problem for gardeners along the Gulf and Southern Atlantic coasts. Every few years the temperature may plummet, but usually not for more than a few days in a row. Schools close down at the first snow flurry because snow is such a rare commodity. This is not to say that oleanders, camellias, and the subtropical perennials don't suffer from the cold. And it's not to say that they won't succumb totally if the winter is particularly nasty.

The danger is that a warm spell may be followed suddenly by a drastic drop in temperature, in which the plants don't have enough warning to shut down.

This happened in December 1989, when gardeners all along the Gulf and Southern Atlantic coasts lost such otherwise reliable shrubs and trees as camellias, sasanquas, loquats, and eucalyptus. The sap was still up and many of the herbaceous perennials hadn't died down yet. On the other hand, in December of 1983 some areas along the coast experienced three days of abnormally cold (12 degree) weather, which didn't do much damage because plants had had time to harden off and the cold spell wasn't prolonged. Although winter wetness kills things on a regular basis, severe cold, by and large, is not a frequent killer in our area.

Summer is a different story altogether. It's not unusual for us to have temperatures of 90 degrees or above for two to three weeks at a time. Taken together with 75 to 80 percent humidity, plants are experiencing the same 105 degree heat index that we are. This also produces a higher soil temperature than in areas with more moderate climates. Because nighttime temperatures remain high, the soil doesn't have a chance to cool down, and it is the soil temperature that will ultimately affect the plant's viability. Trees, shrubs, and perennials planted out optimistically in April can easily turn to burnt sticks by September if not kept well watered and mulched. And in some cases even watering and mulching won't help. Delphiniums, lady's mantle, baby's breath, and peach-leaved campanula — the darlings of the New England garden — may well gasp their way to summer's end like so many tattered refugees, if they survive at all.

In recognition of the need to give equal time to heat in the garden, the American Horticultural Society (AHS) has developed a heat-tolerance map for the United States. This long overdue effort is a welcome addition to the southern gardening arsenal. Whether the AHS map is entirely accurate is open to debate. Some of the writing that attempts to reclassify perennials by heat zone currently errs on the side of understatement. The heat zone concept has not given enough consideration to the impact of elevated nighttime temperatures. Until they have been adjusted and reality-tested somewhat further, it might be wise to view the AHS heat zone ratings on plants as being overly optimistic for our region.

What we need now is for all growers, nurseries, and catalogs to begin to classify plants as accurately as possible by their heat tolerance as well as their cold tolerance, so that gardeners can make more informed decisions before they invest their money. One day it will be just as unthinkable for a gardener in Galveston, Texas, to send away for a dozen peonies as for someone in Montreal to try to grow date palms in her front yard.

Most of this book is written from the perspective of a Zone 7b, 8, or 9 gardener. One way to choose plants that are most likely to do well in your garden is to figure out which zone you're living in and then select plants that are cold tolerant one zone farther north and heat tolerant one zone farther South. This is the most cautious, conservative approach to planting, but one that will avoid the most disappointment in the long run. So, if you're gardening in Zone 8,

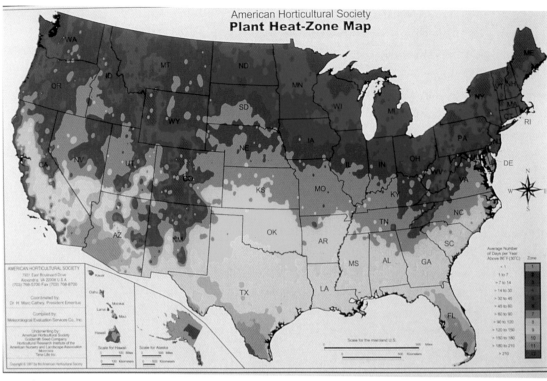

American Horticultural Society
Plant Heat-Zone Map

AHS Plant
Heat-Zone Map

you would look for plants that are cold tolerant to Zone 7 or higher and heat tolerant to Zone 9 or lower. It seems that plants that are rated within a fairly narrow range of tolerance, such as Zones 6–9 (for example, *Aster carolinianus*) or Zones 7–10 (*Ruellia brittoniana*), are the ones most perfectly adapted to our conditions. This is not to say that we have to limit ourselves to those plants, but we may want to rely heavily on them for dependability and performance. The experimenting and "pushing the limits" can then be done with other plants.

In many parts of the country, gardeners are in the habit of closing up shop in the fall with the traditional raking of leaves and planting out of tulip and daffodil bulbs. Fall and winter are the time when most people give gardening a rest and retire inside to sit by the fire and pore over plant catalogs. Sometime in early spring, when warmer days and forsythia call them outside to start the cycle over again, they relocate their gardening gloves and get back to work.

Hibernation is not only unnecessary in the coastal South; it's a missed opportunity. For those of a less than robust nature, in fact, aestivation might be a wiser alternative. Summer along the southern coasts is like winter in the Maine woods, a time of severe, stressful weather for plants and people alike. The times of most people-friendly weather are also the times of most plant-friendly weather, and they are the best time to be outside gardening.

Fall, after the last heat of September has dissipated, is the perfect time for planting, dividing, and transplanting most perennials. This gives them two full months (October and November) to grow lustily before hardening off for winter. Plants established in the fall will have several months of cool, moderate weather with a natural complement of rainfall before they're challenged by the heat and humidity of high summer. They benefit from the seven- or eight-month stretch of favorable conditions to lay down a good root system, which helps them survive their first summer. Fall temperatures and breezes make working in the garden at this time of year pure pleasure. It is, in effect, a second spring for us. It is much better than the near-heatstroke conditions of July and August when, in many people's opinion, only early morning and late afternoon gardening are truly enjoyable.

There are so many mild, pleasant days in winter that there's no reason not to continue gardening right on through. With careful planning you can easily have cool-weather annuals, herbs, ferns, groundcovers, bulbs, vines, shrubs, and even vegetables giving you fragrance and the beauty of foliage and bloom throughout the winter. In our area, winter is one of the most peaceful and potentially renewing times in the garden. Like everything else about gardening in the coastal South, it takes some getting used to and some flexibility, but it rewards us with pleasures our northern neighbors may well envy.

A glorious fall landscape of purple Mexican bush sage (Salvia leucantha) and yellow senna (Cassia alata) with sabal palmettos (Sabal minor) for a backdrop.

HOW TO USE THIS BOOK

This book is intended to be an easy reference source. Chapter 1, "The Seasons," tells what grows and blooms at different times of the year in our area. In this way you can "meet" each of the perennials in its peak season.

Chapter 2, "The Best and Worst Plants for Coastal Gardens," contains a list of the most reliable, fail-safe perennials for the coastal South and, perhaps even more importantly, lists the plants to avoid when gardening in our area.

Chapter 3, "The Types of Gardens," contains charts that classify plants by growing conditions and by category (such as shade plants, bulbs, groundcovers, etc.), which will help guide your selection of what to plant where.

Chapter 4, "The Companion Plants," lists plants that combine well with the recommended perennials.

Chapter 5, "Practical Gardening Tips," constitutes the how-to portion of the book, providing some basic gardening guidelines.

And finally, the "A–Z Plant Guide" allows you to look up cultural requirements, growing habit, and other specifics for all of the perennials recommended here. Hundreds of additional cultivars not mentioned in the main text are described there as well, so it is worth browsing through to learn more about the plants that do well for us. The guide contains information about perennials, vines, bulbs, herbs, hardy palms, groundcovers, and ornamental grasses. For convenience, it also includes a few of the more outstanding annuals and a handful of the best-known flowering shrubs, such as camellias, azaleas, oleanders, and crape myrtles. However, due to the specific focus of this book on perennials and because of space limitations, some of the trees, landscape shrubs, annuals, and vegetables that are mentioned in the narrative portions of the book are not included in the guide.

The book concludes with lists of recommended reading and Internet resources for information about specific plant species and for ordering plants and gardening supplies.

CHAPTER 1
The Seasons

In winter the bones of the garden will show. Here the arching fronds of a sago palm
(Cycas revoluta) are highlighted by a rare blanket of snow.

Winter The Gardener's Secret Pleasures

You may be one of those people who love winter in the garden. Instead of sitting inside and reading about plants, you may wander out and cut camellia blossoms to float in a bowl. You may revel in the intense fragrance of winter daphne. Maybe you keep a disreputable-looking old parka, a woolen hat, and a pair of heavy work gloves by the back door just in case the mood strikes. The secret here is that puttering in the garden is not only possible all winter long; it can be a source of quiet, peaceful pleasure.

The garden in winter is made up of a mixture of evergreen and deciduous shrubs, ferns, herbs, vegetables, bulbs, perennials, and annuals. It won't be the lush, visually stimulating production that a midsummer garden is, but it can be an oasis of beauty on a different scale and with different values.

It requires first and foremost neatening, trimming, and mulching, so that weeds and decaying plant material don't detract from the more subtle design of the minimalist winterscape. Paths, garden beds, and lawn should all be cleaned up and edged, so the winter garden can show through. The British have used the concept of dirt mulch to great effect for generations. And the African tradition of the swept dirt courtyard has the same spare grace. There's something to be said for a bed of neatly raked dirt in which each individual plant is seen to advantage—especially in winter. And winter mulch in the form of bark, pine straw, or other organic material will be the soil of summers to come.

There are a number of ways of creating winter pictures. Large rivers of gold or gray groundcover can offset the silhouettes of deciduous shrubs or small trees and will provide a beautiful backdrop for winter-blooming bulbs. Squared-off plots of salad greens, cabbages, or chard can be combined into tapestries of color and texture. Even a simple pair of cement containers overflowing with tangerine and copper-colored pansies will bring an otherwise drab scene alive. Often winter plants are the last ones we pay attention to because we're so used to focusing our efforts on spring and summer. With some planning, however, a garden can work in all seasons.

Ornamental cabbages add beauty to the winter garden.

TREES AND SHRUBS

The bones of a garden will show in winter. This is when evergreen trees and shrubs such as magnolias, camellias, azaleas, Indian hawthorns, viburnums, hollies, loropetalums, mahonias, and fatsias, among others, provide the all-

There are over 3,000 cultivars of winter-blooming camellia (Camellia japonica). Camellias prefer dappled shade and rich, acidic soil.

important context for the rest of the garden. Each of these gives year-round value for the investment. Probably the most beautiful and classic winter-blooming shrub for the coastal South is the *Camellia japonica*, which produces colorful peony-like or rose-like blossoms for weeks at a time. There are thousands of named cultivars, some blooming as early as November and some continuing on until May. A good place to start to learn about the history and variety of these beautiful shrubs is through your local camellia society.

Another excellent shrub for winter color, *Mahonia* x *media* 'Winter Sun', produces showy yellow flower panicles from November through January. The dark plum-colored leaves of loropetalum (*Loropetalum chinense* 'Rubrum') are often offset by shocking-pink flower tassels in winter. The deciduous holly *Ilex* 'Sparkleberry' will give you plentiful clusters of red berries for months in winter. *Ilex verticillata* 'Scarlet O'Hara', with its male pollinator (guess who?), is an especially outstanding holly for rich, red winter berries.

On a less showy scale, there are a number of viburnums (*Viburnum* spp.) that produce masses of attractive flat white or pink flower umbels in late winter and early spring when flowers of any sort are truly appreciated. Lauristinus (*V. tinus*) is especially reliable, with tight, pink flower clusters opening white. Several cultivars of Lauristinus have been developed, including 'Variegatum' with creamy-yellow-margined leaves. The deciduous, shrubby viburnum *V. grandiflorum* produces clusters of pink-flushed white flowers on bare stems all winter long. If you can't have snow in winter, plant *V. grandiflorum* 'Snow White' for its white flower clusters emerging from dark pink buds.

One evergreen winter bloomer, which is particularly known for its remarkable scent, is winter daphne (*Daphne odora*). Unlike the camellias, hollies, and viburnums, daphne has a reputation for being difficult. It needs perfect drainage, not too much sun or shade, and even in the best of conditions it may drop dead for no apparent reason. This presents the kind of perverse challenge gardeners leap at.

Equally stunning to those who appreciate nature's eclecticism are the dramatic pale green candelabra of the fatsia fruit (*Fatsia japonica*), which stand out beautifully against its large, tropical-looking, dark green glossy leaves for several months beginning in late fall and continue throughout the winter.

*The evergreen fatsia shrub (*Fatsia japonica*) adds great architecture to the garden year-round. In fall and winter it sends up dramatic flowers.*

Other eye-catching and persistent winter fruits include the bright orange hips of rugosa roses (*Rosa rugosa*) and the red-orange fruits of firethorn (*Pyracantha coccinea*). If you have room for it, grow the eight-foot-tall, arching winter honeysuckle shrub, *Lonicera fragrantissima*, and let it perfume the air all winter with the scent of its many, tiny whitish-pink blossoms.

The smaller, more compact *L. nitida* 'Baggensen's Gold' provides golden-colored foliage, a valuable addition to the spare winter garden. Along the same lines is the brightly variegated *Euonymus fortuneii* 'Emerald 'n' Gold', which will stand out brightly at the feet of evergreen shrubs. And the classic gold dust plant (*Aucuba japonica* 'Variegata') will light up even the shadiest, driest corner with its yellow-splotched, glossy evergreen leaves.

Certain outlines can be especially striking in the winter garden when everything else has died back. Palm fronds and the dried blades and plumes of decorative grasses add drama to temporarily depopulated spaces. The variegated Spanish bayonet (*Yucca filimentosa* 'Golden Sword') shows off its creamy, sword-like leaves to advantage at this time of year. An espaliered ivy or camellia against a white stucco wall, a strategically placed topiaried shrub, or the peeling bark of a river birch may become the star players now that the competition is dormant.

SHADE-LOVING WINTER BEAUTIES

When things clear out in December, we come to appreciate those perennials and their companion plants that have been looking good all year but have gone unnoticed against the more colorful summer and fall plants. These include the large, glossy-leaved holly fern (*Cyrtomium falcatum*), the finely incised autumn fern (*Dryopteris erythrosora*), and the various fir-textured club mosses (*Selaginella* spp.), each of which provides an important evergreen anchor to otherwise unstructured bare patches and an excellent accompaniment for winter bulbs. That old Victorian standby, the cast-iron plant (*Aspidistra elatior*), retains its arching foliage year-round, as does the yellow-spotted gold dust plant (*Aucuba japonica* 'Variegata').

Winter is also when the Lenten roses (*Helleborus orientalis*) are at their best. In the shady woodland garden their subtle greenish-white or plum-colored bells hang demurely above and underneath handsomely lobed evergreen foliage just waiting for someone to come and take a peek at their maroon-freckled interiors.

Another treasure is the Italian arum (*Arum italicum*), which sends up its narrow, arrowhead-shaped leaves just in time to take over from where the

*Possibly the most elegant perennial in the winter garden is the Lenten rose (*Helleborus orientalis*) with its subtly colored flowers and lovely foliage.*

hostas have died back and gives us handsome dark green foliage all winter. It, in turn, loses its leaves during the hot months when the hostas resume the point-counterpoint pattern.

WINTER VINES

When the winters are mild, we can enjoy the flowers of the classic trumpet honeysuckle vine (*Lonicera sempervirens*). Flowers can be anywhere from deep yellow to orange-yellow to red. The coral-pink-and-yellow flower clusters of gold flame honeysuckle (*L. heckrottii*) may also appear in winter if the weather is mild.

Winter jasmine (*Jasminum nudiflorum*) can be trained as a vine or as an arching shrub. Its attractive, leafless green branches bear bright yellow, salverform flowers in a sunny spot in late winter. A near relative, downy jasmine (*J. multiflorum*) has woolly gray-green leaves and bears clusters of white starflowers in late winter and early spring. Downy jasmine can be trained as a vine or weeping shrub.

Gold flame honeysuckle (Lonicera heckrottii) *—like its cousin, trumpet honeysuckle* (L. sempervirens)*— will often bloom in winter if the weather is mild.*

WINTER GROUNDCOVERS

Groundcovers also pull their weight in the lean months. They gracefully mask the ground around dormant perennials and provide a nice carpet for jonquils, paperwhites, summer snowflakes, and other winter bulbs. Small-leaved, variegated ivies (*Hedera*), sedums (*Sedum*), low-growing members of the lily family such as monkey grass (*Ophiopogon*) and lily turf (*Liriope*), cream-edged variegated periwinkle (*Vinca*), the cheerful gold of creeping jenny (*Lysimachia nummularia* 'Aurea'), and the soft, silvery carpet of lamb's ears (*Stachys byzantina*) can provide a tapestry of color and shape in the dormant garden, sending the unmistakable message that someone is carefully tending to and nurturing this spot of ground.

And there will be attractive evergreen basal leaves of obedient plant, coneflower, columbine, and other perennials to add interest. Even the artemesias, lavender cotton, and dusty miller—if they haven't been allowed to become too leggy over the summer—can lend an attractive, slightly bushy, evergray presence.

HERBS AND STRAWBERRIES IN THE WINTER GARDEN

If you're looking for a variety of textures and fragrances to combine with your winter bulbs and annuals, you may want to try herbs. Parsley, mint, lemon balm, thyme, chives, Greek myrtle, and Mexican tarragon (in Zones 8b and below) are just a few of the evergreen herbs that can be used in the winter landscape as well as in the stew pot. They can be arranged in an herb garden of their own or in any sunny spot in lieu of a ground-cover, to edge a bed, to fill out a container, or to mix and mingle.

The woody, gray-leaved herbs, rosemary and germander, can be grown as handsome subshrubs and will produce tiny, bright blue flowers to cheer you during the winter months. Borage is a gray-leaved annual herb that grows best in the cooler weather from fall through spring in the coastal South, producing clouds of blue, saucer-like flowers at the end of its growing cycle.

One of the very loveliest edging or groundcover plants for winter is the ornamental strawberry plant (*Fragaria* 'Pink Panda'). The handsome, dark-green, toothed leaves and freely produced delicate pink blooms are outstanding for their fresh appearance in winter and even more useful as an accompaniment to early-blooming bulbs.

*A terrific flowering groundcover for winter, the ornamental strawberry (*Fragaria *'Pink Panda') stays neat and healthy looking in the coldest weather.*

WINTER DELICACIES

Other delicate winter flowers include the simple violet-colored blooms of the evergreen vincas (*Vinca minor* and *V. major*), the classic charm of white or blue tufted violets (*Viola cornuta*), and the pink or white five-petaled flowers of wood sorrel (*Oxalis*). All of these will begin blooming in late winter or early spring depending on the clemency of the weather.

Surprisingly, two cultivars of the perennial pincushion flower, *Scabiosa columbaria* 'Butterfly Blue' and 'Pink Mist', may bloom during mild winter months even though in other places *Scabiosa* is a summer flower. The lilac blue or pale pink pincushion-like flower heads and healthy foliage are a welcome sight, especially if planted in sizable groupings.

Ornamental Swiss chards come in a variety of colors, including yellow, pink, and orange. This deep-plum-colored Swiss chard looks striking with the red winter berries of a deciduous shrub.

WINTER VEGETABLES

Winter is also an excellent time to make room for vegetables in your perennial garden. Cabbages and kales (including the highly ornamental, but not very tasty, frilly pink and purple varieties), the eye-catching rainbow-colored Swiss chards, a wide variety of lettuces, mustard, carrots, broccoli, Brussels sprouts, spinach, collards, onions, and cauliflower all grow very happily in winter and can be incorporated into any garden scheme. Many of them produce interesting flowers just before they bolt into oblivion. Even if you don't grow vegetables in summer, you can make room for them in winter where your hot-weather annuals have died

back. Treat yourself to a freshly picked lettuce and herb salad on New Year's Day!

WINTER BULBS

Paperwhites and Other Early Narcissi

When we're still well and truly into the lean season of short days and long nights, we have the luxury of paperwhites (*Narcissus tazetta* var. *papyracceus*), a plant grown only indoors in other parts of the country. Their nodding white clusters and evocative scent contrast fairly dramatically with the relative spareness of the rest of the winter landscape. They will bloom most prolifically if lifted and replanted more deeply (about six inches deep) every few years. A cream-and-yellow relative of the paperwhite, the Chinese Sacred Lily (*N. tazetta* var. *orientalis*), blooms in winter in the warmer parts of the coastal South. By far the most durable and reliable of the paperwhites is *Narcissus tazetta* 'Grand Primo', which has persisted in southern gardens for generations. It needs no lifting or dividing and can stand both wet and dry conditions. However, since it is hard to come by 'Grand Primo', you may wish to substitute the creamy white, double-flowered *Narcissus tazetta* 'Erlicheer', which will be equally permanent, although it may take a few years to get established.

Another early-blooming *Narcissus* (really a kind of small wildflower) is the Lent lily or *N. pseudonarcissus*. The Lent lily, with its pale-and-deep-yellow blossoms on short stems, seems to thrive on the vagaries of our winters. *N. tazetta* 'Avalanche' with white petals and a lemon yellow cup blooms somewhat later.

The most prolific of all early-blooming daffodils in our climate are the hoop petticoats (*N. bulbocodium*), tiny grassy-leaved gems with narrow star-like petals and rounded cups that can be counted on to form large colonies over the years. Hoop petticoats may bloom any time from midwinter to early spring.

*One of the best bulbs for late winter and early spring is summer snowflake (*Leucojum aestivum*). Each tiny white bell is dotted with green at the tip.*

Spring Starflower and Summer Snowflake

Other late-winter-blooming bulbs include the tiny, milky blue starflower, *Ipheion uniflorum*, its flower a cheerful starry wonder when skies may still be leaden and most perennials still dormant. You will often see *Ipheion* naturalized in lawns and the strips between sidewalk and street. They work equally beautifully among pansies and the late-winter/early-spring bulbs in the perennial garden.

The green-dotted, white clustered bells of summer snowflakes, *Leucojum aestivum* (not to be confused with snowdrops, *Galanthus nivallis*, which are not reliable here), appear on foot-high stems early in the year with the first daffodils. They form grassy clumps and are reliable bloomers year after year if given sunshine and good drainage.

White French-Roman hyacinths, *Hyacinthus orientalis* var. *albulus*, would look wonderful mixed in with summer snowflakes. They produce loose spikes of very fragrant, tiny, white star-shaped flowers beginning in January and continuing for many weeks.

Daffodils

Following the early-blooming *Narcissi*, in very late winter and early spring we move into what most people think of as daffodil season. Gardeners in the coastal South should take some care in selecting the types of daffodils that are best suited to this climate. Some of the more widely distributed bulbs and those most readily available at the local garden centers tend to be the varieties of large trumpet daffodils that don't work as well for us. They are likely to bloom for only one or two seasons, after which the bulbs diminish in size, forever after sending up clumps of useless gray-green leaves. There are many others that are better adapted to our hot summers and mild, wet winters.

The fragrant and diminutive *Narcissus jonquilla* in either single or double form and the antique campernelle (*N.* x *odorus* Linnaeus 'Campernelli') naturalize wonderfully in our area. Among the *Narcissi* in the *jonquilla* hybrid division, there are many excellent choices, including 'Autumn Gold', 'Bell Song', 'Bunting', 'Curlew', 'Divertimento', 'Key Lime', 'Orange Queen', 'Pink Angel', 'Pipit', 'Quail', 'Suzy', 'Trevithian' and many others.

The *N. triandrus* (or angel's tears) hybrids— such as 'Thalia', 'Ice Wings', 'Tuesday's Child', 'Petrel', and 'Hawera', among others—are beautiful and reliable.

Some of the more delicate species of daffodils, such as Narcissus odorus Linnaeus 'Campernelli', *bloom reliably every spring. This little gem will bloom in full sun or light shade.*

The hybrids of *N. cyclamineus*, with their charming reflexed perianths, do well as long as the soil is loose and somewhat sandy. Among those that are fairly easy to find in catalogs are 'February Gold', 'Lemon Silk', 'Peeping Tom', 'Rapture', and 'Tracey'. The miniatures—'Jack Snipe', 'Jetfire', and 'Tête à Tête'—prefer leafy soil and part shade.

The best double-flowered daffodils for the coastal South include 'Abba', 'Bridal Crown', 'Cheerfulness', 'Sir Winston Churchill', 'Telamonius Plenus', and 'Yellow Cheerfulness'. Among the large-cup daffodils, a reliable favorite is 'St. Keverne.' Selecting the right type of Narcissus to plant will go a long way toward helping you create the swaths of late-winter and early-spring color that have come to be emblematic of rebirth in the garden.

LATE-WINTER-FLOWERING SHRUBS AND TREES

Around the time of the first *Narcissi* and before the full-impact glamour of the flowering trees and shrubs has begun, there's space to enjoy some of late winter's more delicate beauties. This is the time when pearly buds and five-petaled, white, red, or coral flowers cover the woody branches of the elegant Japanese quince and when forsythia and green-stemmed winter jasmine enliven the picture with cascades of bright yellow. Witch hazel produces spidery gold tassels on its bare branches, and the saucer magnolia opens its luxuriant, satiny, mauve-and-white flowers, offsetting its handsome leafless silhouette.

WINTER ANNUALS

Finally, no winter garden would be complete without the violets' annual cousins, the pansies (*Viola* x *Wittrockiana*). In containers, in large groupings in the garden bed, or stuck here and there to brighten things up, they are worth planting every year. They are available in every color imaginable, including black. Everyone has their favorites, but the luscious 'Imperial Antique Shades' and the 'Sorbet' series are worth seeking out. Plant pansies in sun to part-sun in well-amended soil in the fall with a sprinkling of slow-release fertilizer. They will bloom all winter, putting on their best show as the weather warms in spring. If the temperature is particularly cold, they will look temporarily frozen and miserable, but experienced gardeners in Zones 8 and below know they will bounce back.

Depending on the severity of the winter, petunias may also bloom for us

The lovely faces of hybrid Johnny-jump-up (Viola tricolor) greet passersby all winter long and through spring. This is an annual that often self-sows.

right on through, especially those cultivars that hate the summer heat. They are not as reliable as pansies, however.

Although pansies and Johnny-jump-ups are probably the best-known cool-weather annuals for the Southern Atlantic and Gulf Coasts, there are more than two dozen others we can use in a similar fashion. The "Annuals" section of Chapter 4 lists these plants and how to grow them. A few examples include English daisy (*Bellis perennis*), wallflower (*Chieranthus cheiri*), stock (*Mattihola incana*), calendula (*Calendula officinalis*), the polyantha primrose (*Primula polyantha*), certain varieties of sweet pea (*Lathyrus odoratus*), larkspur (*Consolida ambigua*), and hollyhocks (*Alcea rosea*).

Spring An Abundance of Beauty

It's impossible not to love spring. It's the only season that leads us to believe perfection is truly possible. The air is cool, breezes are balmy, and the sunlight seems to sparkle. Every day something new is sprouting or opening into bloom. Bulbs you forgot you planted pop up and deliver their miracles for your enjoyment. Spring can be an unbelievably rich time in the coastal South garden.

Depending on where you live in the coastal South, spring here comes a month to two months earlier than in the mid-Atlantic, the Midwest, or northern New England. It's a gradual process, which creeps up on us almost un-

Most azaleas make their biggest splash in midspring. The larger flowered Indica hybrids as well as the Kurumes, shown below, are staples of the coastal spring garden.

aware sometime between a yard full of bright yellow daffodils on Valentine's Day and the first painterly splotch of magenta azalea blossoms in March. By the time we turn around, the entire neighborhood is blanketed with pastel shades—from the blooms of star magnolia, dogwood, shadblow, buckeye, redbud, cherry, pear, peach, plum, apricot, and crabapple to the splashes of gold from forsythia, scotch broom, and shade-loving kerria. And most years we can enjoy this stretch of balmy weather and welcome profusion of flowers for about three months.

SPRING FROM THE GROUND UP

Spring gives us the perfect chance to admire the garden from the ground up, because things haven't yet gotten out of control with overzealous stolons and pestilential weeds. The emerging leaves of perennials, the unfurling fiddle-

One of our most delightful natives is this easy, cooperative columbine (Aquilegia canadensis). It blooms for many weeks in spring and self-sows profusely in the garden.

The delicate-looking evening primrose (Oenethera speciosa) is one of the easiest and most durable of the spring perennials.

heads of ferns, and the fresh blades of ornamental grasses give us hints of perfection on a small scale. Add to this the diminutive, milky blue flowers of *Ipheion*, tiny strawberry flowers (*Fragaria* 'Pink Panda'), miniature *Narcissi*, and summer snowflakes (*Leucojum aestivum*) floating above the burgundy leaves of bugleweed or the gold of creeping jenny, and you have a tableau worth visiting daily.

At the same kneeling-down-to-appreciate-it level, we find the delicate faces of pansies and Johnny-jump-ups (*Viola tricolor*) mixed with tufted violets (*V. cornuta*), the native cherry-and-honey-colored columbine (*Aquilegia canadensis*), pink- or white-flowered wood sorrel (*Oxalis*), and the slightly promiscuous evening primrose (*Oenethera speciosa*), its slender stems topped with the most captivating of shell pink cups. One of the earliest of all the delicate, shade-loving plants for us is the May apple (*Podophyllum peltatum*), its small white flowers dangling underneath its broad, handsomely lobed leaves, where you must bend down to see them.

Creeping buttercup (*Ranunculus repens* 'Pleniflorus'), a vigorous groundcover, gives us bright yellow blooms above shiny, dark green leaves in sun or in shade. Another good, spring-flowering groundcover with similar requirements is goldenstar (*Chrysogonum virginianum*). It bears bright yellow, star-shaped flowers that often reappear when the weather cools back down again in the fall.

The low-growing phloxes are lovely at this time of year as well. In a dry, sunny spot, sand phlox (*Phlox bifida*), moss phlox (*P. subulata*), and trailing phlox (*P. nivalis*) all provide splashes of color—including vivid pinks and purples—at ground level. In a moist spot in partial shade, wild blue phlox (*P. divaricata*) is beautiful mixed with spring bulbs. These species phlox will naturalize to form colonies if the growing conditions are right.

SPRING IN THE SHADE

In shadier spots we can hunt for the flowers of Jack-in-the-pulpit (*Arisaema*) and Lenten rose (*Helleborus orientalis*) as well as the pendent clusters of Spanish bluebells (*Hyacinthoides hispanica*). Given plenty of leaf mold and a moist, partially shady spot, we may be able to grow and enjoy the broken hearts and lovely foliage of *Dicentra*, or bleeding heart. This is, however, not one of our most reliable perennials. A good spring bloomer for part shade is the diminutive bluestar (*Laurentia fluviatalis*), which puts forth sky blue flowers. Bluestar prefers a moist spot and can be used between paving stones in the partially shady garden. It is more reliable in our climate than the prostrate lobelias.

Trillium and Solomon's Seal

Although we associate the three-petaled white or maroon flowers of trillium (*Trillium*) with cooler, woodland habitats, there are some that can stand the heat of the coastal summers as long as they're planted in shade and given

*Southern classics, Spanish bluebells (*Hyacinthoides hispanica*) bloom beautifully in the shady spring garden.*

a rich, constantly moist soil. These include two pink-flowered trilliums, the rosy wakerobin (*T. catesbaei*) and the nodding trillium (*T. cernuum*). The dark maroon whippoorwill flower (*T. cuneatum*) and the purple trillium (*T. erectum*) will also survive down to Zone 9. And our own southeastern native, underwoods trillium (*T. underwoodii*), bears an unusual checkerboard pattern on its foliage in various shades of green. Its flowers are dark purple.

Another lover of cool, woodsy areas is Solomon's seal (*Polygonatum*), with its arching stems and partially hidden clusters of small, bell-like, greenish-white blossoms. If you select the species *P. biflorum*, you will be rewarded with drought- and heat-tolerant plants for the moist, shady garden. Solomon's seal may take a while to get established but will eventually produce delicate flowers each spring and astonishing sprays of cut flowers for the house. The foliage goes dormant in the warm weather of summer.

Cobra Lily

Cobra lilies (*Arisaema*), brothers to Jack-in-the-pulpit, produce fascinating flowers in the shady spring garden. Generally growing one to two feet tall, these tuberous perennials are recognizable by the vase-shaped spathes or pitchers that appear in spring atop short stalks. The tip or hood of the pitcher often curls over in front. Hiding inside, protruding slightly or sticking out wildly (depending on the species), is a pencil-thin tongue or spadix. The green, brown, or red pitchers are usually striped with white on the inside. Give cobra lilies rich soil and ample moisture and they will reward you by forming larger clumps each year.

Peacock Gingers

Some of the more interesting rhizomatous perennials for the partly shady spring garden are the peacock gingers, including the resurrection lily (*Kaempferia rotunda*), the bronze peacock ginger (*K. pulchra*), silverspot ginger (*K. pulchra* 'Silverspot'), and the variegated peacock lily (*K. gilbertii*). Their broad leaves are delicately flushed and marbled in shades of silver, purple, bronze, or maroon. Short spikes of small pink or white, orchid-like flowers arise in late spring, often before the foliage appears. If given rich, moist soil, they will spread out to form a lovely, deciduous groundcover.

SPRING VINES

At eye and sky level, spring presents us with a wide array of flowering vines. The earliest spring-blooming climbers are the February-blooming Carolina jessamine (*Gelsemium sempervirens*), a longtime southern classic. Like the slightly more tender and less well-known primrose jasmine (*Jasminum mesnyi*), it produces masses of small, yellow funnel-shaped flowers on dark, evergreen leaves. An even more dramatic plant that is covered with very fragrant, single, white saucer-shaped flowers in early spring is the evergreen clematis (*Clematis armandii*), a vine whose deep green, glossy leaves add year-round interest.

Another southern spring-blooming classic is crossvine (*Bignonia capreolata*), which has brownish-red trumpet flowers. Crossvine looks like and is related to the later-blooming trumpet creeper (*Campsis radicans*), and they are sometimes confused with one another.

Two climbing species roses come into their once-a-year breathtaking display beginning in early March. The small, butter yellow, pom-pom-like flowers of the thornless Lady Banksia (*Rosa banksiae*) smother fences, walls, and garden bridges for several weeks, symbolizing more than almost any other plant the voluptuousness of spring in the South. The Cherokee rose (*R. laevigata*), a thorny, vigorous climber, is equally captivating, with hundreds of large (3½" across), single, creamy white, cup-like blooms highlighted by bosses of yellow stamens in the center.

Later in the season the garden is awash in the scent and bright colors of Confederate jasmine, honeysuckle, cat's claw vine, and wisteria—all vines that are very much at home in our climate. Confederate jasmine (*Traechelospermum jasminoides*) is the well-beloved evergreen vine of choice for southern gardens, with its starry, fragrant, white blooms and glossy, dark green foliage. It looks wonderful climbing up trellises, arbors, and fences or clipped back to neatly cover a garden arch.

Native American wisteria (*Wisteria frutescens*) and Kentucky wisteria (*W. macrostachya*) drip with sumptuous, romantic bloom clusters in shades of

*The single, creamy white blooms of the Cherokee rose (*Rosa laevigata*) blanket the vine for weeks in early spring—truly a magnificent sight.*

lilac, violet-blue, and purple. More importantly, these two varieties are less likely to take over than the Japanese and Chinese species.

Among the honeysuckles, gold flame (*Lonicera heckrottii*) and trumpet honeysuckle (*L. sempervirens*) are the best choices for gardens in the coastal South. Not only do they have reliable, attractive flowers in shades of pink, yellow, and red, but they are not wildly invasive like the Japanese variety ('Hall's Purple').

Cat's claw vine (*Macfadyena unguis-cati*) behaves like some of the less mannerly honeysuckles and wisterias. Clawing its way up easily to thirty feet high, it also develops very deep roots and sends down new roots wherever the stems touch the ground. For that reason, some gardeners avoid it. But it does bear beautiful two- to four-inch-long, yellow trumpet flowers in early spring.

In late spring, two other classic jasmines come into bloom. Both Chinese jasmine (*Jasminum polyanthum*) and common white jasmine (*J. officinale*) are fast-growing, twining vines with fragrant white flowers. The yellow-edged variety of *J. officinale*, 'Aureovariegatum' is especially handsome even when not in bloom.

SPRING SHRUBS

Between the ground-level, lacy delicacy of columbine and the lofty abandon of wisteria, everything in between seems to be happening at once. Midspring brings out the pastel colors of flowering shrubs such as deutzia, weigela, Indian hawthorn, spireas, and azaleas, along with the continued magnificent flowering of the camellias.

There is nothing more breathtaking than a large swath of blooming azaleas in shades of pink, magenta, lavender, coral, red, or white. Whether it's the large-flowered Southern Indica hybrids or the prolific, smaller-flowered Kurumes, azaleas put on an unbeatable display for several weeks in spring. Unusual shades of gold, burnt orange, creamy yellow, and fiery red are available with the deciduous Florida flame azaleas (*Rhododendron austrinum*), whose blooms appear on the bare stems before the shrubs leaf out. The native honeysuckle azalea (*R. canescens*) has a similar loose habit and fragrant pale pink or white flowers.

In late May and early June the dense-leaved, dwarf, evergreen Gumpo hybrid azaleas extend the season with an abundance of blossom and excellent form. The Gumpos are small enough to mix well in almost any perennial scheme. When they bloom, gumpos are literally covered with flowers—white, pale pink, or coral.

One of the more beloved and quirky spring-blooming southern shrubs is called yesterday-today-and-tomorrow (*Brunfelsia pauciflora*). The pansy-like flowers usually open purple one day, transform to pink the next day, and fade out to white before they're done, hence the common name.

SPRING-BLOOMING BULBS

There's something magical in the conjunction of spring and the treasures that unfold from buried bulbs, rhizomes, tubers, and corms. The process is ancient and inspires awe no matter how many times we witness it.

There are certain traditional spring bulbs that will put on a good show the first year but can't be counted on to bloom in following years. These include many of the bulbs most often advertised in catalogs, magazines, and in-store promotions—tulips, hyacinths, grape hyacinths, crocuses, windflowers, and fritillaria. Claims that these bulbs will perennialize and thrive in our area are exaggerated, to say the least. One solution is to treat these bulbs as annuals here rather than perennials. Once they've finished blooming in the spring, dig them up and toss them on the compost pile. Another solution is to select bulbs that enjoy living here and will give you satisfaction year after year.

In addition to all the *Narcissi* and other late-winter/early-spring bulbs mentioned earlier in this chapter, there are other spring-blooming bulbs that do wonderfully for us. These bulbs will not only produce lovely flowers the first spring but will bring repeat pleasure throughout the years as their colonies increase.

Irises

April is the premier month for irises of all types. Certain old-fashioned strains of bearded iris, if given perfectly dry, uncrowded situations, have persisted for generations in the coastal South. Many of the modern hybrids, however, are susceptible to bulb rot here. (Deal with this disease by scooping out the smelly, mushy, rotten part of the rhizome with a spoon and dousing whatever part is left with a diluted bleach solution. Better yet, plant irises that don't succumb to rot.)

Some of the earliest bloomers of the old bearded hybrids that *don't* rot out are the Italians (*Iris kochii*), which bloom in March in shades of reddish-purple. A somewhat shade-tolerant bearded hybrid is the Dalmation (*I. pallida*), which produces pale lavender blooms in midspring. The tall, purple German (*I. germanica*) and white flag (*I. albicans*) are also excellent candidates for the coastal South.

Among the beardless irises, the best performers

Although some of the older bearded irises do thrive in the coastal South, Louisiana and Siberian are the best irises for our climate.

are the Louisiana iris, yellow flag (*I. pseudocorus*), and Southern blue flag (*I. virginica*), all of which thrive in wet, acidic soil or bogs. We can also grow Siberian (*I. siberica*) and Japanese (*I. ensata*), but they need good drainage in winter.

The large, dramatic blooms of amaryllis (Hippeastrum) stand out in the spring garden. The bulbs will winter over in most parts of the coastal South.

The spring garden is enlivened for many weeks by the colorful blooms of the poppy anemone (Anemone coronaria), shown here with pansies.

Louisiana irises have the honor of being world-renowned natives of the coastal South. The five original native species, gathered by enthusiasts as the swamps around New Orleans were being drained for city building, have been hybridized into hundreds of beautiful colors. Louisiana irises are easy to grow in full or part sun as long as their feet are kept constantly moist. In fact, they can even be grown in a pot submerged in your garden pond.

When the irises begin to bloom, the roses and clematis are never far behind. A rose-draped arch in May, studded with clematis blossoms and with the last of the irises blooming at its feet is a sight to behold. Who could think of going into the office?

Amaryllis

For such an exquisitely elegant flower, the amaryllis (*Hippeastrum*) is a surprisingly easy, carefree bulb in our area. It is hard to imagine more naturally stunning flowers than the huge, outward-facing trumpets, as big as nine inches across, showing off their beautifully hued interiors on top of sturdy, erect stems. The pale pastel pinks, lime greens, and vibrant, fiery reds are all equally beautiful.

Atamasco Lily

The diminutive, bright white Atamasco lily (*Zephyranthes atamasco*) blooms by the hundreds in sunny bogs throughout the coastal South. The crocus-like blooms make a breathtaking sight when massed this way. They can be used in small colonies to add beauty to any damp, sunny niche in the garden.

Poppy Anemones

The giant poppy anemone (*Anemone coronaria*), a tender bulb in cooler climates, has much the same effect in the spring garden as the Oriental poppy would if it were more suited to our climate. The anemone's brilliant scarlet, cup-shaped flower with the dramatic black central eye is a perfect foil for the more delicate, pastel shades of spring. It is equally stunning in its lilac-purple, deep-blue, magenta, bright pink, and white incarnations. Each tuber sends up a succession of eye-catching flowers throughout the spring months. If succeeding winters are fairly mild, it will come back and bloom again for several years in a row. Plant the tubers out around Thanksgiving, and the flowers will begin to appear in March.

Squills

Thick flower spikes loaded with tiny blue bells are a wonderful sight in a naturalized bulb bed in spring. The easy, reliable Spanish bluebells (*Hyacinthoides hispanica*) send up more and more of these charming flower clusters every year. Deep purple, starry flowers clustered into a ball are the hallmark of another reliable squill, the Cuban lily (*Scilla peruviana*). Both of these bulbs make excellent additions to a naturalized bulb garden.

Hardy Gladioli

Corn lilies (*Gladiolus byzantinus*) send up one-sided, reddish-pink flower spikes at this time of year, adding a bright vertical accent among the more relaxed perennial neighbors. They are easy, no-fail bulbs that will form colonies over the years to increase the impact of the colorful display. A lesser known relative, the parrot gladiolus (*Gladiolus natalensis*), contributes three-foot-tall stems of sunny orange and yellow, parrot-like blooms to the spring garden.

Alliums

Alliums are onion relatives that generally have spherical flower clusters, or balls, on top of erect stems. The tiny, individual bellflowers or starflowers that make up each cluster are lilac-blue, greenish-white, or pink. These floating flower balls look wonderful popping up in and amongst other perennials. One of the best lilac-purple-colored alliums for the spring garden is the foot-high *Allium uniflorum*. Bulgarian allium (*A. bulgaricum*) is a much taller plant (three to four feet) with quirky, pendent umbels of greenish-white flowers flushed with purple. Around the same time, in late spring, *A. aflatunense* produces showy, lilac-purple spheres atop two- to three-foot-tall stems. The easiest of the *Alliums* to come by are the small, mauve-pink drumstick chives (*A. schoenoprasum*), a welcome but short-lived addition among the smaller, more delicate perennials and annuals.

Terrestrial Orchids

In a shady spot you may see delicate white or magenta, orchid-like flowers rising up amongst the sword-shaped leaves of the hardy Chinese ground orchid (*Bletilla striata*). When massed and mixed in with plum-colored groundcovers these hardy orchids make a lovely spring carpet for a shady corner.

*The diminutive lavender bloom of hardy Chinese orchid (*Bletilla striata*) appears in a lightly shaded spot with ferns, variegated ivy, and annual begonias.*

SPRING PERENNIALS

In spring the light in the garden is quite different from the glaring haze of midsummer. Spring light tends to be clear and sparkling, refracting off the surfaces it touches. For this reason, the paler, more delicate flower colors and textures are easier to appreciate in the spring garden. Some of the more romantic, old-fashioned flowers can be appreciated during these milder months.

The small, three-petaled flowers of spiderwort (*Tradescantia*) may be dark blue, pale blue, purple, pink, red, or white. The branching stems of spiderwort are somewhat lax and leaning, but this adds to the sense that the spring garden is spilling over with new growth and beauty. For instance, the bright magenta cups of poppy mallow (*Callirhoe involucrata*) spread all over the ground in spring in a wonderfully carefree manner.

Adding to this sense of pleasant abandon are the wiry, lavender-flowered stems of meadow rue (*Thalictrum aquilegifolium*); the yellow, pea-covered spires of Carolina lupine (*Thermopsis caroliniana*); the white lacecaps of Queen Anne's lace (*Daucus carota* var. *carota*); and the pink, daisy-like flowers of swamp gentian (*Sabatia kennedyiana*).

Verbenas of all types begin blooming in the middle of spring and continue on through the summer. The easiest and most reliable of the bunch is the electric purple, prostrate spreader *Verbena canadensis* 'Homestead Purple'. The eye-catching, bright purple flower clusters bloom prolifically on short stems. There are red, pink, and white rose verbena varieties as well. A slightly more temperamental cousin is the lacy-leaved moss verbena (*V. tenuisecta*), which comes in shades of white, pink, lavender, purple, and red. It is somewhat more delicate in foliage and flower.

Tuber vervain (*V. rigida*) is an old heirloom plant, suitable to hot, dry sites and producing purple flower spikes on erect two-foot-tall plants. *V. rigida* 'Flame' is a low-growing, bright red cultivar that forms a mound at ground level, and 'Polaris' is a pale blue cultivar. The upright verbena, *V. bonariensis*, is recognizable by the small clusters of purple flowers it carries on stiff, branching stems. It is a clump-former that mixes well with other plants and blooms all summer long; however, like many of the verbenas, it is susceptible to mildew.

There are some spring-blooming perennial natives that should be used more often in our region. The starry, steel-colored balls of bluestar (*Amsonia tabernaemontana*) will reappear reliably every spring if given a position in full sun. The white pea-spires and black stems of white false indigo (*Baptisia pendula*) are very graceful and romantic mixed in with other spring perennials. *Baptisia* is also valuable for its drought tolerance.

Three native beardtongues (*Penstemon smallii, P. gloxinoides, P. tenuis*) pro-

*This bright purple verbena (*Verbena canadensis *'Homestead Purple') begins its season in spring and keeps up the show all summer long and into the fall. It works well with many colors, including the bright yellow of lantana, shown above.*

duce spring flowers that resemble foxgloves in shades of pink and purple. The last of these, *P. tenuis* or Gulf Coast penstemon, is probably the best one for the coastal South. It produces rosy-purple flower panicles for many weeks from spring to early summer.

Another valuable native, Indian pink (*Spigelia marilandica*), is slow to establish but will eventually form sizable clumps in light shade. The flowers, which appear in spring on erect eighteen-inch-tall stems, are bright, upward-facing red tubes topped with yellow stars.

By mixing flowering shrubs and vines, bulbs, and cool-weather annuals and perennials in the spring garden, it is easy to create a pleasant retreat from the cares of the world. Warm breezes, sparkling sunshine, and constantly unfolding flower treasures—a wonderful season in the coastal South.

COOL-WEATHER ANNUALS AND BIENNIALS

In the coastal South it pays to sow seeds of a number of cool-weather annuals and biennials in the fall. The following spring we can enjoy a host of traditional border flowers as long as the cool weather lasts. For example, old-fashioned annual larkspur and biennial foxglove and hollyhock are easy to grow from seed. Beautiful pale yellow, pink, white, purple, or red foxgloves (*Digitalis*) will bloom the first year from the 'Foxy' series of seeds. The romantic, mallow-type spires of biennial hollyhock (*Alcea rosea*) normally appear the second spring after sowing. However, the old variety 'Indian Spring' produces flowers the first spring after sowing.

A quintessential spring flower, the hollyhock (Alcea rosea) is a biennial. Seed sown in the fall will bloom the second spring.

Biennial rose campion (*Lychnis coronaria*) is a charming, cottagey plant with woolly, gray-green leaves and small, bright pink or red flowers on branching, two-foot-tall stems. It mixes well in the middle of a border with other pastel colors. The erect flower clusters of purple honesty (*Lunaria annua*) have a similar simple, old-fashioned grace. And the paper-thin, wafer-like "money" fruit that stays on the honesty plant after flowering is attractive in the garden or in dried flower arrangements.

Bright orange cups of California poppy, cornflower blue bachelor's buttons, and dozens of other cool-weather annuals can be mixed in with spring-blooming perennials. For a list of terrific choices for spring annuals, see the "Annuals" section of Chapter 4.

Summer Mad Dogs and Salvias

Spring gradually makes way for summer with its longer days, higher temperatures, and increased humidity. Once the days begin to heat up, the cool-weather annuals will wilt and some of the spring-blooming shade plants will go dormant. In place of the Spanish bluebells and wild columbine come the tough, durable perennials and shrubs that make up the backbone of the coastal garden—hibiscus, sage, and subtropical rhizomatous perennials, among others.

The first quality to look for in a summer perennial, annual, shrub, or vine for the coastal South is endurance. This is the time of year when plants are going to be required to run the marathon—or maybe the triathlon (heat, humidity, and intermittent drought). But despite the rigors and sheer length of summer, it is by far the most abundant season of bloom, overwhelming us with choices of plant material.

SUMMER SHRUBS

Perhaps the best way to design a summer garden is to start with the flowering trees and shrubs that will make up the larger outlines of the framework. The tried and true for the coastal South include oleanders, crape myrtles, magnolias, gardenias, hydrangeas, summersweet, abelias, bottlebrush buckeye, chaste tree, and serissa.

The prolific, showy flowers of the oleanders (*Nerium oleander*) in shades of white, pink, coral, red, or yellow can be seen in private gardens and public plantings from Virginia to Florida and across to Texas. These easy, reliable shrubs or small trees bloom all summer long.

Later in the summer the crape myrtles (*Lagerstroemia indica*) deliver the same kind of powerful color impact with their profuse blooms in shades of magenta, white, pink, and lavender—another standout tree for our climate.

In early summer the enormous (ten-inches across), highly perfumed, velvety white blossoms of the classic southern magnolia (*Magnolia grandiflora*) appear against the large, dark green, glossy leaves—as magnificent a sight as

*A seaside garden
planted with bright
green sedum (*Sedum*),
pink yarrow (*Achillea*),
and yellow daylilies
(*Hemerocallis*).*

you ever hope to see in the garden. A mature tree will bear dozens of these blooms for a long period of time.

Nothing compares to walking by a gardenia bush (*Gardenia jasminoides*) in full bloom and smelling the unmistakable, heady perfume of the double white flowers. Dwarf gardenias can be used as a groundcover and mixed in with other shrubs and perennials.

In a shady spot the huge flower trusses or delicate lacecaps of hydrangeas (*Hydrangea*) signal that the lush beauty of summer is in full swing. The colors vary from bush to bush—a range of lavender-blues, sky blues, mauves, pinks,

Unsurpassed for their length of bloom and eye-catching color, crape myrtles (Lagerstroemia) are essential trees for the coastal South.

and greenish whites. Even when not in bloom, the variegated lacecap hydrangea lights up the shade with its creamy-margined leaves.

Chaste tree (*Vitex agnus-castus*) puts on a breathtaking show of color in early summer—lilac-blue, white, or pink, depending on the cultivar. Chaste tree may bloom for months in a row and can be a spectacular focal point for the early summer garden.

Butterfly Bush

Among the very best of the summer-blooming shrubs for the mixed border (and the summer landscape in general) is the butterfly bush (*Buddleia*). These woody, semievergreen shrubs put out bursts of color with dense, terminal flower spikes from early summer through late fall. *Buddleia* colors are mouth-watering blues, lilacs, deep purples, red-purple, pink, white, and yellow-orange. The less well known *B. lindleyana* is an heirloom plant once thought to be lost in the trade but "rediscovered" at an old farm site in Brunswick County, North Carolina. Of particular historical significance, this plant was successfully smuggled into the lower Cape Fear region of North Carolina through the Union blockade of Wilmington in 1864.

Hibiscus

Among shrubby plants, another standout for all-summer bloom and durability in the mixed perennial garden is the hibiscus genus. Although the dark-green, shiny-leaved *Hibiscus rosa-sinensis* sold by florists is tender and must be brought inside if temperatures drop below 50 degrees, it has some noteworthy hardy relatives.

The common mallow, *Hibiscus moscheutos*, produces enormous saucer-shaped flowers on three-foot-tall shrubby plants in a wide range of colors. It

Butterfly bush (Buddleia) is aptly named, attracting the lovely creatures throughout its long blooming season. It begins blooming in late spring and doesn't let up until frost.

The coastal South is home to a large number of hardy hibiscus.

takes full sun and has the unfortunate flaw of being prone to insect damage. A more pest-resistant shrub or small tree is the swamp hibiscus (*H. coccineus*), whose foliage looks a lot like that of the marijuana plant. It grows seven feet tall in full sun, producing attention-getting red flowers all summer long and papery, green seedpods afterwards.

Woolly rose mallow (*H. lasiocarpus*) gets its common name from its furry gray foliage. In summer it bears showy, pale pink or white mallow flowers with dark centers. Woolly rose mallow can stand wet clay soils as well as the salt spray of beachfront gardening.

Virginia mallow, also known as beach mallow (*Kostletzkya virginica*), is in the same family as hibiscus and resembles it. This three- to four-foot-tall shrubby plant is covered with pink flowers from summer through fall. Although it likes boggy soil, beach mallow will perform well in drier conditions and, of course, at the beach. One of the most spectacular mallows is the autumn-flowering Confederate rose (*H. mutabilis*), described in detail later in this chapter.

Bottlebrush and Coral Bean

Lemon bottlebrush (*Callistemon citrinus*) produces stiff, red, bristly flower spikes in late spring and summer. The blooms of this lemon-scented shrub, beloved by hummingbirds, often continue on and off into winter. Lemon bot-

The blooms of the hybrid coral bean tree (Erythrina bidwillii) are standouts in the summer garden.

The decorative hardy orange (Poncirus trifoliata) is quite cold-tolerant and adds a classic, tropical feeling to the garden.

tlebrush can grow from four to twenty-five feet tall, depending on the cultivar. It can also be kept pruned to a smaller size.

If space is not a constraint in your garden, try the thorny hybrid coral bean tree (*Erythrina* x *bidwillii*), which can grow from eight to twenty feet tall. All summer long it shows off its dramatic, bright red flower spikes. Hybrid coral bean has the added advantage of providing masses of plum-colored foliage in the fall. Equally beautiful are its relatives the crybaby tree (*E. crista-galli*), which sends up spikes of velvety, claret-colored flowers, noticeably dripping with nectar, and another red-flowered coral bean tree, *E. herbacea*. All of these shrubs or small trees require full sun. After flowering, they produce elongated bean pods that split open to reveal bright red fruits—attractive but highly poisonous.

Rock Rose

Rock rose (*Pavonia lasiopetala*) will grow in full sun to part shade and doesn't mind being in dry, poor soil. All summer long it produces showy, pink, five-petaled flowers on a five-foot-tall bush. Two of rock rose's relatives, the South American mallow (*P. brasiliensis*) and the Brazilian pavonia (*P. hastata*), have similar habits and cultural requirements and also produce pink, cup-shaped flowers with dark eyes for a long stretch in the summer.

Shrubby Jasmines and Thryallis

Certain plants can be grown as vines or shrubs, depending on how they're pruned and trained. Thryallis, also known as shower of gold (*Galphimia glauca*), with its summer-long yellow flower clusters and blue-green foliage is one such plant. Other vines that can be pruned as shrubs include yellow-flowering Italian jasmine (*Jasminum humile*) and white-flowering Arabian jasmine (*J. sambac*). Italian jasmine has a weeping habit with willow-like leaves. The foliage of all three of these plants is evergreen, an added benefit for the winter garden.

Hardy Orange

Part of the enjoyment we get from gardening in the coastal South is the sense of living near enough to the tropics to take pleasure in some unusual plants. Hardy orange (*Poncirus trifoliata*) is a wonderfully unusual looking small tree with spiny green branches, white flowers, and handsome orange-like fruits. It fits in well with perennials and some of the summer-blooming subtropicals. And though it is very popular along the southern Atlantic and Gulf coasts, it is actually cold tolerant much farther north.

Shrub Jessamines

The genus *Cestrum* gives us a number of excellent flowering shrubs for summer color. Although some of them may suffer from the cold above Zone 9, they are otherwise tough, reliable plants. The two most cold-hardy are willow-leaf jessamine (*C. parqui*), which constantly produces pale yellow flower clus-

*The shade-blooming, pink Brazilian plume (*Justicia carnea*) deserves to be more widely grown in the coastal South. It is shown here next to the yellow bloom of the cold-hardy willow-leaf jessamine (*Cestrum parqui*).*

ters from spring through frost, and the equally floriferous hybrid *C. diurnum* x *nocturnum* with its mustard yellow flowers. The more tender relatives include purple jessamine (*C. elegans*) with rosy-purple flowers, yellow shrub jessamine (*C. aurianticum*) with orangy-yellow flowers, and pink cestrum (*C. roseum*), which blooms later in the summer. The romantic night-blooming jessamine (*C. nocturnum*) is another somewhat tender, late-summer bloomer with highly fragrant white flowers that perfume the night air. Gardeners who live above Zone 9 should take heart from reports that even the more tender *Cestrums* can survive brief spells of weather in the teens!

Shrimp Plant

To mix some faux fauna among the summertime flora, try the shrimp plant (*Justicia brandegeana*). Its flowers, drooping panicles of whitish-lavender covered in copper-colored, overlapping bracts, bear an uncannily convincing resemblance to the marine crustaceans for which they're named. A near relation, Brazilian plume (*J. carnea*), blooms from midsummer to fall with showy clusters of reddish-pink flowers on bushy four- to five-foot-tall plants. There is a white variety (*J. carnea*) that is also quite showy.

Firecracker Shrub and Mexican Cigar Flower

The attention-getting firecracker shrub (*Hamelia patens*) has gray-green leaves and produces bright reddish-orange tubular flowers in summer. Mexican cigar flower (*Cuphea micropetala*) is a somewhat tender, shrubby perennial that also produces clusters of tubular red flowers with yellow tips. In the warmer parts of the coastal South it can grow into a shrub six feet across. Its arching branches are thickly clothed in flower spikes throughout the summer and into fall—a terrific plant for the coastal South.

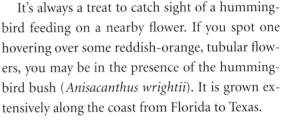

All summer long, fiery red flowers tipped in yellow adorn the Mexican cigar flower (Cuphea micropetala).

Cape Fuchsia and Hummingbird Bush

For a beautiful display of pendent tubular flowers in shades of orange, pink, red, yellow, or salmon from late summer through fall, try the classic Cape fuchsia (*Phygelius*).

The firecracker shrub (Hamelia patens) in the foreground sends up a good display of bright orange flowers throughout the summer months.

It's always a treat to catch sight of a hummingbird feeding on a nearby flower. If you spot one hovering over some reddish-orange, tubular flowers, you may be in the presence of the hummingbird bush (*Anisacanthus wrightii*). It is grown extensively along the coast from Florida to Texas.

LONG-BLOOMING PERENNIALS

The Sages

After selecting the shrubs and trees that can "carry" the garden through summer, you may want to plant the most reliable and long-blooming perennials. The best choices are those that bloom for weeks on end and don't suffer significantly from diseases or pests. At the top of the list for the Gulf Coast and Southern Atlantic coast would be the sages. There are over twenty species that do well for us.

Brazilian sage (*Salvia guaranitica*) is one of those plants you wonder how you ever overlooked. It blooms from late spring through fall and may need only one or two quick deadheading sessions to keep it spiffy looking. It's an upright, slender plant with somewhat mint-like leaves topped with endless spires of delicate, two-lipped flowers in shades of light or dark blue. Hummingbirds love Brazilian sage. It makes itself at home in sunny and partially sunny spots, spreading by underground runners and gives you lots of offspring to donate to friends if you want. It mingles well at the middle or back of a border but would look equally good in large groupings by itself. The hybrid *S.* 'Purple Majesty' bears deep purple flowers and looks very much like *S. guaranitica*.

Another excellent garden sage, *S.* x 'Indigo Spires' begins blooming at the same time as *S. guaranitica* and provides an even more substantial presence with its long, wobbly, deep blue spires on four-foot-tall stems. Whether you deadhead it or not, 'Indigo Spires' will bloom on and on into late fall and early winter, its bloom color deepening as the cool weather approaches.

The native mealycup sage (*S. farinacea*) with its gray-green foliage, sends up two- to three-foot-tall spikes of blue all summer long. Although it may be tender elsewhere, it will generally survive our winters. The best-known mealycup

left:
*Brazilian sage
(Salvia guaranitica)
is unbeatable for its
long blooming season
and ease of care.*

right:
*Another terrific
member of the sage
clan, Salvia 'Indigo
Spires' is a plant that
only gets bigger and
better all summer
long and continues
the show until the
first frost.*

hybrid is the shorter, deep blue cultivar 'Victoria', which produces flowers non-stop all summer long.

The deep red flowers of the bushy, evergreen sage *S. microphylla* add color to the garden from late summer through fall. For this reason, it is widely used in gardens in the hottest parts of the Gulf coast.

The square-stemmed Japanese yellow sage (*S. koyamae*) produces pale yellow flower spikes in moist sun or shade beginning in late summer and into fall. Other sages that bloom all summer and into autumn include the evergreen, coral-colored eyelash sage (*S. blepharophylla*), the bright-blue-flowered bog sage (*S. uliginosa*), and the somewhat shade-tolerant, wine-red sage (*S. vanhouttii*). This last species, however, is tender and may not survive above Zone 9.

The shorter, woody autumn sages (*S. greggii* and hybrids) are not as reliable for us as they are elsewhere. 'Cherry Queen' (dark pink), 'Maraschino' (cherry red), 'Raspberry Royale' (magenta), and 'Faye Chappell' (bright red) are among the best of the autumn sage hybrids for the coastal South.

Beginning in late summer a host of other sages come into their own. Please see the "Fall-Blooming Sages" section below to learn about the late-summer/early fall sages, such as pineapple sage, forsythia sage, Mexican bush sage, Hidalgo sage, azure sage, and rosebud sage.

Verbenas and Lantanas

After the *Salvias*, the next genus to look to for all-summer bloom is *Verbena*. The verbenas tolerate heat, humidity, and drought very well. The best verbenas for our area are listed in the "Spring Perennials" section above.

*The plentiful blooms of lantana (*Lantana camara*) need no deadheading. This hardy perennial, which is available in a large variety of colors, is a must for every summer garden. Here, white lantana mixes with dark purple angelonia, an annual.*

In other parts of the country, lantana (*Lantana*) is used as an annual. For us, it's a surefire perennial as long as it's planted early—in late spring or early summer. It begins blooming in early summer and continues well into the late fall, all the while literally covered with flowers. Lantana will grow into a woody two- to six-foot-tall subshrub (*Lantana camara*) or a prostrate groundcover, called weeping lantana (*L. montevidensis*). In either case, it is clothed in flat, button-like clusters of tiny salverform flowers that are constantly produced in large quantities. In addition to the bicolor pink/yellow, orange/red, orange/yellow, white/yellow, and lilac/white varieties, there are solid-color lantanas as well. Lantanas also adapt very well to container life.

*For months at a time, Mexican petunia (*Ruellia brittoniana*) blooms its head off. There are pink Ruellias as well and dwarf varieties that are perfect for the front of the border or containers.*

Mexican Petunia and Oxford Orphanage Plant

What every gardener needs are a couple of wonderful plants to stick here and there when he or she can't think what else to do. Two good candidates in this region are Mexican petunia and Oxford orphanage plant. Mexican petunia (*Ruellia brittoniana*) is an upright, clump-forming, narrow-leaved plant with funnel-shaped flowers of purple or pink that are produced nonstop from summer through to fall. *Ruellia* never looks raggedy or floppy, needs no deadheading, and mingles well in a see-through kind of way with all its neighbors. Every night it self-cleans by dropping its spent blossoms. *Ruellia* mixes well with salvias, daylilies, annual pentas, and other such stalwarts.

The other gem is the Oxford orphanage plant (*Kalimeris pinnatifida*). Its name conjures up images of children in a Dickens novel clutching fistfuls of flowers against a backdrop of cold stone turrets. In any case, this versatile plant, which was beloved of garden writer Elizabeth Lawrence, deserves more attention. A few sprigs planted four inches apart will fill in, in no time, to make a thick one-foot-tall carpet of delicate, everblooming, small, aster-like white daisies. Use it at the front of the border, to fill in between other plants, or just to put anywhere you can't think of anything else to put. When garden books advise using peach-leaved campanula and baby's breath in a promiscuous fashion throughout your garden, you should disregard that advice and use Mexican petunia and Oxford orphanage plant in their place.

*Double white daisies adorn the Oxford orphanage plant (*Kalimeris pinnatifida*) from spring through fall. This is one of the hardest working perennials in the garden, perfect for mixing with other colors and textures.*

Whirling Butterflies

Another outstanding summer perennial is whirling butterflies, one of the names given to *Gaura lindheimeri*. *Gaura* is a tall, willowy, see-through plant graced with delicate, pale pink, butterfly-like inflorescences all summer long. The wands of *Gaura* move with the passing breezes and sparkle in the sunlight. It's an enchanting, reliable plant to mix in between other midsize to tall plants. Shorter versions can be used closer to the front of the border for an equally nice effect.

DAYLILIES

Before leaving the realm of must-have plants, we need to pay homage to the daylily (*Hemerocallis*)—easy to grow and rewarding. Each erect daylily scape holds numerous flower buds, each one of which opens for only a day at a time. The trumpet flowers may be as large as eight inches across on some of the modern hybrids. More and more daylilies are now being bred for repeat blooming, which is an added joy.

Whatever your color palette, from the palest pastel to the most sizzling hot colors, there are daylilies that will work. There are miniature, dwarf, and extra-tall varieties as well. You have your choice of ruffled or nonruffled petals; single, semidouble, or double blooms; flowers with contrasting "eyes" in the center; as well as freckled and striped blooms. The selection is truly a colorist's dream.

Perhaps the best known and most widely used of all daylilies is the dwarf, long-blooming 'Stella de Oro'. Its color is a deep golden yellow. One of Stella's offspring, 'Happy Returns', has a similar habit, but its clear lemon yellow coloring mixes more smoothly with its neighbors.

The bright orange southern classic, the tawny daylily (*H. fulva*), is among

Nothing can top the beauty of the classic daylilies (Hemerocallis). There are over 30,000 named cultivars to choose from.

the toughest of them all but can also be an aggressive spreader. You can spot it growing wild along roadsides and embankments, but may not find it for sale at your local nursery.

'Hyperion' is considered the standard by which other lemon yellow daylilies are judged. 'Mary Todd' is another beloved clear yellow variety. One of the best near-white cultivars is 'Gentle Shepherd'. If you're looking for pinks, you have a huge selection, including the orchid pink classic 'Catherine Woodbury'. Similarly, there are hundreds of apricot-colored varieties to choose from. 'Ruffled Apricot' has touches of lilac pink.

SOUTHERN HOT-WEATHER FAVORITES

If you choose classic flowering shrubs and trees supplemented by sages, lantanas, verbenas, daylilies, Mexican petunia, Oxford orphanage plant, and *Gaura* as the mainstays of your garden, you will have an abundance of colorful bloom all summer long. Of course, there are a host of other perennials to fill your summer borders, beds, and containers. Some of the plants that work in our gardens are well known and used extensively across the country. Others have a peculiarly southern flavor. We'll start with some of the southern charmers whose constitutions are built to withstand heat and humidity. Give these heat-seekers first dibs on a spot in your garden.

Four O'Clocks

The tuberous-rooted four o'clocks (*Mirabilis jalapa*) must have seemed miraculous to the person who named them. The long tubular flowers—in solid or variegated shades of red, yellow, and white—are borne on three-foot-tall, multibranched stems on a somewhat shrubby framework. They stay tightly closed all day and open up to emit their strong fragrance only when evening arrives—usually well past four o'clock. They are not elegant, but they are durable southern classics, and they bloom from midsummer through fall.

Turk's Cap

Another good, southern hot-weather perennial whose blossoms don't follow standard procedure is the Turk's cap (*Malvaviscus arboreus drummondii*). It produces strangely twisted red flowers with protruding stamens from early summer through fall. The flowers never fully open, but hummingbirds are not deterred. They hover directly over the top of the flowers to sip the nectar. Turk's cap is a shrubby, three- to five-foot-tall plant, which you can keep pruned to any size you like. The white-flowered variety is 'Alba'.

*An old southern classic, the tuberous four o'clock (*Mirabilis jalapa*) gets its name from its habit of opening its blossoms in the late afternoon.*

Cupheas

The genus *Cuphea* includes a number of tender perennials that often overwinter for us or can be treated as annuals if the winter is particularly cold. Mexican heather (*C. hyssopifolia*) with tiny, glossy green leaves grows only about a foot tall. All summer and fall it is covered with small flowers in shades of violet, pink, or white. Cigar plant (*C. ignea*) grows to a similar height with somewhat larger leaves. The flowers of the cigar plant are red tubes with white tips edged in an almost black color, resembling the embers of a glowing cigar.

WELL-KNOWN EVERYWHERE

Yarrow

The summer perennials you're most likely to find in plant catalogs and nurseries are those adapted to the widest range of climates. In many cases the coastal South Zone 8 is at the extreme end of the plants' heat tolerance, but we can still grow them, if not quite as easily as our northern neighbors can. One of the most ubiquitous perennials in the United States — in some cases a weedy pest — is yarrow (*Achillea*). With its ferny foliage and flat umbels of white, pink, red, lilac, or yellow, yarrow is a classic cottage garden perennial. It will do best for us in full, baking sun and fairly poor soil. Yarrow doesn't like to be fertilized, and the drainage must be perfect. Deadhead regularly to keep the blooms coming or cut back severely after the first bloom to get a fall repeat.

*If you look closely at the flowers on the Turk's cap (*Malvaviscus arboreus drummondii*), you will notice that they never open up. This shrubby perennial is guaranteed to produce bright red, turban-shaped flowers all summer long.*

Blanketflower

Yarrow can share its hot, dry position with blanketflower (*Gaillardia* x *grandifora*), a summer bloomer that is a member of the large Compositae family, meaning that its flowers have a daisy-like structure. *Gaillardia* performs well in seashore as well as sunny inland positions. It grows about two feet tall with a burgundy-colored flower center ringed by yellow ray petals with maroon strip-

left:

To do well, yarrow (Achillea) needs a position in full sun and very well drained soil. Cut it back after its first period of bloom to ensure more flowers in the fall.

right:

The colors of blanketflower (Gaillardia) vary from plant to plant. It is a great perennial for a beach garden or a dry, sunny garden farther inland.

ing at the base. It's not a long-lived plant, but it will withstand heat and drought. It needs excellent drainage. The annual or biennial native wildflower, firewheel (*G. pulchella*) is similar in appearance and seeds itself freely along the beach.

Coreopsis

The sunshine yellow, single or double flowers of coreopsis (*Coreopsis*) begin their long season of bloom in late spring or early summer. The flowers are often recognizable by their pinked or incised petal tips. Cultivars of the native lanceleaf coreopsis (*C. lanceolata*), such as 'Baby Sun' and 'Goldfink', and the fully double *L. grandiflora* cultivar 'Early Sunrise' survive our hot, humid summers better than some of the others.

Daisies, Coneflowers, and Black-eyed Susans

Other daisy-like summer flowers include the classic Shasta daisy (*Chrysanthemum* x *superbum*) with its bright white ray petals and golden center. The popular 'Alaska' cultivar tends to be short-lived here and is not guaranteed to do well with our heat, but the cultivar 'Becky' is more reliable, sending up flowers most of the summer on sturdy three- to four-foot-long stems. The cultivar 'Thomas Killian' is the best one for the beach.

We are fortunate to be able to grow the beautiful South African Gerber daisies (*Gerbera jamesonii*) as perennials in our climate. These elegant plants bear large (four to six inches in diameter), single or double, richly colored daisies on ten-inch stems. The range of colors includes white, pink, red, coral, yellow, orange, and cream. Gerbers require full to part sun and perfect drainage or they will rot out.

The common tickseed (Coreopsis) blooms in profusion in late spring and into the summer.

Possibly the most indestructible of all summer perennials, black-eyed Susan (Rudbeckia) comes in various sizes and shapes. The classic cultivar R. fulgida sullivantii 'Goldsturm' is shown here.

On a much smaller scale, tiny, narrow-petaled, magenta-purple daisies appear all summer long at ground level above the narrow, succulent leaves of ice plant (*Delosperma cooperi*), an excellent groundcover for the beach and other hot, perfectly dry areas.

Other members of the *Compositae* family include black-eyed Susans, yellow coneflowers, and gloriosa daisies—all members of the genus *Rudbeckia*. The bloom season of *Rudbeckia* includes early summer (*R. hirta*, the gloriosa daisy, with red bands on yellow petals), midsummer (*R. fulgida*, orange coneflower, the classic golden daisy with a dark eye; *R. lancianata*, green-headed coneflower with drooping yellow rays and a green disk; *R. maxima*, the huge giant black-eyed Susan; and the shade-tolerant *R. triloba*); and late summer into fall (*R. nitida*, 'Autumn Sun' and *R. lancianata* 'Goldrop'). The best *Rudbeckias* for part shade are *R. triloba*, *R. hirta*, *R. lancianata*, and *R. nitida*.

Purple coneflower (*Echinacea purpurea*) is a great butterfly attractant and will bloom from midsummer until fall. This simple, somewhat coarse native likes full sun and excellent drainage. The drooping rays around the dark central disk are generally pink, but there are also white varieties.

The Mexican hat plant (*Ratibida columnifera*), which also loves a dry bake, has possibly the most noticeably protruding central brown cone of all the coneflowers. The cone is surrounded by drooping yellow ray petals, so the overall effect is something like a yellow-and-brown badminton shuttlecock.

Perhaps the most floriferous of all the *Compositae* family is the bush daisy (*Euryops viridens*), with its profusion of yellow daisies lasting from spring through frost. Often you will see bush daisies pruned into a standard form for use in pots so that they look like small daisy trees. Keep *Euryops* well watered and fertilized and give it extra protection during cold spells or you may lose it.

Heavy mulch, cotton sheeting with pine straw on top, or burlap are all good winter protectors for any of your slightly tender perennials. Bush daisy needs perfect winter drainage or it will rot away.

Bee Balm

There are a number of perennials that operate on the theory that more is better. The mints are notorious for making themselves at home everywhere. A close family relative is bee balm (*Monarda didyama*), which sports whorls of red, purple, white, lavender, or pink flowers on two- to three-foot-long stems beginning in midsummer. It spreads rapidly in full sun to part shade and moist soil. The bad news is that it suffers from mildew. Some coastal gardeners also report that this type of *Monarda* stops blooming after the first year or two. If this happens, lift and divide the plants.

A reliable but more subtly colored native, dotted horsemint (*M. punctata*) is a proven plant for late summer bloom in hot, dry sites, including the beach. The yellow flower corollas are spotted with purple and offset by purple bracts. Wild bee balm (*M. fistulosa*) is another heat-tolerant native, which prefers moist soil in part sun. Its pale pink, white, or lavender flowers are less showy than those of *M. didyama*.

Veronica

Speedwell, or veronica, is another summer perennial that's well known across the country. There are both prostrate and erect forms that flower all summer in shades of blue, white, or pink. Gardeners in the coastal South have

Blooming in early summer, Stokes' aster (Stokesia) is an easygoing perennial for the coastal South. It does best when not overly crowded by neighboring plants.

a shot at growing veronica successfully if it is kept very well watered. Spike speedwell (*Veronica spicata*), which grows two to three feet tall, is the best species for our area. Also look for the prostrate *V. peduncularis* 'Georgia Blue' and *V. prostrata* 'Trehane', both of which produce short, spike-like racemes of deep blue flowers on mat-forming plants. *Veronica* 'Sunny Border Blue' produces erect spikes of dark, violet-blue flowers all summer long if it is not allowed to dry out.

Stokes' Aster

Some terrific summer perennials bloom only once but provide several weeks of enjoyment and, if given favorable growing conditions, will increase steadily in the garden. Stokes' aster (*Stokesia laevis*) is a reliable producer of sky-blue, cornflower-like blooms for several weeks in early summer. It prefers full to partial sun and dry feet in winter. There are white, cream-yellow and pink *Stokesias* as well.

Butterfly Weed

Milkweed or butterfly weed (*Asclepias*) is the host plant for the monarch butterfly. The swamp milkweed (*A. incarnata*) thrives in wet soil and full to part sun, producing rosy-purple flowers on two- to five-foot-tall stalks in summer. Two native butterfly weeds (*A. lanceolata* and A. *tuberosa*) bear orangy-red or yellow flowers and require sharp drainage, as does their cousin the red bloodflower (*A. curassavica*). Be careful not to disturb *Asclepias* in spring—they break dormancy quite late.

Patrinia

Also beginning its bloom in early summer is patrinia (*Patrinia scabiosifolia*), which provides three-foot-tall corymbose panicles in a hard-to-find mustard yellow that blends perfectly with almost any other color. The flowers continue to look nice on the plant long past the peak of their bloom. Patrinia is one of those little-known gems that you will be glad you tried.

Keep track of where you plant your butterfly weed (Asclepias tuberosa), because it is late to emerge from its winter dormancy.

Skullcap

The native skullcap *Scuttelaria incana* is a good choice for the summer garden. It grows to a bushy four feet tall with blue, snapdragon-like flowers in sun or part sun and is a favorite of butterflies. The lower-growing skullcaps, *S. suffrutescens* 'Texas Rose' and *S. formosiana* 'Royal Purple', produce, respectively, beautiful pink and purple snapdragon-like flowers for many weeks in summer. *S. suffrutescens* may not be as long-lived as the other two species. All of the *Scuttelarias* prefer light, very well drained soil slightly on the alkaline side. If your soil is acidic, work in a handful of agricultural lime at planting time.

Balloon Flower

Balloon flower (*Platycodon grandiflorus*) got its name from the shape of the deep blue flower buds just before they open. Balloon flower is a long-lived plant once it is established. The taller varieties have a tendency to flop over, but the shorter ones such as 'Sentimental Blue' don't have this problem. There are pink and white balloon flowers as well and some with double petals. Your balloon flower will establish deep roots over time and will not appreciate being moved. Like butterfly weed, it reappears fairly late in the spring, so be careful not to dig it up by mistake. Plant it in a partially sunny or lightly shaded spot in good soil.

A FEW ODD FELLOWS

Red-hot Poker

Red-hot poker (*Kniphofia uvaria*) is not a particularly subtle plant. The torchy flowers on its four-foot-tall stems open red and mature to yellow-green, starting from the bottom of the spike on up, giving the plant a brassy two-tone appearance. The solid-color versions, especially the yellow, are much more demure. But, of course, they're less fun to be around. *Kniphofias* require full sun and perfect drainage.

Voodoo Lily and Pitcher Plant

Different altogether in aspect, but equally quirky, are the shade-loving voodoo lilies (*Amorphophallus*). In early summer the large underground tuber sends up a mottled stem topped with a hooded or flared spathe that encloses a protruding, fleshy-looking spadix. The spathe may be mottled green, white, pink, or purple. A month or so later the tuber sends up a single large leaf. Voodoo lilies generally grow from two to six feet tall, although there are some giants reaching over twelve feet.

Another coastal classic curiosity is the carnivorous pitcher plant (*Sarracenia*), which enjoys sunny bogs, swallows insects, and abhors fertilization. The interesting-looking "pitchers" resemble flared vases. They are often speckled and veined in shades of red, brown, orange, green, or yellow. Although the plants do produce odd spring flower stalks, they are grown for the summer-long interest of their pitchers. In many states it is illegal to cull these natives from the wild, so gardeners should buy only from reputable nurseries.

Parrot Lilies

The restaurant-vase flower we have all seen lined up next to the salt and pepper shakers is really the parrot lily (*Alstroemeria psittacina*). The parrot lily is a mottled, orchid-like flower in various pastel shades. *Alstroemeria* grows well in our area, sometimes even invasively, much to the envy of our northern friends. Grow it in a sandy loam in a spot that gets afternoon shade, and it will colonize for you. When cut, it lasts just about forever in a vase. One well-kept horticultural secret is that there is really only one vase of *Alstroemeria* in the world and it is passed around at night from restaurant to restaurant.

SUMMER SHADE-LOVERS

Hostas

For the shade garden, much of the country relies on hostas (*Hosta* spp.) for variegation in foliage and the blooming wands of lavender or white that appear in early summer. Hostas will grow for us, but they are not "naturals" for the coastal South. One of the largest and healthiest hostas for our climate is 'Sum and Substance', a striking, bright green cultivar with nicely textured leaves. Slightly more reliable, but more costly, are the shade-loving sacred lilies (*Rohdea japonica*).

*Hostas (*Hosta*) flower even in deep shade. Chartreuse-leaved hostas and those with variegation are useful perennials for lighting up dark areas of the garden.*

Lobelia

The best lobelia for the coastal South is the native big blue lobelia (*Lobelia siphilitica*). Growing two to three feet tall, it sends up blue spires in summer in a sunny, moist spot. The bright red, cardinal flower (*L. cardinalis*) is somewhat more finicky in our climate, demanding a rich, constantly moist soil to thrive.

SUBTROPICAL SUMMER DRAMA

Canna Lilies

Canna lilies (*Canna*) are probably the best known of the subtropicals. The classic bright-red- and bright-yellow-flowered varieties have been blooming in southern gardens for generations. The selection has expanded greatly, so that now cannas are available in pastel or bright colors, dwarf or tall habits, and with strikingly variegated foliage. 'Bengal Tiger' has vivid green-and-yellow-striped foliage with tangerine-orange flowers. 'Le Roi Humbert' is grown for its impressive red foliage and red flowers. For a distinctive foliage combination of pink, red, yellow, and green, 'Tropicana' is wonderful. One of the best clear-pink-flowered cannas is 'Tropical Rose'. Cannas grow in part sun to shade in rich, moist soil. They like bogs as well, so you can put them in a pot in your pond if you like. They are remarkably durable, easy plants.

Bananas and Elephant Ears

Gardeners all along the Southern Atlantic and Gulf coasts make great use of the wonderfully oversized bananas (*Musa* and *Ensete*), elephant ears, and taros

*Canna lilies (Canna)
are a staple perennial
for the summer coastal
garden. Available in
a large variety of
flower colors as well
as striking variations
in foliage, they are a
primary source of
nonstop color.*

(*Colocasia*, *Alocasia*, and *Xanthosoma*) in their summer gardens. These terrific
rhizomatous and tuberous perennials add tropical panache and provide architectural structure that few other plants can offer. They can be grown in sun or
part shade, in regular garden soil, in a bog, or in a pond container. In the winter months, they need dry soil.

Two of the largest bananas are the twenty-foot-tall, giant sweet edible banana (*Musa acuminata*) and the fifteen-foot-tall hardy banana (*M. basjoo*).

*The tropical beauty of ginger lilies (*Hedychium*), canna lilies (*Canna*), and black-leaf taro (*Colocasia esculenta 'Illustris'*) is what gardening in the coastal South is all about.*

These plants have huge eight-foot-long leaves that call attention to themselves in any garden. On a slightly smaller scale, in the four- to eight-foot-tall range, are the pink banana (*M. velutina*) and rose banana (*M. ornata*), both of which produce showy flowers in summer. The striking bloodleaf banana (*M. zebrina*) is an excellent addition for its red-splotched foliage.

Some of the larger elephant ears, such as the fifteen-foot-tall giant upright elephant ear (*Alocasia macrorhiza*) and the similar-sized colorful elephant ear (*A. plumbea*), make equally exceptional silhouettes in sun or part shade. The red (*A. plumbea* 'Rubra') and black (*A. plumbea* 'Nigra') cultivars are especially beautiful.

One of the best elephant ears to mix in containers or grow with other perennials is *Colocasia* 'Black Magic'. Its heart-shaped leaves get larger and deeper black as the summer wears on. 'Black Magic' looks terrific next to chartreuse foliage and is an excellent foil for hot oranges and reds. Its cousin, black-stemmed elephant ear (*C. esculenta* 'Fontanesii'), grows six feet tall with dark green, shiny leaves veined with violet-black.

Bananas, taros, and elephant ears grow best in richly amended organic soil that is kept moist during the growing season and dry in winter. The richer the soil, the larger the plant. Of course, plant height is also affected by how far south the plant is grown. In Zones 9 and above these subtropicals will die back to the ground when temperatures drop and will not leaf back out again until early summer. Therefore, gardeners need to design their plantings with this spring "absence" in mind. A thick, dry winter mulch is helpful.

Palms and Cycads

Nothing is quite as emblematic of the coast as palm trees. Even those of us who don't live in the tropics can grow a large number of hardy palms. There are the eighty-foot-tall giants such as the *Washingtonias* that are seen in cities up and down the Southern Atlantic and Gulf coasts. They are most suitable for street plantings. The other common giant is the ninety-foot-tall cabbage palm (*Sabal palmetto*), known for its willingness to transplant under less than perfect circumstances. It even grows on sand dunes. Less colossal but very hardy are the thirty-foot-tall windmill palms (*Trachycarpus fortunei*) and the twenty-foot-tall pindo palms (*Butia capitata*).

The most widely grown of all the hardy palms are probably the dwarf palmettos (*Sabal minor*). Growing three to six feet tall, they are rugged and adaptable in sun or part shade, rich or poor soil. With the typical, deeply divided, fan-shaped foliage that palms are known for, they appear to be trunkless. In summer, ten-foot-tall spikes of white flowers appear above the foliage.

Another handsome, hardy perennial (a cycad rather than a palm) that appears not to have a trunk in its earlier years is the sago palm (*Cycas revoluta*). It grows very slowly to ten feet with arching, deeply cut, fan-shaped fronds. It is a great addition to the sunny perennial border. Other hardy palms that mix in well with perennials include the European fan palm (*Chamaerops humilis*), broadleaf lady palm (*Rhapis excelsa*), and needle palm (*Rhapidophyllum hystrix*).

Phormium

New Zealand flax or phormium (*Phormium tenax*) is an attractive, tropical-looking plant that grows to six feet tall. It sends up sword-shaped leaves, some of which stand erect and some of which arch over. The purple-leaved varieties

*A pindo palm (*Butia capitata*) forms the centerpiece of this well-tended seaside garden.*

left:
*A red-leaved variety
of New Zealand flax
(*Phormium tenax*)
stands out among
palms and other
subtropicals.*

right:
*Lilies of the Nile
(*Agapanthus*) are
among the most
beautiful of all
flowering bulbs.
Plant them in soil
that drains well so
they will have "dry
feet" in winter.*

are especially handsome. New Zealand flax needs full to part sun in rich, well-drained soil to do well.

Cordyline

Cordylines (*Cordyline australis*) start their lives out looking something like phormiums and end up looking more like palm trees once they reach their full, thirty-foot height. The three-foot-long, erect or arching leaves are sword-shaped. Cordyline cultivars are available with dark plum or variegated cream-and-green foliage.

SUMMER BULBS

Lily of the Nile

One thing overlooked in many summer gardens are bulbs, tubers, corms, rhizomes, and other subterranean storers of nourishment. We're fortunate to have a wide choice in this department—from extra large to diminutive. On the large scale—in addition to the bananas, cannas, elephant ears, and gingers already mentioned—there are several substantial, strappy-leaved plants that send up striking flower stalks.

Lily of the Nile (*Agapanthus*) is an elegant plant, often used in containers and overwintered indoors in other parts of the country. For us, it is a hardy perennial, which can be mixed in with other perennials in beds and borders or massed for a dramatic effect. Its handsome, dark green foliage is topped with stunning, rounded or pendent umbels of sky-blue flowers on one- to five-foot-tall stalks, depending on the variety. There are also white *Agapanthus*. All agapanthus like a partially sunny spot with rich soil and good drainage. In winter it's especially important that they have dry feet, but they appreciate getting plenty of water in summer.

The large corms of
crinum lilies (Crinum)
should be planted
shallowly, with the top
third above ground.
After that you can sit
back and expect
glorious blooms year
after year.

Crinum Lily

Other strappy-leaved giants include the southern classic crinum lily (*Crinum*), which produces huge (four- to six-inch-long), trumpet-shaped or spidery flowers all summer long once it's gotten itself well established. Crinums like full to part sun and good moisture, but they do remarkably well at the beach. Plant your crinum corm so that the top third is sticking out of the ground. The *Amarcrinum* is a cross between an amaryllis and a crinum, with the typical strappy leaves and the tall scapes of trumpet-shaped flowers blooming all summer. It is an excellent bulb for the coastal South.

Tuberoses and Gladioli

Moving down the scale heightwise, fragrant tuberoses (*Polianthes tuberosa*) are still in the category of stately bulbous plants. Their three-foot-tall, waxy, white spires appear in late summer. The best variety for the coastal South is 'Mexican Single'.

Hardy Abyssinian gladiolus (*G. callianthus*) also sends up spires in summer and can be left in the ground from year to year. The flowers are white with rich brown markings.

Crocosmia and Liatris

Bright spikes of summer color are what crocosmia (*Crocosmia*) is all about. Landscapers often use these easy bulbs because they have the same healthy constitution and relative flexibility as the daylily and thrive in very similar conditions. Depending on the variety, *Crocosmia* sends up red, orange, gold, or pale-yellow spikes above erect, sword-shaped foliage. It looks neat and stays neat and is especially dramatic en masse from a distance. The bright red cultivar 'Lucifer' is a tried and true performer for us. The flowers of 'Golden Fleece' are a beautiful, soft, primrose yellow.

Another well-known and widely used member of the bulb clan is the blazing star or gayfeather (*Liatris spicata*), which sends up two- to three-foot-tall purple spikes for several weeks in summer. *L. spicata* has a tendency to rot out in our wet winters. Some gardeners may find that thick-spiked gayfeather (*L. pycnostachys*) performs slightly better in our area.

Summer Daffodils

So-called summer daffodils come in two varieties in the coastal South, neither of which are in the *Narcissus* genus. The Peruvian daffodil (*Hymenocallis* 'Sulfur Queen') has something of the look of a daffodil morphing into a spider lily. The lovely, pale yellow blooms are borne on two-foot-tall stems above strappy leaves in summer. Peruvian daffodils need full to part sun and rich, well-drained soil. Like other bulbs, they abhor winter wetness. Also known as Peruvian daffodil and sharing the same cultural requirements are the white-flowered *H. narcissiflora* and *H.* x *festalis* 'Advance'.

*Sometimes called summer daffodils, spider lilies (*Hymenocallis*) are durable southern classics. The bulbs will persist and increase in coastal gardens with very little attention.*

The sea daffodil (*Pancratium maritimum*) is shorter but otherwise not too dissimilar, with strappy leaves and white, whiskery flowers appearing in summer. Sea daffodils demand full sun and a hot, baking, perfectly drained location to survive.

Summer Hyacinths and Irises

With your summer "daffodils" why not plant some summer hyacinths? *Galtonia candicans*, the summer hyacinth, sends up two- to four-foot-tall scapes of white pendent bells in summer. Give it full sun and keep it watered in summer, dry in winter.

And we have irises for summer, too. The copper iris (*I. fulva*) will put forth striking reddish-copper blooms in midsummer in full to part sun as long as its feet are wet. The African iris or fortnight lily (*Dietes vegeta*) produces white flowers above sword-shaped leaves from spring through fall. It grows best in moist soil but will tolerate a poor, dry spot. African iris is somewhat tender and may do best in the lower parts of the coastal South.

Dahlias

Dahlias (*Dahlia*) are known all over the gardening world for their long season of bloom and the huge variety they provide in terms of color, size, and

left:

In the warmer parts of the coastal South, dahlias (Dahlia) may overwinter in the ground as long as they are not allowed to get too wet. The bright red 'Roodkapje' (or 'Little Red Riding Hood') adds excellent color to the perennial garden.

right:

The lavender blooms of society garlic (Tulbaghia violacea) mix well with other perennials in a sunny or partially sunny location.

configuration. They are widely planted in the coastal South in spite of the fact that they are not particularly trouble-free. Dahlias may overwinter if the cold is not abnormally severe and if they are given perfectly dry winter situations. Lifting the tubers and storing them in a dry place until the following spring is always a safe bet.

Plant dahlia tubers in spring in a sunny, well-drained spot in a fairly rich soil, and they will bloom into the fall if they're regularly deadheaded and sprayed. Use Bt (an insecticide made of the bacterium Bacillus thuringiensis) and neem oil to ward off pests that are fighting you for your prize blooms.

Society Garlic and Chinese Chives

The onions and their look-alikes also have some blooms to offer in summer. Society garlic (*Tulbaghia violacea*), which is not a true garlic, holds up very well to our heat and humidity, increasing its clump size each year. Its small, lavender, ball-shaped inflorescences appear from early summer straight through fall. The variegated society garlic has handsome, white-striped, gray-green leaves.

Chinese or garlic chives (*Allium tuberosum*) is a rhizomatous bulb that increases rapidly and is extremely reliable in our climate, blooming from late summer into fall. Chinese chives' white umbels of star-shaped flowers are valued for their ability to mix well with other perennials. Both of these vampire-slayer bulbs prefer full to part sun and perfect drainage.

Rain Lilies and Fairy Lilies

Among the very small bulbs with dainty, ground-level flowers are some of the treasures of summer. Not used nearly as much as they should be in our gardens, rain lilies, fairy lilies, and copper lilies are all worth getting to know. Two genera, *Habranthus* and *Zephyranthes*, harbor these delicate funnel- or star-shaped bloomers in a wide range of colors—white, pink, coral, copper, and various yellows from pale to orangy. Most of them prefer full to part sun in rich soil with absolutely perfect drainage so they won't rot out in winter. These gems will bloom sporadically during the summer and into the fall and deserve a place in every garden. Rain lilies have the charming habit of bursting into bloom after thunderstorms.

After a summer thunderstorm, rain lilies (Zephyranthes and Habranthus *spp.) burst into bloom. The grassy foliage remains attractive year-round. Shown here is the delicate, lemon yellow bloom of four-inch-high Z. citrina.*

Lilies

Last, but definitely not least, in this list of summer bulbs are the gorgeous lilies (*Lilium* spp.). There are so many lilies, each more tantalizing than the next, that it's hard to imagine a summer garden without them. It's not necessary to become an expert on the differences among all the lilies to plant them and enjoy them. Lilies like full to part sun, rich soil, and excellent drainage. Certain types are more suited to the coastal South than others, but lilies generally are not hard to grow.

It's important to remember that the juicy, scaly lily bulbs have no protective skin or coating, so when they're dug from the ground they immediately run the risk of becoming desiccated. Try to stick them back in the ground right away. When you receive mail-order lily bulbs, plant them as soon as possible. The Asiatic hybrids, of which there are hundreds to choose from, do slightly better for us than the oriental hybrids (also with a huge selection). Asiatics are often the first lilies to bloom in summer and orientals are among the last.

Several beautiful white species lilies do well for us, including the Easter lily (*L. longiformium*), the madonna lily (*L. candidum*), and the Formosa lily (*L. formosanum*). Regal lilies (*L. regale*) are especially stunning with their tall, sturdy stems and huge wine-and-cream-colored trumpets highlighted by yellow shading. Regals bloom fairly early in the summer. Lilies are generally inexpensive, easy to care for, and multiply into sizable colonies over the years. They are always a beautiful addition to the garden. If you have a problem with pine voles eating your lily bulbs, try planting them in small, homemade chicken-wire "cages."

*Asiatic hybrid lilies (*Lilium*) bloom in full to part sun in early summer in almost every shade of the rainbow.*

SUMMER VINES

The lush abandon of summer wouldn't be complete without vines clambering over walls and fences and attracting bees and hummingbirds with their profusion of blossoms. There are hundreds to choose from. Most vines do best in full to part sun and appreciate water during periods of drought. Some vines tolerate partial shade but won't bloom as well in shade as they will in a sunny position.

Clematis

Of the more delicately stemmed summer vines, clematis (*Clematis* spp.) heads the list. There are over 200 species of clematis and even more hybrids, many with spectacular flowers. Among the large-flowered hybrids, the white 'Henryi', pink 'Comtesse de Bouchard', red 'Ernest Markham' and 'Ville de Lyon', purplish-pink striped with crimson 'Nelly Moser', and the deep purple *C. jackmanii* are probably among the best known. The choice of size, color, and bloom time is ultimately enormous. All clematis, including both the small-flowered species and the large-flowered hybrids, appreciate the richest soil you can give them, attention to watering, roots protected by a mulch or groundcover, and regular fertilization during the growing season. One trick is to plant your clematis under an upside-down terra cotta pot, allowing the stem and leaves to work their way up through the drainage hole. This way the roots are permanently shaded. Or try planting your clematis very deeply, so that six to eight inches of the stem is covered. This keeps the roots moist and cool and protects the stem.

Virgin's bower clematis, *C. viticella* and its hybrids, work well for us either alone on a trellis or twining up a nearby rosebush or shrub. *C. viticella* is known by its open, bell-shaped flowers in shades of blue, lavender, pink, and deep purple. It will bloom on and off all summer once it has become established.

Flowering clematis (Clematis) is a good vine to mix with roses and shrubs. The flowers may take the shape of a large saucer, a star, a bell, or, as here, a reflexed inverted vase.

Passionflower Vine and Trumpet Creeper

We're lucky to be able to enjoy the spectacularly sculptural blooms of passionflower vine (*Passiflora* spp.) in its many species and hybrids all summer long. 'Byron Beauty' is a particularly stunning, blue, white, and purple cultivar. The southeastern native maypop (*P. incarnata*) is a very hardy, deciduous vine. Growing twenty to thirty feet long and producing beautiful pale lavender blossoms with purple and pink markings, this passionflower vine can be more invasive than some of the other species. There are passionflower vines with red, blue, greenish-white, pink, and salmon-colored flowers as well. The Gulf fritillary butterfly feeds on these vines, so if you see red caterpillars about, let them enjoy their feast.

Showy red, yellow, orange, or apricot-colored trumpet vine (*Campsis*) is an extremely vigorous southern classic. Reaching to forty feet and producing bright, colorful trumpets all summer once established, it may take a few years to start blooming heavily. Once a trumpet vine takes hold, however, it may make itself more at home than you want. *Campsis* spreads both stoloniferously and by seeding itself about. 'Madame Galen' is an old-time hybrid with larger, more open flowers. It is much more decorative than the native *Campsis* found along roadside fences.

Honeysuckle and Jasmine

Trumpet honeysuckle (*Lonicera sempervirens*) and gold flame honeysuckle (*L. heckrottii*) continue to display their fragrant fans of narrow tubular flowers on and off during the summer months.

There are also some evergreen and semievergreen summer-blooming jasmines. These can be used as vines, groundcovers, sprawling shrubs, or hedges—depending on how they are pruned and

*Violet-blue tepals form the base from which the ovary and stamens of the passionflower (*Passiflora*) protrude dramatically. A contrasting ring of deep blue filaments completes this work of art.*

trained. Generally they have small, glossy green leaves and clusters of salverform flowers. Arabian jasmine (*Jasminum sambac* 'Grand Duke of Tuscany') is a classic, double-flowered white variety for the coastal South. Italian jasmine (*J. humile*) bears yellow flowers in summer, and the long-blooming Spanish jasmine (*J. grandiflorum*) produces white flowers tinged with pink. South African jasmine (*J. angulare*) has clusters of pale pink summer flowers.

Coral Vine

If you've traveled in the lower South in the summer, you may have seen the pink flower sprays and heart-shaped leaves of coral vine (*Antigonon leptopus*) draped along fences and walls. Coral vine is a somewhat airy, deciduous southern classic that loves the heat and is especially well suited to Zones 9 and southward. It can grow to forty feet easily.

Kiwi, Star Jasmine, and St. Vincent's Lilac

Planting a male and female fuzzy kiwi vine (*Actinidia deliciosa*) may well reward you not only with creamy flowers but also with egg-sized, fuzzy kiwi fruit in late summer and fall. This vigorous, twining vine, which grows to thirty feet, needs a strong support and regular pruning each winter.

And speaking of fruits and vegetables, the potato and eggplant clan gives us several summer-blooming vines. These include the somewhat tender, lilac-blue St. Vincent's lilac (*Solanum seaforthianum*), which blooms all summer and into fall. It will do best in Zones 9 and southward. Hardier than St. Vincent's lilac is *S. crispum* 'Glasnevin', which produces dark blue flowers in late summer and fall.

Their near relative, the star jasmine (*S. jasminoides*), has a very long blooming period, from early summer through fall, with white, star-shaped flowers with prominent yellow stamens. It is often evergreen for us, providing handsome foliage all winter long.

Climbing Hydrangeas

In the coastal South we do somewhat better with the native climbing hydrangea *Decumaria barbara* than the better-known *Hydrangea petiolaris*, which is not particularly well-suited to our area. Given full to part shade and rich, moist soil, *Decumaria barbara* will produce fragrant white flower clusters in early summer once it has had a chance to establish itself. It is a very vigorous, woody vine that climbs by aerial holdfasts or makes its way along the ground for thirty feet or more. Give it plenty of room to roam.

One other climbing hydrangea, Japanese hydrangea vine (*Schizophragma hydrangeoides*), blooms in full sun to part shade as long as it is given fertile, well-drained soil that is kept well watered. Showy, cream-colored bracts surround the small white flowers. It is another vigorous climber, up to forty feet, which attaches by aerial roots.

FROST-TENDER VINES

Mandevilla and Bougainvillea

Finally, there are dozens of tender perennial or annual vines that add months of color to the summer garden. Used all over the coastal South for its large (two-inch-diameter), trumpet-shaped blooms in shades of pink, white, and yellow, the tender Chilean jasmine vine or mandevilla (*Mandevilla laxa*) is a plant worth having even if it means bringing it inside every winter. If given full sun, rich soil, and ample moisture, mandevilla will bloom constantly and prolifically with glossy green leaves and dramatic, eye-catching flowers.

Similarly stunning is bougainvillea (*Bougainvillea*) with its pink, red, gold, white, or purple petal-like bracts bringing color to the garden all summer long. Bougainvillea likes frequent fertilization and is tender above Zone 9. It is much more shy to flower than mandevilla if conditions aren't perfectly to its liking. There are a number of bougainvillea theories—imprison the roots in a container one size too small, beat the roots regularly with a baseball bat. It may be that this plant is better suited to outdoor life in the tropics than to life in the coastal South.

In historic Charleston, two classic southern vines, Bougainvillea (on the left) and mandevilla (Mandevilla laxa), adorn a wrought-iron fence.

Cypress Vine, Morning Glories, Moon Vine, and Some Sweet Potatoes

One of the most delightful annual vines used for many years in the South is the classic humming-bird attractant, the cypress vine (*Ipomoea quamoclit*). It has extremely delicate-looking, thread-like foliage and tiny, bright red, tubular flowers. This vine interlaces with and complements heavier vines and shrubs and may be the airiest plant you can grow. It reseeds so freely that it can almost be considered an honorary perennial.

The somewhat similar-looking star quamoclit or star morning glory (*I. coccinea*) has larger, red, tubular flowers and larger, boldly toothed foliage.

In the same genus we have the deep-purple-flowered perennial morning glory vine (*I. indica*) as well as the annual morning glories (*I. purpurea* and *I. tricolor*) with their funnel- or trumpet-

The laciest foliage in the garden may belong to the cypress vine (Ipomoea quamoclit), an annual that reseeds itself vigorously. Its bright red tubular flowers attract hummingbirds.

shaped flowers. Annual morning glories are available in shades of sky blue, purple, magenta, lilac, white, and pink—some double varieties and some striped—and all are fast-growing, reliable, all-summer bloomers. Morning glories can be planted with their night-blooming cousin, the moonflower vine (*I. alba*), whose large, bright white cups are visible even in the dark.

A Gulf Coast native, salt marsh morning glory (*I. sagittata*) produces rosy-purple blooms all summer long in a sunny spot. It tolerates both wet and dry conditions. The highly useful annual sweet potato vines (*I. batatas*) are also members of the *Ipomoea* genus. Although they don't provide flowers in our cli-

left:
*The annual
morning glory vine
(Ipomoea purpurea)
thrives in poor,
well-drained soil.*

right:
*The bright chartreuse
leaves of the annual
'Margarita' sweet
potato vine (Ipomoea
batata 'Margarita')
contrast beautifully
with the dark leaves
of a basil plant.*

mate, their lobed foliage looks handsome spilling out of a containers or cover-ing the ground in an area of sun or part sun. 'Margarita' has bright chartreuse foliage that contrasts well with other greens in the garden. 'Blackie' has un-beatable, dark plum, almost black-colored foliage. For a variegated pink, white, and green vine, try the sweet potato 'Tricolor' (also sold as 'Pink Frost'). 'Lady Fingers' is a rich, mid-green color.

Summer Gourds

If you're looking for an easy way to create drama with vines in your summer garden, try planting gourd-bearing vines. They grow quickly from seed, and if you dry the mature fruits slowly in a cool, well-ventilated spot, you can use them for indoor decorations. Gourd vines generally reach ten to fifteen feet tall, producing flowers of yellow or white. The gourds themselves may be round, cylindrical, bottle-shaped, crook-necked, spatulate, and a number of other shapes. There are solid and striped varieties. Gourds generally ripen to shades of yellow and brown.

HOT-WEATHER ANNUALS
Classic Annuals

It would be difficult to sustain a garden all summer long with only flower-ing trees and perennials to the exclusion of annuals. Annuals often keep the garden going, supplying color and interest when perennials are lagging. Grow hot-weather annuals from seed started six to eight weeks before the frost-free date or buy them started in six-packs. They are worth the small investment every year because their bloom season is so long.

We can grow all the well-known annuals such as geraniums, begonias, impatiens, portulacca, nicotiana, salvia, ageratum, coleus, cosmos, marigolds, alyssum, zinnias, celosia, purslane, and vinca. All except shade coleus and impatiens prefer a position in full sun. Begonias will flower in full sun or full shade. Summer annuals should be given rich soil, slow-release fertilizer in the planting hole, and ample water all summer long. Some will need more deadheading than others to keep blooming well.

New Guinea impatiens and petunias tend to melt out in the hot weather unless kept constantly watered and given some protection from afternoon sun. The best petunias for hot weather are 'Purple Wave' and 'Pink Wave' and other cascading varieties. *Petunia integrifolia*, which is considered a short-lived perennial in our area, does well for some folks and not for others. Its flowers are reddish-purple.

Among the lesser-known summer annuals, there are some that work especially well in our hot, humid summers. These annuals are better suited to the coastal South than some of the traditional standbys.

Pentas

At the top of the list is the old southern favorite, pentas (*Pentas lanceolata*). If you plant pentas, you will enjoy nonstop white, red, lilac, or pink starry flower umbels all summer long until the first hard frost. Flowers are borne on erect two- to three-foot-tall stems, and the plant often grows to the size of a small bush by summer's end. Pentas need little attention apart from an occasional deadheading. Plant them in a sunny or partially sunny spot with good soil and keep them watered. In the southernmost regions of the coastal South, pentas may perennialize.

Tithonia

Tithonia or Mexican sunflower (*Tithonia rotundifolia*) is a torchy, coarse kind of flower that stands up to heat, drought, and humidity. A member of the composite family, it bears bright orange or orangy-red daisy-like flowers on three- to six-foot-tall stems. This bushy, self-sower is beloved of butterflies and hummingbirds. Grow tithonia in full sun and well-drained soil.

Globe Amaranth

Globe amaranth (*Gomphrena globosa*) is a prolific bloomer, which laughs at heat and humidity. It makes fairly neat mounds about a foot high, topped with a profusion of round, pompon flowers in shades of pale lilac, dark purple, strawberry red, or white. It does not require deadheading.

If you can choose only one summer annual, plant pentas (Pentas lanceolata). It blooms through heat and humidity, retaining its glossy green health until the first frost.

left:
Another outstanding summer annual for the coastal South, globe amaranth (Gomphrena globosa) *is a strong performer, needing little or no attention. There are cultivars available in bright purple, white, lilac, and strawberry red.*

right:
*Once established, the annual butter daisy (*Melampodium paludosum*) produces abundant blooms for months with no deadheading.*

Annual Salvia

Another summer stalwart is annual sage (*Salvia splendens*). It is widely available at garden centers and nurseries, and its colorful nonstop spikes atop two-foot-tall stems mingle well at the middle of the border. Although the fire engine red form is most common, the dark plum, lavender, white, and coral-colored annual salvias are also attractive and useful to mix in with perennials.

Butter Daisies

Melampodium or butter daisy (*Melampodium paludosum*) is one of those remarkable plants that looks good for months and months on end and never stops blooming even without deadheading. Its flowers are a bright, cheerful yellow and the plant stays compact and neat looking with healthy, bright green foliage. It grows one to two feet high.

Ornamental Okra

Once you try ornamental okra (*Abelmoschus moschatus*), you may be hooked every year. *Abelmoschus* is a mallow relative with the typical showy, open mallow blossoms on a one- to two-foot-tall, handsomely foliaged plant. It blooms in deep red or pink with white eyes that emphasize the black stamens. This is a floriferous, drought- and heat-tolerant plant that begins blooming only late in the summer but will keep up the show until frost. It often reseeds itself. Its larger relative, *A. manihot*, is equally well suited to our hot, humid summers. *A. manihot* grows five feet tall and produces yellow mallow flowers with maroon eyes.

Spider Flower

Spider flower (*Cleome hasslerana*) is named for the spidery look of the flowers' long, protruding stamens. *Cleome* grows to five feet tall and blooms sequentially farther and farther up its flower stalk, leaving behind slender seedpods as the summer progresses. The spidery flowers are mauve, pink, or white, and each plant will become somewhat bushy if given well-drained, sandy soil. *Cleome* is quite famous for its tendency to self-sow. Pruning in late spring will make it bushier.

Angelonia

Angelonia (*Angelonia angustifolia*) is another annual that works well for us. Growing only a foot and a half tall, it has narrow, pointed, dark green leaves and bears racemes of rich, violet-blue or white flowers all summer long. It needs a partially sunny spot, rich soil, and plenty of moisture to do well.

The Toughest Zinnias

More resistant to heat and humidity than the larger-flowered, more common zinnias are the narrow-leaved zinnias (*Zinnia linearis*). They form mounds to sixteen inches tall topped with small, single blooms in bright orange, white, or yellow. *Zinnia linearis* are very long-blooming annuals that need no deadheading. They perform well at the beach.

Vinca

One of the best known and most widely grown hot-weather annuals is vinca or Madagascar periwinkle (*Cathranthus roseus*). It is valued for its nonstop

The narrow-leaved zinnias (Zinnia linearis) are much more vigorous and healthy looking throughout the summer than other types of annual zinnia.

Although this vinca (Cathranthus roseus) is an annual, it reseeds reliably in the coastal South. It's a tough, dependable annual with nonstop flower production.

flowering and healthy green foliage. Vinca grows from four inches to two feet high, depending on the variety. It has a somewhat bushy, spreading habit. Flowers are white or pink. Vinca does well in full to part sun in well-drained soil and has good drought tolerance.

The long-blooming, colorful hot-weather annuals, together with the flowering summer shrubs, bulbs, perennials and subtropicals will create a lush, vibrant scene in your summer garden. With very little effort you can have constant bloom and fascinating, tropical-looking foliage all summer long.

Fall Rebirth

It's hard to say with any certainty exactly when we have fall. But we don't like to think that we're short one season, so we call fall the period between the last ninety-degree day in October and Christmas. During this period the garden gets a second wind. The cooler nights, the milder daytime temperatures, and the respite from stress stimulate many plants. They reward us by putting on new fresh growth. A number of plants will rebloom in fall as though they'd just been waiting, biding their time. For many plants this is their very best time of year. Some would argue, for example, that roses are more beautiful in the fall in the coastal South than at any other time.

As the weather cools, it's a pleasure to be out in the garden. Fall is the perfect time for planting and transplanting most perennials and for starting cool-season annuals. A fall garden in the coastal South can be as lovely and fresh as a spring garden. All it takes is a little foresight and planning.

Cool fall weather provides the perfect environment for planting and transplanting most perennials.

FALL SHRUBS

After the fireworks of summer have died down, fall-blooming shrubs and subshrubs play an especially important role in keeping the show going. Beginning in October, the sasanquas (*Camellia sasanqua*) put forth hundreds of beautiful white, red, or pink rose-like blossoms. Sasanquas are cousins to the later-blooming *Camellia japonicas*. Their leaves are dark, glossy green like those of the camellias, but they are somewhat smaller and narrower.

Confederate Rose

The Confederate rose (*Hibiscus mutabilis*), as its scientific name suggests, is full of transformation. It's an herbaceous plant, growing eight to ten feet tall, which looks something like a multitrunked maple tree decorated with peony blossoms. Confederate rose is one of the South's most glorious natives. From September through November, large, fully double blossoms cover the plant. The flowers of 'Flora Plena' change from pale pink to deep red each day. The flowers of the cultivar 'Rubrus' remain red.

Senna

The spectacular, golden-yellow peaflowers of senna or cassia plants are visible from a distance and beautiful to observe close at hand. One senna shrub in flower can make a whole garden. Sennas (*Cassia bicapsularis, C. splendida, C. alata,* and *C. corymbosa*) are often the stars of the fall garden, growing to ten feet tall with a bushy shape and handsome, glossy green foliage. Although

left:
Fall is the season when the Confederate rose (Hibiscus mutabilis) is covered with rose-like blossoms in various shades of pink. Shown above is an unusual, single variety of this southern coastal classic.

right:
Even from a great distance, the sunshine yellow clusters of senna flowers (Cassia corymbosa) bring a fall garden alive.

senna may take a few years to get established it will eventually reward you with a bountiful display. Golden senna (*C. corymbosa*) is the most cold-hardy of the group.

Glorybowers

The glorybowers (*Clerodendrum* spp.) are southern fall-blooming classics for the partially shady garden. Cashmere Bouquet plant, aka "Stink Plant" (*C. bungei*), grows three to six feet tall and produces dark pink flower cymes in late summer and fall. Around the same time, its near relation, the blue butterfly flower (*C. ugandense*), bears lavender and white flowers that resemble butter-flies.

The white-and-red-flowered bleeding heart vine (*C. thomsoniae*) is a twin-ing evergreen shrub that can grow to six feet in height. In late summer and fall it is covered with white and red bellflowers.

Clusters of bright, aquamarine-blue berries are one of the excellent features of the harlequin glorybower plant (*C. trichotomum*). They follow upon the heels of the late summer blooms, which are cymes of fragrant, white, salver-form flowers with red sepals.

Blue bean pods follow the bright red flowers of the tender pagoda flower (*C. speciosissimum*). Growing to twelve feet tall with velvety green leaves, pagoda flower thrives in the warmer areas of the coastal South.

Finally, the multicolored production of the electric light plant (*C. indicum*) gives a spark to many lower coastal gardens in late summer and throughout the fall. The red and green flower bracts of this somewhat leggy plant are surmounted with purple fruits in the fall. Like many of the *Clerodendrum* species, this one tends to be invasive, so be forewarned.

If you thought nothing bloomed in the shade in the fall, try the lovely pink Cashmere Bouquet plant (Clerodendrum bungei).

American Beautyberry

Among the southern classics for fall is a somewhat unsophisticated shrub with arching branches and coarse leaves that often look ratty by the end of summer. The beauty in American beautyberry (*Callicarpa americana*), however, is not the foliage or flowers but the abundance of bright, shiny, magenta berries that are borne for weeks in late summer and fall. Gardeners who make the effort to pick off the tired-out foliage and expose the berry-covered branches will create a truly beautiful spectacle that will stand out among the other shrubs and perennials. Beautyberry can even be used as a specimen plant, planted on its own as a focal point in the garden.

Japanese beautyberry (*C. japonica*) has smaller leaves and a denser display of berries. It would be interesting to juxtapose the aquamarine berries of Harlequin glorybower with the rich, purple-magenta berries of the beautyberry shrubs.

Another shrubby fall bloomer, the butterfly bush (*Buddleia*), mentioned in more detail in the "Summer Shrubs" section above, will keep up its show of brightly colored flower panicles right up until frost. In fact, fall is a good time to sit and drink in the vision of dozens of yellow sulfur butterflies gently pulsating their wings over the lilac-colored blooms.

Tibouchina

One of the most glorious of all the fall-blooming shrubs is the tibouchina, or princess flower (*Tibouchina urvilleana*). Profuse, single, rich, royal purple blossoms and velvety, ovate leaves make this a spectacular plant. In coastal Zones 8 and 9 it tends to reach three to four feet tall, blooms late in the summer and autumn, and then dies back to the ground each winter. It needs a protected spot and a good winter mulch.

Although it doesn't look like much the rest of the year, in fall the American beautyberry (Callicarpa americana) makes up for it with its brilliant, magenta-purple fruits.

Cape Plumbago

In summer and fall, Cape plumbago (*Plumbago auriculata*) is smothered in striking, sky blue flower clusters for weeks on end. It is grown as a two- to six-foot-tall shrub or trained up a fence to a height of ten to twenty feet. It looks beautiful spilling over a wall or bursting out from behind wrought iron bars.

Like tibouchina, this woody perennial will have a much longer bloom season and will be taller the farther south it grows.

LONG-BLOOMING PERENNIALS

There are some perennials that just don't give up. Among the more resolute bloomers (described in more detail in the "Southern Hot-Weather Favorites" section above) are the verbenas, the lantanas, the cannas, and the sages. *Salvia guaranitica*, *S.* 'Indigo Spires', *S. uliginosa*, *S. coccinea*, and the hybrids like 'Cherry Queen' will still be in bloom, having started their work in early summer.

Mexican petunia (*Ruellia brittoniana*) will also continue to bloom heavily in the fall, as will Oxford orphanage plant (*Kalimeris pinnatifida*), especially if it has been cut back once. Royal catchfly (*Silene regia*), a reliable southeastern native, sends up eye-catching, red-orange flowers on two- to three-foot-tall stems in August.

One of the more breathtaking flowers in the fall garden is the princess flower (Tibouchina). In warmer parts of the coastal South it will bloom from summer through fall.

In the warmer parts of the coastal South, clouds of sky blue flowers clothe Cape plumbago (Plumbago auriculata) from summer through fall. Farther north it will bloom later and be more tender.

Among the bulbous plants, society garlic (*Tulbaghia violacea*) continues to send up slender stems topped with lilac-colored umbels all fall. White-flowered garlic chives (*Allium tuberosum*) look quite similar and bloom for several weeks in the fall. Both of these plants mix well with other perennials.

And the cool days of autumn may be the best season for lamb's ears (*Stachys byzantina*), when the plant sends out a fresh batch of woolly gray-green leaves.

Many roses, both the climbers and the shrub types, will rebloom for weeks once the cool weather returns. Fertilize your roses in late summer in anticipation of the fall blooming period. Some of the repeat bloomers will put out perfect blossoms straight through to Christmas.

BACK-OF-THE-BORDER BLOOMS

Over the course of the summer, while we're not paying much attention, certain perennials gradually get taller and taller. And then these back-of-the-border beauties suddenly burst into flower at the tag end of summer and into fall. They may be somewhat floppy and rangy, they may be less than sophisticated, but we are glad to have them when September rolls around. Generally, the colors that predominate naturally in these tall, fall-blooming perennials are white, shades of purple, blue, lavender, and golden yellow. A splash of red or orange will bring the picture into dazzling focus.

Joe Pye Weed and Hardy Ageratum

One of the easiest and weediest of all the fall bloomers is hardy ageratum (*Eupatorium coelestinum*). It is guaranteed to spread where you don't want it and will look rangy and leggy all summer long. However, hardy ageratum will reward you with long-lasting, bright blue flowers for many weeks when the garden is in need of color. The blooms look terrific no matter where they happen to pop up, keeping good company with all sizes and colors of neighbors. If you take the time to keep hardy ageratum pinched back, it will be much bushier come fall and will have more stems for blooming purposes.

Several other *Eupatoriums*, all known by the common name Joe Pye weed, bloom in fall on tall, plain-looking plants. The name Joe Pye weed conjures up something out of Lil' Abner, and that's not far off the mark. Sturdy, six- to nine-foot stems of *E. purpureum* will be clothed in purple leaves and topped with rosy purple flowers in the fall. *E. hyssopifolium*, on the other hand, produces shorter, four-foot stems and a more see-through effect with its delicate, white blooms. Giant Joe Pye weed (*E. fistulosum*) blooms earlier than all the others, usually in midsummer. It can grow twelve feet tall and produces massive lavender blooms. Butterflies love all the Joe Pye weeds.

With a name like Joe Pye weed (Eupatorium), you wouldn't expect such a lush, presentable flower display. Joe is flanked by a red Turk's cap (Malvaviscus arboreus drummondii) and orange coneflowers (Rudbeckia).

Ironweed

Another somewhat weedy-looking, back-of-the-border plant is ironweed (*Vernonia*). It can grow to ten feet tall but is also available in shorter varieties. The stems of ironweed are sturdy; the flower heads are bright purple. Like many of these tall fall-bloomers, ironweed benefits from a few sessions with the clippers during the summer.

Goldenrod, Boltonia, and Aster

The bright, golden spires of the goldenrods (*Solidago*) mix beautifully with the fall sages and Joe Pye weeds. Seaside goldenrod (*S. sempervirens*) is well

*Goldenrod (*Solidago*) is a beautiful fall-blooming perennial with an undeserved reputation for causing hay fever. The real culprit is ragweed.*

suited to beach as well as inland coastal conditions. Mixed in with all of these simple, back-of-the-border plants, the small, white daisies of native boltonia (*Boltonia asteroides*) or the lavender-blue daisies of the asters (*Aster* spp.) work well. The best asters for our area are the giant, seven-foot-tall tatarian aster (*A. tataricus*), the shorter, four-foot-tall smooth aster (*A. laevis*), the three-foot-tall great aster (*A. grandiflora*), and some of the New England asters (*A. novae-angliae*).

Montecasino aster (*A. pringlei* 'Montecasino') is a billowy white aster that is especially resistant to mildew, the bane of the genus. 'Fanny's Aster' is an excellent hybrid cultivar among the Michaelmas daisies.

Perennial Sunflowers

Swamp sunflower (*Helianthus angustifolius*) is the kind of plant that is so captivating it can cause automobile accidents if it's planted near a busy street. It grows six to ten feet tall and bursts with bright yellow flowers in early fall. As its name implies, it prefers rich, moist soil and full sun. Willow-leaf sunflower (*H. salicifolius*) tolerates drier conditions and grows even taller than swamp sunflower, with similar bright yellow daisy flowers. For paler, more buttery yellow blooms in a hot, dry, baking spot, try *H.* x 'Lemon Queen'.

Fall-Blooming Sages

The fall garden wouldn't be complete without the beauty of the late-blooming sages. Most eye-catching of the bunch is Mexican bush sage (*Salvia*

left:
Swamp sunflower (Helianthus angustifolius) grows in regular garden soil as well as in the swamp. It is a dynamite fall perennial.

right:
Every garden in the coastal South should have at least one Mexican bush sage (Salvia leucantha) with its stunning spires of felt-like, deep purple flowers.

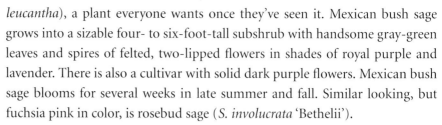

*opposite:
The huge,
pendulous blooms
of angel's trumpet
(Brugmansia)
are among the
showstoppers of
the fall garden.*

leucantha), a plant everyone wants once they've seen it. Mexican bush sage grows into a sizable four- to six-foot-tall subshrub with handsome gray-green leaves and spires of felted, two-lipped flowers in shades of royal purple and lavender. There is also a cultivar with solid dark purple flowers. Mexican bush sage blooms for several weeks in late summer and fall. Similar looking, but fuchsia pink in color, is rosebud sage (*S. involucrata* 'Bethelii').

Bright-yellow forsythia sage (*S. madrensis*), growing six to seven feet tall, joins its sage cousins to put on a gorgeous show all fall and up until a hard frost. If you like magenta, try the four-foot-high *S. puberula*. Hidalgo sage (*S. regla*) will give you bright reddish-orange, tubular flowers on a similar size plant.

One of the best fall bloomers is the southeastern native azure sage (*S. azurea*). Tough and adaptable, azure sage has dense blue spikes on three- to four-foot-tall plants.

Finally, the fiery-red flower spikes of pineapple sage (*S. elegans*), rising up on delicate two- to four-foot stems, add excellent exclamation points among the purples and golds of the other fall flowers.

Angel's Trumpet

Arguably the most spectacular of all the flowering perennials we can grow in the coastal South are the magnificent angel's trumpets (*Brugmansia*). These herbaceous perennials can reach ten feet tall in the warmest areas. In late summer, enormous (ten- to twelve-inch-long), pendulous, bell-shaped flowers hang down from the branches. These monster flowers give off a scent at nighttime. Perennial angel's trumpet is one grand, awe-inspiring plant when it's in bloom. Flower colors include white, yellow, orange, and pink. All parts of the plant are poisonous if ingested.

Chrysanthemums

Fall immediately brings to mind chrysanthemums (*Chrysanthemum* spp. and hybrids). Every grocery store and garden center in America will be stocked with field mums (*C. x morifolium*) soon after Labor Day. These plants will do best if you plant them quite shallowly in full sun in very rich soil. If you leave them to their own devices, they'll bloom again the next spring and then grow tall and leggy and probably bloom once more in the fall. If you want, you can cut them back before they bloom in the spring and then repeatedly all summer to achieve a bigger fall bloom and a denser plant. In many cases these mums will peter out on their own after a couple of years unless they're lifted and divided and replanted in enriched soil.

To find chrysanthemums that are longer-lived and more graceful in habit, you may have to do a little searching in nurseries and catalogs, but it's worth the trouble. For example, there are a number of lovely pale pink, daisy-like mums with yellow centers that bloom in late summer and fall. Among them are *C. x weyrichii* 'Pink Sheffield', *C. x* 'Ryan's Daisy' or 'Ryan's Pink', and *C. x rubellum* 'Clara Curtis'.

*It wouldn't be
fall without mums
(Chrysanthemum,
Leucanthemum,
Dendranthema,
Pyrethrum, and
others). For a really
big flower show in
the fall, keep your
mums pinched back
during the spring
and summer.*

Montauk daisies (*C. nipponicum*), which grow well at the beach, are fall-blooming white daisies with handsome, leathery foliage. Their stalks are somewhat naked looking, so you may want to hide them behind other plants. *C. x* 'Single Apricot' produces an abundance of single daisy mums in a lovely pale apricot shade for several weeks in the fall.

MORE FALL-BLOOMING PERENNIALS

There are a few other notable perennials that come into their own in autumn. At the top of the list are the Japanese anemones (*Anemone* x *hybrida*),

*The inaptly named obedient plant (*Physostegia virginiana*) will get away from you unless you corral it. But the lilac-colored blooms compensate for its wayward tendencies.*

with their incised basal leaves and delicate, foot-high stalks topped with clusters of delicate, white or pink, single or double flowers. Japanese anemones appreciate filtered sunlight and rich, moist soil.

Obedient plant (*Physostegia virginiana*), a somewhat lax, cottagey plant, blooms in lilac or white for a long period of time beginning in late summer. It adds a soft touch to the garden composition all fall. Obedient plant spreads rapidly, taking over a large area unless you thin it out each year.

Two of the late-blooming coneflowers include the classic, yellow mophead (*Rudbeckia lanciniata* 'Gold Drop') and the green-and-yellow-flowered *R.* 'Autumn Sun'.

Perennial Marigold

Two perennial marigolds, Mexican mint marigold and shrub marigold, produce bright yellow-orange flowers for many weeks in autumn. Shrub marigold (*Tagetes lemonnii*) grows four feet tall and wide, blooming best in full sun and well-drained soil. Its healthy, eye-catching button flowers combine beautifully with the dark blue sages. The cultivar 'Copper Canyon Daisy' has the added advantage of blooming in spring as well as fall. Mexican mint marigold (*T. lucida*) is a much shorter plant, growing only one to two feet tall, and is often grown for its tarragon-flavored leaves.

FALL-BLOOMING VINES

Flowering vines contribute as much to the fall garden as their counterparts do in spring. The vigorous southern classic, coral vine (*Antigonon leptopus*), with its rich pink sprays continues to bloom in late summer and fall in the warmer parts of the coastal South.

Another fall classic is sweet autumn clematis (*Clematis terniflora*), which smothers fences and arbors with clouds of white blooms whose place is later taken up by decorative, spidery seed heads that keep the vine looking interesting for many more weeks. The orange peel clematis (*C. tibetana*) also waits until fall to put out its deep-yellow, recurved bellflowers, which are followed by attractive white seed heads.

Climbing aster (*Aster carolinianus*) is a lovely, long-blooming autumn vine with small, mauve, daisy-like flowers with yellow disks. This native reaches ten to fifteen feet high and can take up a lot of space if not kept trimmed back. The semievergreen butterfly vine (*Stigmaphyllon ciliatum*) produces beautiful yellow, orchid-like flowers at the same time of year. It blooms in part shade and will benefit from a winter mulch.

CONTINUING BLOOMS FROM VINES

Some vines will have been blooming all summer and continue on and off through until frost. Described in the "Frost-tender Vines" and "Summer Vines" sections above are the tender mandevilla or Chilean jasmine (*Mandevilla laxa*), Asiatic jasmine (*Trachelospermum asiaticum*), star jasmine (*Solanum jasminoides*), St. Vincent lilac (*S. seaforthianum*), and *S. crispum* 'Glasnevin'.

The expansive and vigorous trumpet creeper (*Campsis* spp.) also blooms right on through fall, as do star quamoclit (*Ipomea coccinea*) and cypress vine (*I. quamoclit*). In addition, the tubular yellow flowers of swamp jessamine (*Gelsemium rankii*) reappear at this time of year, having taken a rest after their first season of bloom in late winter and early spring.

left:
*You will see the hardy trumpet creeper vine (*Campsis radicans*) blooming even in abandoned lots from late summer through fall.*

right:
*An extremely vigorous and hardy vine, sweet autumn clematis (*Clematis terniflora*) is blanketed with flowers in the late summer and early fall. When the flowers are finished, the vine is covered with fluffy seed heads.*

EXCELLENT TENDER VINES FOR THE FALL

Hyacinth bean vine (*Dolichos lablab*) grows extremely easily from seed sown in the spring. All summer long it is clothed in handsome plum-colored foliage that contrasts well with many other garden colors. In late summer it produces showy lavender and white flower clusters. But the real showstoppers are the otherworldly, bright-purple-colored bean pods that hang down along autumn fences. A remarkable sight. Those who garden in the lower parts of the coastal South can treat this vine as a perennial.

Black-eyed Susan vine (*Thunbergia alata*) is another annual, fall-blooming vine that may perennialize in warmer areas. It is covered for many weeks with flared tubular flowers in shades of deep gold, creamy white, or butter yellow. The flower throats are brownish-purple. It blooms best in full sun and rich, moist, well-drained soil.

Its cousin, the sky vine (*T. grandiflora*) wins the prize in many peoples' book as the most beautiful of all the fall-blooming vines. Clusters of stunning, two- to three-inch-long, sky blue, flared, trumpet flowers are borne profusely on this twenty-foot-long twiner. The interior of each flower is tinted yellow. Unfortunately, blue sky vine doesn't work well as an annual, because it takes a year to get established, but those in Zones 9b and below have the chance to grow it as a perennial.

left:
The annual hyacinth bean vine (Dolichos lablab) is easy to grow from seed. In the fall it is covered with purple bean pods and lavender flowers.

right:
In the warmest parts of the coastal South the stunning sky vine (Thunbergia grandiflora) will be perennial.

BULBS THAT BLOOM IN FALL

Spider Lilies

Like spring, fall is an excellent time for flowering bulbs in the coastal South. Around Labor Day a number of wonderful spidery flowers appear in the garden as if from nowhere. Red spider lilies (*Lycoris radiata*) and their yellow counterparts, hurricane lilies (*L. aurea*), send up one- to two-foot-tall stems of bloom before the foliage appears. Their earlier blooming, pink relative, *L. squamigera*, is named naked ladies for just this reason. Although they may take a year or two before they bloom, *Lycoris* will eventually become reliable institutions in the fall garden, increasing in flower production over the years.

Oxblood Lilies

Clusters of rich, wine red trumpets on slender, foot-high stalks pop up before the foliage of the oxblood lily (*Rhodophiala bifida*), another southern classic. It is a durable bulb that can stand poor sandy soil or clay, sun or part shade. It will colonize nicely if left alone.

Ginger Lilies

Fall is the peak season for many of the ginger lilies. They are interesting not only for their tropical-looking foliage but also for their unique floral displays. Colorful bracts add to the beauty of the true flowers. All of the gingers prefer a spot in part shade in rich, moist soil during the growing season. In winter they

*Like aliens from outer space, red spider lily flowers (*Lycoris radiata*) shoot up out of the ground in the fall before their leaves appear.*

left:
*The subtropical
bottlebrush ginger
lilies* (Hedychium
densiflorum) *are
among the glories
of the late summer
and fall garden.*

right:
*The diminutive
blooms on this
subtropical perennial,*
Globba wintii, *look
like dancing ladies,
hence the common
name.*

need dry feet. The *Hedychiums* grow from five to eight feet tall with showy flowers in the shape of butterflies, orchids, or bottlebrushes in a wide variety of colors, from the palest pastels to the brightest red-orange. Their strong, perfumed scent is especially welcome in the fall garden.

Spiral ginger (*Costus*) is equally dramatic, with its pink or orange crepe flowers and purple-red flower bracts on four- to ten-foot tall plants. The gingers in the *Zingiber* genus have pine-cone-shaped inflorescences, some at ground level.

Among the most diminutive of the fall-blooming gingers are the delicate pink and yellow dancing girls (*Globba wintii*). Not impressive at a distance, this is one plant you have to examine up close. The dancing girls are visible as recurved pink bracts from which elegant, attenuated yellow flowers burst forth and tumble down the plant.

More Fall Bulbs

Several small bulbs send up lovely, open-cupped blossoms in fall. Autumn daffodil (*Sternbergia lutea*), which looks like a yellow crocus rather than a daffodil, sends up flowers before foliage.

On the same scale, the rain lilies and fairy lilies (*Zephyranthes* and *Habranthus* spp.) produce ground-level blossoms in shades of white, yellow, pink, and copper throughout the fall. Especially beautiful are the clumps of starry white *Z. candida*, which appear prolifically in September. Their reed-like foliage remains all winter.

A delight to behold, these bright white rain lilies (Zephyranthes candida) appear at ground level in the fall.

The fall-blooming kaffir lily (*Schizostylus coccinea*) originates in South Africa. It is a strong clump-former with sword-shaped leaves and two-foot-tall spikes of crimson flowers that somewhat resemble gladioli. There are white, pink, and salmon-colored cultivars as well.

Irises for Fall

Finally, the *Iris* genus has some fall bloomers that do well in the coastal South. The tall, pink iris 'Pink Classic', with its bright orange "beard," re-blooms in the fall, as does the shorter, reddish-purple, bearded Italian iris (*Iris kochii*).

Some gardeners enjoy growing *Iris foetidissima* for its fall seedpods, which split open and reveal bright reddish-orange seeds, adding a splash of color to the garden that persists into the winter months.

GRASSES AND OTHER SOURCES OF FALL COLOR

Although bright yellows, golds, white, lavenders, blues, and purples abound in the fall garden, an even more subtle beauty comes from the blending of coppery reds, muted yellows, and soft oranges. These tones are visible in the changing foliage of shrubs and trees and the earth tones of the ornamental grass seed heads. There are also subtle golds, bronzes, wines, and russets in certain fall-blooming perennials, such as *Sedum* x 'Autumn Joy', goldenrod, oxblood lily, and late-blooming, earth-toned daylilies. Although the coastal South doesn't enjoy the drama of leaf turn the way its northern and western neighbors do, we can rely on Japanese maples, viburnums, dogwoods, barberries, loropetalums, witch hazels, and red maples to provide a subtle tapestry of color to weave in amongst fall blooms.

The ornamental grasses generally tend to be at their best in fall and the gen-

The gentle light of autumn catches the subtle texture and color of ornamental fountain grass (Pennisetum).

The imposing, variegated 'Cosmopolitan' maiden grass (Miscanthus sinensis 'Cosmopolitan') will be topped with white plumes from fall through winter.

tler fall sunlight catches their awns and spikelets and dances through them. From the reddish tints of hairy awn muhly grass (*Muhlenbergia capillaris*) to the pale golds of feather reed grass (*Calamagrostis* x *acutiflora* 'Stricta'), there are dozens of grasses to choose from. Please see Chapter 4 for more information on ornamental grasses.

FALL GARDENING TIPS

Fall is the time for dividing and transplanting most perennials. This gives them months of cool, generally moderate weather to get established before they are faced with the stress of summer. In mid- to late August you can start the seeds of cool-weather annuals inside so that by mid-October they will be ready to transplant into the garden. Or sow the seeds directly in the garden where they will wait until cooler weather to germinate. Some may bloom dur-

An explosion of fall color includes the orange Canna *'Bengal Tiger', deep red wine sage (*Salvia vanhouttii*), midnight blue of Brazilian sage (*S. guaranitica*), royal purple Mexican bush sage (*S. leucantha*), pink roses, and sunny yellow senna (*Cassia alata*).*

ing the winter months, but most will flower in the warmer weather of spring. Once the temperature heats up in early summer, they melt away, which is why they need to be started in the fall rather than spring. See Chapter 4 for more details on cool-weather annuals.

A few words to the wise about fall gardening. If you intend to grow bearded iris, this is one plant that would rather not be planted or transplanted in the fall. They prefer that you do the work in July or August, so their rhizomes can get a good baking. Clematis, lantana, and any perennials that are slightly frost-tender are another exception to fall planting. They need to be planted in early spring, so they will have all summer to establish a good root system.

Although you may safely cut back and tidy up the remains of most spent perennials after the first hard frost (to neaten the garden and prevent pests and diseases from overwintering), save the trimming and tidying up of butterfly bush and Mexican bush sage *(Salvia leucantha)* until the following spring.

CHAPTER 2

The Best & Worst Plants for Coastal Gardens

Fail-Safe Perennials   The Horticultural Survivalists

If you're just starting a perennial garden or if you're adding to an existing design, it makes sense to invest your time and money in plants that are known survivors in the coastal South. Given the right setting and a few minimal cultural requirements, these plants will increase in size and/or number and will bloom reliably year after year. Generally not subject to chronic diseases, they should remain fairly healthy except for the occasional pest invasion, which can be treated with environmentally friendly remedies.

Deciding which perennials to include in this list was, as they say in the law, somewhat arbitrary and capricious. Arguments could be made for including others. In any case, you will find in this list plants that will give you a variety of foliage, height, texture, season of bloom, color, form, and garden location, so that you'll have a wide range of potential garden designs. There are bulbs, vines, ferns, ornamental grasses, groundcovers, herbs, herbaceous perennials, and a couple of woody shrubs on the list. All of them are suited to perennial beds, mixed borders, and general landscape use. For more details and an explanation of the plants' cultural requirements, consult the A–Z Plant Guide.

In a dry, baking location, the lacy gray leaves of the artemesias (Artemesia) remain handsome from spring through frost. They are an excellent foil for pastel or bright colors.

Agapanthus (lily of the Nile). These strappy-leaved plants are topped with showy blue or white flower umbels on erect stalks for several weeks in summer. No fuss and lovely.

Artemesia (artemesia). Artemesias provide beautiful, lacy, gray foliage year-round, a great complement to many other plant colors. The best ones for us are 'Powis Castle', 'Silver King', 'Valerie Finnis,' 'Huntington', and southernwood (*A. abrotanum*).

Aster (aster). For reliable fall color, there are several excellent asters, including the great aster (*A. grandiflorus*), smooth aster (*A. laevis*), and tatarian aster (*A. tataricus*). The native climbing aster (*A. carolinianus*) is a vigorous vine with the classic yellow-centered, purple or blue daisy blooms.

Buddleia (butterfly bush). *Buddleias* begin blooming in early summer and continue right through to frost. Each shrub is covered with richly colored spires that, as the name suggests, attract butterflies all summer long. Shades include lavender, purple, pink, mauve, white, and yellow.

Canna (canna lilies). Generally, these tropical-looking plants will bloom from the beginning of summer through to the first frost and require little or no

overleaf:
Gardeners in the coastal South rely on a slightly different plant palette than gardeners elsewhere. Shown here are huge, hardy bananas (Musa), blue Cape plumbago (Plumbago auriculata), and red roses.

above left:
Butterflies do love their namesake butterfly bush (Buddleia). Give this shrub a position in full sun, but water it regularly.

above right:
Many of the fall-blooming asters (Aster) have purple or blue daisy flowers with yellow centers. They work well with goldenrod (Solidago) and hardy ageratum (Eupatorium coelestinum).

below left:
There are many excellent hardy palms that work well on their own or mixed in with perennials. Shown here is European fan palm (Chamaerops humilis) with dark plum annual salvia (Salvia splendens).

maintenance. They are available in shades of white, pink, red, salmon, yellow, and orange. Foliage may be solid green or dramatically variegated with yellow, white, pink, or red.

Cassia (cassia, senna). Glorious clusters of golden yellow flowers appear on these shrubs from late summer to fall. A spectacular show in and of themselves and great with the deep purple sages.

Chamaerops humilis (Mediterranean fan palm). These hardy, reliable palms add a handsome, tropical design element to any garden. Multistemmed with blue-green, fan-shaped foliage and a bushy habit.

Chasmanthium latifolium (inland sea oats, river oats). In the summer this handsome, easy-to-grow ornamental grass produces oat-like seed heads. They mature from green through shades of pink and copper in the fall.

Clematis terniflora (sweet autumn clematis). Among the easiest and most vigorous of all clematis vines, in early fall it produces clouds of white flowers followed by whirly seed heads.

The deep plum foliage of Colocasia *'Black Magic' adds beauty to any scene, as it does here, where it has been planted in a pot submerged in water. On land it can grow to six feet tall.*

*A cottage garden classic, sweet William (*Dianthus barbatus*) blooms during the cooler months, often all winter long when the weather is mild.*

Clerodendrum (glorybower). Excellent shrubby plants for the shady garden. The genus includes a variety of flower types: flat pink cymes, red spikes, violet-blue butterflies, or showy, multicolored flower bracts, depending on the species.

Colocasia, Alocasia, and Xanthosoma (taro, elephant ear). The tropical-looking, heart-shaped foliage may be solid green, solid dark-plum-colored, veined with violet-black or silver, or flushed with an overall red or black tint. The giant varieties are especially striking. Black taros mix very well with other plant colors.

Coreopsis (tickseed). Coreopsis gives us eye-catching yellow blooms starting in late spring and continuing for many weeks into summer. Some flower all summer long. Best bets for our area include 'Zagreb', 'Early Sunrise', 'Baby Sun', 'Goldfink', Chipola River (*C. integrifolia*), mouse ear coreopsis (*C. auriculata* 'Nana'), and beautiful coreopsis (*C. pulchra*).

Crocosmia (montbretia, crocosmia). A plant-it-and-be-done perennial corm that reliably produces bright red, yellow, or orange, zigzag flower spikes for several weeks in summer. It adds an orderly vertical accent to any design.

Cuphea (cigar plant). The shrubby *Cupheas* bloom from summer through fall, reliably producing red and orange tubular flowers above glossy green foliage. Mexican heather (*C. hyssopifolia*) is lower growing and sports tiny lavender, pink, or white flowers.

Cyrtomium falcatum (holly fern). The holly fern is extremely well adapted to the coastal South. The glossy, bold, rich green leaves remain healthy-looking throughout the winter, giving a lift to even the most troublesome corner of your shady garden.

Dianthus (pinks). Lacy, gray-green-leaved cheddar pinks (*D. gratianopolitanus*) and cottage pinks (*D. plumarius*) can stand a baking-hot, hell-strip position (between the sidewalk and the street) or can grow next to their cousin sweet William (*D. barbatus*) in the garden. *Dianthus* flowers may be pale to deep pink, white, or red.

Dryopteris erythrosora (autumn fern). This evergreen fern makes a beautiful fountain of foliage in a shady spot, growing larger and more impressive with

above left:
Autumn fern (Dryopteris erythrosora) earns its keep all year long. Its handsome evergreen foliage stays healthy looking throughout winter, and the emerging bronze crosiers are a treat to watch in spring.

above right:
The crybaby tree (Erythrina crista-galli) blooms in spring and then on and off through summer and fall. The name comes from the nectar that drips from the flowers.

below left:
Although gardeners along the coastal South don't generally succeed in growing baby's breath (Gypsophylia), a compensation is whirling butterflies (Gaura lindheimeri) with its delicate wands of pale pink flowers appearing from spring through fall.

age. The lovely copper-colored fiddleheads, which emerge in spring, are an added delight. This is an outstanding fern for us.

Erythrina (coral bean plant, crybaby tree). These woody shrubs or small trees produce eye-catching red flower spikes for a long period of time in summer. Classics for our area.

Eupatorium (Joe Pye weed). This genus includes a number of tough, easy, native plants valued for their fall flower show in shades of lavender, pink, white, or deep blue.

Gaura lindheimeri (whirling butterflies). This wonderful, see-through plant produces tiny white or pink blossoms on branching flower spikes from mid-spring into fall. *Gaura* adds delicacy and movement to your garden.

Gelsemium sempervirens (Carolina jessamine). Beginning in late February, this native vine treats us to cascades of tiny, bright, forsythia-yellow blossoms for weeks on end. Its shiny evergreen leaves are handsome year-round.

Hedychium, Costus, and Curcuma (ginger lilies). The taller ginger lilies add tropical drama and good fall color to the shady garden. Blooms resemble butterflies, orchids, or bottlebrushes and are often fragrant.

Helianthus angustifolius (swamp sunflower). This perennial sunflower grows five to ten feet tall over the course of the summer and then explodes in a profusion of eye-catching yellow flowers in early fall. A real showstopper and very easy.

Helianthus debilis (beach sunflower). Blooming all summer long, this tough perennial forms a low-growing mat topped with a profusion of brown-eyed, yellow daisies.

Helleborus orientalis (Lenten rose). In late winter the deep-green, lobed, and serrated leaves of these shade lovers provide a background for greenish-white or plum-colored inverted bells, sprinkled on the inside with maroon

The scent of white butterfly ginger (Hedychium coronarium) is a heady mix between gardenia and honeysuckle.

What the garden needs in the heat of summer is a tough, nonstop flowering plant like the beach sunflower (Helianthus debilis)—as beautiful as it is sturdy.

freckles. Often these blooms will continue until early summer. Easy and deer-proof!

Hemerocallis (daylily). These tough, easy, and reliable perennials come in a rainbow of colors—from the brightest orange to the palest ivory. Repeat bloomers and those with an extended flowering season give extra value. A perfect choice for the coastal South.

Hibiscus and Kosteletzkya (mallows). Many plants in the mallow family perform very well in the coastal South by giving us months of bright, showy blooms and requiring little care. Among the best bets are Texas star or scarlet mallow (*Hibiscus coccineus*), rose of Sharon (*H. syriacus*), woolly rose mallow (*H. lasiocarpus*), Confederate rose (*H. mutabilis*), and seashore mallow (*Kosteletzkya virginica*).

Hymenocallis (spider lily, Peruvian daffodil). These bulbous perennials send up fragrant, greenish-white, spidery flowers in spring or summer. They multiply readily.

Ipheion uniflorum (starflower). Distribute these little bulbs by the hundreds if you want to cheer up your late-winter/early-spring landscape. The tiny, star-shaped flowers, held only a few inches above the ground, are a milky blue, visible even from a distance.

Iris (Louisiana iris, Siberian iris, Japanese iris, Southern blue flag, yellow flag). Easy and reliable, Louisiana irises bloom in an impressive array of colors in early summer where the ground is constantly moist. Other easy, moisture-loving irises for our area include Siberian iris (*I. sibirica*), Japanese iris (*I. ensata*), yellow flag (*I. pseudacorus*), and Southern blue flag (*I. virginica*).

Jasminum (jasmine). Evergreen jasmine vines provide fragrant flowers in shades of white, yellow, or pink. Bloom times range from early spring to summer.

Hibiscus of all sorts are at home in the coastal South. Shown here is the striking red bloom of Texas star (Hibiscus coccineus).

The delicate pale blue presence of starflower (Ipheion uniflorum) is one of the cheeriest sights of late winter. Plant these small bulbs by the dozen and watch them increase over the years.

Many evergreen jasmines (Jasminum), such as this variegated cultivar, earn their keep in the garden as handsome groundcovers or climbing vines.

Mondo grass or monkey grass (Ophiopogon) is one of the most ubiquitous of all groundcovers in the coastal South. Here it is blooming in conjunction with pale pink annual impatiens.

Justicia (Brazilian plume, shrimp plant). *Justicias* are shrubby perennials valued for producing showy flower plumes in partially shady spots. They bloom over a long period of time in late summer and fall. Flower colors include pink, yellow, and white.

Kalimeris pinnatifida (Oxford orphanage plant, Genghis Khan aster, false aster, Japanese aster). Although it may be unprepossessing, this small, white, double daisy flower is one of the very best filler plants for us. It blooms from spring through fall.

Lantana (lantana). Lantanas bloom nonstop from early summer through fall. They are grown as woody subshrubs or groundcovers, depending on the variety. Colors include combinations of white, yellow, pink, orange, and red.

Leucojum aestivum (summer snowflake). Don't be confused by the common name. *Leucojum* is an easy, reliable spring bloomer. The flowers are white bells with tiny green dots that mix well with pansies and early-blooming *Narcissus*.

Lilium (lily). The elegant, trumpet-shaped flowers of summer lilies are among the most delightful perennials in the garden. The most reliable lilies for our climate include the madonna lily (*Lilium candidum*), the Formosa lily (*L. formosanum*), the Easter lily (*L. longiformium*), the tiger lily (*L. lancifolium*), the regal lily (*L. regale*), and the Asiatic hybrids.

Liriope and Ophiopogon (lily turf, monkey grass or mondo grass). The evergreen, grassy foliage of these two often-confused perennials will survive in almost any location. Both are widely used in our area as groundcovers or edging plants. They are virtually indestructible.

Lonicera (honeysuckle). Two excellent honeysuckles for the coastal South are trumpet (*L. sempervirens*) and gold flame (*L. heckrottii*). They bloom intermittently year-round, provide a touch of fall foliage coloration, and sport bright red berries in winter.

Lycoris radiata (spider lily). In late summer, red, spidery flowers appear on foot-high stems as if from nowhere. *Lycoris* gives no advance warning of its arrival because its leaves don't emerge until after it has bloomed.

Lysimachia (moneywort, creeping jenny). These spreading groundcovers add a bright chartreuse-yellow color to the garden palette. Two excellent choices are *L. congestifolia* 'Outback Sunset' and *L. nummularia* 'Aurea'. In mild winters the foliage persists as a welcome addition to the winter garden and excellent carpet for spring bulbs.

Mandevilla laxa (Chilean jasmine). These vines are not hardy perennials above Zone 9, but they are powerful annual additions to the summer garden. The foliage is a glossy deep green, and the exotic-looking flowers are pink, white, yellow, or red.

Miscanthus sinensis (maiden grass). A gently weeping habit and fluffy beige feathers (seed heads) in the fall make this tough ornamental grass a softening addition to the garden.

Creeping jenny (Lysimachia nummularia 'Aurea') makes a river of chartreuse foliage beside the plum-colored variegation of bugleweed (Ajuga reptans 'Burgundy Glow').

Monarda (bee balm). Colorful whorled flowers appear for many weeks in summer on these easy perennials. Two good choices for the coastal South are wild bee balm (*M. fistulosa*) and spotted bee balm (*M. punctata*), both with attractive purple flower bracts.

Muhlenbergia (muhly grass). This tough ornamental grass has a graceful, weeping habit and clouds of pink or purple seed heads in fall. Very drought- and heat-tolerant.

Narcissus (daffodils, jonquils, and paperwhites). Choosing carefully will ensure years of pleasure from these wonderful bulbs. The most reliable bloomers for our climate include the early-blooming, bunch-flowering narcissus or paperwhites (*N. tazetta*), the reflexed jonquil hybrids (*N. cyclamineus*), the tiny hoop petticoats (*N. bulbicodium*), angel's tears (*N. triandrus* hybrids), and classic jonquils (*N. jonquilla* and hybrids). See the "Winter Bulbs" section of Chapter 1 for recommended cultivars.

Plumbago auriculata (Cape plumbago). The sky blue clouds of bloom of this woody shrub light up the garden for months in the summer and fall. A glorious plant.

Rosmarinus officinalis (rosemary). Grow rosemary as a handsome evergray shrub, as a hedge around the herb garden, or let one of the creeping varieties trail over the top of a container. Tiny winter flowers and the aromatic foliage are added bonuses.

Rudbeckia (coneflower, black-eyed Susan). In addition to the classic brown-eyed, yellow daisy flowers, there are green-eyed coneflowers, gold- and red-banded daisies, and yellow mopheads. Short and tall, adaptable and easy— a genus of worthy garden perennials.

Ruellia brittoniana (Mexican petunia). *Ruellia* is adorned from midsummer through fall with purple, upward-facing, funnel-shaped flowers that fall

There are many varieties of yellow coneflower (Rudbeckia) ranging from tall to dwarf, all of them excellent perennials for our area.

above left:
Another of the outstanding sages for the coastal South is the long-flowering mealycup sage (Salvia farinacea).

above right:
Stonecrops (Sedum) *add year-round textural interest to the garden. In the coastal South they prefer a position in part sun with adequate moisture.*

below right:
The large palmate leaves of Fatsia japonica *on the left are echoed by the imposing foliage of rice paper plant* (Tetrapanex papyriferus).

gracefully to the ground each evening. A healthy, easy perennial that will increase readily in the garden.

Sabal (palmettos). A genus of native, cold-hardy palms that thrive in the coastal South and provide tropical drama in the landscape. Fan-shaped foliage. Easy and tough.

Salvia (sage). Probably the best single genus of perennials for the coastal South, the sages are invaluable additions to any garden. Colors include many shades of blue and purple, pink, red, coral, yellow, and white. Among the classics for our area are the midnight blue Brazilian sage (*Salvia guaranitica*), the indigo blue *S.* 'Indigo Spires', the royal purple Mexican sage (*S. leucantha*), bright red pineapple sage (*S. elegans*), Japanese yellow sage (*S. koyame*), bright blue bog sage (*S. uliginosa*), scarlet sage (*S. coccinea*), and the classic blue mealycup sage (*S. farinacea*). Sages love it here!

Sedum (sedum). The rounded, succulent leaves of sedums form attractive rosette patterns. Creeping varieties like *Sedum acre* make delicate groundcovers. The larger varieties like the classic 'Autumn Joy' are handsome, easy perennials spring through fall.

Tetrapanex papyriferus (rice paper plant). This reliable, fast-growing giant makes a dramatic canopy with deeply lobed, gray-green leaves that are furry white underneath. Creamy-white flower spikes add interest in the fall.

Trachelospermum jasminoides (Confederate jasmine). An evergreen vine with glossy foliage and fragrant white flower clusters in early summer, this is a southern coastal classic. Let it climb fences and arbors or clip it into a thick covering for an archway.

Tulbaghia violacea (society garlic). A dependable filler plant with blue-green, grassy foliage and small, lilac umbels on foot-high stems.

Verbena (verbena). Verbenas are valued for their long season of constant bloom during the hottest months of the year. The best bets for us are the rose verbenas (*V. canadensis*), especially 'Homestead Purple'.

Zephyranthes and Habranthus (rain lilies, fairy lilies). Easy, tough bulbs that produce grassy leaves and cup- or star-shaped flowers at ground level intermittently from spring through fall. Colors include white, pink, yellow, salmon, and copper.

When the air is rich with the scent of Confederate jasmine (Trachelospermum jasminoides), summer has officially arrived in the coastal South.

Perennials to Avoid
Don't Even Think of Growing These Plants Here

Can you grow these plants here? Yes. Will they thrive and stay healthy looking, come back the next year, bloom nicely, and generally earn their keep in the garden? Probably not. For every plant listed here, there are a dozen people who will tell you that they have figured out a way, with a little patience and ingenuity, to make it grow. They will tell you there's no problem. Be forewarned—these plants are not naturally suited to the coastal South. Whether you can beat the odds is another question. Whether you want to attempt it is a matter between you and your garden genie.

There are exceptions within every rule. In this case, there may be a particular species, variety, or cultivar of an otherwise nonrecommended genus that has been proven to survive under our climatic conditions. These are noted where appropriate. Finding these particular plants may require delving into the more arcane catalogs, which is worth it if you absolutely must have, for example, a peony in your garden. Part of gardening is nostalgia. All of gardening is emotion. If you have to have it, you have to have it.

Some of these plants, especially the Dutch bulbs, are used extensively in our area as annuals: new bulbs or plants are set out each year and then thrown on to the compost pile when they've finished blooming. For that purpose, they're fine. But they're not going to perennialize. Also, keep in mind that there are areas along the coast that are far enough inland that they experience a Zone 7 climate, which is much more amenable to growing certain heat-intolerant plants.

Here are some plants to avoid if you want to save energy, money, and disappointment:

Aconitum (monkshood). Monkshood or aconite requires cool summer nights with temperatures below 70 degrees in order to do well. And guess what? We don't have near enough of them.

Alchemilla mollis (lady's mantle). This plant looks so seductive in those pictures of gardens in England, New England, and the Pacific Northwest. It grows so easily in those places. The bad news is, it's not happy here. The good news is, if you're looking for that wonderful chartreuse color effect to offset other plants in your garden, you can use the annual sweet potato vine (*Ipomea batata* 'Marguerite'), the spring-blooming spirea 'Lemon-Lime Mound', golden stonecrop (*Sedum acre*), creeping jenny (*Lysimachia aurea*), or chartreuse-colored annual coleus instead. If you try lady's mantle, give it shade and moisture.

Astilbe arendsii (astilbe, false spirea). You will find astilbe prominently displayed in garden centers throughout the coastal South in springtime. The plants will be topped with beautiful plumes of pink, white, red, or lavender. Of course, these astilbes have been trucked in from Elsewhere at the peak of their bloom. Try to resist. Our climate is too hot for astilbes to thrive—even in moist shade. If you feel like experimenting, try planting them in a shaded spot with constant moisture. Better yet, save your money.

Brunnera macrophylla (brunnera). Brunneras don't appreciate our summer evenings, much preferring a lightly shaded garden somewhere near Asheville, N.C. If you want to experiment with brunnera, try the cultivar 'Langtrees', but keep it moist.

Campanula (bellflower). Much as we may court her, campanula prefers cooler climates. Instead of wasting your effort on this tempting charmer, try Mexican petunia (*Ruellia brittoniana*), a plant with a somewhat similar display (purple upright funnels instead of pendant blue bells) that does wonderfully for us over a very long season of bloom. Like campanula, it's a good mixer.

Delphinium hybrids (delphinium). We all know they're tricky. In the coastal South they're beyond tricky. Try growing them as annuals here by planting them out in the fall and enjoying them during the coolest months of spring. Instead of delphinium in the summer garden, use *Salvia* x 'Indigo Spires' for tall, deep-blue spikes of color all summer long.

Geranium (cranesbill geranium). The true perennial geranium (as opposed to the common annual *Pelargonium*, planted successfully in pots and window boxes) doesn't thrive in our hot summers. The cultivar *G.* x *cantabrigiense* 'Biokovo' is reputed to be more heat-tolerant than most, but chances are it won't be long-lived. *G.* x 'Robert Worth' is also reputedly heat-tolerant but can become weedy. Worth trying may be the less well-known tuberous geranium *G. malviflorum*, which produces its first foliage in November and December after a summer's dormancy. Blue flowers appear in spring. But don't count on cranesbill.

Gypsophilia (baby's breath). Weddings, Valentine's Day, perfect innocence — baby's breath conjures up all these images. Would that we could grow it well here. Word has it that the Israelis have developed a heat-tolerant baby's breath, 'Festival White'. The jury is still out on that one. A better bet is to use the see-through wands of palest pink, almost white *Gaura lindheimeri* or the delicate lavender sprays of *Thalictrum aquilegifolium* instead.

Imperata cylindrica 'Red Baron' (Japanese blood grass). Don't bother with this grass, which neither gets very red nor very far beyond pathetic-looking in our climate. Although it's not in any way red, you might want to try black monkey grass (*Ophiopogon nigrescens*) as an alternative. Black monkey grass is a slow spreader, but it is terrific-looking, unusual, and can be just as dramatic if juxtaposed with golden foliage or just about any bright-colored flower. Better yet, try one of the bronze-leaved New Zealand flaxes (*Phormium*), such as 'Rubra' or 'Bronze Baby'.

Lavandula (lavender). The addition of lavender to this list is bound to cause much wailing and gnashing of teeth. It's such a popular, must-have plant. Nothing is more beautiful than a Mediterranean hillside covered with this silvery-white-foliaged herb in bloom. Unfortunately, lavender likes dry climates. In the coastal South it tends to rot and suffer fungal disease. You can experiment with lavendin (*Lavandula intermedia*) and fernleaf lavender (*L. multifida*), which are the most heat- and humidity-tolerant of the lavenders. Try a spot away from other plants in full, baking sun, and keep the lavender dry, with its roots surrounded by the alkalinity of cement or bricks. Adding a handful of garden lime and giving it a raised bed will also help. Good luck.

Linum (blue flax). Too hot for blue flax. If you're trying to achieve a tall, airy effect with dainty, blue flowers, try *Salvia guaranitica* instead.

Lupinus Russell hybrids (lupine). Lupines of some sort were the flowers that the fictitious Miss Rumphius spread all over Maine, and the Russell hybrids, which are commonly sold in the trade, are truly beautiful plants. Although some native species dotting local graveyards (*Lupinus perennis*) do well, the hybrid lupines don't like the coastal South. A good alternative, which is not hard to locate, is the Carolina lupine (*Thermopsis carolinia*), a tall, yellow, and very lupinesque plant. It does admirably here. Mother Nature threw us a nice bone when she gave us *Thermopsis*. False indigo (*Baptisia*) is another excellent substitute, reliably sending up showy white, blue, or yellow spires in late spring and early summer.

Pachysandra (pachysandra, spurge). This groundcover, so ubiquitous in the north, tends to look scraggly here, but this is no great loss. There are at least a dozen outstanding groundcovers we can use in its place. For suggestions, see the "Groundcovers" section in Chapter 4.

Paeonia (peony). Peonies must be among the most gorgeous herbaceous perennials in the world. Unfortunately, they need the enforced dormancy of a cold winter to produce their magnificent flowers. Gardeners in Zones 7b and 8 may have some luck with the early-season single cultivars by planting them where they have protection from afternoon sun. If you're going to try to grow peonies, avoid the semidouble, double, and late-season varieties. Although there's no substitute for the splendor of peonies, the mallows in the *Hibiscus* and *Pavonia* genera give us a chance to choke the garden with an equally lush, if different, display of big, dramatic blooms for several months in the summer.

Papaver orientalis (poppy). Oriental poppies are such wonderfully romantic-looking flowers, and they are so unhappy in our climate. A very good substitute for midspring to early-summer bloom are the giant poppy anemones (*Anemone coronaria*) usually recommended for greenhouse use in the north. Rich, deep petal colors of carmine, purple, blue, rosy-pink, or white with dramatic, contrasting black centers give the plants a look remarkably similar to poppies. In addition, certain cool-season annual poppies such as California, Iceland, and others can be seeded or planted in the late fall for a beautiful show during the cool weeks of spring. (Note that *Meconopsis* or woodland poppies don't like it here either.)

Primula (primrose). Most primroses will find our climate too hot. The brightly colored polyantha primrose, which is sold in garden centers in late winter, makes a nice addition to the garden, but it should be thought of as an annual. Plants with a similar name, the delicate evening primroses and prairie primroses (*Oenothera*), are very happy in the coastal South, often spreading like weeds. Cowslip (*Primula veris*) may survive in moist, shady areas.

Rhododendron (rhododendron). Azaleas, of course, are classified in the genus *Rhododendron* and they thrive in the coastal South. We're talking here about the larger-leaved shrub that everyone commonly calls a "rhododendron." This shrub is much happier and healthier in a slightly cooler climate than ours. Reputedly the most heat- and humidity-tolerant are those developed by David Leach. But instead of a rhody, why not try the deciduous cashmere bouquet plant (*Clerodendrum bungei*)? It has large, dark green, ovate leaves and puts forth large, pink flower clusters in summer in a partially shady spot.

Syringa (lilac). It doesn't get cold enough in winter for lilacs to produce their flowers. Try crape myrtle (*Lagerstroemia*) or chaste tree (*Vitex agnus-castus*) instead. Crape myrtles are available in a wide array of colors. They're as easy as can be, and they bloom their heads off for weeks and weeks in even the hottest of summers. Chaste tree puts on an impressive show for months in summer, with lilac-type flowers in blue, white, or pink.

And now about those bulbs. Just about any bulb will bloom the first year. The question is, will it bloom again in subsequent years, and will the mother bulb produce a host of daughter bulbs, thereby giving you more and more flowers as the years go by, as you would like it to? The best bulbs for the coastal South are described in detail in the "Bulbs" section of Chapter 4. The following bulbs have minor or major drawbacks and should be avoided or else treated as disposable annuals.

Anemone blanda (Grecian windflower). Our winters are not cold enough for reliable flower production, and our summers may be too hot even for minimum survival. Instead, try windflower's relative, the readily available *A. coronaria*.

Chionodoxa (glory of the snow). It grows very well in alpine meadows.

Convallaria majalis (lily of the valley). Another heartbreaker. There's nothing quite like lily of the valley for early spring daintiness and evocative scent. Although it's listed in some catalogs as surviving in Zone 8, this is by no means a sure bet. We can grow colonies of summer snowflakes (*Leucojum aestivum*) instead. They don't have the powerful scent, but they do have charming, nodding white bells similar to lily of the valley.

Crocus vernus (Dutch crocus). The standard, spring-blooming Dutch crocuses, so readily available for sale, will not bloom reliably in subsequent years because our winters are not cold enough. However, the early-blooming lavender crocus, *Crocus tomasinianus*, and the lavender autumn crocus (*C. goulimyi*) work somewhat better for us. Better yet, try the wild Easter lily (*Zephyranthes atamasco*), which produces white, crocus-like flowers.

Fritillaria (fritillary). Generally not happy campers. Try other showy bulbs, like Peruvian daffodil (*Hymenocallis narcissiflora*), amaryllis (*Hippeastrum*), lily of the Nile (*Agapanthus*), and tuberose (*Polianthes tuberosa*) instead.

Galanthus nivallis (snowdrops). It doesn't get cold enough here in winter for adequate flower production after the first year. Instead of snowdrops, try the starry-flowered *Ipheion uniflorum*, which naturalizes and increases from year to year in sun or part-sun in late winter and early spring. *Ipheion* makes a lovely carpet, as snowy as you could want.

Hyacinthus orientalis (Dutch hyacinth). If you love the look and smell of the common Dutch hyacinth in spring, plant it out each fall as an annual and throw it on the compost pile when it's finished blooming. The only reliable hyacinths for perennializing in our area are the French-Roman forms (*H. orientalis albulus*), which may be harder to come by.

Muscari (grape hyacinth). The traditional grape hyacinth sold by the bushel load for spring bloom will not do well for us. Try Cuban lilies (*Scilla peruviana*) instead.

Scilla siberica (Siberian squill). Even if you didn't know better, the name might give you a big clue as to how this little bulb would react to eighty-degree evenings. Try its near relative, the Cuban lily (*S. peruviana*), with its starry blue balls of flowers in late spring, or Spanish bluebells (*Hyacinthoides hispanica*), with its dangling blue bells.

Tulipa (tulips). Before everyone starts screaming, let's set some parameters. Should all tulips be banned from our garden? Absolutely not. Most tulips, especially the hybrids, are going to bloom for only one season, but they will be glorious for that short period of time. They should be chilled for ten to twelve weeks in a perforated bag in the refrigerator (away from ripening fruits and vegetables) and planted out in November or December, either in the ground or in containers. Tulips need a sunny spot and good drainage so they won't rot. After they've finished their show in the spring, dig them up and toss them on the compost pile where they will eventually turn into a nice soil amendment. If you want to take a stab at perennializing a "naturalized" area of tulips, try some of the old species, like *T. clusiana*, *T. bakerii* 'Lilac Wonder', *T. tarda*, or *T. batalinii*. All of these are smaller and more delicate than many of the hybrids, and they have a better chance of persisting for a few years if given full sun, good soil, perfect drainage, and an annual spring application of bulb booster. But here's the bottom line with tulips: (1) they need sufficient cold every winter to grow up to their appointed height; (2) they go dormant as soon as the weather gets hot, which is before the bulb has had a chance to bulk up as it's supposed to; (3) hot summer nights deplete the food storage reserves; (4) the depleted bulbs shrink; (5) bulbs that are too small will not bloom; and (6) pests and diseases can get them more readily in the South than in the North.

CHAPTER 3

The Types of Gardens

Location, location, location. The most important consideration that any gardener faces is what his or her local growing conditions are. Is the prospective garden exposed to the full brunt of the sun for most of the day, or is the entire space deeply shaded by large trees? Maybe the sunlight filters in gently all day. Are there some spots that get morning sun and afternoon shade? It's very important to consider these factors before choosing your planting material.

The vast majority of perennials that work for us in the coastal South prefer partial sun, rich soil, ample moisture, and good drainage. However, there are some plants that can stand full, baking sun all day long, and some that flourish in the shade. In addition there is a wide variety of subtropical plants—that is, plants native to warmer climates that can withstand some frost— that work very well in most coastal southern gardens. The charts in this chapter will help you find plants for each of these special needs.

The Dry Sunny Garden and Gardening at the Beach
Egg-frying Hot

Imagine it's three o'clock in the afternoon, July 23rd, at Wrightsville Beach, North Carolina. The temperature is ninety-six degrees Fahrenheit. There's been no rain for the past ten days. Not a breeze is stirring. Heat is rising in waves from the blacktop. The only sound is the rasping of cicadas. Not even the birds are out. The sunlight is so bright it hurts. Everyone is inside with air conditioning or submerged in the Atlantic Ocean. What—from a horticultural point of view—can not only live but look good under such conditions?

Think gray leaves first. Think narrow leaves, succulent leaves, spiny or hairy leaves, rough, dull, or dusty-looking leaves. Think grasses. The following are some of the most heat-tolerant perennials for the coastal South. But remember they must be kept dry and given soil that's not overly rich. The leaves especially do not want to be wet—so a soaker hose or drip irrigation is a good idea. If they're planted in very rich, constantly moist soil, these sturdy plants will end up like those rugged cowboys in the movies who waste away when they're dragged into high society. Let them show how tough they are by planting them in full sun in dry, perfectly drained soil. Some people even put a layer of sand or gravel as a mulch around these plantings to help them drain quicker and prevent the splash back of fungus spores from the ground during rain or watering.

DROUGHT TOLERANCE

All of these plants are drought tolerant. However, there may be some confusion about just what "drought tolerant" means. It doesn't mean you can just stick a plant in the ground and not water it and expect it to live. Drought-tolerant plants need about one year of semipampering to get themselves estab-

overleaf:
A child's plush toy duck adds a touch of whimsy to this partially sunny cottage garden bed.

opposite:
Full sun in the coastal South is a much more serious proposition than full sun elsewhere. Only true sun worshippers like the annual sunflower (Helianthus annuus) can take it.

lished before they can do without water for extended periods of time. Also, plants in containers are not going to exhibit the same amount of drought tolerance as those in the ground, because generally they won't have enough room to develop the strong root system that is needed to help them through dry spells.

Summer temperatures in the coastal South can stay in the nineties for weeks at a time, with extremely high humidity.

CHART 1

Best Plants for Dry, Sunny Gardens and Gardening at the Beach

☼ REQUIRES FULL SUN

○ GROWS IN FULL OR PART SUN

◑ GROWS BEST IN PART SUN OR LIGHT SHADE

≋ DOES WELL AT THE BEACH AS WELL AS FARTHER INLAND

Drought-Tolerant Gray-Leaved Plants

≋☼ Artemesia (*Artemesia* x 'Powis Castle'; *A. ludoviciana* 'Silver King'; Southernwood, *A. abrotanum*; Beach wormwood, *A. stelleriana*)

≋☼ Beach evening primrose (*Oenethera drummondii*)

≋☼ Beach rosemary (*Conradina canescens*)

☼ Cheddar pinks (*Dianthus gratianopolitanus*)

☼ Cottage pinks (*Dianthus plumarius*)

≋☼ Dusty miller, senecio (*Senecio*)

☼ Germander (*Teucrium fruticans*)

☼ Giant hyssop (*Agastache*)

≋☼ Groundsel bush (*Baccharis halimifolia*)

≋☼ Hummingbird plant (*Dicliptera suberecta*)

☼ Lamb's ears (*Stachys byzantina* 'Countess Helen Von Stein')

≋☼ Lavender cotton (*Santolina incana*)

left:
*Gray-leaved artemesia (*Artemesia*) withstands poor, dry conditions and demands full sun. 'Powis Castle' is one of the best for us.*

above:
*The silvery gray foliage of lamb's ears (*Stachys byzantina*) is beautiful on its own or as a foil for other colors in the garden.*

left:
*The sharp blades of Spanish bayonet (*Yucca filamentosa*) make an excellent accent in the garden, but encountering them can be painful.*

above:
*Ice plant (*Delosperma cooperi*) is a low-growing succulent that thrives in full sun and sharp drainage.*

≋☼ Rosemary (*Rosmarinus officinalis*)
≋☼ Stemodia (*Stemodia tomentosa*)
≋☼ Woolly yarrow (*Achillea tomentosa*)

Drought-Tolerant Hairy and Spiny Plants
☼ Wine cups (*Callirhoe* spp.)
≋☼ Sea holly (*Eryngium*)
≋☼ Yucca (*Yucca*)

Drought-Tolerant Succulents
≋☼ Century plant (*Agave americana*)
≋☼ Hen and chicks (*Sempervivum tectorum*)
≋☼ Ice plant (*Delosperma cooperi*)
≋☼ Myrtle euphorbia (*Euphorbia myrsinites*)
≋☼ Prickly pear cactus (*Opuntia*)

Drought-Tolerant Plants with Fine-Leaved Foliage
☼ Lemon marigold (*Tagetes lemmonii*)
☼ Moss phlox (*Phlox subulata*)
≋☼ Sand phlox (*P. bifida*)
○ Threadleaf coreopsis (*Coreopsis verticillata* 'Zagreb')
○ Yarrow (*Achillea* spp.)

Drought-Tolerant Composites
○ Asters (*Aster*)
≋☼ Beach sunflower (*Helianthus debilis*)

left:
*Blanketflower
(Gaillardia) is so
tough it grows even
in sand dunes.*

right:
*The bright spires of
Crocosmia stand out
even in the glare of
midsummer.*

○ Black-eyed Susan (*Rudbeckia fulgida* var. *deamii*;
  R. fulgida var. *sullivantii* 'Goldsturm')

≋☼ Blanket flower (*Gaillardia*)

○ Boltonia (*Boltonia asteroides*)

≋☼ Gazania (*Gazania*)

○ Giant coneflower (*Rudbeckia maxima*)

○ Golden glow (*Rudbeckia lanciniata* 'Golden Glow')

☼ Mexican hat coneflower (*Ratibida columnifera*)

≋○ Montauk daisy (*Nipponantheum nipponicum*)

○ Perennial sunflower (*Helianthus* x 'Lemon Queen'; *H. giganteus*; *H. pauciflorus*)

○ Willow-leaved sunflower (*Helianthus salcifolius*)

≋○ Seaside goldenrod (*Solidago sempervirens*)

≋○ Shasta daisy (*Leucanthemum* x *superbum* 'Thomas Killian')

Other Good Drought-Tolerant Perennials

≋○ Bushy lantana (*Lantana camara*)

○ Red-hot poker (*Kniphofia uvaria*)

≋☼ Sea lavender (*Limonium latifolium*)

○ Wild foxglove (*Penstemon coboaea*)

Drought-Tolerant Groundcovers

≋☼ Beach sunflower (*Helianthus debilis*)

≋☼ Beach hypericum (*Hypericum reductum*)

≋☼ Dune sunflower (*Sanvitalia procumbens*)

≋☼ Mexican daisy (*Erigeron karvinskianus*)
≋○ Purple heart (*Tradescantia pallida*)
≋○ Rose verbena (*Verbena canadensis*)
≋○ Weeping lantana (*Lantana montevidensis*)

Drought-Tolerant Bulbs
☼ Bearded iris
○ Copper lily (*Habranthus texanus*)
≋○ Crinum lily (*Crinum*)
○ Crocosmia (*Crocosmia x crocosmiflora*)
≋○ Daylily (Hemerocallis)

Drought-Tolerant Shrubs and Subshrubs
≋☼ Beach rosemary (*Conradina canescens*)
☼ Firecracker plant (*Russelia equisetiformis*)
☼ Hummingbird bush (*Anisacanthus wrightii*)
≋☼ Lemon bottlebrush (*Callistemon citrinus*)
≋☼ Rugosa roses (*Rosa rugosa*)

Best Drought-Tolerant Annuals
≋○ Angelonia (*Angelonia angustifolia*)
≋☼ Blanketflower (*Gaillardia pulchella*)
≋☼ Butter daisy (*Melampodium*)
≋○ Globe amaranth (*Gomphrena*)
≋☼ Mexican sunflower (*Tithonia rotundifolia*)
≋☼ Narrow-leaved zinnia (*Zinnia angustifolia*)
≋○ Ornamental Okra (*Abelmoschus moschatus*)
≋○ Pentas (*Pentas*)
≋◑ Porterweed (*Stachytarpheta jamaicensis*)
≋☼ Purslane (*Portulacca oleracera*)
≋○ Vinca (*Catharanthus roseus*)
≋○ Wheat celosia (*Celosia spicata*)

*The arching, needle-fine foliage of the firecracker plant (*Russelia equisetiformis*) presents a lovely counterpoint to its bright red tubular flowers.*

*Although it resembles the more common annual portulacca, annual purslane (*Portulacca oleracera*) has larger leaves and showier flowers. It is also a superior performer in the coastal South.*

VINES IN THE SUN

With the notable exception of clematis and climbing bleeding heart—both of which like a cool, moist root run—most of the vines we can grow in the coastal South will do fine in hot sun with relatively sparse watering once they've gotten themselves established. Vines are a good answer to what to do with a bare fence, and if they're trained over an arch or arbor, they will provide shade under which other less sun-loving plants can flourish. See Chapter 4 for information on specific vines.

GARDENING AT THE BEACH

Not only does the sun beat down unrelentingly at the beach in the summer, but the soil is sandy, the wind can be merciless, and the salt spray of the ocean often reaches the plants. Sometimes the ocean itself reaches the plants. In the aftermath of Hurricanes Allison, Andrew, Bonnie, Dennis, Diana, Floyd, Fran, and Hugo, we have learned just which plants can stand a saltwater bath and which can't.

If you garden at the beach, the very first thing to do is bring in a truckload or two of shredded pine bark or other compost and dig it into your soil. Professional landscapers who create gardens for beach residents always create

In summer, the pindo palm (Butia capitata) produces fantastic clusters of yellow, edible dates.

new, viable soil first before planting anything. You might also consider building a windbreak or installing plants that will shield your perennials from the brunt of the wind. Beach garden soil will need amending much more frequently than the soil in a garden ten miles inland. The whole bed should, optimally, be dug up and heavily amended every three years at the beach.

It's the opinion of some very experienced gardeners in this area that the best thing to do with a beach garden is turn it over completely to the survivalists—the grasses and gray-leaved subshrubs—and not think in terms of mixed perennial arrangements. However, that seems a harsh fate for those who love and want to grow a variety of shrubs and perennials. There are certain large and small trees, evergreen and deciduous shrubs—many with beautiful flowers—and a good number of perennials that tolerate maritime life quite well. By using a combination of trees, shrubs, and perennials, you should be able to achieve year-round color and interest even in a salty, windswept environment.

Word has it that pittosporum and Indian hawthorn were among the only shrubs that were not killed by standing salt water after the hurricanes. Note that sweet pepperbush (*Clethra alnifolia*) and hydrangea (*Hydrangea*) are often grown at the beach, but they need to be in a shaded location.

CHART 2

Best Trees and Shrubs for the Beach

☼ REQUIRES FULL SUN

◯ GROWS IN FULL OR PART SUN

● REQUIRES FULL OR PART SHADE

≋ DOES WELL AT THE BEACH AS WELL AS FARTHER INLAND

In addition to the trees and shrubs listed below, some hardy palms also do well at the beach. For suggestions, see "The Subtropical Garden" in Chapter 3.

≋◯ American holly (*Ilex opaca*)

≋◯ Barberry (*Berberis thunbergii*)

≋◯ Bayberry (*Myrica pensylvanica*)

≋◯ Butcher's broom (*Ruscus aculeatus*)

≋◯ Cotoneaster (*Cotoneaster*)

≋◯ Evergreen euonymus (*Euonymus japonica*)

≋● Fatsia (*Fatsia japonica*)

≋◯ Flowering quince (*Chaenomeles*)

≋◯ Indian hawthorn (*Raphiolepis indica*)

≋◯ Japanese black pine (*Pinus thunbergiana*)

≋◯ Japanese pittosporum (*Pittosporum tobira*)

≋☼ Lemon bottlebrush (*Callistemon citrinus*)

≋◯ Live oak (*Quercus virginiana*)

≋◯ Magnolia (*Magnolia grandiflora*)

≋☼ Oleander (*Nerium oleander*)

≋☼ Petite Scotch rose (*Rosa spinosissima*)

≋◯ Privet (*Ligustrum*)

≋◯ Rose of Sharon (*Hibiscus syriacus*)

≋☼ Rugosa roses (*Rosa rugosa*)

≋◯ Sand pine (*Pinus clausa*)

≋◯ Scrub oak (*Quercus ilicifolia*)

≋◯ Shore juniper (*Juniperus conferta*)

≋◯ Southern yew (*Podocarpus macrophyllus*)

≋☼ Spirea (*Spirea*)

≋◯ Tamarisk (*Tamarix*)

≋☼ Texas sage (*Leucophyllum frutescens*)

≋◯ Thorny eleagnus (*Eleagnus pungens*)

≋◯ Wax myrtle (*Myrica cerifera*)

≋◯ Yaupon holly (*Ilex vomitoria*)

THE MOIST SUNNY GARDEN

Many perennials require full or part sun to perform best. If a plant is not listed among the drought-tolerant plants above, however, it may not appreciate a baking-hot, dry position. Check the A–Z Plant Guide at the end of this book to see what the plant's cultural requirements are. If the plant takes "full sun to part sun" or "full sun to part shade," it can get by with half a day of sun in the coastal South—morning sun is best. Gardeners in our area should also take care to give those plants rich soil, ample moisture, and a good layer of mulch during the hottest times of the year. It's especially important to guard against the brutal afternoon sun in the summer. In winter and early spring, the effects of day-long exposure to the sun are not as much of a problem. Caution: Other sources of information may tell you that a plant takes full sun. Full sun in Connecticut is not the same thing as full sun in Texas. Part sun may be the wiser course.

Plants that are bog dwellers are unique, in that they live with constantly wet feet and their heads in the sun. To create a bog, choose a spot in full sun and line the ground beneath your plants with plastic set about one to two feet deep. Give bog plants rich soil and don't let them dry out.

Coastal Shade Gardens Shady Doesn't Always Mean Cool

One of the mistakes we make in the coastal South is to think that plants traditionally suggested for shade will do well in *our* shade. Many of those plants are leaf-mold-loving woodlanders whose natural habitat is nestled away in a fresh mountain nook somewhere next to a babbling stream at an elevation of several thousand feet. They are delicate creatures enjoying nature's kindlier ways—cool nights, frequent waterings, and humus-rich soil from various rotting neighbors. The plants that are going to thrive in shade in the coastal South, on the other hand, will often have to deal with hot, poor, sandy soil or hardpan clay in addition to the lack of direct sunlight. This is a quantum leap that a plant like lady slipper, for example, isn't going to make.

Given these real-world limitations, we can still grow dozens of foliage and flowering plants in shade. In many cases it will be helpful to make the soil as rich and moisture-retentive as possible by adding generous amounts of compost, leaf mold, and/or rotted manure and by mulching well. Another idea that works well is to excavate all or part of the shade garden and line it with plastic (heavy-gauge pond liner works well, but is more expensive) or large plastic tubs. Even a child's wading pool will do the trick. After doing this, you poke a few holes to allow for sufficient drainage. Poking the correct number of holes is an art form unto itself, but if you get it right you'll have the moist soil and cooler root run that many shade plants appreciate.

Many plants will bloom in light shade more readily than in heavy, deep shade. To lighten up a heavily shaded spot, consider removing a tree or lopping off as many of the lower branches as you can.

opposite:
Red-leaved Cannas *and other subtropical corms and tubers such as giant elephant ear (*Colocasia*) and bananas (*Ensete*) are flexible plants. They will grow in full sun or part shade.*

CHART 3

Best Plants for Shady and Partly Shady Gardens

○ GROWS IN FULL OR PART SUN

◐ GROWS BEST IN PART SUN OR LIGHT SHADE

● REQUIRES FULL OR PART SHADE

◉ TOLERATES A WIDE RANGE OF CONDITIONS, FROM FULL SUN TO FULL SHADE

Bulbs, Corms, and Tubers for Shade and Light Shade

The diminutive pink flowers and plum-colored foliage of this wood sorrel (Oxalis regnellii 'Triangularis') are a nice addition to the partially shady garden.

*Hardy tuberous begonia (*Begonia grandis*) blooms in deep or light shade from spring through fall. The heart-shaped foliage is a deep green tinged with red.*

- ○ Canna lilies (*Canna*)
- ○ Crinum lily (*Crinum*)
- ● Cuban squill (*Scilla peruviana*)
- ○ Elephant ears (*Alocasia*; *Colocasia*; *Xanthosoma*)
- ○ Fortnight lily (*Dietes vegeta*)
- ◐ Ginger lilies (*Hedychium*; *Globba*; *Costus*; *Curcuma*; *Zingiber*)
- ● Hardy begonia (*Begonia grandis*)
- ● Hardy orchid (*Bletilla striata*)
- ● Spanish bluebells (*Hyacinthoides hispanica*)
- ○ Spider lily (*Hymenocallis*)
- ○ Star of Bethlehem (*Ornithogalum umbellatum*)
- ● Voodoo lily (*Amorphophallus*)

- ◖ Walking iris (*Neomarica gracilis*)
- ○ White French Roman hyacinth (*Hyacinthoides orientalis* var. *albulus*)
- ○ Wood sorrel (*Oxalis*)
- ○ Yellow flag iris (*Iris pseudocorus*)

Flowering Vines for Light Shade
- ◖ Bower vine (*Pandorea jasminoides*)
- ○ Carolina jessamine (*Gelsemium sempervirens*)
- ◖ Climbing hydrangea (*Decumaria barbara*)
- ○ Confederate jasmine (*Trachelospermum jasminoides*)
- ○ Evergreen wisteria (*Milletia reticulata*)
- ○ Honeysuckle (*Lonicera heckrottii*; *L. sempervirens*)
- ○ Jasmine (*Jasminum*)
- ○ Sweet autumn clematis (*Clematis ternifolia*)
- ○ Trumpet vine (*Campsis*)

Flowering Shrubs for Part Shade or Filtered Sunlight

*Sasanquas (*Camellia sasanqua*) begin blooming in the fall and are followed by their cousins the camellias (*Camellia japonica*). Both sasanquas and camellias bloom beautifully in filtered shade.*

- ● Azaleas (*Rhododendron* spp.)
- ○ Beautyberry (*Callicarpa*)
- ● Camellia (*Camellia japonica*)
- ○ Cape fuchsia (*Phygelius capensis*)
- ○ Cape honeysuckle (*Tecomaria capensis*)
- ● Fatsia (*Fatsia japonica*)
- ○ Firespike (*Odontonema strictum*)

An exquisite bloom of variegated lacecap hydrangea (Hydrangea macrophylla 'Variegata') graces the shady garden in early summer. Fertile, four-petaled white flowers surround the central corymb of blue, sterile flowers, creating a true work of art in nature.

○ Flowering maple (*Abutilon*)
○ Flowering quince (*Chaenomeles*)
◑ Glorybower (*Clerondendrum*)
○ Himalayan honeysuckle shrub (*Leycesteria formosa*)
○ Hummingbird bush (*Anisacanthus wrightii*)
● Hydrangea (*Hydrangea*)
◑ Kerria (*Kerria japonica*)
● Mahonia (*Mahonia*)
● Sasanqua (*Camellia sasanqua*)
○ Shower of gold (*Galphimia glauca*)
◑ Shrimp plant (*Justicia brandegeana*)
○ Winter honeysuckle shrub (*Lonicera fragrantissima*)
○ Yellow shrimp plant (*Pachystasis lutea*)
○ Yesterday-today-tomorrow (*Brunsfelsia pauciflora* 'Floribunda')

Groundcovers and Foliage Plants for Shade and Part Shade
◑ Bugleweed (*Ajuga reptans*)
● Chameleon plant (*Houttuynia cordata*)
● Club moss (*Selaginella*)
○ Creeping buttercup (*Ranunculus repens* 'Pleniflora')
◑ Creeping celery (*Oenanthe javanica* 'Flamingo')
○ Creeping raspberry (*Rubus calcynoides*)
◑ Golden creeping jenny (*Lysimachia nummularia* 'Aurea')
◑ Golden moneywort (*L. congestifolia* 'Outback Sunset')

The bright blue spires of bugleweed (Ajuga) play off the ruffled, acid green foliage of the dwarf Hosta 'Chartreuse Wiggles' in a lightly shaded part of the garden.

○ Golden star (*Chrysogonum virginianum*)
● Hosta (*Hosta*)
● Italian arum (*Arum italicum*)
◉ Ivy (*Hedera helix*)
◉ Lily turf (*Liriope*)
◑ Mazus (*Mazus reptans*)
◉ Monkey grass (*Ophiopogon*)
◑ Peacock ginger (*Kaempferia* spp.)
◉ Periwinkle (*Vinca major*)
● Persian shield (*Strobilanthes dyeranus*)
◑ Purple velvet plant (*Gynura aurantiaca* 'Purple Passion')
◑ Self-heal (*Prunella grandiflora*)
◑ Stonecrop (*Sedum acre* 'Aureum')
◑ Strawberry geranium (*Saxifraga stolonifera*)
● Tovara (*Tovara virginiana* 'Painter's Palette')
◑ Violet (*Viola hederacea*)
● Wild ginger (*Asarum* var. 'Shuttleworthii')
◉ Wintercreeper (*Euonymus fortunei*)

Grasses for Light Shade
◑ Golden satin grass (*Hakonechloa macra* 'Aureola')
○ Inland sea oats (*Chasmanthium latifolium*)
○ Muhly grass (*Muhlenbergia*)
◑ Sedges (*Carex*)

*Variegated lily turf grass (*Liriope muscari*) blooms even in deep shade.*

Flowers for Shade and Part Sun

left:
*This shady composition is made up of Solomon's seal (*Polygonatum*), holly fern (*Cyrtomium falcatum*), hostas (*Hosta*), variegated sparkler sedge (*Carex phyllocephala 'Sparkler'*), Lenten roses (*Helleborus orientalis*), and Virginia sweetspire (*Itea virginica*).*

below:
*Ginger lilies (*Hedychium*) produce spectacular blooms even in light shade.*

- ◐ Bee balm (*Monarda*)
- ○ Cigar plant (*Cuphea ignea*)
- ◐ Creeping phlox (*Phlox stolonifera*)
- ◐ Fringed bleeding heart (*Dicentra exemia*)
- ◐ Indian pink (*Spigelia marilandica*)

- ◑ Japanese anemone (*Anemone x hybrida*)
- ◑ Japanese sage (*Salvia koyame*)
- ● Leopard plant (*Ligularia dentata*)
- ● Lenten rose (*Helleborus orientalis*)
- ● May apple (*Podophyllum peltatum*)
- ◑ Meadowsweet (*Filipendula ulmaria*)
- ○ Mexican cigar flower (*Cuphea micropetala*)
- ○ Mexican heather (*Cuphea hyssopifolia*)
- ◑ Native columbine (*Aquilegia canadensis*)
- ◑ Parrot lily (*Alstroemeria psittacina*)
- ● Solomon's seal (*Polygonatum odoratum*)
- ○ Spiderwort (*Tradescantia*)
- ● Toad lily (*Tricyrtis*)
- ○ Turk's cap lily (*Lilium martagon*)
- ○ Turk's cap (*Malvaviscus drummondii*)
- ◑ Wild blue phlox (*Phlox divaricata*)
- ○ Wine sage (*Salvia vanhouttii*)

Ferns

For a list of ferns that thrive in the coastal South, see Chapter 4.

The shady garden doesn't have to be a boring place. Here a bright chartreuse hosta mixes with ferns, trillium, ginger (Asarum), and the electric purple foliage of Persian shield (Strobilanthes dyeranus).

The Subtropical Garden

To some people, a garden based primarily on foliage may seem like not a garden at all. "Where are the flowers?" a visitor may ask. But others may appreciate the erect, fleshy, blue-green foliage of the American century plant or the black, kid-glove foliage of *Colocasia* 'Black Magic' as much as the most perfect 'Don Juan' rose blossom. The foliage and structure of plants are important considerations because, in most cases, the colorful blossoms of perennials are short-lived.

A satisfying garden design juxtaposes plants with different textures, leaf shape, and foliage color so the eye and the mind are kept intrigued. Variegated foliage and the moving grace of ornamental grasses add instant variety to any garden. The erect, sword-shaped foliage of plants like Spanish bayonet (*Yucca*), cordyline (*Cordyline australis*), and New Zealand flax (*Phormium tenax*) can add a sense of order and architecture to an area populated by more lax, sprawling plants. Palms of any type immediately add a tropical dimension.

There are many reasons to use subtropicals in the garden: they are hardy, beautiful, and well suited to our climate.

Some of the biggest, boldest foliage plants demand that you look at them. Many of these are subtropicals. There are a number of reasons for gardeners in the coastal South to weave subtropicals into their landscapes. First, barring those unpredictable arctic cold snaps that surprise the plants in midsap, most subtropicals are winter hardy here, with a protective mulch. Secondly, they

stand out in the hazy, overly bright summer garden while their more delicate neighbors may look exhausted and insubstantial. Thirdly, they provide a wonderful variety of texture, leaf shape, and foliage color. Finally, they are relatively easy to grow and require little attention during most of the growing season.

Many of these plants are averse to a wet, cold winter. One solution is to create raised beds for them, which will provide excellent drainage. Those gardeners whose passion is growing the subtropicals use a soil made up of one-half composted cow manure and one-half finely shredded mulch to provide the richest, best quality soil possible. After the first heavy frost, you can cut your subtropicals to the ground and scatter another two-inch layer of compost or other soil amendment on top.

True tropicals live in Zones 11 and 12 and will give up the ghost if the temperature falls much below forty-five degrees. The hardy subtropicals, though, can withstand thirty-degree weather without much problem and some survive down to zero. In our area, the roots may survive and the tops die down, so that we will not have any significant above-ground showing until mid-May or mid-June. In addition, plants like the banana may not bear fruit except in Zone 9 climates. However, the biggest danger to these plants is root rot from overly wet soil in winter, so give them good drainage. If you live in the northernmost range for the more tender subtropicals—such as *Alocasia, Colocasia, Musa*, and *Xanthosoma*—you may want to dig them up every few years and replant them deeper (about six inches) to insulate them from the cold. They tend to do themselves a disservice by rising up over time.

If you're looking for drama, look no further than the hardy giant bananas (Musa), shown here at the foot of a stately live oak.

CHART 4

Best Subtropicals, Cycads, and Palms for the Coastal South

☼ REQUIRES FULL SUN

○ GROWS IN FULL OR PART SUN

◑ GROWS BEST IN PART SUN OR LIGHT SHADE

● REQUIRES FULL OR PART SHADE

Subtropicals and Dramatic Foliage Plants

above:
What could be more exotic looking than the yellow shrimp plant (Pachystachys lutea)?

left:
The mauve and yellow inflorescences of the hidden ginger lily (Curcuma petiolaris) are treasures just waiting to be discovered.

*Doll-size fruits sprout from between the leaves of the hardy pink banana (*Musa veluntina*).*

- ◐ Alligator plant (*Acanthus montanus*)
- ○ Banana (*Musa, Ensete*)
- ◐ Bear's britches (*Acanthus* x 'Summer Beauty')
- ○ Canna lily (*Canna*)
- ☼ Castor bean (*Ricinus communis*)
- ☼ Century plant (*Agave americana*)
- ☼ Cordyline (*Cordyline australis*)
- ○ Elephant ear (*Alocasia*; *Colocasia*; *Xanthosoma*)
- ◐ Ginger lily (*Hedychium*; *Costus*; *Curcuma*; *Zingiber*)
- ● Leopard plant (*Ligularia dentata*)

○ New Zealand flax (*Phormium tenax*)
◑ Peacock ginger (*Kaempferia*)
◑ Pinecone ginger (*Zingiber zerumbet*)
☼ Plantain (*Plantago*)
○ Rice paper plant (*Tetrapanex papyferus*)
○ Yellow shrimp plant (*Pachystachys lutea*)

Cold-hardy Palms and Cycads
○ Broadleaf lady palm (*Rhapis excelsa*)
○ Butia palm (*Butia capitata*)
○ Cabbage palm (*Sabal palmetto*)
☼ Desert fan palm (*Washingtonia filifera*)
○ Dwarf palmetto (*Sabal minor*)
○ European fan palm (*Chamaerops humilis*)
○ Hispaniola palmetto (*Sabal blackburniana*)
○ Needle palm (*Rhapidophyllum hystrix*)
○ Sago palm (*Cycas revoluta*)
○ Texas palmetto (*Sabal mexicana*)
☼ Thread palm (*Washingtonia robusta*)
○ Windmill palm (*Trachycarpus fortunei*)

CHAPTER 4
The Companion Plants

The delicate pink blooms of Rosa 'The Fairy' keep good company with bright, acid yellow Patrinia scabiosifolia.

Companion Plants for Perennials What Are They?

If we were to plant nothing but perennials, we would have to forgo a lot of wonderful companion plants. Gardening with perennials always involves incorporating other plants, whether large or small into an overall composition or garden scheme. In this chapter, we will meet some terrific companion plants. Most of them—with the obvious exception of the annuals and some of the herbs and vines—will increase and persist in your garden for many, many years to come. So, in that sense, they are perennial in nature just as true perennials are. These companion plants add enormous value to the garden. Gardeners in the coastal South should make extensive use of these plants in order to have a full and varied gardening experience.

For example, a garden will be a richer, more satisfying place with a few ferns gracing a shady corner and maybe one or more beautiful, no-fail roses where there's full sun. And, if you want color in your garden—which most gardeners do—you will have to rely on annuals to "carry" the garden during those stretches when one perennial has finished blooming and the next one hasn't started yet.

In this chapter we also look at the ceiling and the floor of the garden. Groundcovers are very useful for filling in troublesome spots and for helping

Perennials need company in the garden, whether it be mingling with ferns or sharing the glory with a beautiful wall of creeping fig (Ficus pumila).

unify your garden design. Vines can add romance and an airy feeling to an otherwise earthbound garden scene.

Bulbs are terribly underutilized in the coastal South for two reasons. First, gardeners in our area have had bad experiences with the traditional Dutch bulbs; and, secondly, most gardeners are unaware of the fantastic bulb choices we have. We can grow so many bulbs that people in other parts of the country cannot grow that it would be a shame not to include some in every garden.

Ornamental grasses are often an afterthought, but designing your perennial plantings with these stately, vertical accent plants in mind can open up all sorts of new possibilities. And, finally, herbs don't need to be relegated to the herb garden. They are so varied in color, size, and texture that they can and should be combined with your perennials—and then enjoyed in the kitchen as well.

It should come as no surprise that not *all* ferns, vines, bulbs, herbs, groundcovers, grasses, annuals, and roses do well in the coastal South. Some of the most common ones that appear regularly in gardening books and at the larger garden centers may not be at all suited to our climate. As with perennials, it pays to learn which ones are the best for our area. In the long run, you will save time, money, and frustration. You'll also be on your way to having the kind of garden you have dreamt about.

Note: Because of space limitations we have not provided detailed descriptions of the larger companion plants in the garden, such as the trees and landscaping shrubs. You will find some trees and flowering shrubs mentioned in Chapter 1, "The Seasons."

Bulbs The Food Storage Experts

Bulbs are underused in the southeastern coastal area. In large part that's because we're unfamiliar with the ones that grow well for us. It may also be that some of us have had bad experiences with the Dutch bulbs that don't perennialize well here. The advantage we have in the coastal South is that we can grow many bulbs in our gardens that are restricted to the greenhouse in other parts of the country. Within the broad category of bulbs, we are talking about all geophytes, which includes rhizomes, corms, and tuberous roots, all of which are enlarged parts of the plant's tissue used to store food during periods of drought or cold. In addition to the late winter and spring bulb season, summer and fall are also excellent times of the year for bulbs in the South. The sterile hybrids, or "mules," do best for us.

BULB BASICS

There are only a few things to keep in mind about bulbs. First, some bulbs need a good, long chill every year in order to bloom. Of course, we avoid these bulbs like the plague. Or, if they happen to be tulips or some other romantic

Truly a glorious flower in all ways, the gloriosa lily (Gloriosa superba 'Rothschildiana') climbs to six feet tall and will need some support. Wonderfully showy stamens protrude from the colorful, wavy-edged tepals.

bulb we can't bear to pass up, we chill them for ten weeks in the vegetable drawer of the refrigerator (keep them away from ripening fruit), plant them out in November, cross our fingers and enjoy whatever flowers they produce on a one-time-only basis. When they've finished flowering, they go on top of the compost pile.

But, in general, we should stick to the dozens of bulbs that don't need a cold winter chill and don't mind a hot, humid summer. These can stay in the ground forever and multiply happily, making us truly glad of their company. Luckily, we have a huge number to choose from.

The next rule about bulbs—almost all bulbs—is that they hate having their feet wet. Most especially in winter they *hate* sitting in wet soil. They will rot out and disappear if you do this to them. The exceptions to this rule are certain rhizomes and bulbs like Japanese, Siberian, and Louisiana irises; yellow flag iris; swamp spider lily; colocasias; and cannas, all of which thrive in standing water during the growing season. In general, however, unless you specifically know differently, you should keep your bulbs well drained in the winter months.

Most bulbs also require full or part sun to do their best. Bulbs that bloom in winter or spring can survive on the sunlight that exists under deciduous trees because they will have finished photosynthesizing and will go dormant around the time the trees leaf out. Most bulbs that bloom in summer or fall, however, won't do well under the shade of a tree. The exceptions to this rule are those summer-flowering bulbs that tolerate light shade, such as the cannas, the ginger lilies, martagon lilies, and the crinums.

One of the simplest facts about bulbs is that they must be a certain size in order to bloom. Of course, what this minimum bulb mass is will depend on whether it's a crocus or a crinum. In order to grow to that minimum flowering size, stay that size, and form what are called "daughters," a mother bulb must have adequate fertility and the opportunity to fully photosynthesize over a long enough period to create food for herself. That's why a handful of bulb booster isn't a bad idea once a year. Apply the bulb booster around or just before the time the bulb blooms.

It's also important to let bulb leaves turn yellow before you do away with them. They are the plant's built-in food production mechanism. If you clip them down neatly while they're still green, you'll diminish the bulb's size and eventually make flower production an impossibility. What's really undesirable is a bunch of uninteresting green leaves appearing year after year with no flowers. That's just what you'll get if you fail to let the leaves senesce before removing them.

Planting bulbs is a fairly straightforward affair. The depth of planting is directly proportional to the size of the bulb. With a few exceptions, big bulbs are planted deeper than little bulbs. For example, the tiny *Ipheion uniflorum* should be planted so that the top of the bulb is about an inch below the surface, and the hefty amaryllis bulb should be planted about six to eight inches below the surface. The top of the bulb is usually somewhat pointier than the bottom. The bottom will have evidence of last year's roots on it. If you can't tell the bottom

This bright red poppy anemone (Anemone coronaria 'The Governor') is every bit as stunning in the garden as its namesake, the oriental poppy (Papaver orientalis), but better suited to our climate. It is shown here with pale blue starflowers (Ipheion uniflorum) and 'Antique Shades' pansies.

from the top, plant the bulb on its side and it will figure it out on its own. Certain tubers like anemones look like large hard raisins and it's impossible to tell, so don't even worry about those.

It's nice to break up and amend the ground with manure or compost before you plant, but bulb expert Brent Heath of Brent and Becky's Bulbs has a technique he uses for planting out hundreds of bulbs an hour—which he and his wife are often required to do for major public plantings—and it involves sticking bulbs in the ground when you can't or don't want to dig up the whole bed first. Here's how their method works: (1) stick your trowel in the ground; (2) work it back and forth once or twice in an upward motion so that you are slightly lifting the ground directly *in front of* the trowel; (3) where the ground has been loosened (in front of the trowel), slip your bulb in the way you would hide your valuables under the mattress of your bed; (4) give the earth a brief pat and keep moving on with the rest of your bulbs. This takes something over three nanoseconds to accomplish. Plant the bulbs as thickly as possible because almost all bulbs (except maybe the giants like crinum and amaryllis and such) look much better en masse rather than scattered here and there.

The very best source for learning about bulbs that will do well in our area is Scott Ogden's *Garden Bulbs for the South*, which is a treasure trove of information. We should be using these southern classics abundantly and lobbying the nurseries and mail-order catalogues to carry more of them. See "Internet Sources for Information and Ordering Plants" for some excellent mail-order sources for bulbs and "Recommended Reading" for further reading on the subject.

left:
Delicate starflowers (Ipheion uniflorum) mix well with dark blue pansies, cream-colored daffodils (Narcissus 'Curlew'), and magenta poppy anemones (Anemone coronaria 'Sylphide').

right:
In the coastal South it is important to choose daffodil bulbs wisely. One of the best large-cup, solid yellow cultivars for our area is Narcissus 'Saint Keverne'.

CHART 5

Best Bulbs for the Coastal South

☼ REQUIRES FULL SUN

◯ GROWS IN FULL OR PART SUN

◑ GROWS BEST IN PART SUN OR LIGHT SHADE

● REQUIRES FULL OR PART SHADE

Fall Blooms

◑ Ginger lily (*Hedychium*)

☼ Kaffir lily (*Schizostylis coccinea*)

◯ Naked ladies (*Lycoris squamigera*)

◯ Oxblood lily (*Rhodophiala bifida*)

◑ Pinecone ginger (*Zingiber zerumbet*)

◯ Spider lily, red (*Lycoris radiata*)

◯ Spider lily, yellow (*L. aurea*)

◑ Spiral flag, ginger lily (*Costus*)

◯ White rain lily (*Zephyranthes candida*)

Late Winter and Early Spring Blooms

☼ Paperwhite narcissus
(*Narcissus tazetta* var. *papyracceus*)

● Spanish bluebell (*Hyacinthoides hispanica*)

◯ Spring starflower (*Ipheion uniflorum*)

◯ Summer snowflake (*Leucojum aestivum*)

◯ Wood sorrel (*Oxalis*)

Spring Beauties

◯ African iris (*Dietes vegeta*)

☼ Amaryllis (*Hippeastrum*)

☼ Bearded iris

◯ Blue flag iris (*Iris versicolor*)

☼ Copper iris (*Iris fulva*)

☼ Daffodil, jonquil (*Narcissus*)
(See Chapter 1 for recommended varieties.)

☼ Dutch iris

● Hardy Chinese orchid (*Bletilla striata*)

◯ Japanese iris (*Iris ensata*)

◯ Louisiana iris

☼ Poppy anemone (*Anemone coronaria*)

◯ Siberian iris (*Iris siberica*)

◑ Walking iris (*Neomarica gracilis*)

◯ Wood sorrel (*Oxalis*)

◯ Yellow flag iris (*Iris pseudocorus*)

Summer Blooms

◑ Achimenes (*Achimenes* 'Purple King')

☼ Abyssinian gladiolus (*Gladiolus callianthus*)

top:
*Most bulbs demand "dry feet" in winter, but the yellow flag iris (*Iris pseudocorus*) grows just as happily in a pot submerged in water. This rhizomatous perennial spreads rapidly.*

bottom:
*The walking iris (*Neomarica gracilis*) blooms in full sun or light shade. Roots form where the stems bend to the ground with newly emerging plantlets. In this way, the iris "walks" around the garden.*

In summer the hardy Abyssinian gladiolus (Gladiolus callianthus) produces spikes of white flowers with reddish-purple markings at the throat.

○ African iris (*Dietes vegeta*)

☼ Allium (*Allium*)

   A. schoenoprasum (garden chives)

   A. tuberosum (garlic chives)

   A. uniflorum

   A. bulgaricum

   A. aflatunense

☼ Asiatic hybrid lily (*Lilium*)

○ Blackberry lily (*Belamcanda chinensis*)

☼ Corn lily (*Gladiolus byzantinus*)

○ Crinum (*Crinum*)

○ Crocosmia (*Crocosmia*)

☼ Dahlia (*Dahlia*)

○ Daylily (*Hemerocallis*)

○ Easter lily (*Lilium longiformium*)

○ Formosa lily (*L. formosanum*)

○ Gloriosa lily (*Gloriosa superba* 'Rothschildiana')

☼ Hybrid garden gladiolus

☼ Liatris (*Liatris spicata*)

○ Lily of the Nile (*Agapanthus*)

○ Madonna lily (*Lilium candidum*)

○ Peruvian daffodil (*Hymenocallis*)

○ Rain lily, fairy lily (*Zephyranthes* and *Habranthus*)

○ Regal lily (*Lilium regale*)

☼ Sea daffodil (*Panacritum maritimum*)

○ Society garlic (*Tulbaghia violacea*)

☼ Summer hyacinth (*Galtonia candicans*)

○ Tuberose (*Polianthes tuberosa* 'Mexican Single')

The coastal South abounds with fascinating vines. Above, the chartreuse seed pods of lavender orchid vine (Mascagnia lilacina) appear in autumn after the yellow flowers are spent.

Jack had no idea what he was getting into when he planted those magic beans. He probably wasn't an Englishman at all. He and his mother and their cow probably lived somewhere in coastal Zone 9. Garden writers, who should know better, tell us that there's always room for a vine no matter how crowded the garden. The theory is that a vine is a vertical element and takes up only air space and not much ground space. However, vines in our climate are a law unto themselves. With the exception of some forms of clematis and climbing bleeding heart, which have been known to behave politely and demurely, you have to be prepared for vines carrying on somewhat boorishly in this region. This includes the innocent little annual vines grown from seed, such as the moonflower, the morning glory, and the hyacinth bean vine. Flowering vines, like nothing else in the garden, give you the feeling that you are in the presence of palpable growth—life moving forward and increasing before your very eyes.

Most of the vines you might want to grow with your climbing roses, for example, will have smothered them by midsummer. It's usually not fatal. But you may end up ripping out one vine and trying another in hopes that it will be less vigorous. One conclusion is that vines should be given a place of their own and left to do their very glorious thing undisturbed. Keep in mind that by midsummer a vine growing on an arch, trellis, or pergola will have produced approximately (unscientifically speaking) a billion leaves and will shade its neighbors just as if it were a small tree.

HOW VINES CLIMB

Vines climb in one of three ways: they can cling to vertical supports by means of curly tendrils, the way passionflower vine and clematis do; they can burrow themselves into the wood or cement with their tenacious holdfasts, as ivy and creeping fig do; or they can wrap themselves around a vertical structure by simply twining upward—wisteria and honeysuckle are good examples of this choke-it-to-death method of gaining height. Other so-called "climbing" plants, like roses, have to be attached along the way up with the help of the gardener or else they will sprawl in a heap on the ground.

There are dozens of wonderful vines to choose from in a rainbow of colors and a variety of bloom times. All except the Carolina jessamine (*Gelsemium sempervirens*), swamp jessamine (*G. rankii*), confederate jasmine (*Trachelospermum jasminoides*), climbing hydrangea (*Decumaria barbara*), and honeysuckle (*Lonicera*) need full sun or a goodly amount of part sun to put forth blooms. Generally speaking, the sunnier the spot the more profusely they will bloom. Well-amended soil is always appreciated.

CHART 6
Best Vines for the Coastal South

☼ REQUIRES FULL SUN

◯ GROWS IN FULL OR PART SUN

◖ GROWS BEST IN PART SUN OR LIGHT SHADE

◉ TOLERATES A WIDE RANGE OF CONDITIONS, FROM FULL SUN TO FULL SHADE

[A] ANNUAL

[E] EVERGREEN

[H] HERBACEOUS PERENNIAL

Best Spring- and Summer-Blooming Honeysuckles

[E]◯ Trumpet honeysuckle (*Lonicera sempervirens*)

[E]◯ Gold flame honeysuckle (*Lonicera heckrottii*)

Classic Spring-Blooming Vines

[H]☼ Anemone clematis (*Clematis montana*)

[E]◯ Carolina jessamine (*Gelsemium sempervirens*)

[E]◯ Cat's claw vine (*Macfadyena unguis-cati*)

[E]◯ Crossvine (*Bignonia capreolata*)

[E]☼ Evergreen clematis (*Clematis armandii*)

[E]◯ Pink jasmine (*Jasminum polyanthum*)

[E]◯ Swamp jessamine (*Gelsemium rankii*)

[H]◯ Wisteria (*Wisteria*)

Summer-Blooming Clematis

[H]☼ Golden clematis (*Clematis tanguitica*)

[H]☼ Hybrid clematis (including *Clematis jackmanii*)

Clusters of the coral-pink-and-yellow flowers of gold flame honeysuckle (Lonicera heckrottii) embroider a white picket fence in midsummer. This semievergreen vine blooms from spring through fall.

[H]☼ Italian clematis (*Clematis viticella*)
[H]☼ Portuguese clematis (*Clematis campaniflora*)
[H]☼ Texas clematis (*Clematis texensis*)

Summer-Blooming Jasmines
[E]○ Arabian jasmine (*Jasminum sambac*)
[E]○ Common white jasmine (*Jasminum officinale*)
[E]○ Confederate jasmine
        (*Trachelospermum jasminoides*)
[E]○ Italian jasmine (*Jasminum humile*)
[E]○ Asian star jasmine (*Trachelospermum asiaticum*)
[H]○ Spanish jasmine (*Jasminum grandiflorum*)

Best Climbing Hydrangeas
[H]◗ Japanese hydrangea vine
        (*Schizophragma hydrangeoides*)
[E]◗ Climbing hydrangea (*Decumaria barbara*)

The large-flowered clematis (Clematis), such as 'Ernest Markham', bloom in early summer on fences, trellises, and arbors.

More Excellent Summer Vines

The small white flowers of the potato vine (Solanum jasminoides) *cover the vine in spring and appear again less profusely in summer and fall.*

[E]◑ Bower vine (*Pandorea jasminoides*)

[E]☼ Coral vine (*Antigonon leptopus*)

[A]☼ Cypress vine (*Ipomoea quamoclit*)

[H]○ Kiwi vine (*Actinidia deliciosa*)

[A]☼ Morning glory (*Ipomoea nil*)

[A]☼ Moonflower vine (*Ipomoea alba*)

[H]☼ Orchid vine (*Mascagnia lilacina*)

[H]○ Passionflower vine (*Passiflora incarnata*)

[H]○ Perennial sweet pea (*Lathyrus latifolius*)

[E]○ Potato vine (*Solanum jasminoides*)

[E]○ St. Vincent Lilac (*Solanum seaforthianum*)

[A]○ Sky vine (*Thunbergia grandiflora*)

[A]☼ Star quamoclit (*Ipomoea coccinea*)

Vines for Late Summer and Fall Color

*Cape honeysuckle (*Tecomaria capensis*) is beloved of hummingbirds. It can be grown as a shrub or allowed to climb up as a twenty-five-foot-long vine.*

[A]○ Black-eyed Susan vine (*Thunbergia alata*)

[E]○ Butterfly vine (*Stigmaphyllon cilatum*)

[E]○ Cape honeysuckle (*Tecomaria capensis*)

The annual moonflower vine (Ipomoea alba) opens its opulent white trumpet flowers at the end of the day and closes them back up when morning comes.

[H]☼ Climbing aster (*Aster carolinianus*)

[E]○ Evergreen wisteria (*Milletia reticulata*)

[A]○ Hyacinth bean vine (*Dolichos lablab*)

[H]☼ Muscadine grape vine (*Vitis rotundifolia*)

[H]☼ Orange peel clematis (*Clematis tibetana*)

[H]○ Porcelain berry vine (*Ampelopsis brevipedunculata*)

[H]○ Sweet autumn clematis (*Clematis ternifolia*)

[H]○ Trumpet creeper (*Campsis*)

Tender Vines for Summer and Fall Color
[H]☼ Chilean jasmine (*Mandevilla laxa*)

[E]☼ Bougainvillea (*Bougainvillea*)

Vines for Winter Color
[E]○ Trumpet honeysuckle (*Lonicera sempervirens*)

[E]☼ Firethorn (*Pyracantha coccinea*)

[E]○ Gold flame honeysuckle (*Lonicera heckrottii*)

Useful Foliage Vines

Ivy (Hedera helix) works as a groundcover and as a climbing vine. It attaches to buildings and other surfaces by tenacious rootlets or "holdfasts." There are dozens of beautiful leaf shapes, colors, and sizes to choose from.

[E]○ Chocolate vine (*Akebia quinata*)

[E]○ Creeping fig (*Ficus pumila*)

[H]○ Golden Hop vine (*Humulus lupulus* 'Aureus')

[E]◉ Ivy (*Hedera helix*)

[H]○ Kiwi vine (*Actinidia deliciosa*)

[H]◉ Virginia creeper (*Parthenocissus quinquefolia*)

Groundcovers   Watching Jenny Creep

If there's one group of plants that's generally yawn-producing, it's got to be groundcovers. They are, by and large, short. Visitors rarely stop to admire them. Often they have no flower to speak of, and they seem to remain unchanged month after month, year after year. They're so willing to please by making more and more of themselves that gardeners immediately take them for granted and begin to behave scornfully toward them. We adopt a somewhat cavalier attitude about whether they live or die because we know they will live no matter what we do. We might say the same thing about our toenails. And yet, the truth is, what would we do without them?

Groundcovers are useful in many ways. Here dwarf mondo grass (Ophiopogon japonicus 'Nana') adds sophistication to a paved driveway.

Groundcovers come in various colors, shapes, heights, and habits. They range from teensy to bushy, from orderly to sprawly, and include the meek as well as the show-offs. They can be mixed in with flowering perennials to provide a source of color in winter when deciduous plants have died back. They're useful at the feet of taller, more leggy or woody plants, to provide a kind of skirt. You can use them in pots to create soft effects with annuals and perennials or along paths to create neat borders. They can provide essential, perfectly orderly elements in a highly formal gardening scheme. Vining groundcovers with blossoms or groundcovers with unusual foliage coloring—cream, chartreuse, burgundy, gold, red, pink, gray, blue-gray, and even black—can mingle in the perennial bed, adding interesting complements and contrasts. For most groundcovers, a few starter plants will multiply to cover a large area in a few years. They're worth the investment. Use the following groundcovers in part sun or light shade except as noted. (See the list of "Groundcovers for Difficult Places" for those that can stand full sun as well as full shade.)

CHART 7

Best Groundcovers for the Coastal South

☼ REQUIRES FULL SUN

○ GROWS IN FULL OR PART SUN

◐ GROWS BEST IN PART SUN OR LIGHT SHADE

● REQUIRES FULL OR PART SHADE

◉ TOLERATES A WIDE RANGE OF CONDITIONS, FROM FULL SUN TO FULL SHADE

Burgundy and Variegated Foliage

The colorful variegations of tovara (Tovara virginiana 'Painter's Palette') will light up a shaded part of the garden.

◐ Bugleweed (*Ajuga reptans*)
● Chameleon plant (*Houttuynia cordata*)
◐ Creeping celery (*Oenanthe javanica* 'Flamingo')

○ Creeping raspberry (*Rubus calcynoides*)
◐ Purple velvet plant (*Gynura aurantica* 'Purple Passion')
● Tovara (*Tovara virginiana* 'Painter's Palette')

Gold and Chartreuse Foliage

Golden creeping jenny (Lysimachia nummularia 'Aurea') can be used to enliven almost any color scheme. It prefers part sun and ample moisture.

Variegated chartreuse foliage topped by yellow daisy flowers make this ground daisy (Wedelia trilobata 'Outenreath Gold') an excellent choice for a blooming groundcover.

◐ Golden creeping jenny (*Lysimachia nummularia* 'Aurea')
○ Golden oregano (*Origanum vulgare* 'Aureum')
☼ Golden lemon thyme (*Thymus* x *citriodorus*)
○ Ground daisy (*Wedelia trilobata* 'Outenreath Gold')
● Variegated dwarf hosta (*Hosta* x 'Chartreuse Wiggles';
   H. sieboldii 'Kabitan' and others)
○ Dwarf golden sweet flag (*Acorus gramineus* 'Ogon')

- ◉ Variegated ivy (*Hedera helix* 'Gold Heart' and others)
- ◉ Variegated wintercreeper (*Euonymus fortunei* 'Emerald 'n' Gold')

Groundcovers with Noticeable Flowers

Wood sorrel (Oxalis) makes an excellent flowering groundcover in sun or part shade, blooming on and off all year long, including winter.

On the coldest day in winter you may find ivy-leaved violets (Viola hederacea) in bloom. Even without the flowers, the foliage remains healthy and attractive looking.

- ☼ Beach hypericum (*Hypericum reductum*)
- ◗ Bugleweed (*Ajuga reptans*)
- ○ Creeping veronica (*Veronica peduncularis* 'Georgia Blue')
- ○ Creeping winter savory (*Satureja procumbens*)
- ◗ Golden creeping jenny (*Lysimachia nummularia* 'Aurea')
- ○ Goldenstar (*Chrysogonum virginianum*)
- ◗ Griffith's leadwort (*Ceratostigma griffithii*)
- ○ Hummingbird plant (*Dicliptera suberecta*)
- ☼ Ice plant (*Delosperma cooperi*)
- ◗ Mazus (*Mazus reptans*)
- ☼ Moss phlox (*Phlox subulata*)
- ☼ Moss verbena (*Verbena tenuisecta*)
- ○ Ornamental strawberry (*Fragaria* 'Pink Panther')
- ◉ Periwinkle (*Vinca major* and *V. minor*)
- ○ Rose verbena (*Verbena canadensis*)
- ○ St. Andrew's Cross (*Hypericum hypericoides*)

If you are looking for a tough, flowering groundcover to choke out the weeds, try mazus (Mazus reptans)—shown here growing between slate stepping-stones.

◑ Self-heal (*Prunella grandifolia*)
◑ Stonecrop (*Sedum*)
◑ Strawberry geranium (*Saxifraga stolonifera*)
○ Trailing lantana (*Lantana montevidensis*)
◑ Violet (*Viola*)
○ Wedelia (*Wedelia trilobata* 'Outenreath Gold')
○ Wood sorrel (*Oxalis*)

Groundcovers for Difficult Places

Periwinkle (Vinca) is another reliable midwinter-blooming groundcover. The variegated cultivars are especially helpful for lighting up shady areas.

○ Asiatic jasmine (*Trachelospermum asiaticum*)
◉ Ivy (*Hedera helix*)
◉ Lilyturf (*Ophiopogon jaburan*)
◉ Mondo grass (*Ophiopogon japonicus*)
◉ Periwinkle (*Vinca major* and *V. minor*)
◉ Wintercreeper (*Euonymus fortunei*)

Ornamental Grasses Beyond Pampas Grass

Twenty years ago it was considered very bold to incorporate clumps of tall grasses into a perennial border or into the landscape in general. Due largely to the influence of designers Wolfgang Oehme, James van Sweden, and Kurt Bluemel, this has now become an accepted basic of garden design. The taller ornamental grasses add height, substance, movement, and a certain graceful elegance to a landscape. The thin blades and airy inflorescences catch the sunlight and refract it into a thousand particles. Even the more diminutive grasses can sparkle when the sun hits them. You might want to select a grass for sheer drama, to give added depth to a color scheme, to loosen up a tight composition, to add height to an otherwise uniform planting, or to vary the texture and sameness of the foliage of what's growing nearby. Most grasses are extremely easy to grow. Most prefer a sunny to partly sunny location with moisture-retentive soil, but there are some that will thrive in shade or in extremely dry conditions. And some live out their lives in bogs.

Color and variegation in grasses is generally fairly subtle, but if a number of plants of one variety are massed together or if the blade and flower color of the grass is placed where it can pick up on similar nearby hues, the effect can be very beautiful.

Some grasses have a serious job to do. Sea oats (Uniola paniculata) prevent sand dune erosion along much of the coastal South.

CHART 8

Best Ornamental Grasses for the Coastal South

☼ REQUIRES FULL SUN

◯ GROWS IN FULL OR PART SUN

◑ GROWS BEST IN PART SUN OR LIGHT SHADE

◉ TOLERATES A WIDE RANGE OF CONDITIONS, FROM FULL SUN TO FULL SHADE

*Ornamental grasses provide a variety of textures and subtle coloration to the garden. Use them to add height, movement, and softness, as well as fall and winter interest. Top row, left and center: two examples of panic grass (*Panicum virgatum*), right: an example of muhly grass (*Muhlenbergia*); bottom row, left: another example of muhly grass, center: Northern sea oats (*Chasmanthium latifolium*), right: maiden grass (*Miscanthus sinensis*).*

Yellow and Gold Tones in Foliage or Flowers

◗ Golden satin grass (*Hakonechloa macra* 'Aureola')

◗ Golden sweet flag (*Acorus gramineus* 'Ogon')

○ Hybrid New Zealand flax (*Phormium tenax*)

◗ Japanese sedge (*Carex morrowii* 'Aureovariegata')

☼ Needle grass (*Stipa*)

◗ Sparkler sedge (*Carex phyllocephala* 'Sparkler')

◉ Variegated lily turf grass (*Liriope muscari*)

Pink, Red, and Purple Tones in Foliage or Flowers

○ Dwarf maiden grass (*Miscanthus sinensis* 'Adagio')

○ Feather reed grass (*Calamagrotis* x *acutiflora* 'Karl Foerster')

○ Hairy awn muhly grass (*Muhlenbergia capillaris*)

○ Hardy purple fountain grass (*Pennisetum alopecuroides* 'Purpureum')

○ Hybrid New Zealand flax (*Phormium tenax* 'Atropurpureum'; 'Rubrum')

○ Inland sea oats (*Chasmanthium latifolium*)

○ Maiden grass (*Miscanthus sinensis* 'Positano'; 'Rotsilber'; 'Condensatus')

○ Purple fountain grass (*Pennisetum setaceum* 'Rubrum')

White Highlights in Foliage or Flowers

○ Variegated maiden grass (*Miscanthus sinensis* 'Cosmopolitan'; 'Silberfeder'; 'Variegatus')

○ Feathertop grass (*Pennisetum villosum*)

☼ Pampas grass (*Cortaderia selloana*)

☼ Variegated giant reed (*Arundo donax* 'Variegata')

Blue Tones in Foliage or Flowers

○ Panic grass (*Panicum*)

○ Blue muhly grass (*Muhlenbergia lindheimeri*)

◗ Sedge (*Carex glauca*)

☼ Blue paspalum (*Paspalum glaccifolium*)

☼ Bluestem (*Andropogon capillipes* 'Valdosta Blue')

☼ Bushy blue stem (*Andropogon glomeratus*)

☼ Broom sedge (*Andropogon virginicus*)

○ Hardy sugar cane (*Saccharum arundinaceum*)

Black Tones in Foliage or Flowers

○ Black fountain grass (*Pennisetum* 'Moudry')

◉ Black mondo grass (*Ophiopogon planiscapus* 'Nigrescens')

Ferns Easy and Rewarding

Many ferns thrive in the coastal South in spite of the heat. Although most need the cooler temperatures of deep or dappled shade, some can tolerate a partially sunny position. Those ferns that keep their foliage year-round are a great boon to the winter garden. Ferns add the kind of texture, leaf color, and shape to a garden that gives it interest and definition. They can act as a foil for more striking neighbors or as a transition between contrasting colors. They solve a remarkable number of problems.

Ferns are extremely easy plants to grow. They appreciate an annual top-dressing of well-rotted compost or manure to keep the caudex, or crown, cool

Though they appear delicate, ferns are tough plants, able to survive under less than optimal conditions.

and moist. Some of them like boggy conditions and some don't, but they all like to be kept moist. They really need no fertilization unless they are in pots. Even then, adding a fresh batch of good potting soil would be more welcome than adding a chemical fertilizer. If treated well, ferns will reward you by growing larger and more luxuriant year by year. They are easy to propagate by division almost any time of year except midsummer or at the height of winter, both of which times would be too stressful for them. Propagation by cultivating the spores is a more ambitious and painstaking process.

There are hundreds of ferns to choose from. Their sizes vary from tiny to imposing. Described here are a few of those that do especially well in our area, but the list is ultimately much larger. There's no reason not to experiment beyond those mentioned here. Also, bear in mind that within each of the genera or species listed here there are many varieties and cultivars that will give you variation in height, color, and frond configuration. Refer to the A–Z Plant Guide at the end of this book for more details about these ferns.

CHART 9
Best Ferns for the Coastal South

● REQUIRES FULL OR PART SHADE

Excellent Evergreen Ferns and Fern Relatives

*One of the most rewarding ferns for the coastal South, the holly fern (*Cyrtomium falcatum*) retains its glossy, dark green foliage throughout the winter.*

- ● Arborvitae fern (*Selaginella braunii*)
- ● Autumn fern (*Dryopteris erythrosora*)
- ● Golden trailing spikemoss (*Selaginella kraussiana* 'Aurea')
- ● Holly fern (*Cyrtomium falcatum*)
- ● Peacock moss (*Selaginella uncinata*)
- ● Tassel fern (*Polystichum polyblepharum*)

Frost-tender, Fern-like Plant for Dry or Moist Shade
- ● Asparagus fern (*Asparagus denisflorus* 'Sprengeri')

Some of the more beautiful shade plants, sometimes mistaken for ferns, are the Selaginellas. In detail at left is the finely etched foliage of trailing spikemoss (S. kraussiana).

Well-adapted Deciduous Ferns

- Chain fern (*Woodwardia*)
- Cinnamon fern (*Osmunda cinnamomea*)
- Japanese climbing fern (*Lygodium japonicum*)
- Japanese painted fern (*Athyrium niponicum* var. *pictum*)
- Lady fern (*Athyrium filix-femina*)
- Male fern (*Dryopteris affinis*; *Dryopteris filix-mas*)
- Royal fern (*Osmunda regalis*)
- Southern maidenhair fern (*Adiantum capillus-veneris*)
- Southern shield fern (*Thelypteris kunthii*)
- Sword fern (*Nephrolepis cordifolia*)

Ferns don't need to be ostracized. They mix beautifully with other plants—as here, with the shrubby orange Lantana 'Tangerine'.

For various reasons, some purely practical, herbs in the past have often been relegated to gardens of their own. A well-designed herb garden is a wonderfully appealing sight, whether surrounded by a low, clipped hedge of Greek myrtle, germander, santolina, or rosemary or, on a larger scale, by a white picket fence. But if you're short on space, you may not want to dedicate one whole area to herbs. One common alternative is to grow herbs in containers where they can be moved around to prime locations while they're at their peak, changed out when they've done all they can do, or brought inside for the winter to keep from freezing if they are not frost-tolerant.

However, in addition to their place in the herb garden or in pots, herbs can be incorporated with perennials in mixed garden beds to add a variety of texture, color, and plant habit. They are a pleasure to come into contact with when you're down on your hands and knees weeding and accidentally crush them, releasing their fragrant oils. And, of course, you can clip them to use in cooking, for making potpourri and sachets, for restorative infusions, or to make dried arrangements.

This section is not meant to be an exhaustive review of all plants used for culinary, medicinal, or cosmetic purposes. Its much more modest aim is to suggest a few herbs that will mix and mingle well with your other perennials. Whether you use them simply for their good looks and fragrance in the garden or also cut them for use in stews, salads, and closet sachets, you will get pleasure from planting herbs. The A–Z Plant Guide at the end of this book gives details about the herbs listed below.

Herbs mingle well with perennials of all sorts. This display at the Gourd Garden in Seagrove Beach, Florida, offers a variety of fragrant mints (Mentha)— pineapple, orange, chocolate, and more!

HERB CULTURE

One common piece of misinformation is that herbs don't like the same kind of soil as other plants. The truth is that they appreciate a well-excavated hole filled with a mixture of garden dirt and compost and/or rotted manure. For those herbs that prefer a more alkaline soil (such as lavender, sorrel, lemon balm, rue, thyme, and the summer and winter savories), mix a handful of agricultural lime in with the planting soil and amend well with organic material.

Herbs generally like soil that drains very well. Rosemary, lavender, anise hyssop, santolina, winter savory, and the artemesias particularly need sharp drainage and full sun in order to prosper. If you don't have this kind of fast-draining soil, consider building a raised bed or planting your herbs in containers. Most herbs thrive in full sun, but some will tolerate part sun (especially angelica, lemon balm, sweet cicely, and chervil). The most shade-tolerant herbs are the mints and bee balms. In general, the more you clip your herbs back the fuller, more compact, and less woody they will become. Stop clipping your perennial herbs in midfall to give them a chance to harden off before the first frost.

CHART 10

Best Herbs for the Coastal South

☼ REQUIRES FULL SUN

◯ GROWS IN FULL OR PART SUN

◉ TOLERATES A WIDE RANGE OF CONDITIONS, FROM FULL SUN TO FULL SHADE

*One of the very best herbs for the coastal South is rosemary (*Rosmarinus*). Here it has been pruned into a standard and planted in a container with colorful annuals at its feet.*

Gray-leaved Herbs

☼ Artemesia (*Artemesia*)

☼ Germander (*Teucrium fruticans*)

☼ Lavender cotton (*Santolina incana*)

☼ Rosemary (*Rosmarinus officinalis*)

☼ Rue (*Ruta graveolens*)

Lemon-scented Herbs

☼ Lemon balm (*Melissa officinalis*)

☼ Lemon basil (*Ocimum americanum*)

◯ Lemon catnip (*Nepeta cataria* 'Citriodora')

◯ Lemon grass (*Cymbopogon citratus*)

◯ Lemon-scented geranium (*Pelargonium crispum*)

☼ Lemon thyme (*Thymus x citriodorus*)

◯ Lemon verbena (*Aloysia triphylla*)

More Herbs to Mingle with Perennials

☼ Anise hyssop (*Agastache foeniculum*)

◉ Borage (*Borago officinalis*)

◯ Catmint (*Nepeta*)

*Bronze fennel (*Foeniculum vulgare *'Purpureum') keeps good company with anise sage (*Salvia guaranitica*) and the annual, pink-bloomed wheat celosia (*Celosia spicata*).*

☀ Dill (*Anethum graveolens*)

○ Fennel (*Foeniculum vulgare*)

○ Lovage (*Levisticum officinale*)

☀ Ornamental mustard (*Brassica nigra*, *B. hirta*)

☀ Pineapple sage (*Salvia elegans*)

○ Sweet marjoram (*Origanum majorana*)

Low-growing Herbs

○ Creeping marjoram (*Origanum vulgare* 'Humile')

☀ Nasturtium (*Tropaeolum majus*)

○ Oregano (*Origanum vulgare*)

☀ Thyme (*Thymus*)

Herbs as Edging Plants

☀ Chives (*Allium schoenoprasum*)

☀ Dwarf bush basil (*Osimum basilicum* 'Dwarf Bush Fineleaf'; 'Minette'; 'Minimum'; 'Nano Compatto Vero'; 'Spicy Globe')

☀ Garlic chives (*Allium tuberosum*)

☀ Germander (*Teucrium fruticans*)

○ Greek myrtle (*Myrtus communis*)

○ Parsley (*Petroselinum crispum*)

☀ Rosemary (*Rosmarinus*)

☀ Rue (*Ruta graveolens*)

○ Salad burnet (*Sanguisorba minor*)

☀ Santolina (*Santolina*)

○ Scented geranium (*Pelargonium*)

Invasive Herbs (Pot Them Up)

◉ Mint (*Mentha*)

☀ Tansy (*Tanacetum vulgare*)

Some herbs can go formal. In this knot garden, germander (Teucrium fruticans) is clipped into a low-growing hedge.

Summer is the time to grow fresh basil (Ocimum) for all your culinary needs. Grow it in full sun, either in a pot or in the ground.

Easy, Excellent Basils for Hot Weather (Ocimum basilicum)

☼ *Compact and bushy:* 'Dwarf Bush Fineleaf', 'Minette', 'Minimum', 'Nano Compatto Vero', 'Spicy Globe'

☼ *Dark-leaved:* 'Anise', 'Dark Opal', 'Purple Ruffles', 'Purpurascens', 'Red Rubin'

☼ *Ruffled:* 'Crispum', 'Green Ruffles', 'Lettuce Leaf', 'Purple Ruffles'

☼ *Uniquely scented:* anise ('Anise', 'Licorice', 'Siam Queen'); camphor ('African Blue'); cinnamon ('Cinnamon'); clove (*O. gratissimum*); lemon/lime (*O. americanum*); pesto basil ('Genovese'); Thai cooking basil ('Thyrsiflora'; 'Siam Queen')

Herb Substitutes

☼ * For French tarragon (*Artemesia dracunculus* var. *sativa*),
   substitute Mexican mint marigold (*Tagetes lucida*).

☼ * For cilantro (*Coriandrum sativum*), substitute Mexican coriander
   (*Eryngium foetidum*).

○ * For another oregano flavor, try Mexican oregano
   (*Lippia graveolens*).

Herbs and vegetables can be grown in a fenced-off garden of their own or allowed to mingle informally with flowering annuals and perennials.

Annuals Easy Come, Easy Go

One gardener's perennial may be another gardener's annual, and vice versa. One definition of an annual might be a plant that won't make it through the cold of the local winter or the heat of the local summer. There are certain perennials and bulbs that grow easily elsewhere but which we generally treat as annuals, tossing them out after they've done their bit. Delphiniums, oriental

Hollyhocks (Alcea rosea) grace an informal summer garden.

poppies, Dutch hyacinths, polyantha, and English primroses are examples of perennials that don't survive our heat from one year to the next. In the coastal South we grow them instead as annuals. Sometimes the best place for this type of annual is in a container, where it can be given exactly the situation it needs and removed when it's finished.

Plant your annuals in soil that has been amended with aged manure or compost. Add a slow-release fertilizer at planting time, because annuals are heavy feeders. With few exceptions most annuals will need regular watering in order to thrive.

THE BEST HOT-WEATHER ANNUALS

Once again, gardeners in the Southern Atlantic and Gulf Coast regions have a challenge to face—choosing the right annuals for those long, hot days of summer. Happily there are a number of outstanding plants that fit the bill. The annuals listed in the chart below are exceptionally tolerant of heat, humidity, and drought. They also flower nonstop and require little or no attention. They are the first-choice for summer annuals.

CHART 11

Best Hot-Weather Annuals for the Coastal South

☼ REQUIRES FULL SUN

○ GROWS IN FULL OR PART SUN

◐ GROWS BEST IN PART SUN OR LIGHT SHADE

● REQUIRES FULL OR PART SHADE

◉ TOLERATES A WIDE RANGE OF CONDITIONS, FROM FULL SUN TO FULL SHADE

One of the best hot-weather annuals for the coastal South is wheat celosia (Celosia spicata), seen here in a two-tone pink variety.

Best Flowering Hot-Weather Annuals

Another standout hot-weather annual for our area is pentas (Pentas), available in shades of white, red, pink, and mauve.

- ○ Angelonia (*Angelonia*)
- ☼ Blanketflower (*Gaillardia pulchella*)
- ☼ Butter daisy (*Melampodium*)
- ○ Globe amaranth (*Gomphrena*)
- ☼ Mexican sunflower (*Tithonia rotundifolia*)
- ☼ Narrow-leaved zinnia (*Zinnia angustifolia*)
- ○ Ornamental Okra (*Abelmoschus moschatus*)
- ○ Pentas (*Pentas*)
- ◑ Porterweed (*Stachytarpheta jamaicensis*)

- ☼ Purslane (*Portulacca oleracera*)
- ○ Vinca (*Catharanthus roseus*)
- ○ Wheat Celosia (*Celosia spicata*)

Good Hot-Weather Foliage Annuals

Certain annuals are valued for the texture and coloration of their foliage. Swedish ivy (Plectranthus) *makes a great addition to any container arrangement.*

In addition to the annuals that produce showy flowers all summer long there are some excellent annuals grown primarily for their foliage. Use them in containers or in the garden to add color and textural interest.

- ☼ Alternathera (*Alternathera ficoidea* 'Joseph's Coat')
- ○ Annual sweet potato (*Ipomoea batata*)
- ● Caladium (*Caladium bicolor*)
- ○ Castor bean (*Ricinus communis*)
- ◐ Chocolate plant (*Pseuderanthemum alatum*)
- ☼ or ● Coleus (*Coleus hybridus*), depending on the variety
- ◐ Swedish ivy (*Plectranthus*)
- ○ Wild basil (*Perilla frutescens*)

Best Annual Flowering Vines for Hot Weather

Once established, many vines tolerate heat, humidity, and drought very well. For maximum flower production, they need a spot in full sun. Add a slow-release fertilizer at planting time. The annual vines listed below are tried and true classics for the coastal South.

- ☼ Morning glory (*Ipomoea nil*)
- ☼ Moon vine (*Ipomoea alba*)
- ☼ Cypress vine (*Ipomoea quamoclit*)
- ○ Black-eyed Susan vine (*Thunbergia alata*)

○ Hyacinth bean vine (*Dolichos lablab*)
☼ Star quamoclit (*Ipomoea coccinea*)

Hot-Weather Annuals That Require Special Attention

During the hottest months of the year, many of the traditional annuals available at garden centers will experience extreme stress in our region. This leaves them more vulnerable to pests and diseases. Even though the cultural tag says "grow in full sun," they will probably need some protection—especially from the punishing afternoon sun. These annuals need more attention to watering than those in the previous lists. Some gardeners add soil polymers to the planting mix to increase water retention. Once again, enriched soil and a slow-release fertilizer are advised. You may also need to spray to combat fungus or insect damage.

*The flower heads of annual sunflowers (*Helianthus annuus*) turn to follow the sun.*

☼ Ageratum (*Ageratum houstonianum*)
○ Annual salvia (*Salvia splendens*)
◉ Begonia (*Begonia*)
☼ Blue daze (*Evolvolus glomeratus*)
☼ Celosia (*Celosia argentea*)
☼ Cosmos (*Cosmos bipinnatus*)
☼ Flowering tobacco (*Nicotiana*)
☼ Geranium (*Pelargonium*)
● Impatiens (*Impatiens*)
☼ Lisianthus (*Eustoma grandiflorum*)
☼ Marigold (*Tagetes*)
☼ Moss rose (*Portulacca grandiflora*)

- ☼ Petunia (*Petunia hybrida*)
- ☼ Rose campion (*Lychnis coronaria*) — biennial
- ☼ Scaevola (*Scaevola aemula*)
- ☼ Spider flower (*Cleome hasslerana*)
- ☼ Sunflower (*Helianthus annuus*)
- ☼ Sweet alyssum (*Lobularia maritima*)
- ☼ Zinnia (*Zinnia*)

THE BEST COOL-WEATHER ANNUALS

Some of the hardy and half-hardy cool-weather annuals, biennials, and perennials that bloom beautifully all summer in cooler climates will be overcome by the heat in the coastal South around the middle of June. It seems a shame to miss out on this profusion of classic flowers. Instead, gardeners can start this kind of plant outside in the fall and enjoy the flowers in the spring. These cool-weather plants can be started from seed sown directly in the ground, from home-grown seedlings, or from purchased six-pack plants.

If you're sowing seed directly in the ground, do this sometime between the beginning of September and the end of December. The seeds need enough time to germinate, grow, and flower before the hot weather sets in. If you're planting out home-grown seedlings, aim for putting them in the ground some time between the cooler days of October and the end of November. Purchased six-pack plants with well-developed root systems can be planted out any time from September through March.

Unless we have one of our once-every-five-years, freak, extra-cold winters, the seeds, seedlings, or small plants (depending on what you planted) will winter over and bloom from March through early or mid-June. The following is a list of those annuals, biennials, and perennials that do best for us in cool weather.

CHART 12

Best Cool-Weather Annuals and Biennials for the Coastal South

- ☼ REQUIRES FULL SUN
- ○ GROWS IN FULL OR PART SUN
- ◑ GROWS BEST IN PART SUN OR LIGHT SHADE

- ☼ Bachelor's button (*Centaurea cyanus*)
- ☼ Bells of Ireland (*Moluccella laevis*)
- ☼ Calendula (*Calendula officinalis*)
- ☼ California poppy (*Eschscholzia*)
- ☼ Chinese forget-me-not (*Cynoglossum amabile*)
- ☼ Corn poppy (*Papaver rhoeas*)

above left:
Biennials like foxglove (Digitalis purpurea) do not bloom until their second year. However, they often self-sow.

above right:
To enjoy annual spring poppies (Papaver spp.), gardeners in the coastal South must sow the seed in the fall. This is the secret to growing all cool-weather annuals.

left:
Plant pansies (Viola wittrockiana) in the fall in full to part sun with a slow-release fertilizer. They will bloom on and off all winter, putting on their biggest show from early spring until the beginning of summer.

- ☼ English daisy (*Bellis perennis*)
- ☼ Feverfew (*Chrysanthemum parthenium*)
- ◑ Foxglove (*Digitalis purpurea*)
- ☼ Godetia (*Godetia*)
- ○ Honesty (*Lunaria annua*)
- ○ Hollyhock (*Alcea rosea* 'Indian Spring')
- ☼ Horned poppy (*Glaucium*)
- ☼ Iceland poppy (*Papaver croceum*)
- ○ Johnny jump-up (*Viola tricolor*)
- ☼ Larkspur (*Consolida ambigua*)
- ☼ Love-in-a-mist (*Nigella damascena*)
- ○ Pansy (*Viola wittrockiana*)
- ☼ Prickly poppy (*Argemone*)
- ○ Queen Anne's lace (*Daucus carota*)
- ☼ Snapdragon (*Antirrhinum majus*)
- ☼ Stock (*Matthiola incana*)
- ☼ Sweet pea (*Lathyrus odoratus*)
- ☼ Wallflower (*Erysimum cheiri*)

NASTURTIUMS: A SPECIAL CASE

*Easy to grow from seed, nasturtiums (*Tropaeolum majus*) have beautiful flowers and foliage. They make an elegant, edible addition to any salad.*

Nasturtiums are cool-weather annuals that cannot be planted out until the frost-free date in early spring. Soak the seeds overnight, plant them in poor soil and full sun, and enjoy the edible foliage and flowers. Unlike most spring-planted seeds, they don't like the hot weather and will probably wither away by midsummer.

Gardening with annuals in winter can be a creative experience. Geometric parterres of ornamental cabbage, Swiss chard, lettuce, spinach, mustard, and other edibles are often very beautiful.

WINTER VEGETABLES AS ANNUALS

And, finally, annuals work very well during the coldest months of the year in the coastal South—especially winter vegetables. Many of these edible and ornamental vegetables can be purchased at garden supply centers in the fall as small started plants. Plant them in September or October. Give them full sun, well-amended soil and make sure the soil drains well. Try beets, broccoli, Brussels sprouts, cabbage, carrots, cauliflower, collards, kale, lettuce, mustard, onions, peas, radishes, snow peas, spinach, and Swiss chard.

Roses Timeless Beauties

Roses have gotten an undeservedly bad reputation for being finicky and requiring constant attention. Blame it on the hybrid tea rose people, whose passion for creating long-stemmed, uniquely colored, "perfect" blossoms spilled over into the home gardening trade and somehow took over. This was to the detriment of the tried and true old roses that have survived over the centuries

The climbing
Noisette roses like
'Old Blush' were
developed in the 1800s
by two Charlestonians,
Phillipe Noisette and
John Champneys.
Noisettes are well
suited to the coastal
climate.

in ditches, fields, and farmyards with sometimes no more attention than what Mother Nature had to offer. Even in the hot, muggy South, there are roses that perform as well as any other plant in the garden. Roses add a grace and charm that no other plant can provide. They're romantic. They link us with gardens from past centuries and from the farthest corners of the world.

Before buying any rose, you should check for two important factors: can it withstand especially hot summers, and is it disease-resistant—or, better yet, disease-free? If the answer to both questions is yes, you move on to matters of color, size, fragrance, and whether or not the flowers will be produced repeatedly over a long season of bloom. Black spot is a major problem for us. If you don't choose heat-tolerant, disease-resistant, or disease-free varieties, you will be faced for most of the year with an unsightly show of bare green branches sprinkled with the occasional sickly, yellowing, spotted leaf and not a bloom in sight. Or you will chain yourself to a weekly toxic spray program that promotes cancer and environmental damage.

THE BEST ROSES FOR HEAT AND HUMIDITY

Happily, there are many heat-tolerant, disease-resistant roses for the coastal South and some that are totally disease-free, that never require spraying. The best bets are the species roses, the Albas, the Chinas, the Teas (not to be confused with the Hybrid Teas, which are generally not low-maintenance plants), the Noisettes, the Bermudas, and the Rugosas (which also do very well at the beach). There are dozens of roses within these categories. There are also some new hybrids that combine the best qualities of the old roses. However, many of these "new old-fashioned roses," such as those bred by David Austin and Graham Thomas, may perform outstandingly in England but not so well in the coastal South unless they are specifically labeled as being highly disease-resistant.

If a rose is described as "hardy" and "vigorous," this refers only to cold tolerance and growth habit, not to heat and disease tolerance. A terrifically hardy and vigorous rose might suffer and do very poorly in our area unless it also happens to be very disease-resistant. Oddly enough, a hybrid series of roses developed in Canada, the Canadian Explorer Series, works very well for us because of its excellent disease resistance. Other excellent modern hybrids for our area include the series of Meidiland landscape roses.

Charleston, South Carolina, takes pride in having developed the Noisette roses, which are grown primarily in Zone 7 southward. Phillipe Noisette and John Champneys, both Charlestonians, introduced a number of classics that have been popular since the 1800s. The Noisettes tend to be cluster-forming, highly fragrant climbers, with the best blooms coming in spring and fall. These disease-resistant southern treasures have abided for generations.

CLIMBING ROSES

Climbing roses sometimes take longer to establish themselves than the shrub or bush type. Don't be discouraged if blooms are scarce the first few years. Eventually they will be abundant. Some of the bush-type roses that reach seven or eight feet in height can also be trained as low-growing climbers. Another insight into southern rose growing: roses grown on their own rootstock do better for us than those that are grafted.

PLANTING YOUR ROSES

Roses must receive a minimum of five to six full hours of direct sunlight every day in order to bloom. The exceptions to this are the handful of shade-tolerant roses. Although the shade-tolerant roses can put up with something

All roses need at least five hours of direct sunlight each day.

less than the optimum amount of sunlight, they would still prefer the full five to six hours. Roses should be planted in deep, wide holes with plenty of good compost, manure, and/or peat moss mixed in with your garden soil. If your soil is mostly clay, add some gypsum as well. Give your roses good drainage because they do not appreciate having wet feet—especially in winter. If the rose is grafted, be sure to plant the graft above the soil line. Water in the planting very well, eliminating any air pockets in the soil.

If you add new compost every year and keep the plant watered during periods of drought, you can get by with little chemical fertilization. Some gardeners believe that constant fertilization of the old roses makes them more prone to disease. Many devoted rosarians, however, use a slow-release rose food (labeled as such) two or three times a year, beginning in the spring, for the repeat-blooming varieties. Many of the repeat bloomers will begin their show in April and continue putting out buds until the first frost. If you head outside on Christmas Day, you may discover a nose-high blossom of the fragrant, pale-peach-colored 'Gruss an Aachen' just beginning to unfurl.

BLACK SPOT

There are a number of nontoxic products on the market that you can use to combat black spot. The main ingredients are lime sulfur, copper sulfate, and neem oil. These sprays work best during the cooler months of spring and fall and tend to be less effective in the muggiest days of summer. If possible, avoid getting your rose foliage wet. Use drip irrigation, pick off all affected leaves, and destroy them. Don't let diseased leaves accumulate on the ground under your roses or the cycle will continue. Another good prophylactic measure is to carry around a small bucket of bleach and water in which to dip your pruners as you clip your roses.

SUMMER HEAT

In midsummer, when the heat is particularly intense, rose production on the repeat bloomers will fall off. This is normal, and you shouldn't try to compensate for this by stoking the plant up with fertilizer. That will only stress the plant further. Be patient and wait for cooler weather, when the roses will get a second wind and put out many beautiful blooms for weeks and weeks in the fall.

RECOMMENDED ROSES

Listed below are some of the most reliable roses for the coastal South, arranged by bloom color. Pink roses sometimes open white, red roses sometimes deepen to purple, white roses may have traces of red or yellow, and so on. Ambient temperature and location also play a role in what color the blooms will be. Seeing pictures in a specialized rose catalog or on the Internet will give you the best idea of what each rose really looks like. All of the roses listed here are hardy, disease resistant, and heat tolerant. If they are completely disease-free, this is noted. Most of these roses begin their show in late spring or early summer. The repeaters

An extremely disease-resistant, floriferous rose, 'Knockout' is a standout in the summer and fall garden.

may bloom more or less abundantly during the summer, depending on the cultivar. And once the weather cools off in fall, all of the repeat bloomers will put on another good show. There are many cultivars listed here that do not repeat but which are excellent for us because they are disease-free. In addition, most of the species roses listed have one bloom season. The most well-known species roses in the south are the Lady Banks rose (two weeks bloom in mid-spring), the Cherokee rose (two weeks in early spring), the Sweetbrier (several weeks in early summer), and the Swamp Rose (six weeks in summer). See "Internet Sources for Information and Ordering Plants" for Internet sources for roses.

CHART 13

Best Roses for the Coastal South

☼ REQUIRES FULL SUN

○ GROWS IN FULL OR PART SUN

≋ DOES WELL AT THE BEACH AS WELL AS FARTHER INLAND

♥ DISEASE FREE

ʊ BLOOMS ONLY ONCE A YEAR

Rosa *'Marie Van Houtte' is a pale yellow suffused with pink.*

All roses listed here are hardy, heat tolerant, and disease resistant or disease free. Unless otherwise noted, all are repeat bloomers, blooming heavily in spring and fall and intermittently in between.

White Shrub Roses

☼ 'Alba'

≋☼♥ 'Blanc Double de Coubert'

☼ 'Boule de Neige'

☼ 'Glamis Castle'

☼♥ʊ 'Hebe's Lip'

☼ 'Ivory Fashion'

☼❦↻ 'Leda'

☼❦↻ 'Madame Hardy'

☼❦↻ 'Madame Plantier'

☼❦↻ 'Maxima'

☼ 'Nastarana'

☼ 'Out of Yesteryear'

☼ 'Pax'

☼❦↻ *Rosa multiflora*

≈❦☼ *Rosa rugosa alba*

☼ 'Sevillana'

≈☼ 'Sir Thomas Lipton'

☼ 'Somebreuil'

White Climbers

☼ 'Aimée Vibert'

☼❦↻ Cherokee rose (*Rosa laevigata*)

☼❦↻ 'City of York'

☼❦↻ 'Félicité et Perpétue'

○ 'Madame Alfred Carrière'

☼❦↻ Memorial Rose (*Rosa wichuraiana*)

☼❦↻ *Rosa soulieana*

☼ 'Sally Holmes'

☼ 'Sea Foam'

☼❦↻ 'Silver Moon'

Yellow Shrub Roses

☼❦↻ Father Hugo's Rose (*Rosa hugonis*)

☼❦↻ 'Frühlingsgold'

☼ 'Gold Badge'

☼ 'Marie Van Houtte'

☼ 'Mrs. Dudley Cross'

☼ 'Topaz Jewel'

☼ 'Toulouse Lautrec'

Yellow Climbers

☼ 'Albéric Barbier'

☼ 'Celine Forestier'

☼❦↻ Lady Banks Rose (*Rosa banksiae*)

☼❦ 'Leverkusen'

☼ 'Maréchal Niel'

☼ 'Mermaid'

☼ 'Sunny June'

Peach/Coral/Apricot/Shrub Roses

☼❦ 'All That Jazz'

☼ 'Auguste Renoir'

Rosa 'Eden' blooms profusely in May and repeats intermittently throughout the summer and fall.

☀ 'Bishop Darlington'
☀ 'Collette'
☀ 'Country Life'
☀ 'Perdita'
☀ 'Tamora'

Peach/Coral/Apricot Climbers
○ 'Desprez à Fleurs Jaunes'
☀ 'Gloire de Dijon'
☀ 'Rêve D'Or'

Purple/Lavender/Magenta Shrub Roses
☀ 'Angel Face'
☀❦ 'Bayse's Purple'
☀ 'Lilac Rose'

Red Shrub Roses
☀ 'Europeana'
☀ 'Linda Campbell'
☀ 'Little Buckaroo'
☀ 'Louis Phillipe'
☀ 'Martha Gonzales'
☀❦↺ *Rosa moyesii*
☀ 'Red Fairy'
☀ 'Scarlet Meidiland'
☀ 'Traviata'

Red Climbers
☀ 'Altissimo'
☀ 'Cramoisii Superieur'
☀ 'Don Juan'
☀❦ 'Dortmund'
☀ 'Red Cascades'

Orange/Tangerine Shrub Roses
☀ 'Abbaye de Cluny'
○ 'Playboy'

Pink Shrub Roses
☀ 'Amiga Mia'
☀❦↺ 'Belle Amour'
☀ 'Betty Prior'
☀ 'Burbank'
☀ 'Caldwell Pink'
☀ 'Catherine Mermet'
☀ 'Cécile Brunner'
☀❦↺ 'Celestial'

☼❤↻ 'Celsiana'

☼ 'Centennaire de Lourdes'

☼ 'Cherry Meidiland'

◯❤↻ Chestnut rose (*Rosa roxburghii plena*)

☼❤↻ 'Chloris'

☼❤↻ 'Conrad Ferdinand Meyer'

☼ 'Country Fair'

☼ 'Dainty Bess'

☼ 'Duchesse de Brabant'

☼❤↻ 'Ferdy'

☼❤≈ 'Frau Dagmar Hastrup'

☼❤↻ 'Frühlingsmorgen'

☼ 'Geisha'

☼❤↻ 'Gloire de Guilan'

◯ 'Grüss an Aachen'

☼ 'Guy de Maupassant'

☼ 'Hawkeye Belle'

☼ 'Hermosa'

☼ 'Honey Chile'

☼ 'Honoré de Balzac'

☼❤↻ 'Ispahan'

☼ 'Johann Strauss'

☼❤↻ 'Königin von Danemark'

☼❤↻ 'La Noblesse'

☼ 'La Reine Victoria'

☼❤↻ 'La Ville de Bruxelles'

☼❤↻ 'Maiden's Blush'

☼ 'Maman Cochet'

☼ 'Marie Pavié'

☼ 'Maybelle Stearns'

☼ 'Old Blush'

☼❤↻ Pasture rose (*Rosa carolina*)

◯ 'Playgirl'

☼❤↻ *Rosa roxburghii normalis*

☼❤↻ *Rosa rubrifolia*

☼❤≈ *Rosa rugosa*

☼❤≈ *Rosa rugosa rubra*

☼❤≈ 'Roseraie de l'Hay'

☼ 'Rosette Delizy'

☼ 'Royal Bonica'

☼ 'Sarah Van Fleet'

◯❤↻ Swamp rose (*Rosa palustris*)

☼❤↻ Sweetbrier (*Rosa eglanteria*)

☼ 'The Fairy'

☼ 'Therèse Bugnet'

☼❤↻ 'Tour de Malakoff'

☼ 'Vanity'

☼❣ 'William Baffin'

☼ 'Wind Chimes'

☼❣☯ 'York and Lancaster'

☼ 'Yves Piaget'

Pink Climbers

☼ 'Belle Portugaise'

☼ 'Champneys' Pink Cluster'

☼ 'Climbing Cécile Brunner'

☼ 'Climbing Old Blush'

☼ 'Eden'

☼ 'Kathleen'

☼❣☯ 'May Queen'

☼ 'New Dawn'

Multicolored (Pink, Orange, Yellow, and Crimson) Shrub Rose

☼ Butterfly rose (*Rosa mutabilis*)

CHAPTER 5

Practical Gardening Tips

*Deep purple Mexican bush sage (*Salvia leucantha*) and bright pink coneflowers (*Echinacea purpurea*) work together to create a rich landscape design at Water Color near Seaside, Florida.*

Using Perennials in the Landscape
Where Do You Want Me to Put This?

There's no place like a dirt-smudged, idea-jammed piece of scrap paper for creating a perfectly tended, color-coordinated perennial border. On the other hand, one spring foray to the nursery may destroy the picture. It may be an encounter with an infant *Cestrum parqui* covered with clusters of pale, butter yellow flowers that undoes the entire blueprint. The unplanned-for newcomer will grow eight feet tall and six feet wide, hogging six times the space allotted for it. Or, in another scenario, the gardener's best friend gives him a whole clump of fire-engine-red crocosmia to put somewhere, and he'd been planning an all-white border. Or birds deposit something interesting that another gardener has never seen before in her life, and she wants to wait and see what it turns out to be. So much for the plan on the scrap paper.

The goal for most gardeners is to temper impulse with as much planning as they can stand. The following suggestions are the most basic considerations for using perennials in the landscape:

- **Decide what garden style appeals to you.** Perennials can be used in the most formal of gardens in the same way the other plant materials are used—with great control. A knot garden hedge of clipped germander filled with a solid carpet of *Lysimachia nummularia* 'Aurea' can be stunning in its simplicity. Or you may want a wild, tropical look. Consider giant elephant ears, bananas, and cannas. If you like the feeling of a ro-

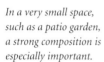

In a very small space, such as a patio garden, a strong composition is especially important.

mantic, cottage garden with plants spilling over onto the pathways, you may want to include weeping and billowing plants such as *Gaura*, roses, and some of the sages. A completely natural, almost wild look can be created with grasses, native perennials, and bulbs. Alternatively, you may decide to create your own eclectic mix and experiment with everything that's out there. There is no right or wrong way to garden.

· **Know your site.** Your site may be all sun, all shade, or may have a series of different microclimates that you come to understand after several seasons of gardening. Group plants with the same cultural requirements near one another so that those that don't enjoy wet feet can hang out together and all those boggy creatures can wallow in the muck with one another.

· **What does "full sun" mean?** Full sun means that your plant is getting five hours or more of direct sunlight in an open area unobstructed by overhanging limbs, nearby building walls, garden structures, or large neighboring plants. Interestingly, some of the plants best adapted to full sun have minimal need for water while others are bog dwellers.

Reminiscent of an Italian garden, this lovely formal landscape at the Cummer Museum of Art in Jacksonville, Florida, incorporates annuals and perennials for year-round color.

Many plants that thrive in full sun farther north will not do so in the coastal South without constant watering. Often it's better to plant them in part sun instead. If you want to grow plants that require full sun, such as roses and many of the gray-leaved perennials, and your garden is too shady, consider removing a tree or eliminating overhanging branches. You can also plant in containers and move them to where they will get full sun.

· **What does "part sun" mean?** Part sun means that your plant is getting some sunshine every day. This might be a long period of exposure to the lightly dappled sunshine under very tall overhead branches or it might be several hours of unobstructed full sun in the morning followed by shade in the afternoon. Usually plants that like part sun are not going to be happy if that sun is primarily afternoon sun because afternoon sun tends to be scorching and too harsh. Some call it the "killing sun" for this reason.

· **What does "part shade" or "light shade" mean?** Part shade or light shade can mean several things. Maybe diffused sunlight is reaching your

In Charleston, South
Carolina, sages, canna
lilies, and senna mix
with other plants
to form a magical
landscape.

Sometimes the simplest
compositions are the
most striking. Here
perennial firespike
(Odontonema strictum)
and the dark-leaved
annual sweet potato
vine 'Blackie' (Ipomoea
batata 'Blackie') are a
perfect match for the
silvery gray tree bark.

plant for most of the day because the plant is at the edge of a shady area or is under a fairly heavy canopy of foliage through which sunshine still manages to penetrate to some degree. Part shade can mean that most of the day the plant is in shade, but it receives an hour or two of sun during the day.

- **What is "full shade" or "deep shade"?** Full shade or deep shade is usually an area where a large building and/or dense overhead growth completely blocks out the sun. Of course, there is light in these areas, but it is never direct sunlight. Year-round the full shade area remains cooler and darker than any other place in the garden. Successful gardening in deep shade requires selecting plants that have specifically adapted to this low-light environment.

- **Put your hardscape in first.** If at all possible, figure out beforehand where your paths and garden structures are going to go. Lay the brick or flagstone, build the walls and fences, situate the pergola, the pond, or the rose arch before you plant if you can. This will save untold heartache and moving around of plant material later. Planning the hardscape first also gives you a starting point, something to work around when you begin to decide which perennials you want and where.

When designing a garden, it pays to lay out the hardscape first. This garden comes together around a well-designed brick path.

- **Decide ahead of time if you want a low-maintenance garden.** The easiest gardens to maintain will be those consisting of evergreen trees, shrubs that don't require pruning, and some sort of evergreen groundcover that needs little or no tending to. Plants such as Lenten roses, daylilies, *Rudbeckia*, crinum lilies, hardy palms, crocosmia, lantana, monkey grass, liriope, rosemary, daffodils, sedums, evergreen ferns, Confederate jasmine or Carolina jessamine, the ornamental grasses, and small bulbs such as *Ipheion* and the rain and fairy lilies (*Zephyranthes* and *Habranthus* spp.) would all work well in a low-maintenance landscape.

- **Decide if you want your garden to peak at a particular time of year or have something in bloom year-round.** Because it is so easy and pleasant to enjoy gardening year-round along the coastal South, many gardeners plan and plant for fall and winter color as well as the more traditional spring burst and summer fireworks. Having all the shrubs and perennials bloom at once has a dramatic impact but leaves nothing much to look at for the other nine or ten months of the year.

- **We all have permission to throw the color wheel out the window.** Color in the garden is a very personal choice. The color police aren't going to

left:
*A small garden that
incorporates evergreen
shrubs and ferns will
be easy to maintain.*

right:
*At the Mercer
Arboretum in Humble,
Texas, color rules.
Chartreuse sweet
potato vine (Ipomoea
batata 'Margarita')
mixes it up with
annual coleus in
shades of crimson
and gold.*

come around and tell you that magenta and lemon yellow don't go together. The traditional combinations of lavender-pink-and-white, gold-
orange-and-purple, red-yellow-and-blue are fine, as are any number of
other colors you want to combine. In gardening (as in interior decorat-
ing or fashion design), certain colors complement one another, certain
colors seem to have an emotional feel to them, and certain juxtapositions
can be either soothing or jarring. Once you figure out what kind of mood
or sensation you're trying to create, you can play with color accordingly.
Or, like many gardeners, you can just plant whatever seems to grow well.
The nice thing about living in the coastal South is that we have the potential for year-round bloom. If you want, you can have a red and white
garden in winter, a pink and lavender garden in spring, an orange and
yellow garden in summer, and a gold and purple garden in fall. The color
possibilities are almost endless. One thing to keep in mind is that color in
summer will be perceived differently from color in the cooler months,
when the light is gentler. Summer sun puts so much glare into the at-
mosphere that only the brightest, most strident colors are "easy" to see.
Pastel colors may not stand out except in the early morning and late afternoon in the summer garden.

Some of the neutral tones that blend well with many other colors in
the garden include butter yellow, deep plum, mustard yellow, gray, and
chartreuse. Bright white isn't as neutral as ivory. There is color in leaves,

The giant banana (Musa) towering over the vine-clad fence and Cape plumbago shrub (Plumbago auriculata) provide a sense of tropical scale to this coastal South garden.

stems, stamens, twigs, mulch, pavement material, house walls, fences, and birdbaths. It's all part of the garden canvas.

- **Mix perennials with other plants.** A bed or border made up entirely of perennials can be spectacular, but it's almost always incorporated into a larger garden in which walls, trees, shrubs, vines, and groundcovers provide a framework or backbone. This architectural garden structure should be able to stand up on its own when the perennials aren't doing their thing. Winter is a good time to look at the "bones" of your garden and make adjustments. Perennials don't have to be given a bed or border all their own. They can be incorporated into the overall landscape design to provide variety in foliage, color, and texture. A particularly handsome perennial can be showcased on its own as a specimen, especially in a small garden.

- **Try to imagine how big everything will get (eventually).** A forty-foot juniper slammed up against the side of a small bungalow is disconcerting. Unless your intention is to throw proportion to the wind (and to disconcert your audience—whoever they may be), you need to leave enough space for things to grow or, alternatively, to pull them out if they overshoot what you had in mind. Gardens aren't static places, and a garden design isn't meant to last forever.

- **Without repetition, there's a tendency toward chaos.** It is said that chaos theory is the basis for some great gardens, including the traditional

above:
One of the reasons this summer garden at Wrightsville Beach, North Carolina, works so well is that plant material has been repeated at regular intervals.

right:
In every garden there should be at least one uncluttered space. A stretch of lawn, an open patio, or a simple water garden can serve this purpose.

opposite:
Containers can be used for portable color or to create minigardens for plants that have particular cultural needs. In this garden in Savannah, Georgia, the arrangement of terra cotta pots adds a feeling of harmony and order.

Japanese garden. But if you don't feel comfortable with chaos theory, try repetition. Repeat plant material, color, form, and texture. Repeat elements of the hardscape. Repetition is the key to a lot of good fairy tales. Why is that? We don't know exactly, but it works. Threes and fives work better than ones and twos. One of something works best if it is dramatic and you are trying to call attention to it.

- **Allow space for nothing.** In his book *Elements of Garden Design*, landscape designer and author Joe Eck writes about the need for "repose" in a garden. If there's nowhere for the eye to rest, the viewer doesn't get the whole picture. The eye moves restlessly about, coming back again and again to the beginning. Ultimately the viewer is unable to process the garden as more than a collection of individual plants. Repose can be created by a lawn, a patio, an expanse of blank wall, the still water of a pond, or an area of uninterrupted groundcover. It's the blank space on the canvas that makes the other elements form a pleasing picture.

- **Make good use of containers.** Containers can be used not only on your deck or patio but along garden paths, inserted at various spots in the border to mask decaying foliage, to fill in blank spots, to raise a plant up to where it shows off or to add a particular color or foliage accent. Think of containers as miniature gardens in themselves where you can give particular plants exactly the cultural requirements they need—something you might not be able to do in the rest of your garden. Containers can greatly broaden the spectrum of plants you choose to experiment with (up and down the zone limits). It's important to remember that a plant overwintering in a container is experiencing at least one zone (or twenty degrees) colder than the plants in the ground. Plants living in containers will also dry out much more rapidly and need more frequent fertilization than plants in the ground.

Soil Basics The One with the Best Dirt Wins

There's a very well known saying that a gardener shouldn't put a ten-dollar plant in a ten-cent hole because she is just wasting her money that way. All plants need an appropriate growing medium. The better the growing medium, the better chance they will become a real presence in the garden and not just some unidentifiable collection of brown sticks or dull green basal leaves that never seem to do anything.

The vast majority of plants that grow well in the coastal South enjoy rich,

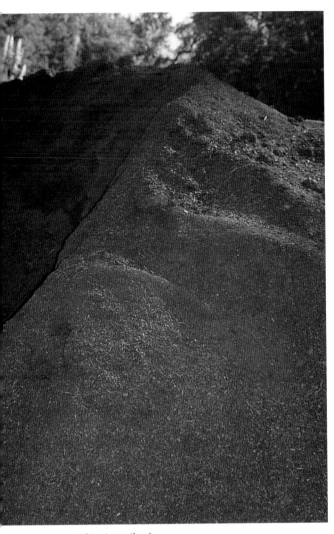

This giant pile of mulch is a gardener's dream. Use a two-inch layer of mulch around your plantings to insulate against heat and cold, to help retain moisture, and to discourage weeds.

moist, well-drained soil. One way of creating this situation is to grow them in a raised bed. Raised beds have the advantage of allowing gardeners to create wonderful soil from scratch.

Creating good soil isn't that hard. There are some frighteningly complex soil formulas out there. Mostly they are propounded in English gardening books. They might involve bat guano, washed silver sand, three-sixteenth-inch grit, or other such daunting ingredients. However, a much simpler formula works just fine. Mix three parts of garden soil with one part of any of the following: compost, shredded bark, aged manure, leaf mold, humus, or any other organic material. (If your soil is particularly sandy or full of clay, increase the formula to half and half). Mushroom compost, chicken manure, and coffee bean hulls all tend to be costlier than other organic amendments and don't necessarily perform better.

Adding a layer of organic mulch on top of the soil (such as pine bark) will help retain moisture, insulate the soil from temperature extremes, keep out weeds and eventually decompose to enrich the soil further. Choose a fairly fine-textured mulch and go with whichever one is cheapest in your area. Find out if your city or town sells recycled, shredded garden waste or shredded bark. (Note: Shredded cedar takes longer than other mulches to break down into a soil amendment.)

Good garden soil is maintained by this kind of repeated organic enrichment. Because we experience such consistently high temperatures in our area the organic matter we put in and on top of our soil disappears much more rapidly than in cooler parts of the country and therefore needs to be replenished more often. The organic material actually decomposes into water and carbon dioxide, which evaporate.

Along the Texas and Louisiana coasts many gardeners have "gumbo" soil— a black clay that's hard to dig and doesn't drain well. Gardeners with gumbo soil need to sprinkle a layer of agricultural gypsum on top, water it in well, wait a few days, and then turn the soil over. At that time the soil should be amended with sand and large amounts of organic matter. In any kind of clay soil, the addition of sand plus organic matter will help to break it up, change the texture, and allow breathing room for the plant's roots.

If your soil is very sandy, the incorporation of organic matter will improve the soil's tilth (good texture for plant growth) and give the roots a chance to make use of the water and nutrients they receive. Ideal soil for many plants is a sandy loam, which consists of equal parts clay, sand, and silt. A sandy loam gives the roots the best access to water, air, and nutrients for proper growth.

To find out how close to ideal your soil is, try this simple test. Squeeze a handful in your fist. If it won't hold any shape at all and runs through your fingers, it's too sandy. If it forms a hard, tight ball and won't crumble between your fingers, you've got clay. Loam is dark in color, smells good, and forms a loose ball. That's black gold!

Most perennials are adaptable to a fairly wide pH (5–7). The addition of compost usually will bring the soil to a 6 or 6.5 pH from either too alkaline or too acidic. In this way it acts as a chemical buffer. Local agricultural extension agencies offer soil tests that will help you determine your soil's pH and tell you whether it is missing any essential minerals. For example, you might find an unsuspected, anomalous soil condition such as cement mortar mixed in with your soil (pH 8–9) or a bed of black sand (pH 3.5)—both conditions so severe as to deprive plants of the ability to take up needed nutrients.

To make an acidic soil more neutral for plants such as Louisiana iris, add ground limestone or ground oyster shells. Plants that like truly alkaline soil will do well next to a concrete path or inside a concrete block. To create a more acidic soil, mulch with pine bark or add aluminum sulfate or elemental sulfur dust to the soil according to the package directions.

Well-amended soil is the secret to successful gardening, and it is an ongoing process. The most experienced and knowledgeable gardeners spend money and time where it counts the most—in making and maintaining *great* dirt.

The Care, Feeding, and Propagation of Plants
Ignore Them and They Will Go Away

PLANT MAINTENANCE

The time when the wisdom of your choice of plant material becomes apparent is when it comes to garden maintenance. That's when you'll be glad you've chosen plants suitable to the coastal South. As a general rule, the better adapted the plant, the less fussing you'll have to do. Well-adapted plants will (1) be less susceptible to diseases and pests, (2) be strong enough to do battle against would-be weed competitors, (3) be able to adapt to the vagaries of our rainfall, and (4) naturally increase and multiply on their own. That said, the gardener still has some work to do.

Watering

All plants, even those that tolerate drought, need watering. Those that appreciate constantly moist soil can be placed together in an area excavated one to two feet deep, lined with a piece of plastic sheeting or a plastic children's

left:
One of the secrets to keeping weeds and pests to a minimum is to select plants that are well suited to the local climate.

below:
Growing the right plants will also reduce the need for watering. This giant watering can presides over flower beds at Longue Vue Gardens in New Orleans.

wading pool (poke holes in whatever you use), and filled back up with a good dirt/compost mixture. Examples would be swamp milkweed, lobelia, or cinnamon fern. If the plants are true bog dwellers, such as Louisiana iris, you could even skip the holes.

Plants that need perfect drainage and constant moisture (like some of the small sedums) should be given loose, sharp (fast-draining) soil and a spot underneath the automatic sprinkler system or next to a source of constant drip. Plants that have average water requirements should receive about an inch of water per week either from rainfall or irrigation.

Plants that require dry conditions—such as bearded iris, lamb's ears, and yarrow—should be planted outside of the automatic sprinkler system/hose watering routine and watered only if there is a severe and persistent drought.

Soaker hoses, which can be disguised with bark mulch, do the job of getting water to the plant roots without losing any to evaporation. They also help to prevent black spot on roses and fungal diseases on other susceptible plants, because the water doesn't touch the leaves.

Container plants need constant checking to make sure they don't become completely dry, unless they are plants that require very dry conditions, like cactus. Try working some soil polymers into the potting mix to extend the length of time between waterings. These tiny granules absorb hundreds of times their weight in water and release it back into the soil as the container dries out. The advantage of polymers is that they tend to keep the soil evenly moist. Put a small amount of granules in a large bucket of water and let it sit overnight. You will have a bucket full of blue Jell-O in the morning and can work this into the soil when you pot up your plants.

Weeding

A weed is any plant growing where we don't want it. Weeds steal water and nutrients from our favorite plants, they seem to increase the minute we turn our back, and, like death and taxes, no one can avoid them. There are several reasons not to use weed killers. They are toxic to the environment, carry health risks, and often kill the good plants with the bad.

If you're preparing a large area for the first time, try putting a layer of newspaper or black plastic on top and leaving it for several weeks until most of the weeds have died. The best defense against weeds is to fill your empty spaces with things you love, including groundcovers, so the weeds have (almost) no room to wangle their way in. Over time, weeding duty should decrease, especially if you pull the rascals up before they have time to set seed. A good layer of mulch will also make it easier to pull the weeds up because it will improve the soil. Weeding is much easier just after a rainfall.

MULCHING

Mulch is a layer of material that goes on top of the ground to insulate the plant against temperature extremes, to help retain moisture, to keep down weeds, and to make the garden look neater. Organic mulches are excellent be-cause they improve the soil as they decompose. You can use pine straw, shred-ded pine bark, compost, or other organic materials. Coastal Bermuda hay is an excellent, inexpensive mulch, which has no viable seeds to cause trouble. Peb-bles or rocks can act as a mulch, but they won't benefit the soil, and they may hamper the plants from increasing in size or spreading out as much as they would with an organic mulch. They are best used only on plants that need ex-tremely dry soil.

When you apply mulch, put down a thick enough layer to completely hide the dirt underneath. This keeps the weeds in the dark and discourages them for a while. To ward off rot and pests, keep the mulch away from the crown of the plant. Mulch should be renewed regularly in spring and fall, but keep in mind that a heavy layer of mulch applied at just the wrong time will prevent the germination of those self-seeding perennials, biennials, and annuals you may want more of (such as Queen Anne's lace, cleome, Brazilian bachelor's buttons, hollyhock, foxglove, or columbine). To avoid smothering the off-spring of a desirable plant, wait until there are viable seedlings before renew-ing the mulch around it or just don't mulch at all in that space.

Fertilizing

Gardeners who give their plants wonderfully amended dirt will need to do relatively little fertilizing. Most perennials benefit from a once-a-year appli-cation of balanced fertilizer in the spring, just as they start to put on their big growth spurt. A balanced fertilizer is one in which the ratio of nitrogen-phosphorous-potassium is equal, such as 8-8-8 or 10-10-10. A high-nitrogen fertilizer encourages leaf growth (good for lawn grasses). A super phosphate fertilizer encourages blooms and is often sold as a "super bloom" fertilizer. There are also fertilizers specifically designed to stimulate root development. A weak solution of root stimulator can be helpful when you are setting out transplants.

The least expensive synthetic fertilizers are the dry types available in large bags. If you use this type, sprinkle the granules lightly around your plants, work them into the soil, and water heavily. Plants that aren't watered heavily may burn up. The more expensive time-release granules present less of a dan-ger of plant burn. Time-release granules may be sprinkled in the planting hole at the time of planting or worked into the top layer of soil after planting. They usually don't begin to release their nutrients until the soil warms up in the spring. They will continue to provide the plant with food for three to six months, depending on the product and how hot the weather is. (The hotter the weather, the sooner the fertilizer will be used up).

Time-release fertilizers are particularly helpful for heavy feeders such as long-blooming annuals and repeat-blooming roses. Perennials that bloom in the fall—such as the ginger lilies, chrysanthemums, perennial sunflowers, and angel's trumpet—will benefit from periodic fertilization during the summer, although this is not absolutely necessary.

Hose-end sprayers can be used to give plants an instant fertilizer infusion. There are balanced synthetic fertilizers available for hose-end sprayers and there are super-bloom powders as well. When you're using a liquid fertilizer on container plants, use it at half the recommended strength, but use it often.

Organic fertilizers such as manure, fish emulsion, cottonseed meal, and others generally rely on soil organisms to release their nutrients, and the process occurs over a longer period of time than with synthetic fertilizers. It may be hard to gauge exactly what nutrients your plants are getting and when they're getting them. Talking with other organic gardeners, reading on the subject, and experimenting will help determine which organics work best for your garden.

To make manure tea for your perennials, fill a burlap bag or old pillowcase with manure (composted or not), tie it closed, and let it soak for several days in a large container full of water. Use one part manure to twenty parts water. When it has finished steeping, you can use it on your plants the way you would a liquid fertilizer.

Certain plants enjoy rich soil but prefer not to be subjected to the annual fertilization routine. These include butterfly bush, bearded iris, ferns, and some herbs. Some plants, such as yarrow, prefer poor, sandy soil and don't want to be fertilized at all. Pitcher plants (*Sarracenia*) and Venus flytrap (*Dionaea*) can be damaged by overfertilization.

Bulbs benefit from an application of bulb booster in the spring. This is a specially formulated fertilizer developed after many years of research. Some bulb experts believe that bone meal is of little or no use to a bulb. This may be because what is currently sold as bone meal has been stripped of whatever fertilizer the old-fashioned version used to have—when there were actual meat scraps on the bone.

Trimming and Deadheading

The general rule is that any time of year is the right time to trim off the "3-Ds"—dead, diseased, or damaged parts of your perennials, shrubs, and trees. There are some exceptions to this rule. Ferns, for example, would rather you leave their ratty-looking, spent fronds attached until the new, fresh foliage appears in spring. The old ones protect the new ones waiting in the crown. Mexican bush sage (*Salvia leucantha*) is another plant to leave intact until spring.

Bulb foliage must be allowed to yellow naturally in order for the plant to have blooms in future years. If it's too unsightly for your taste, try interplanting the bulbs with other perennials that will hide the foliage as it senesces. Ornamental grasses are often left in place all winter, when their dried blades and attractive seed heads can be enjoyed as part of the winter landscape. Cut them back to a few inches from the ground in early spring when the new green shoots start to appear.

With the foregoing exceptions in mind, it's a good idea to clean up and dispose of the foliage and flowers of plants once they've started to yellow, dry up, or otherwise indicate they've had it. Leaving decaying plant material on the plant or on the ground invites insects and disease.

Trimming flowering shrubs should generally be done as soon after they bloom as possible because many of them set their new buds fairly quickly. For most azaleas, this will be in the late spring or early summer; for hydrangeas and gardenias, in the late summer and early fall; for camellias and sasanquas, the early spring.

Trimming nonflowering evergreen shrubs can be done any time from early spring until midfall. Trimming should be completed by the end of October to avoid the danger of new growth being killed by a sudden freeze.

Deadheading is the process of removing (with fingers or clippers) the flowers of annuals, perennials, and roses that have finished blooming. Deadheading is not necessary for all annuals or perennials, but for many plants it promotes continued blooming, because it frustrates the plant's natural desire to set seed and reproduce itself. The A–Z Guide at the end of this book indicates which plants benefit most from deadheading.

Certain plants tend to get leggy as the summer wears on, with a resultant sparse flower production. They can be kept bushier and more floriferous if they're pruned or pinched back on a regular basis. Examples include some of the artemesias, chrysanthemums, perennial ageratum, swamp sunflower, purple coneflower, *Rudbeckia* 'Autumn Sun', the glorybowers and some of the sages. In some cases, if you cut a plant back fairly dramatically after its first season of bloom, it will bloom again later in the summer or early fall. Good examples of this include spiderwort, phlox, and yarrow.

Pests

Gardeners who make a habit of inspecting their plants on a regular basis are able to catch infestations before they get out of control. Natural insect predators such as ladybugs, grasshoppers, lacewings, trichogoma wasps, and others are terrific allies in the pest war. (Organic gardening catalogs sell them.) The following are some nontoxic alternatives to chemical pesticides.

In the winter and early spring you can apply a dormant oil spray on deciduous plants to smother the insects and their eggs that overwinter. A summer oil spray such as Sun Spray will kill aphids, mites, and scale the same way—by smothering. Volck oil can be applied in winter or summer. Horticultural oil is especially effective against whitefly if used repeatedly over a period of several days.

Snails and slugs are a problem in the coastal South. They like to feed at night in damp, shady spots. Control them with diatomaceous earth (a dust containing sharp particles, which they prefer not to crawl over), shallow dishes of beer (in which they drown), or a wooden board set an inch off the ground (pick them off from underneath in the early evening).

Insecticidal soaps are effective, nontoxic weapons to use against scale, spider mites, mealy bugs, and aphids. Thoroughly wet the plant, including the undersides of the leaves. The soap must come into contact with the insects to be effective.

A variety of wormy pests and caterpillars with chewing mouthparts will eat their way quickly through leafy plants such as hollyhocks, hibiscus, mullein, and angel's trumpet in no time. One good control is Bt (*Bacillus thurengiensis*). It is sold under the names Dipel, Javelin, and Thuricide and is an effective, nontoxic pesticide that paralyzes the pests once they've consumed it on the leaf. Rotenone is another plant-derived pesticide that controls chewing insects. Don't use rotenone near a pond, because it will kill the fish.

Neem spray will stop many pests in their tracks and also works as a fungicide against black spot and powdery mildew. Neem oil controls whitefly, spider mites, mealy bugs, scale, leaf miner, beetles, leafhoppers, and fruit flies, among others.

Sprays containing pyrethrins derived from certain chrysanthemum species have low human toxicity and are effective against mites, thrips, aphids, mealy bugs, whiteflies, scales, certain beetles, and a number of wormy pests. Again, be sure to coat the plant thoroughly.

Environmentally friendly pest control includes encouraging natural predators like chameleons, ladybugs, trichogoma wasps, and others.

The best time to apply pesticides, whether organic or synthetic, is in the early morning or late afternoon, when the temperature is cool. Otherwise you run the risk of burning the plant. Dilute insecticidal soap and/or bleach solutions can be used on cuttings and transplants.

Diseases

The coastal South is hospitable to many kinds of fungus and rot. They come with the territory. Black spot and powdery mildew are the most prevalent diseases, because they thrive in heat and humidity. For black spot, the first step is to keep an eye on your plants and remove all affected leaves and stems before they fall to the ground. On the ground (and even in the compost pile) the fungus lives on to reproduce itself inexorably. Dispose of the affected plant material elsewhere. Another preventative measure against all kinds of fungus is to try to keep water off the leaves as much as possible (soaker hoses work well for this). Some gardeners carry around a bucket of water-and-bleach solution to dip their shears in when they're pruning susceptible plants such as roses.

There are some organic alternatives for combating fungus. In the winter and early spring you can mix dormant oil with lime sulfur as a preventative. Sulfur dust or wettable powder is also a preventative. And, finally, neem oil applied on a regular basis will cut down on the incidence and spread of fungal diseases. Use the same guidelines for application as with pesticides. Avoid spraying in the heat of the day and don't use full-strength fungicides on the newly transplanted.

If bearded irises develop rot, use a spoon to scrape out the mushy, rotten part of the rhizome and treat the remaining part with a mild bleach-and-water solution to prevent the condition from getting worse. Try growing those beardeds that are most suitable to the coastal South. (See Chapter 3 and the A–Z Plant Guide for suggestions.) Keep the rhizomes as dry as possible and plant them high, with the top of the rhizome showing. Plant them away from their neighbors. Leave the ground around them bare—no mulch!

Note: Gardeners who use any of the heavy-hitting synthetic chemicals like diazanon, malathion, daconil, captan, maneb, dursban, kelthane, lindane, sevin, cygon, or others of this type should wear long sleeves, long pants, socks and shoes, some kind of covering for their hair, heavy rubber gloves (not the kind for washing dishes), and a specially designed mask. A shower immediately afterward is also advised. These chemicals and the containers in which they are mixed or sprayed should be kept in a separate location inaccessible to children and disposed of safely.

Even when using natural, organically derived pesticides and fungicides, gardeners should still use care not to inhale or swallow them or saturate skin or clothing with them. It's a good idea to wash off thoroughly after applying them. Edibles such as vegetables, fruits, or herbs should be rinsed thoroughly before eating if organic pesticides or fungicides have been applied.

PLANT PROPAGATION

One of the joys of gardening is increasing your supply of plants by propagating them yourself. The easiest method of propagation is by division. Growing plants from cuttings or seed takes a little more time and effort but is a relatively inexpensive way to have all the plants you need. You don't need a special grow lab or expensive supplies to succeed.

From Division

Division is a way of propagating new plants, but it's also a way of reinvigorating plants such as mums, which will otherwise become weary and skimpy with their blooms if they're not dug up every three years or so. Propagation by division works with certain tuberous plants (for example, gloriosa lily and *Liatris*), with plants that produce new shoots from the central crown (such as *Stokesia* and Oxford orphanage plant), and with rhizomatous plants like cannas. The large majority of perennials can be propagated by division. To divide a plant, dig it up completely, use your fingers or a knife to divide it into viable sections (each with enough roots to survive on its own and some new shoots or growth buds on top), and replant the divisions in well-amended soil. Water them in and treat them as you would any other new transplants. Clump-forming bulbous plants like daffodils and *Oxalis* can be divided by separating out the daughter plants from their mothers. Division is easy and very satisfying.

Don't divide or transplant anything in the heat of summer unless you plan to tend to it religiously thereafter. In very hot weather, new transplants may transpire faster than their roots can take up the water they need and they will struggle to survive. This kind of stress makes the plant a more attractive target for pests and diseases. Much better choices would be fall or early spring, when the temperatures are cool and the transplants will have a good long period of moderate weather to get established.

From Cuttings

You can create an exact replica of a plant you like by taking a cutting from the stem, leaf, or root of the plant and planting it in a suitable potting mixture until it forms roots, stems, and leaves of its own. Although there are many ins and outs to this process, depending on the nature of the plant, the general steps for a stem cutting are as follows: (1) cut off the soft, pliable leaf tip of the plant just below a leaf node, retaining several pairs of leaves so that your cutting is three to four inches long; (2) remove the bottom one-third of the leaves; (3) dip the stem in a rooting hormone; (4) plant it in a loose potting mix containing perlite; (5) keep it moist and warm until it develops a good root system.

If you take cuttings of the plant's roots, use thick roots close to the crown and follow these steps: (1) cut the end of the root nearest the crown straight across; (2) cut the other end at a slant so that you end up with a piece two to

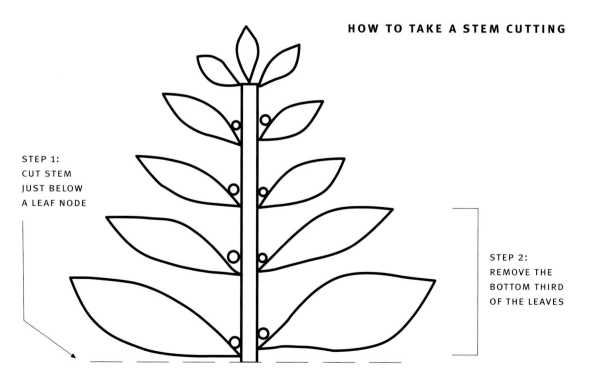

HOW TO TAKE A STEM CUTTING

STEP 1:
CUT STEM
JUST BELOW
A LEAF NODE

STEP 2:
REMOVE THE
BOTTOM THIRD
OF THE LEAVES

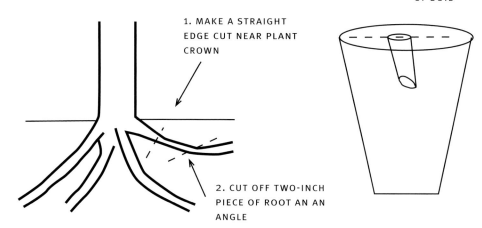

1. MAKE A STRAIGHT
EDGE CUT NEAR PLANT
CROWN

2. CUT OFF TWO-INCH
PIECE OF ROOT AN AN
ANGLE

four inches long; (3) stand the cutting up straight in moist potting mix with the straight edge flush with the top of the soil; (4) don't water it until it develops roots.

For information on leaf cuttings, hardwood cuttings, and other more specific details about this kind of propagation, consult a general garden encyclopedia, such as *The American Horticultural Society A–Z Encyclopedia of Garden Plants*, listed in the Recommended Reading.

From Seed

Most seed catalogs will send you excellent instructions on propagation techniques, and, of course, there are guidelines on all seed packets. In general, you should sow the seeds in a loose growing medium that contains perlite. Although vermiculite is often recommended, some gardeners believe it tends to get waterlogged and thereby promotes damping-off. Other propagators swear by it. In any case, use a clean seed tray or other container with drainage holes. If you are reusing old trays, soak them in a dilute bleach mixture and then thoroughly rinse them before you begin. Cover the seeds thinly with growing medium unless they are very tiny. Keep the growing medium moist but not wet. The best way of doing this is to put the growing container in a pan or tray that will hold water and let the water wick up from the bottom rather than watering from the top.

Cover the seed tray with transparent plastic wrap to keep the seeds moist until they've germinated. Seeds germinate at differing temperatures depending on their climate of origin. Some need a period of cold (stratification) in order to germinate. You will have to determine this for each type of seed, although most will germinate at room temperature. As soon as the seeds sprout, place them in a south-facing window or under a grow light. When they've be-

Keep newly sown seeds moist by covering the tray with plastic wrap until they have sprouted.

come strong enough to move (usually when they have their first real leaves but sometimes before this), thin them out so that they have enough space between them to develop a good root system and to leaf out. This usually means leaving two to three inches between seedlings.

Some people will take the extra step of potting each seedling up in its own small pot before planting it out. If you start with plantable seed starter pots or divided trays, you can skip this step. When you're ready to move them outdoors to the garden, give the plants about a week of hardening-off first, by taking them outside to a sheltered spot during the day and bringing them in at night. If you're growing seeds outdoors either directly in the ground or in seed trays, be sure to protect them from the full intensity of the sun until they're well established, and be sure to keep the ground or growing medium moist.

A–Z Plant Guide

All plant entries in this guide begin with the scientific name, followed by the common name (if any) in parentheses. USDA cold-hardiness zones are denoted by the letter Z followed by a range of numbers. For example, *Abutilon* is commonly known as flowering maple. The coldest USDA zone in which it normally survives is Zone 8, the warmest is Zone 10. When the phrase "southern classic" is used in this guide, it refers to plants that have been grown by gardeners in the South over many generations because of their outstanding performance in our climate.

ABELMOSCHUS (ornamental okra, silk flower, musk mallow). These heat- and drought-resistant plants are well adapted to our coastal summers. Foliage is dark green and deeply lobed. The showy flowers are open, five-petaled, mallow-type blooms. They have contrasting "eyes" and prominent, curved stamen. *Abelmoschus* will grow in sun or part shade in well-amended and well-drained soil.

A. *manihot*. Z7–10. This somewhat tender perennial grows 4'–6' tall with large (6" diameter), pale yellow flowers highlighted with dark maroon eyes. Deadhead to encourage continuous bloom. Self-sows dependably. Also known as *Hibiscus manihot*.

A. *moschatus*. Annual. Grows 14"–18" tall with pink or red flowers with pale yellow or white eyes. These bushy annuals are treated by some gardeners as honorary perennials because of their habit of reseeding freely. Also known as *Hibiscus abelmoschus*.

ABUTILON (flowering maple, abutilon). Z8–10. There are a number of beautiful flowering maples that thrive in the coastal South. The large (2"–3" wide), pendent, bell-shaped inflorescences are made up of colorful calyxes from which protrude flower petals (often of a different color) and showy stamens. Give abutilon a position in light shade or filtered sunlight, in fertile, well-drained soil. Prune it regularly to keep it within bounds. Abutilons are beloved of hummingbirds. The following species bloom nonstop summer through fall.

A. 'Kentish Belle'. A semievergreen, arching shrub, 8' tall by 8' wide, with inflorescences of red, buff yellow, and purple.

A. *megapotamicum*. A semievergreen, arching shrub 6' tall and wide, which bears inflorescences of bright red, yellow, and purple.

A. x *milleri*. An evergreen, arching shrub growing 8' tall by 8' wide, with inflorescences of pink and apricot flushed with red.

ACANTHUS (bear's britches). Grown for their deeply cut foliage, these perennials like a partially shady location with good drainage. After the flower spikes appear in late spring or early summer, cut them off and water the plants well. Keep them watered during dry spells.

A. *mollis* (common bear's britches). Z7–9. Flower spikes reach 2'–3' tall. The pale lilac or pink flowers are surrounded by spiny green or purple bracts.

A. *montanus* (alligator back plant). Z8–11. The foliage of this spiny-leaved plant, which can grow 6' tall, has a leathery texture and silver markings. It bears mauve-pink, thistle-like flowers in the fall.

A. *spinosus* (spiny bear's britches). Z6–10. This evergreen species, which is spinier and has more deeply divided leaves than *A. mollis*, survives our heat and humidity better. Its late spring flowers are similar to those of *A. mollis*.

A. x 'Summer Beauty'. Z6–10. Deeply cut, dark, glossy green leaves on a 6'–8'-wide, clump-forming perennial. Spires of white and purple flowers appear in early summer. This may be the best *Acanthus* for our climate.

ACHILLEA *millefolium* (yarrow). Z3–9. This is an 18"-tall yarrow with dark green, lacy foliage. The first flush of flowers appears in late spring or early summer. Staking may be required because of our hot nights, which prevent stalks from becoming rigid. Yarrow won't flourish unless it's grown in dry, sandy, or generally poor soil in full, baking sun. Don't fertilize it. Deadhead the plants for continuous bloom. Tolerates seaside conditions. Cultivars: 'Cerise Queen'—spreads rapidly with a profusion of deep rosy-pink flowers; 'Lilac Beauty'—pale purple flowers on strong stems; 'Paprika'—beautiful crimson and

Creeping fig (Ficus pumila) *surrounds a garden cherub.*

yellow flowers, excellent color; and 'White Beauty'—creamy white flowers. Certain yarrow species and cultivars (such as 'Moonshine') do poorly in the coastal South, so select carefully.

ACHIMENES (achimenes). Z8–10. These rhizomes can be planted directly in the ground, where they will overwinter in all but the coldest parts of the coastal South. More often they are grown in containers in a light soil mixture. They bloom during the warm months of summer and fall, bearing flared, tubular flowers in shades of pink, purple, and lavender. 'Purple King' is an especially cold-hardy, deep purple variety. Give achimenes a protected spot in light shade.

ACIDANTHERA. *See* GLADIOLUS *callianthus.*

ACORUS *gramineus* **'Ogon'** (dwarf golden sweet flag). Z5–10. This 8"–10"-tall, slow-spreading, dwarf ornamental grass has bright chartreuse foliage. 'Variegatus' is similar to 'Ogon' but with creamy striped leaves. Grow sweet flag in full sun to part shade in a pond or in a bog. Grow it in regular soil only if you can provide plenty of water.

ACTINIDIA (kiwi vine). Give these twining, fruiting vines a sturdy support to grow on, and prune them in winter to two or three principal trunks. Don't let the shoots twine around these main branches. Kiwi blooms and fruits on old wood. You may want to thin the vine by one-third every year, cutting back the very oldest wood each time, to keep it manageable. Kiwi takes full to part sun and rich soil. Look for the varieties that do not require a period of chilling in order to produce fruit.

A. *arguta* (hardy kiwi). Z3–9. These kiwis are hairless, so you can eat the skin. If you obtain the cultivar 'Issai', you will have a self-fertile vine, so you don't have to worry about having a male-female duo.

A. *deliciosa* (fuzzy kiwi). Z7–9. This is an extremely vigorous deciduous vine, growing to 30' tall, that produces creamy flowers in spring or early summer and kiwi fruit in the fall. The leaves start out red and fuzzy then mature to dark green with a fuzzy white underside. The skin of the fruit is also fuzzy. To produce fruit, you will need a male and a female.

ADIANTUM *capillus-veneris* (Southern maidenhair fern). Z7–10. This is a delicate, 12"-tall, native fern that spreads slowly by creeping rhizomes and loses its foliage in winter. Plant it in light shade in rich compost with plenty of moisture and good air circulation. Southern maidenhair also grows in damp cracks and crevices of walls. Its pinnules

(the smallest segment of the fern frond) are fan-shaped, which gives it a unique appearance.

AGAPANTHUS (lily of the Nile, agapanthus). Z7–10. This dramatic, tropical-looking plant produces beautiful blue or white flower umbels on erect stalks in summer. It flowers in part sun to light shade in rich, moist soil. Certain agapanthus rot away during our wet winters, so be sure to give these tuberous plants a well-drained position. You will often see agapanthus used in containers or as specimen plants in a small garden. Note that the Headbourne hybrid series of agapanthus do not do very well in our region.

A. *africanus.* This is a widely known and loved evergreen species that bears blue flowers on 1'–2'-tall stalks and strappy green foliage. Recommended cultivars: 'Blue Baby', a dwarf variety that has light blue, bell-like flowers on 15"–24" scapes in early summer; 'Blue Nile', a vigorous, clump-former in moist or regular soil that produces 5'-tall stalks topped with umbels of sky blue flowers; and 'Peter Pan', an excellent blue-flowering dwarf with evergreen foliage that grows 1'–2' tall.

A. *inapertus.* This species sends up 2'–3'-tall scapes with up to a hundred bright blue, tubular flowers in summer. The foliage dies back in winter.

AGASTACHE *foeniculum* (anise hyssop). Z6–10. This 2'–3'-tall plant is covered in colorful, dense racemes of purple flowers all summer long. The leaves have a licorice scent, and the plant attracts bees and butterflies. It is used in herbal infusions, as a cut flower, and for dried arrangements. Plant these decorative herbs in full, baking sun in a perfectly drained situation.

AGAVE *americana* (American century plant, agave). Z7–10. This huge, striking succulent—grown for its glaucous, blue-green, spined foliage and spectacular, chandelier-like bloom—is native to the Southwest. The leaves grow up to 6½' long and 10" wide. Also look for variegated varieties. Grow agave in hot, baking sun with perfect drainage.

AJANIA *pacifica* (silver and gold)—Z5–9. Not the longest lived plant, but useful throughout the spring and summer as a 2'–3'-tall groundcover or subshrub. The lobed green leaves have silver margins. In late fall the golden button flowers are a welcome addition to the garden. This plant can stand serious, repeated cutting back up until mid-August. It also works well at the beach. 'Pink Ice' is a pink and yellow, daisy-like version. Also known as *Pyrethrum marginatum* or *Dendranthema pacificum;* formerly *Chrysanthemum pacificum.*

AJUGA reptans (carpet bugleweed). Z3–10. *Ajuga* is a stoloniferous, evergreen groundcover or edging plant that looks something like the leaves of baby Bibb lettuce but is much darker in color. It performs well from full shade to part sun and tolerates almost any soil except under extremely wet or extremely dry conditions. In full sun it will need extra watering. In spring, *Ajuga* produces small, deep blue flowers on short spikes. The bronze-leaved and variegated forms of *Ajuga* add an interesting color to the garden. *Ajuga* spreads semirapidly and can be very easily propagated by division. Recommended varieties: 'Braunherz'—deep-burgundy-colored leaves with 6"-long lavender flower spikes in spring; 'Burgundy Glow'—purple, green, pink, and white variegated foliage with blue flowers in late spring to early summer; 'Caitlin's Giant'—large-leaved variety with bronze-colored leaves and 8"-long spikes of blue flowers; 'Jungle Beauty'—splotched gold and purple leaves in a calico pattern that is most prominent in early spring, blue flowers; 'Pink Surprise'—bronze leaves with pink flower spikes.

AKEBIA quinata (five-leaf akebia vine, chocolate vine). Z5–9. Grown in full sun or light shade in well-drained soil, this delicate-leaved, semi-evergreen vine can easily grow to 40'. Vanilla-scented, dusky purple, three-petaled flowers appear in early summer, followed by purple fruits in late summer. Fruits will appear only if there is a male pollinator nearby.

ALCEA rosea (hollyhock). Z3–9. These quintessential cottage garden flowers, with their 3'–6' stems bearing racemes of outward-facing mallow-type flowers or double-rose-like blooms, come in a variety of pastel colors and even dark chocolate. They bloom in late spring and early summer. Generally hollyhocks are treated as cool-weather annuals or biennials in our area, self-sowing if the pods are left to dry on the plant and scattered in fall. A very old hollyhock variety, 'Indian Spring', has been brought back into commerce and is now available through heirloom seed catalogs. It is an annual that blooms the first year from seed planted in the fall. Give your hollyhocks full to part sun, rich soil and good air circulation. If the leaves are chewed by caterpillars, dust with Dipel.

ALLIUM (ornamental onions). A genus of bulbs and rhizomes with over 500 species, including garlic, onions, and chives. These are good plants to interlayer with other bulbs or to squeeze in among your perennials. They are reliable minglers that require full sun and well-drained soil. Bees and butterflies love them, and you can snip the leaves and flower heads to add to your salads or other culinary creations. Propagate by seed or from bulblet offshoots. Some of the more popular *Alliums* are not suited to our area, but the following do well.

A. aflatunense. Z5–9. This 2'–3'-tall *Allium* blooms in early summer with dense balls or umbels of magenta-colored flowers.

A. bulgaricum. Z6–10. Blooming in late spring or early summer, the stems of these *Alliums* reach 3'–4' tall and are topped with umbels of pendent, bell-shaped, greenish-white flowers, flushed purple. Grow them in sun to part shade in fertile, well-drained soil. They will self-seed where they are contented. Also sold as *Nectaroscordum siculum* subsp. *bulgaricum*.

A. schoenoprasum 'Forescate' (drumstick chives). Z5–9. This is a clumping plant that produces 18"-high, lilac-pink, drumstick flower heads in early summer. It tends to suffer from the heat but is easy to plant annually from seed.

A. triquetrum (triangle garlic, three-cornered onion). Z5–9. For several weeks in early summer this plant produces drooping sprays of green-striped, white bells on foot-high, three-sided scapes.

A. tuberosum (garlic chives). Z7–10. Rounded umbels of greenish-white stars are produced freely in July and August on 1'–2' stems. The leaves are gray-green. This *Allium* spreads to form sizable clumps and works well among other perennials. Also a dependable reseeder.

A. unifolium. Z5–9. This small *Allium* grows about 12" tall with gray-green leaves that disappear neatly. It is topped by showy umbels of lilac-purple-to-pink, bell-shaped flowers in the spring.

ALOCASIA (elephant ear). These rhizomatous perennials are wonderful, dramatic additions to the partially shady garden.

A. macrorhiza (giant upright elephant ear, giant taro). Z7b–10. This is one of the largest elephant ears, boasting 3'–4'-wide, arrow-shaped leaves on equally long petioles. In the warmest parts of the coastal South, these plants grow 12'–15' tall with a 6'–8' spread in sun or part shade in ordinary garden soil, bog, or aquatic conditions. A definite presence in the garden. Give them a good winter mulch.

A. plumbea (colorful elephant ear). Z8–10. Similar in height and spread to *A. macrorhiza*. 'Nigra' (black elephant ear) has black-green-tinted foliage and multiplies rapidly. 'Rubra' (red elephant ear) has reddish foliage and is easy to grow.

ALOYSIA triphylla (lemon verbena). Z8–10. This somewhat tender, deciduous, woody shrub has lanceolate, hairy leaves that give off a distinct lemon fragrance. Pale lavender flower spikes appear in summer. Plants reach 5'–10' tall, depending on how far south they are grown. Give them a position in sun or part shade, in good, well-drained soil, and keep them watered during the growing season, dry in winter. Lemon verbena has many culinary uses, including in beverages, salads, and marinades.

ALSTROEMERIA psittacina (parrot lily, lily of Peru). Z8–10. This species grows 2'–3' tall and bears tubular red flowers with touches of green at the tips and purple on the inside. Hybrids have been developed in shades of white, yellow, pink, purple, and red, with bloom seasons ranging from spring through fall. Generally parrot lilies prefer a moist loam in a partially sunny position and may go temporarily dormant in summer when the temperatures become extremely high. Where it is happy, *Alstroemeria* can become weedy.

AMARCRINUM memoria-corsii (amarcrinum). Z7–10. This large, bulbous perennial is a cross between an *Amaryllis* and a *Crinum*, with trumpet-shaped flowers and strappy foliage. Once established, it will bloom midsummer through frost with dramatic flowers borne on 2'-tall stalks. It also does well in containers. The cultivar 'Fred Howard' has handsome, fragrant, pink flowers. Amarcrinum prefers to be planted shallowly in full sun and well-drained soil.

AMORPHOPHALLUS (voodoo lily, snake palm). Z7b–10. Once they've become well established in a moist, partially sunny to shady position with organically enriched soil, these very large tubers produce otherworldly spathe and spadix flowers. In spring, 2'–8'-tall mottled stalks arise to showcase the eye-catching, flared, vase-like spathe and erect, often wildly protruding spadix. Colors of spathe, spadix, and stems include greenish-white, pale pink, burnt orange, peach, wine-purple, rusty red, dark brown, and more—a large color spectrum that includes dark blue and shocking-pink berries on some plants. After flowering, the plant rests for a while before sending up one large leaf that remains until frost. In addition to their strange behavior and appearance, they are renowned for being (briefly) malodorous. Plant the tubers 4"–6" below the surface. Do not let these tubers suffer from wet feet in winter or you may lose them. Mark the planting spot well, because they are late to emerge.

AMPELOPSIS brevipedunculata (porcelain berry vine). Z6–9. The leaves and berries of this rambunctious vine look something like those of a grape vine. Climbing by twining tendrils, porcelain berry can reach 20' tall in full sun to part shade. The berries turn from a porcelain ivory color to metallic blue in late summer and fall. The leaves will take on a reddish tint at the same time. This is a vine that can get out of control if left unchecked. 'Elegans' is a variegated variety, with leaves marbled in shades of white, ivory, yellow, and pink.

AMSONIA (bluestar flower). Grow these disease- and insect-free natives in full sun in any garden soil. They are prized for their starry blue flowers in spring and the golden color of their foliage in fall.

A. hubrichtii (narrow-leaf bluestar, willow-leaf bluestar). Z5–9. The foliage of this excellent 3'-tall *Amsonia* is thread-like. The flowers are sky blue, and it tolerates drought.

A. tabernaemontana (bluestar). Z3–9. In full sun, this 2'-tall native stays round and compact. In moist, partial shade, it may need some support. This somewhat larger-leaved *Amsonia* is also a dependable spring flower for us.

ANDROPOGON (bluestem). These native ornamental grasses originated in the prairies. They prefer fertile, perfectly drained soil in full sun but will tolerate drought and wet feet. Divide the clumps every few years when the centers die out.

A. capillipes 'Valdosta Blue'. Z3–9. This 3'–4'-tall, blue-green grass maintains a rigid upright stance even into fall and winter when other ornamental grasses are sprawling uncouthly.

A. glomeratus (bushy blue stem). Z3–9. This is an excellent grass for our climate, making an upright, narrow 6'–7'-tall clump in full to part sun. The billowy seed heads are especially beautiful in the fall.

A. virginicus (broom sedge). Z6–9. This 1'–5'-tall southern classic grows tallest where it is kept constantly moist, but it also tolerates drought. The blades are blue-green in summer, turning to bright orange in fall. It is especially tolerant of poor, rocky soil.

ANEMONE (anemone). Although the well-known Greek windflowers (*A. blanda*) are not suited to the coastal South, the following species and cultivars work well for us.

A. coronaria (poppy anemone). Z6–9. Looking very much like their namesake the poppy, these single or double saucer-like flowers—in brilliant shades of blue, red, pink, and white with dramatic, black central stamens—grace 10"-tall plants for many weeks in the spring. The finely lobed foliage remains attractive all season. Plant these tubers in sun to part sun in November or December and keep them watered. Because they cannot be counted on to bloom well for more than a few seasons, you may want to plant out new tubers each year. These anemones make good cut flowers also.

A. x hybrida (Japanese anemone). Z4–9. Japanese anemones are excellent late-summer- and fall-blooming plants. They like light shade or filtered sunlight and rich, moist soil where they will multiply once they've had a year or two to get established. They won't tolerate hot sun, especially the midday variety. Flowers can be single, semi-double, or double in shades of white or pink. The white cultivar 'Honorine Jobert' tolerates heat well.

A. tomentosa (grape-leaf anemone). Z5–9. This fall-blooming anemone has healthy, lobed foliage that remains attractive throughout the growing season. It produces many offspring by sending out stolons. Single, pale pink flowers appear on 2'–6' scapes in August and September. Recommended: 'Robustissima'—delicate mauve flowers from August to October on 2–3'-tall plants. (Also sold as *A. vitifolia* 'Robustissima'.)

ANGELONIA angustifolia (angelonia). Annual. When the winter is mild, angelonia will act as a perennial, but it is generally tender above Zone 9. This bushy, 12"–18"-tall plant has narrow, attractive, dark green foliage. It sends up racemes of dark violet, white, or bicolor flowers all summer long. Angelonia takes full sun to part shade and rich, well-drained soil. It will tolerate some drought and makes a good container plant.

ANISACANTHUS wrightii (hummingbird bush, flame acanthus). Z8–10. This semievergreen, twiggy, glossy-leafed shrub grows to 3' tall and blooms nonstop from early summer through to frost, sporting clusters of bright reddish-orange or yellow tubular flowers. It takes full sun to light shade and perfect drainage to do well. Cut it back by one-third in late winter/early spring. As its common name suggests, it is beloved of hummingbirds (and also butterflies).

ANTIGONON leptopus (coral vine). Z8–10. This vigorous, semievergreen, drought-tolerant vine is an old southern favorite, with its sprays of coral pink flowers from midsummer through fall. Plant it in full sun in perfectly drained soil. It will climb to 40' by twining and use of its tendrils. There are also white and red varieties available. In the cooler parts of the coastal South, protect the roots with a thick winter mulch.

AQUILEGIA (columbine, doves-in-a-ring, meeting houses). Z3–9. These spring-blooming delicacies should be planted in part sun or light shade with plenty of moisture and excellent drainage. Although they may live for only a few years, they are truly beautiful plants. Their unique flowers, which are attached to the stem by a petiole, are five-petaled, with a frontward-projecting petal tube, a surround of sepals, and rearward-projecting hollow spurs (some spurs being longer than others, depending on the species). Often the foliage has a silvery underside, with green or gray-green on top. A good plant for hummingbirds. The most reliable columbine for our area is the native *A. canadensis*.

A. canadensis (wild columbine). This excellent native boasts 2'-long spikes of flowers shooting off a base of delicate, plentiful, many-lobed leaves. The flowers are a beautiful contrast of crushed raspberry calyx and clear, lemon yellow petals. This plant self-sows readily.

A. flavescens (Corbett's columbine). This is a shorter, pale yellow version of the wild columbine.

A. x hybrida (hybrid columbines). Short- and long-spurred hybrids are available in a large variety of pastels and vibrant shades. They have the same cultural requirements as the species.

ARGYRANTHEMUM frutescens (marguerite daisy). Z8b–11. These bush-forming daisies may have finely or coarsely dissected leaves, depending on the variety. They are extremely floriferous from spring through fall, producing corymbs of white, pink, coral, or primrose yellow daisies. They have a woody base and should not be cut back severely but rather pruned lightly and consistently. They are often used as annuals elsewhere and will probably be short-lived, needing to be replaced every few years. They may need their lower legs hidden as they get taller. Marguerites are good seashore flowers. They prefer full sun and well-drained, fertile soil. Give them a thick, dry winter mulch. Where winters are mild, they may continue to give you blooms into January and February. (Formerly known as *Chrysanthemum frutescens*.)

ARISAEMA (jack-in-the-pulpit, cobra lily, green dragon). Z4–9. These native, tuberous or rhizomatous woodlanders are known by their inflorescences: hooded green or purple spathes and protruding, fleshy spadices that appear above the foliage in spring. They thrive in shade with rich, moist soil. Although the coastal South is not *Arisaema*'s preferred habitat, *A. dracaonitum*, *A. quintatum*, and *A. triphyllum* are known survivors in our area.

ARTEMESIA (wormwood). *Artemesias* are grown for their narrow-leaved or finely dissected gray foliage, which blends well with other textures in the perennial garden and acts as a transition between contrasting colors. They need full baking sun, not overly rich soil, and absolutely perfect drainage or they will rot in our humid weather. The woodier ones thrive in the coastal Southeast even in beach conditions and during periods of drought. The woody *Artemesias* can be revitalized by light, intermittent pruning, but don't prune in the fall or winter or you will kill the plant. Wait until the warmer weather of spring or summer. Unfortunately, the furry-looking, mat-forming varieties such as 'Silver Mound' do poorly here and should be avoided.

A. abrotanum (Southernwood). Z4–8. This sturdy, easy-to-grow plant is somewhat less gray than the others and has pinnately divided foliage. It does well in our area and can grow to 4' tall. It is known for its pungent scent.

A. ludoviciana 'Silver King' (white sage). Z4–9. This disease-resistant plant is well suited to our area, where it will form a 2'–3'-tall clump of gray-white, woolly leaved foliage. 'Valerie Finnis' is another excellent, silvery gray, deepy incised cultivar for our climate.

A. x 'Huntington'. Z5–9. Plants reach anywhere from 18" to 4' tall with soft, silvery foliage that is deeply cut. An excellent hybrid for our area.

A. x 'Powis Castle'. Z5–9. This is a tall, bushy, semi-evergray subshrub that may be the very best *Artemesia* for our climate. Its delicately filigreed, pale silver foliage is always fresh looking, and the more you shear it, the bushier it gets. Prune in spring or summer only.

A. stelleriana (beach wormwood, perennial dusty miller). Z4–8. These 2½'-tall, hairy-leaved, whitish-gray plants do well at the beach, producing panicles of yellow flowers in summer. Try the cultivar 'Silver Lace'.

ARUM italicum 'Pictum' (Italian arum). Z6–9. Grown for their glossy, deep green, marbled leaves shaped like arrowheads, these tuberous plants play a unique role in the garden. The 10"-tall arum foliage doesn't appear until the fall, around the time the hostas are getting ready to bite the dust, and the foliage remains handsome all winter. In the spring, flowers appear in the form of pale yellow spathes. The plant then goes dormant for the summer. If they are in a cool enough spot, arums will offer up spikes of orange berries in autumn. Arums mix well with hostas, deciduous ferns, and hellebores, all of which enjoy moist, rich soil in a shaded spot.

ARUNDO donax 'Variegata' (variegated giant reed). Z7–10. This tall (6'–10'), rhizomatous perennial grass is grown for the drama of its blue-green-and-white-striped foliage and erect, bamboo-like stems, which are topped in fall with pale-green-to-purplish spikelets. It takes full sun and moist soil. Cut it back to the ground in late winter. Leaf edges are sharp, so take care! This is an invasive plant that must be planted within firm boundaries.

ASARUM (wild ginger). Grown as evergreen groundcovers, the wild gingers each boast a unique leaf pattern, with no two being alike. In spring, brownish, jug-shaped flowers are borne on the undersides of the leaves, hidden from sight unless you know where to look. *Asarums* are rhizomatous plants that prefer a shady, constantly moist site with good drainage. *A. canadense* and A. *europaeum* are not as happy in our hot summers as those listed below.

A. arifolium (arrow-leaf ginger). Z4–8. Evergreen, arrow-shaped foliage. Reliable for upper coastal South.

A. shuttleworthii (Shuttleworth ginger). Z6–9. Evergreen, mottled, heart-shaped leaves. Reports are that it tolerates our hot summers.

A. splendens. Z6b–9. Arrow-shaped foliage is dramatically mottled with silver, and the leaves are larger and the flowers are showier than in other *Asarums*. This is an attractive, evergreen groundcover for our area.

ASCLEPIAS (milkweed, butterfly weed). Butterflies love the brightly colored umbels of these summer-blooming plants, which are the host plants for the beautiful Monarch butterflies. They are slow to emerge, so mark their place well. Plant *Asclepias* in full to part sun. They don't like to be moved once they're established, but they will self-sow. Please note that, depending on the species you select, *Asclepias* may require very well drained soil or bog-like conditions.

A. curassavica (blood flower, Indian root). Z8b–10. This tender perennial grows to 3' tall with umbellate cymes of reddish-orange and yellow flowers borne all summer long. It is particularly long blooming and requires good drainage. Look for the yellow cultivar 'Silky Gold'.

A. incarnata (swamp milkweed). Z3–9. This native can grow 2'–5' tall. It needs ample moisture and can stand wet feet. The foliage has a purple cast and the flowers are a rosy-purple. Cultivars: 'Soulmate'—dusty pink flowers; 'Ice Follies'—pure white flowers.

A. lanceolata (butterfly weed). Z3–9. This 4'-tall native bears bright red, yellow, or orange flower cymes in summer. It likes part sun and good drainage.

A. tuberosa (butterfly weed). Z4–9. This species bears saffron orange to orangy-red flowers on 2'–3'-tall plants for many weeks beginning in midsummer and needs well-drained soil. Cultivars: 'Gay Butterflies'—a mixture of reds, oranges, and yellows; 'Hello Yellow'—a unique, vibrant yellow.

ASPARAGUS densiflorus 'Sprengeri' (hardy asparagus fern). Z9–10. Although it is commonly called a fern, this is actually a flowering plant. It may be the laciest plant you can grow; its needle-like formations, which look like leaves, are actually tiny stems. Growing 2'–4'-tall, this spreading non-fern looks good all year round where it is hardy. Red berries are produced in late summer. This tender plant does well in deeply shaded, dry spots and neglected containers, as well as in rich, moist soil.

ASPIDISTRA elatior (aspidistra, cast-iron plant). Z7–10. The cast-iron plant gets its name from its unflappable constitution. Able to survive dry, deep shade, poor soil, and extreme heat, this 2'-tall plant is used primarily for its arching, glossy foliage. Cast-iron plant will do even better in rich, well-watered soil. In any case, situate it in deep or filtered shade in the coastal South. The creamy-white-striped 'Variegata' will light up a shady corner.

ASTER (aster). These tall, fall-blooming plants join boltonia and goldenrod at the back of the border to put on a good display when the rest of the garden is flagging. Like boltonia, they need a sunny, dry spot with perfect drainage and excellent air circulation. They are subject to mildew, but you can cut the plant back several times during the summer to alleviate this problem and still reap the benefits of prodigious flower production. The secret about asters is that they are really annuals that set out baby offsets just before they die each year.

A. carolinianus (climbing aster). Z6–9. This native vining plant needs a big space, up to 10'–15'. Its lavender blooms with yellow central disks appear in late fall but may continue on through January, depending on the weather. Shear it back in early spring.

A. x 'Fanny's Aster'. Z4–9. Blue flowers with yellow central disks proliferate late in the fall on this 2'–4'-tall Michaelmas daisy. It will eventually form a clump 4' wide.

A. grandiflorus (great aster). Z5–9. Large, violet-blue flowers are borne on 3'–4' plants in late fall. Bob McCartney, the native plant expert in Aiken, South Carolina, lists this as one of his all-time favorite plants.

A. x 'Hella Lacy'. Z4–9. This 3'-tall Michaelmas daisy does well for us in the coastal South. In late summer it's covered with deep blue, yellow-centered flowers.

A. laevis (smooth aster). Z4–9. Bright lavender-blue flowers with yellow centers are born on gray-leaved, purple-stemmed plants. They bloom late summer through fall. This robust, 4'-tall, vase-shaped clumper does well for us.

A. novae-angliae (New England aster). Z4–9. Give these drought-tolerant asters a position in full to part sun. The species grows 3'–6' tall in shades of pink and purple. There are also many hybrids (Michaelmas daisies) in shades of pink, red, white, blue, violet, and purple.

A. pringlei 'Montecasino' (Montecasino aster). Z4–9. This is a mildew-resistant, 3'–6'-tall white aster that blooms in September and October. It has a billowing habit with thread-like leaves.

A. tataricus (tatarian aster). Z3–9. This easy-to-grow, 7'-tall by 6'-wide giant is good for the back of the border. It produces sprays of lavender-blue daisies in late summer.

ASTERMOEA. See *KALIMERIS pinnatifida*.

ATHYRIUM

A. felix-femina (lady fern, wood fern's wife). Z3–8. This deciduous fern emerges in late spring, displaying arching, sharply pointed fronds and red or green stems. The spore clusters are arranged in double rows in a herringbone pattern on the underside of the frond. Lady fern colonizes by both rhizomes and spores. Like all ferns, she prefers moist to wet soil in full to partial shade, but she can stand a tad of sunlight and an occasional dry spell. There are dozens of selections of *A. felix-femina* available.

A. niponicum var. pictum (Japanese painted fern). Z4–8. Perhaps the most beautiful fern in the moist, partially sunny to partially shady garden, this deciduous gem has burgundy stems and tinted pinnae that are a mixture of gray, green, and silver. It colonizes where it is happy.

AUCUBA japonica 'Variegata' (gold dust plant). Z6–9. This slow-growing (to 6' tall), evergreen shrub is used to light up dark, shady corners. The glossy, toothed leaves are dark green splotched with yellow. Gold dust plant tolerates poor soils and competes well with tree roots in dry shade. Give it a position in full to light shade and prune to keep it in shape. Keep it from getting waterlogged in winter.

BACCHARIS halimifolia (groundsel bush, sea myrtle). Z3–9. This gray-leaved, native subshrub is valued as a windbreak at the beach. It grows wild in roadside ditches and sand dunes. In warmer areas it can grow to 10' tall. It produces white or yellowish-white flower corymbs in late summer and fall, followed by decorative silver seed heads. Groundsel bush demands full sun and perfect drainage. Cutting it back now and then will help keep it bushy.

BAPTISIA (false indigo). These lovely spring-blooming natives look something like lupines. Where happy, they will form large clumps. Plant *Baptisia* in full to part sun in porous, sandy, well-drained soil. Although they dislike being moved, you may divide the clumps every few years if you wish.

B. alba (white false indigo). Z4–9. This bushy perennial grows 2'–4' tall with attractive, blue-green foliage. It bears plentiful white flowers in early summer.

B. australis (blue false indigo). Z3–9. This native perennial takes several years to develop but, once developed, does well here, forming a large drought-tolerant clump 3'–4' tall. In early spring, blue, lupine-like flowers appear. The blue-green leaves are also very attractive. Black seedpods appear after the flowers have finished blooming.

B. pendula (white false indigo). Z5–8. In spring, tall spires of white pea-like flowers make an interesting contrast with the black stems and blue-green leaves. Grows 36" to 40" tall.

B. perfoliata. Z5–9. This fairly low-growing false indigo (12" high) has perfoliate, gray-green leaves and sprouts bright yellow flowers at its leaf axils in summer. It will form an erect groundcover, spreading to about 4' across.

B. x 'Purple Smoke'. Z3–9. Especially notable for its charcoal gray stems and smoky purple flowers with dark eyes. Once established, this is a very floriferous, drought-tolerant plant. It grows 4'–5' tall.

BEGONIA grandis (hardy begonia). Z6–10. Hardy begonias have copper-tinted, heart-shaped leaves and sprays of pink or white flowers in summer. This tuberous perennial grows into a 3'-tall branched plant in a rich, moist soil in filtered sunlight. Give it a good winter mulch.

BELAMCANDA chinensis (blackberry lily). Z5–10. These easy rhizomatous plants grow well under conditions similar to what daylilies like. They need full to partial sun and prefer a rich, well-drained soil, but they will tolerate clay and sandy soil. The loose flower clusters appear in July and August atop sturdy 3'–4' stalks in shades of yellow and orange with darker spots. The fans of foliage resemble iris leaves. The common name derives from the black seeds that appear when the fall seedpods split open.

BIGNONIA capreolata (cross vine). Z6–10. This vigorous southern native climbs easily to 30', using a combination of clinging tendrils and tiny, burrowing holdfasts. In spring it is covered with large, trumpet-shaped flowers that are brownish-red on the outside and yellow-orange on the inside. It will grow in full sun or light shade in rich, moist, well-drained soil. This is a semi-evergreen vine whose shiny, dark green leaves may acquire a purple-red tinge in winter. Prune your cross vine back after flowering to keep it under control. The cultivar 'Tangerine Beauty' provides a long season of bloom.

BIGNONIA jasminoides. *See* PANDOREA *jasminoides.*

BLETILLA striata (hardy orchid, Chinese ground orchid). Z5–10. This clump-forming bulb has upright, sword-shaped foliage that is noticeably pleated. It is a slow spreader, growing 12"–15" tall and producing white and magenta wands of orchid-like flowers in late spring. Plant the hardy orchid in part sun to light shade, in rich, well-drained soil that is kept moist. For best results, the soil should be made up of a mixture of sand, peat moss, and leaf mold. Hardy orchid also works in containers.

BOLTONIA asteroides (boltonia). Z4–9. This tall native produces clouds of small daisy-like blooms in August and September. It prefers full sun in good soil in a well-drained position. It seems to perform well in either moist or dry situations and can tolerate the occasional drought. For best results, cut your boltonia back by half in early summer and by half again in late June. Recommended varieties: 'Killer'—an excellent boltonia for our area, a 4'–5' bushy, prolific bloomer, with white daisy flowers; 'Snowbank'—masses of white flowers on 3'–4'-tall, multibranched plants; 'Pink Beauty'—pink starry flowers on multibranched plants that can reach 5' tall.

BOUGAINVILLEA (bougainvillea). Z9–11. This tender perennial vine or woody shrub may or may not survive our winters. To guard against this, you can grow it in a container and bring the plant inside when temperatures drop below freezing. Otherwise, plant it in a protected spot next to a sunny wall. It needs well-drained, sandy soil and full sun. Add some dolomitic limestone to the soil to increase the pH. It blooms best when it is root-bound. Keep it watered and give it a monthly application of fertilizer during the growing season.

The colorful bracts of these evergreen climbers appear in shades of white, pink, red, yellow, orange, purple, and coral. Be careful not to break off the fragile roots at planting time. Prune it back drastically after flowering to encourage more blooms and to keep it in shape.

BRUGMANSIA (angel's trumpet). Z8–10. A mature specimen of angel's trumpet will be laden with hundreds of huge (10"–12" long), pendulous, trumpet-shaped flowers, scenting the evening air from midsummer to fall. These shrubby, semi-evergreen or deciduous perennials grow 8'–10' tall with large, tropical-looking leaves. Angel's trumpet flower colors include pink, gold, orange, white, apricot, and pale yellow. Plant in full to part sun in rich, moist, well-drained soil. Prune back in early spring. Note: All parts of the plant are poisonous if ingested.

BRUNFELSIA *pauciflora* 'Floribunda' (yesterday-today-and-tomorrow). Z8b–10. This glossy-leaved, semievergreen perennial is tender and may not survive above Zone 9. Its name comes from its habit of producing clusters of spring flowers that usually start out purple, turn lavender, and end up white before they're finished. The flowers are tubular, opening to a flat disk. *Brunfelsia* prefers very rich, well-drained soil in a protected spot in part shade. Keep it evenly watered. It performs best when its roots are crowded, making it a good container plant. Fertilize it regularly during the growing season. It can grow 10' tall or can be kept pruned as a low shrub.

BUDDLEIA (butterfly bush). These terrific plants are excellent in the sunny summer garden. They produce months of nonstop bloom all the way into the fall and ask practically nothing in return. Prune them hard in early spring to keep them in shape and to encourage bloom, which occurs on new wood. Deadheading now and then during the summer will also give you more continuous bloom. Plant them in full sun in rich, well-drained soil, and water them during periods of drought. If you feel you must fertilize them, use alfalfa pellets rather than your regular by-the-bag fertilizer. And, yes, butterflies do adore these plants!

B. *alternifolia* (fountain buddleia). Z5–10. This butterfly bush needs a lot of space. If given its druthers, it reaches 10'–15' tall and equally wide. Arching branches that weep onto the ground are covered in slender, mauve racemes in late spring only. Because this one blooms on old wood, prune it lightly immediately after blooming.

B. *davidii* (summer lilac). Z5–10. This is an excellent species for our area. It can grow 5'–20' tall if left

on its own but can be kept pruned without much effort. Generally the leaves are small and gray-toned. The variegated forms may scorch in full sun and prefer a little shade. Cultivars: 'Black Knight'—deep purple panicles, smaller-leaved than other *Buddleias*; 'Harlequin'—gold-splashed green leaves and striking, large burgundy blossoms, this *Buddleia* grows only 6'–8' tall; 'Pink Delight'—a large-growing variety with green leaves and large trusses of true pink flowers; 'Potter's Purple'—clear violet flowers; 'Royal Red'—large maroon flowers; 'White Bouquet'—a highly floriferous white *Buddleia*; 'White Harlequin'—variegated foliage and white blossoms on a 5'-tall plant.

B. *davidii* var. *nanhoensis*. Z5–10. The Nanhos are somewhat smaller plants than other *Buddleias*, growing 4'–5' tall with smaller leaves. Cultivars: 'Nanho Blue'—large, periwinkle blue panicles and narrow, blue-gray foliage; 'Nanho Purple'—wine-colored flowers.

B. *lindleyana*. Z8–10. This heirloom butterfly bush differs from others in that it is semievergreen, spreads by underground stolons, does not require cutting back to the ground each year, and is much more drought tolerant than the *davidii* hybrids. In late summer the arching branches are covered with long, deep violet flower panicles. The shrub reaches 6' tall.

B. x 'Lochinch'. Z5–10. A fragrant, profusely blooming plant clothed in lilac-blue flowers with orange throats from summer through late fall. It reaches only 4'–5' tall and has silvery gray foliage.

B. x *weyeriana* 'Sungold'. Z5–10. This vigorous, large-leaved *Buddleia* blooms in a range of yellows from orangy to buttery. Prune this one in the middle of November. Some coastal gardeners find that this *Buddleia* doesn't hold up as well as the others, possibly because it is a favorite host of nematodes—especially in sandy soil.

BUTIA *capitata* (Butia palm, jelly palm). Z8–11. This hardy palm grows slowly 10'–20' tall. The pinnate, deeply divided, gray-green palm fronds arch out from the top of the thick trunk. Unless it is neatened up, the trunk will hang on to the remnants of the spent fronds. Up to 5'-long, yellow flower panicles are followed in summer by purple and yellow ovoid fruits. Give this palm full sun to part shade and perfectly drained soil.

CALAMAGROSTIS X *acutiflora* (feather reed grass). Z6–9. This slow-spreading grass grows 2'–6' tall with arching blades and erect stems topped with inflorescences in shades of silver, brown, and purple. The "feathers" appear in midsummer and last through winter. Feather reed grass grows in full sun to part shade and prefers wet feet, even enjoying clay. It tolerates hot summers. 'Karl Foerster' is a 6'-tall clumper that shows off in September with plentiful 3'-long, pinkish-bronze plumes, which turn pale brown as they age.

CALLICARPA *americana* (American beautyberry). Z6–10. This deciduous, native shrub takes full sun or part shade and prefers poor soil. It grows 5'–15' tall. In the fall its stems are clothed in a profusion of shiny, round, magenta fruits. Any leaves that are still hanging on at this point can be picked off to let the berries show to best effect. Flowers and fruit appear on new wood, so prune well in early spring. Plant beautyberry in groups for greater berry production. There are dwarf varieties and even some beautyberries that bear white fruit. Some of the Asian beautyberries, such as *C. bodinieri* var. *giraldii* 'Profusion', *C. rubella*, *C. dichotoma*, and *C. japonica*, produce purple berries in the fall that tend to stay on the plants longer than the American species.

CALLIRHOE (poppy mallow). Z6–9.

C. *involucrata* (poppy mallow, wine cups). This native perennial demands full, hot, baking sun with absolutely perfect drainage in order to perform well. It thrives on poor soil and inattention. Producing magenta-colored, cup-shaped flowers from late spring through early summer on 6"–18" stems, its stems and leaves are hairy, and the plant has a somewhat lax habit. Although it is a spreading plant, the stems do not root where they touch the ground; instead, the plant grows from a carrot-like tuber.

C. *digitata* (wine cups). This is an upright version of wine cups, with similar shaped flowers and finely dissected foliage on 4'-tall plants. A see-through plant, which may need staking.

CALLISTEMON *citrinus* (lemon bottlebrush). Z8b–11. This tender shrub or small tree grows 5'–25' tall, depending on how far south it is growing and how it is pruned. The narrow, lanceolate foliage is lemon-scented. In spring and summer, it bears showy, bottlebrush-shaped spikes of bright red flowers with prominent stamens. In Zones 9 and southward it blooms on and off year-round. Grow it in full sun in moist, well-drained, fertile soil. Although this is the most cold-hardy of the bottlebrushes, it will benefit from a good winter mulch. Also known as *C. lanceolatus*.

CAMELLIA (camellia, sasanqua). Z7–9. These are some of the most beautiful and reliable evergreen shrubs for the coastal South. The handsome leaves are dark green and glossy. There are hundreds of named cultivars in shades of white, pink, red, and bicolors. Blossoms may be single, semidouble, or double. Some blossoms resemble roses; others look more like peonies or anemones. Give your camellias and sasanquas a spot in shade or filtered sunlight and rich, moist, well-drained, acidic soil. Fertilize in early spring with an azalea-camellia fertilizer. Camellias and sasanquas generally grow 6'–10' tall, but over time they can become 20'–25'-tall trees. Prune, if desired, after flowering.

C. *japonica* (camellia). Depending on the cultivar, blooms anytime from December through March.

C. *sasanqua* (sasanqua). Leaves of the sasanquas are often slightly narrower and smaller than those of *C. japonica*. Their bloom season is from fall through early winter.

CAMPSIS (trumpet vine, trumpet creeper). This fast-growing, vigorous vine (25'–40') will grow in sun or shade but has fewer flowers in shade. The brightly colored, flared, tubular flowers are borne in clusters in summer. Trumpet vine prefers moist, well-drained soil but will tolerate dry conditions. As with other climbers, it may take a few years before the flowers appear. A major food source for hummingbirds, this plant may become invasive.

C. *grandiflora* (Chinese trumpet creeper). Z7–9. This 30'-long climber produces scarlet trumpets from early summer through frost. 'Morning Calm' is a particularly nice pink-tangerine-colored *grandifora*.

C. *radicans* (common trumpet vine). Z5–11. This 40'-long native bears clusters of orange and red, flared, tubular flowers from late summer through fall. The variety 'Flava' has yellow flowers. Also known as *Bignonia radicans*.

C. x *tagliabuana* 'Mme. Galen'. Z5–11. Considered by many to be the best trumpet creeper, 'Mme. Galen' has large, showy clusters of orangy-apricot-colored flowers in the late summer through fall. Another of Mme. Galen's pleasing attributes is that she is less invasive than *C. radicans*.

CANNA (canna lily, Indian shot). Z7b–10. Cannas are tuberous perennials, grown for the drama of their large (12"–24"-long), paddle-shaped leaves and dramatic flower spikes. The most familiar are the bright red and bright yellow varieties, which have been flowering in the South for generations. Cannas bloom nonstop from summer through frost with very little attention. They prefer full sun, rich compost, and wet feet but can tolerate light shade and poor soil. They don't suffer terribly from drought. By fall some of the outer leaves may become ratty looking, but they can be removed with no harm to the plant. If canna leaf rollers become a problem, dust with Dipel. Cultivars: 'Bengal Tiger'—6' tall with orange flowers, green-and-yellow-striped leaves with maroon edge (also sold as 'Pretoria'); 'Durban'—4'–5' tall, reddish-purple foliage striped with yellow and reddish-orange flowers; 'Le Roi Humbert'—red leaves and red blooms, 4'–8' plant; 'Minerva'—4' tall with green-and-white-striped leaves, red buds opening to butter-yellow flowers; 'Pink Sunburst'—4' tall with peach-colored blooms and variegated, cream-and-green-striped leaves with a pink cast; 'Pfizer's Chinese Coral'—2'–3' tall, coral pink flowers; 'Tropical Rose'—2' tall, rosy-pink flowers; 'Tropicana'—variegated red, pink, and yellow foliage with bright orange flowers. Note: The multicolored 'Stuttgart' is one of the few cannas that does not thrive in our climate; for best results, keep it in full shade.

CAREX (sedge). Z6–9. These clump-forming, low-growing ornamental grasses remain neat and tidy and can be used for edging and mixing with plants like hostas and ferns in part sun to full shade in constantly moist soil or in a pond or a bog. The golden (*C. elata* 'Bowles Golden') and variegated (*C. morrowii* 'Aureovariegata') sedges are especially good for lighting up dark areas. *C. glauca* is a small (6"-tall) blue sedge that stays compact.

CASSIA (cassia, senna). These tropical-looking, flowering shrubs put forth glorious yellow or gold blooms late in the summer. They combine well with Mexican bush sage, especially the all-purple variety. Plant cassia in full sun to part shade, and keep it watered during droughts. The following cassias may reach 10' in warmer parts of the coastal South. Prune them back severely after blooming to keep them in line. *Cassias* are in the process of being reclassified as *Sennas*. Whatever the name, butterflies love them.

C. alata (candlestick senna). Tender Z10. Gardeners along the coastal South grow this cassia as an annual because of its spectacular show of yellow flower spikes in the fall. Truly beautiful. Fertilize it regularly during the summer. If the winter is mild and your candlestick senna survives, prune it back the following spring to ensure more bloom.

C. bicapsularis. Z8–10. This is a semievergreen shrub that will die back to the ground in a hard frost. Spiky clusters of bright yellow flowers appear in late summer and fall.

C. corymbosa (golden senna). Z8–11. Rounded clusters of yellow flowers may appear anytime from late summer through fall. This is the hardiest of the cassias, growing to 7' tall. It may take a while to establish itself before flowering.

C. splendida (golden wonder). Z8–10. Loose clusters of orangy-yellow flowers are produced in late fall and into winter, depending on the severity of the weather.

CATHARANTHUS roseus (annual vinca, Madagascar periwinkle). Annual. One of the easiest, toughest, most heat-tolerant of all the summer annuals, annual vinca produces attractive, five-petaled flowers nonstop all summer long. The leaves on this spreading, somewhat bushy annual are a healthy, glossy green. Flower colors include white, pale pink, and shocking pink. Hybrids are available in varying heights, from 4" to 24". Give annual vinca a spot in full sun to part shade in fertile, well-drained soil. This is a drought-tolerant plant that doesn't need deadheading. It self-sows readily. Also known as *Vinca rosea*.

CELOSIA spicata (wheat celosia). Annual. Growing 3'–4' tall, this celosia looks more like an ornamental grass than the more familiar cockscomb celosias. The white or pink flower spikes resemble wheat sheaves. The purple-leaved varieties are especially handsome. Plant this tough annual in full sun.

CERATOSTIGMA (plumbago, leadwort). These groundcovers and shrubs provide deep blue flowers in late summer and fall.

C. griffithii (Griffith's leadwort). Z7–9. This evergreen groundcover does well for us. It grows 15" tall and spreads about 3', producing bright blue flowers from late summer through fall. The small, rounded leaves take on a reddish hue in fall. Best planted in part sun to light shade.

C. plumbaginoides (dwarf plumbago). Z6–9. This 6"–18"-tall semievergreen, rhizomatous groundcover is used widely along the coastal South. In the late summer and fall it produces dark, gentian blue flowers and the foliage turns a good reddish-bronze color. Give it a partially sunny position (protected from afternoon sun) and well-drained, moist soil, and it will spread readily. Cut it back after it finishes flowering. It is slow to leaf out in the spring, so be patient. Also known as *Plumbago larpentiae*.

C. willmottianum (Chinese plumbago). Z8–9. This 2'–4'-tall deciduous shrub likes perfect drainage and full sun. It is prized for its deep blue flowers in late summer and fall.

CESTRUM (cestrum). These fast-growing, somewhat tender shrubs can grow 8'–10' tall if you let them, but they can also be cut back regularly to keep them lower and bushier. Plant cestrum in full to part sun in a warm, protected spot in good garden soil. Mulch well in winter. Once established, they will tolerate some neglect. Cestrum tends to be herbaceous except in the warmest parts of the coastal South.

C. diurnum x nocturnum (hybrid jasmine). Z7–11. This very floriferous, 5'–7'-tall cestrum may be the hardiest of the group. It bears mustard yellow flowers all summer, followed by dark purple berries.

C. nocturnum (night-blooming jasmine). Z8b–10. This 6' tall, late summer and early fall bloomer has fragrant, tubular white flowers that give off a powerful scent at night. The flowers are followed by white berries.

C. parqui (willow-leaf jasmine). Z8–10. Pale yellow to yellow-green flower cymes bloom from spring through fall. Violet-brown berries follow.

C. roseum (pink cestrum). Z8b–10. Cymes of tubular pink flowers appear all summer, followed by red berries.

CHAMAEROPS humilis (European fan palm, Mediterranean fan palm). Z7–11. One of the hardiest of the palms for the coastal South, this is a good choice for containers or for adding drama to the perennial garden. With deeply lobed, blue-green, palmate fans 2'–3' long, this palm has a somewhat bushy habit. As it gets older, it spreads by suckering. This is an extremely slow growing palm that reaches 6'–20' tall, depending on how far south it is grown. It prefers a position in full sun with fertile, well-drained soil, however it tolerates poor soil and part shade.

CHASMANTHIUM latifolium (inland sea oats, river oats). Z5–9. This native ornamental grass grows about 3' tall and 2' wide in full sun to full shade but prefers a lightly shaded spot with rich, evenly moist soil. It will tolerate dry soil and beach conditions. The foliage is somewhat bamboo-like, and the stems are topped with nodding, green, oat-like seed panicles in late summer. The color of these spikelets moves from green to reddish purple and then to copper as the weeks wear on. These spikelets are often cut for dried flower arrangements. This grass self-sows, or you may propagate it by division. Cut plants to ground level in winter. Note: The sea oats that are grown extensively along the beaches to stabilize the sand dunes are *Uniola paniculata*.

CHRYSANTHEMUM (chrysanthemum). Almost all chrysanthemums have been reclassified into other genera. There are many chrysanthemums we can grow successfully in the coastal South. We do have to use some discretion, however, in which ones we choose. Plant them not too deeply in full sun with excellent drainage, keep them watered, and

fertilize them in spring and summer. All chrysanthemums benefit from at least one pinching back during the summer to keep them from getting leggy. Deadheading promotes a longer bloom season. Wet feet in winter may be fatal, so take care. If you venture beyond the standard fall grocery store mums, you may be rewarded by more delicate and more perennial plants.

C. frutescens. *See* ARGYRANTHEMUM *frutescens*.

C. leucanthemum. *See* LEUCANTHEMUM *vulgare*.

C. x morifolium (florist's chrysanthemum). Z5–9. This is what we normally think of when we think of chrysanthemums in all their hundreds of shapes, colors, sizes and habits. Mums have an internal flowering clock that responds to the length of the nights. In our area they may bloom during the long nights of spring as well as in the fall. It's best, however, to thwart this tendency and keep them pinched back until fall (stop pinching around mid-August). Divide the clumps every few years when the centers threaten to die out. These mums like very rich soil and routine fertilization. Protect them from the worst of the summer sun by giving them a slightly shaded spot. Also known as *Dendranthema grandiflora*.

C. nipponicum. *See* NIPPONANTHEMUM *nipponicum*.

C. pacificum. *See* AJANIA *pacifica*.

C. parthenium. *See* TANACETUM *parthenium*.

C. x rubellum (hybrid red chrysanthemum). Z4–8. These 2'–3'-tall, multibranched, woody clump-formers produce attractive pink to reddish flowers with yellow centers in late summer and early fall. They do well in our area and have a more relaxed, delicate appearance than florist's mums. In some cultivars, the foliage is silvery-gray. 'Clara Curtis' is a very floriferous, easy, pink cultivar with a raised yellow center. 'Mary Stoker' has peachy-yellow ray flowers with a greenish-yellow central disk. Also known as *Dendranthema zawadskii*.

C. x 'Ryan's Pink Daisy'. Z6–9. Unlike most chrysanthemums, this plant remains fairly bushy and compact without cutting back. In late summer and fall, large, single, pink daisies are produced on 1'–2' stems. This has proven to be a tough, dependable survivor in our area as long as it is given perfect drainage. Full sun or part shade.

C. x superbum. *See* LEUCANTHEMUM *superbum*.

C. x weyrichii. *See* DENDRANTHEMA *weyrichii*.

CHRYSOGONUM virginianum (golden star, green and gold). Z5–9. This low-growing (10"-tall) evergreen native is useful as a groundcover in sun or part shade. Five-petaled, bright yellow, star-shaped flowers appear mostly during the cooler weather of spring and fall. Planted in rich, moist, well-drained soil, it will spread rapidly.

CLEMATIS (clematis). There are hundreds of species and hybrids in the *Clematis* genus. Most are vines; some behave as herbaceous groundcovers. Install your clematis in rich, well-drained, moist soil with plenty of sunlight. The necessity for and timing of pruning varies with the cultivar. Many of the hybrid clematis take years to start blooming and are not known to be easy in our climate. However, when and if they do bloom, they are romantic and spectacular. Mix them with roses; let them ramble up shrubs, trees, and arbors; trail them from large containers. Some of the best-known cultivars are 'Henryi' (white), 'Comtesse de Bouchard' (pink), 'Nelly Moser' (pale pink and reddish-striped), 'Earl Markham' (rosy red), and *C. jackmanii* (deep blue), but there is no reason not to experiment with the many other varieties available. The following are the species clematis that do best for us.

C. armandii (evergreen clematis). Z8–9. This handsome vine grows to 25' with dark, glossy green, lanceolate leaves, which need only an occasional tidying up. In early spring *C. armandii* produces an abundance of highly fragrant, large, white cruciform blooms that perfume the garden with their scent. It does not require pruning and blooms on old wood.

C. montana (anemone clematis). Z6–9. In late spring this vigorous vine (15'–30' high) is covered with pale pink or white flowers highlighted by showy yellow anthers. To keep it in line, prune it back immediately after it finishes flowering. Anemone clematis is available in dark pink and mauve cultivars as well.

C. tangutica (golden clematis, Russian virgin's bower). Z6–9. Climbing 15' high, this gray-green clematis is highly floriferous. From midsummer to fall, it bears bright, golden yellow, bell-shaped flowers. Attractive, fluffy seed heads follow. Prune it back seriously after it finishes flowering or in early spring.

C. terniflora (sweet autumn clematis). Z4–9. Massive clouds of fragrant, starry white blossoms smother this native vine in late summer and early fall, followed by very attractive, fluffy seed heads. This is a durable, very easy, vigorous grower, which blooms in sun to part shade. Also known as *C. dioscoreifolia, C. paniculata,* and *C. maximowicziana.*

C. texensis (Texas clematis). Z4–9. From midsummer to fall this 8'–10' vine bears red, orange, or pink tulip-shaped flowers. Prune it back hard in late winter or early spring. The flowers of 'Gravetye Beauty' are a beautiful crimson-red. 'Duchess of Albany' has open, pale pink blooms with dark pink centers.

C. tibetana (orange peel clematis). Z6–9. This species is named for the way the thick yellow flower petals curve back from the center when the bell-like flowers appear in October. From late fall through winter the vine is smothered in striking, fluffy white seed heads. The foliage is blue-green. Prune in early spring.

C. viticella (virgin's bower, Italian bower vine). Z5–9. Open, bell-shaped flowers in colors ranging from purple to pink to blue adorn these semiwoody vines in summer. They are often grown through roses and other shrubs or up trellises. There are many named cultivars. Prune back hard in late winter or early spring.

CLERODENDRUM (glorybower). Plant *Clerondendrum* in good, moist soil in part shade. They tend to be multistemmed bushes that die back in the winter like herbaceous perennials. They spread by suckering and may eventually take over a large area. Intersperse medium-height companion plants with your *Clerondendrum,* to hide their somewhat awkward, adolescent-looking legginess. These are excellent plants for the coastal South.

C. bungei (stink plant or cashmere bouquet—take your pick). Z6–9. This old farmyard shrub, growing 3'–6' tall, deserves to be used more in the coastal South. It produces pleasantly fragrant, rosy-pink cymes in summer and fall. The heart-shaped leaves have a purplish cast in spring and have an unpleasant odor when crushed. It is stoloniferous and will spread readily if the soil is rich and moist. Hummingbirds love it.

C. indicum (electric light plant, Turk's cap). Z8–10. The common name for this evergreen plant comes from its striking red and green flower bracts. Purple fruits are produced in late summer and fall above these bracts. It grows to 8' tall but does best if cut back repeatedly during the summer to encourage bushiness. Some gardeners find it invasive.

C. speciosissimum (pagoda flower, glorybower, Java glorybean). Z8–11. This tender evergreen shrub with velvety leaves can grow to 12' tall. With a little attention, it can be kept pruned to a third that height. It bears bright red flower panicles from summer through fall, followed by blue, bean-shaped fruit. This is a good coastal plant.

C. thomsoniae (glorybower, bleeding heart vine). Z8–11. This twining, evergreen shrub grows to 6' tall. In late summer and fall it bears striking red and white flowers. Give it rich, loose soil.

C. trichotomum (Harlequin glorybower). Z8b–10. This is a southern classic, a multistemmed shrub growing to 10' and dying back in winter. Fragrant white and red tubular flowers are borne in late summer and fall, followed by beautiful, turquoise-blue berries. The red calyx portion of the flower remains on the shrub. A variegated-leaf form, 'Carnival', is also available.

C. ugandense (blue butterfly flower). Z8b–11. This somewhat tender evergreen shrub, with glossy green leaves, grows 6'–10' tall and bears five-petaled, violet-and-white flowers that resemble butterflies. The lower lip of each flower is long, and the stamens arch above the flower petals like butterfly antennae. Flowers are borne from August through October. This plant may not survive winter above Zone 9.

COLOCASIA (taro, elephant ear). Use these tuberous perennials for their terrific foliage in partially sunny to partially shady spots in wet to regularly watered, very rich garden soil. The more fertile the soil, the larger the leaves. They are late to emerge, so watch out for where you planted them. *Colocasias* also work well in containers and in aquatic settings.

C. x **'Black Magic'**. Z7b–10. Deep plum to black leaves on a 3'–6'-tall clumping, herbaceous plant. By midsummer the leaves will have turned almost black and will be very large (2' long). This is one of the most wonderful plants you can grow in your perennial garden!

C. esculenta **'Fontanesii'** (black- or violet-stemmed elephant ear). Z7b–10. This giant grows 6'–7' tall, with 4'-long leaves that always have a slick, oiled-looking sheen. The stems are dark violet-black and the leaves have violet-black veins and margins. This tuberous plant is stoloniferous. The tubers are used in Polynesian cooking to make the food staple, poi.

C. esculenta **'Illustris'** (black-leaf taro). Z7–10. Notable for the black zones on the leaves outlined with green veins. This 2'–3'-tall, tuberous taro takes full sun to full shade, but the color will be darker in sun.

C. fallax (silver-leaf taro). Z7–10. This dwarf, groundcover-type taro boasts a silver stripe down the middle of its leaf and silver veining. Give it shade and rich, moist soil for best results. It grows 18" tall.

CONRADINA canescens (beach rosemary). Z5–9. It is not always easy to find gray-leaved plants that don't succumb to our summer humidity. Happily, beach rosemary thrives in our climate. This southeastern native, woody subshrub has fragrant gray leaves and tubular lavender flowers in spring. It is an excellent, drought-tolerant beach plant. Growing 1'–2' tall, it needs a position in full sun or light shade with perfect drainage. Widely used along the Gulf Coast.

CONSOLIDA ambigua (larkspur). Annual. The annual larkspur (also known as *Delphinium ajacis*) substitutes for the perennial delphinium in the coastal South. Gardeners sow the seeds in the fall in rich, slightly alkaline soil in full sun. From late spring to early summer we can enjoy the 1'–2'-tall delphinium-like spires in shades of blue, white, pink, or purple. The plants are such reliable reseeders that larkspur can become a quasi-perennial member of the garden. The old-fashioned strains work best for us.

CORDYLINE australis (giant dracaena, cordyline, New Zealand cabbage palm). Z8–10. Cordylines are striking accent plants for the perennial garden. When they are young, their 1'–3'-tall, light green, sword-shaped leaves, some erect and some arching, give the plant a resemblance to the phormiums. A mature cordyline can reach 10'–30' tall and looks more like a palm tree. If you want to create a multitrunked plant, cut cordyline back while it is young. In summer, panicles of small, cream-colored flowers appear. Cordylines can take full sun or light shade and prefer well-drained, fertile soil. 'Atropurpurea' is a handsome bronze-leaved variety. 'Variegata' has creamy-white striped foliage. 'Purple Tower' is flushed a dark plum color.

COREOPSIS (coreopsis, tickseed). There are over a hundred species of this common garden perennial. They do not tend to be long-lived for us, but they are useful nevertheless. Their cultural requirements vary depending on the species, but they all prefer full or part sun.

C. auriculata **'Nana'** (mouse ear coreopsis). Z4–9. This 1'–2'-tall native blooms from late spring through summer if given exactly the right conditions—ample moisture and loose, fast-draining soil.

C. integrifolia (Chipola River coreopsis). Z7–9. This 2'–3'-tall native makes a blanket of bright yellow flowers with dark eyes in late summer and fall. It prefers rich, very moist soil and can stand boggy conditions. A good performer in our area.

C. grandiflora (tickseed). Z4–9. The best known of the coreopsis plants, *grandiflora* does best if it is given a hot, sunny location in perfectly drained, poor soil. It will thrive on full, baking sun and minimal watering. Remove spent flower stalks for continuous bloom from late spring to midsummer. 'Early Sunrise', an 18"-tall plant that produces double, bright yellow flowers all summer, is one of the first coreopsis to bloom and is one of the best for us because of its drought tolerance.

C. helianthoides (swamp tickseed). Z7–10. This native of eastern North Carolina grows 2'–3' tall in bogs and in regular soil. In late summer and fall it is covered with yellow daisy flowers.

C. lanceoata (lanceleaf coreopsis). Z3–8. This species is quite similar to *grandiflora* and has the same cultural requirements. This native, 1'–2'-tall coreopsis is an excellent plant for the coastal South. It may take a year or two to get firmly established. It can also tolerate a location in part shade. Recommended varieties: 'Baby Sun'—dense, 12"–18"-tall plants with orangy-yellow flowers; 'Goldfink'—short, 9"-tall plant with single yellow flowers with orange centers.

C. pulchra (beautiful coreopsis). Z6–9. This durable native produces lemon yellow flowers with a red eye all summer long. The foliage is fine-leaved. Give it hot, baking sun with perfect drainage.

C. verticillata (threadleaf coreopsis). Z5–9. These delicate, feathery beauties must have dry, baking sun. Where they are happy, they will form sizable clumps and bloom for a long time in summer. If you shear them back, you may get a second bloom in the fall. Recommended varieties: 'Golden Showers'—a 2'-tall plant producing large, bright yellow flowers; 'Zagreb'—a good, tough plant for the South, it grows to about 18" tall and stays fairly compact, bearing flowers of orangy-yellow. Note: *C. verticillata* 'Moonbeam' (moonbeam coreopsis) and *C. rosea* (pink coreopsis) are extremely poor performers in our climate. They are not recommended.

CORTADERIA selloana (pampas grass). Z6–9. This sharp-edged, incredibly durable ornamental grass is the signature plant of many beach communities. Large showy plumes emerge on 4'–7'-tall plants in summer and persist throughout the winter. Look for dwarf and variegated varieties as well as those with pink plumes. Pampas grass is easy to grow in full sun in regular to sandy soil. The old foliage can be removed in spring if you feel like neatening it up. Propagation by division is no laughing matter and requires an axe (no joke).

COSTUS (spiral ginger, crepe ginger). Z7b–10. These subtropical beauties grow in part sun to full shade in rich, moist, well-drained soil. The common name comes from the way the leaves spiral around the stems. These clumping, rhizomatous perennials appreciate a few applications of manure or fertilizer and plenty of water during the summer to help them out with their showy late summer and fall blooms. The inflorescences consist of a pinecone-like clutch of colored bracts at the end of each flowering stem, from which the actual flowers appear. The visual interest comes from the combination of the color, shape, and texture of the bracts and the flowers. Keep these plants dry in winter and protect them with a good winter mulch. They can be used in containers. Their habit is somewhat lax and spreading.

C. barbatus (red tower ginger). With stems growing to 6' tall, this ginger bears bright red bracts topped with yellow flowers.

C. igneus (fiery costus). Showy yellow or orange flowers appear at the end of 2'-long stems. Also known as *C. cuspidatus*.

C. specisosus (spiral ginger, crepe ginger). This is one of the largest spiral gingers, growing 4'–10' tall. Felty, elliptical leaves appear in spiral formation on the top half of the stems. The inflorescences consist of reddish-purple bracts and white or pink crepey flowers. The interiors of the flowers are flushed yellow.

C. spiralis (spiral flag ginger). This 4'–6'-tall ginger produces inflorescences of orange cones with pink or red flowers.

CRINUM (crinum lily). Z8–11. There are many species and hybrids of these herbaceous, perennial bulbs. Dramatic spidery or trumpet-shaped flowers 4"–6"-long appear on erect, 1'–5'-tall stalks between spring and fall. Colors include white, pink, lavender, and red. In some cases the flower trumpets are striped with pink or maroon. Foliage is dark green, long, and strappy. Crinums will bloom in sun to part shade. They prefer rich, moist soil. They even enjoy bog conditions. Plant them with the neck of the bulb slightly above soil level. Because they develop a huge root system, they need plenty of room to spread. Don't dig up your crinums if you can help it—they resent being disturbed. Although crinums are tough, reliable plants for the coastal South, they may take several years to get established before they begin to flower.

C. americanum (Southern swamp lily, Florida crinum). This native crinum will bloom in full shade. Its natural habitat is in swamps and at the water's edge.

C. asiaticum (grand crinum, St. John's lily). Fragrant, spidery, white flower umbels appear atop 2' stalks in spring and summer in sun or shade. This plant is huge and so is its root system.

C. x powelliii 'Album' (Powell's white hybrid crinum). This stately, 5'-tall crinum bears flared, pendent, white flower trumpets in late summer and fall.

CROCOSMIA X crocosmiflora (crocosmia, montbretia). Z5–11. These easy, cormous perennials have erect, sword-shaped foliage and 2'–3'-tall zigzag stems that are covered with small, funnel-shaped flowers in early summer. Colors range from buttery to golden yellow through the reds and oranges. Plant the corms about 3" deep in full sun to light shade in well-drained soil. Excellent as cut flowers also, they benefit from bulb booster in spring. For best flowering, divide every few years. Cultivars: 'Golden Fleece'—clear, primrose yellow flowers on 2'–3' stems; 'Lucifer'—one of the most widely grown crocosmias, with brilliant scarlet flowers.

CUPHEA. Z8–10. Grow these long-blooming, somewhat tender perennials in full sun to part shade in fertile, moist, well-drained soil. In most areas of the coastal South they will die back to the ground in the winter and should be given a protective winter mulch.

C. cyanea. This 3'-tall subshrub bears racemes of orange tubular flowers tipped in a yellowish-green from summer through fall.

C. hyssopifolia (Mexican heather). From spring through fall, tiny lavender, pink, or white flowers appear on this shrubby 6'–12'-tall plant with small, glossy green leaves. Useful in containers or as an edging plant.

C. ignea (cigar plant). This compact, shrubby perennial grows to 1'–3' tall with glossy, lanceolate foliage. From summer through fall it bears single, bright red, tubular flowers with a white band and tiny, dark petals at the tip.

C. micropetala (Mexican cigar flower, cigarette plant). Another wonderful *Cuphea* for the coastal South, this arching shrub grows 3'–5' tall with shiny, dark green foliage. From summer through fall it is covered with orangy-red tubular flowers with yellow edging.

CURCUMA (hidden cone ginger). These rhizomatous ginger relatives, grown for the tropical look of their foliage and flowers, are hardy for us. They prefer part sun to light shade and rich, moist soil. These are just several of the dozens of varieties that will work for us.

C. elata (giant pink ginger, giant plume ginger). Z8–10. These large-leaved, 5'-tall, erect plants sprout dramatic, pinecone-like pink and yellow flowers at their base in early summer.

C. petiolata (hidden lily). Z8–10. The hardiest of all the *Curcumas*, this may be the easiest one to find in the trade. It is an excellent plant for the coastal South, growing to 2'–3' tall with striking, tropical-looking foliage. The midsummer inflorescences are made up of spikes of deep violet and green bracts surrounding small yellow and white flowers. You may have to look carefully among the leaves to see the inflorescences, hence the common name. This is a southern classic. The variegated-leaf version is also excellent.

C. zedoaria (pride of Burma). Z8–10. These huge, 7'-tall plants have green-and-maroon-striped leaves. Red and yellow pinecone-like flowers are produced on 1' spikes in early summer.

CYCAS revoluta (sago palm). Z8b–11. These slow-growing, somewhat tender evergreen plants are cycads rather than palms, but in maturity they look like palms. They begin life looking trunkless, with stiff, leathery, feather-shaped leaves arching out from a central crown. Eventually they grow to 10' tall, with a single trunk and a classic palm-like appearance. With age, the trunk tends to lie on the ground. Sagos may not be able to withstand temperatures below 10°. They are adaptable to full sun, part sun or part shade with rich, well-drained soil. Give them a protective winter mulch.

CYRTOMIUM falcatum (holly fern). Z6–10. This is a large (2' to 3' tall and wide), handsome, dark green, glossy-leaved fern that retains its fronds in a very presentable condition all winter long and puts forth bright green, fresh ones in spring. Plant in rich, moist soil in light to deep shade. Carefree and durable, this is a good plant for pulling together those otherwise troublesome, blah spots in the neglected shady garden.

DAHLIA (dahlia). Z4–8. These well-known tubers produce flowers in a large variety of colors, sizes, and shapes. When they are happy, they flower nonstop from early summer through frost, either in the garden or in containers. Unfortunately, they are not particularly suited to our climate. They suffer from fungal disease and pests. If you decide to grow them, give them full sun, rich soil, perfect drainage, and a protective winter mulch. During the growing season they appreciate deep, regular watering, a low-nitrogen fertilizer, and a top dressing of aged manure. Pinching back will encourage bushiness. Deadheading will promote continuing blooms. Taller varieties need to be staked to keep them upright. In Zones 8 and below we can leave them in the ground over winter as long as the drainage is perfect. Gardeners north of Zone 8 lift them in the fall and replant again in the spring.

DAUCUS carota var. carota (Queen Anne's lace). Z3–10. This classic wildflower is known for its lacy umbels of tiny white flowers, which bloom from late spring through early summer. Foliage is finely dissected and resembles carrot tops. Queen Anne's lace grows 3'–6' tall, depending on the location and growing conditions. A biennial that will freely reseed itself if given the opportunity, it will grow in just about any type of soil, in sun or part shade.

DECUMARIA barbara (climbing hydrangea). Z6–10. Plant this vigorous, 40', semievergreen, native climber in full or part shade in rich, loamy soil. It prefers moist spots but can stand to be dry. It climbs by aerial roots into trees or up other supports, producing fragrant white flower corymbs in summer above glossy, dark green leaves. It can also be used as a groundcover.

DELOSPERMA cooperi (ice plant). Z7–10. Ice plant has small, needle-shaped, succulent leaves that will form a 5"-tall, mat-like groundcover or spill over the side of a container. The flowers are showy, magenta-purple daisies that complement the foliage perfectly. Ice plant's main season of bloom is from midspring through midsummer, but it will bloom on and off well into the fall and winter. There is a yellow-flowering species that is not nearly as successful for us as the purple. Plant *Delosperma* in full, baking sun with perfect drainage.

DENDRANTHEMA grandiflora. *See* CHRYSANTHEMUM *morifolium*.

DENDRANTHEMA weyrichii (pink daisy). Z3–8. These foot-high, mat-forming perennials were formerly classified in the genus *Chrysanthemum*. They produce 2"-wide daisy flowers in late summer and fall. The ray petals may be white or pink, and the central disks yellow. Foliage is glossy green and lobed. They will perform well for us if given fertile, loose, sandy soil, perfect drainage, and full sun. 'Pink Sheffield' is an excellent old-fashioned variety with pale pink ray petals. (Also known as *Chrysanthemum weyrichii*.)

DENDRANTHEMA zawadskii. *See* CHRYSANTHEMUM *x rubellum*.

DIANTHUS (pinks, carnations, Sweet William). There are such a large number of excellent species and hybrids of *Dianthus* that every garden should make room for at least a few of these old cottagey plants. The cottage pinks survive extreme heat in summer, and the Sweet Williams give us color in winter and early spring when little else is in bloom. Most all *Dianthus* need full sun, perfect drainage, and good air circulation. The gray-leaved varieties especially will thrive in poor soil in parched conditions. If your soil is extremely acidic, you may want to mix in some agricultural lime. Flower production will increase if the plant is left in the same spot over a period of several years.

D. x alwoodii (modern pinks). Z4–9. This species is noted for its blue-gray foliage and neat pink, red, or white flowers. Pinks grow from 3"–18" tall. Some gardeners use a gravel mulch around these perennials to help prevent fungal disease in our hot, humid summers. Cultivars: 'Frosty Fire'—a diminutive 6"-tall variety with brilliant red, double flowers; 'Helen'—grows 12" tall and sports fragrant, deep salmon-pink flowers.

D. barbatus (Sweet William). Z3–9. These excellent biennials prefer full sun but will tolerate some shade. They tend to perennialize in our climate, especially if lifted and divided every few years. Their flat-topped flower clusters bloom in shades of white, pink, and red, often flowering during the warm spells of winter. Their narrow, dark green foliage is evergreen. The main season of bloom for Sweet William is spring through early summer. Some are low spreaders and some have erect stems to 18" tall. Great plants for the coastal South.

D. deltoides (maiden pinks). Z3–9. These pinks are particularly good for our climate as they won't melt out the way others might. This is a low-growing, mat-forming plant with grassy green leaves that take on a reddish tinge in cool weather. Pink or purple flowers appear atop 18" stems for many weeks in summer. Shear them after flowering for an additional flush of flowers.

D. gratianopolitanus (cheddar pinks). Z3–9. These are blue-green or gray-leaved mat-forming plants that need baking sun and a dry position to do well. Given the right conditions, they will bloom in spring and again in summer. The shorter varieties can be used as a groundcover or for edging, for planting between pavers, and for situating along the harsh heat of sidewalks and hell strips. Recommended: 'Bath's Pink'—a good, tough plant with evergray foliage and fragrant, light pink flowers; 'Firewitch'—a neat, compact, blue-gray-foliaged plant with single magenta flowers that withstands our summer heat admirably.

D. plumarius (cottage pinks, grass pinks). Z3–9. Cottage pinks have gray-blue foliage similar to cheddar pinks and similar cultural requirements.

DICENTRA (bleeding heart). These well-loved favorites with their delicate, pendulous, heart-shaped blooms need rich, moist soil in a shady spot in order to survive. They are not as well suited to our area as they are to cooler climates, but some gardeners in the coastal South are able to grow them.

D. eximia (fringed bleeding heart). Z3–9. Dangling, pink, heart-shaped blooms are borne on 12"–18" stems above delicately dissected, gray-green leaves. This plant loves a rich loam with a top dressing of leaf mold and must be kept moist. It does better for us than *D. spectabilis*. 'Alba' is a white cultivar.

D. x 'Luxuriant'. Z4–9. This is a good bleeding heart for our area, with cherry red flowers from midspring to early summer on a 10"–15"-tall plant.

D. scandens (climbing bleeding heart). Z7b–9. If you can get it to grow for you, climbing bleeding heart will reward you with racemes of butter-yellow flowers from late spring through fall. This very delicate-looking vine climbs by wrapping its tendrils around whatever is nearby. It can grow to 10' in light shade to full sun. Give it rich soil and keep it watered.

D. spectabilis (common bleeding heart). Z2–8. The foliage of this bleeding heart will go dormant in our hot summers. Pink and white hearts appear in spring. Make sure this plant gets ample moisture or you will lose it.

DICLIPTERA suberecta (hummingbird plant). Z7b–11. In late spring and summer reddish-orange tubular flowers adorn this 2'-tall, arching, woody subshrub. The gray-green, woolly foliage is attractive as well. Give *Dicliptera* a position in full sun or light shade with excellent drainage. Use it in a mixed perennial border, in a container, or as a deciduous groundcover. This is a survivor. It needs no attention, no pruning, no pesticides, and it likes the beach.

DIETES vegeta (African iris, butterfly iris, fortnight lily). Z8–10. This 4'-tall, cormous plant blooms from spring through fall, sending up waxy white blossoms with yellow and purple spots, somewhat resembling Japanese iris. The plant forms fan-shaped clumps with branched, flowering stalks that somewhat resemble crocosmia. The common name fortnight lily comes from the plant's habit of blooming approximately every two weeks. Blooms will continue to appear from spring through fall and occasionally even during the winter, if temperatures are not severe. This is a somewhat tender perennial and needs a protected spot in sun or part shade with a good winter mulch, especially in the northern reaches of the coastal South. *Dietes* performs well in both wet and dry soils. Also known as *D. iridoides*.

DIGITALIS (foxglove). These storybook biennials or cool-weather annuals are grown best in moist, rich, well-drained soil in partial sun to light shade.

They send up freckled pastel flower spires in late spring and early summer. The most commonly grown foxglove is the self-seeding biennial *D. pupurea*, but strawberry foxglove (*D. mertonensis*) is somewhat longer lived.

D. grandiflora (yellow foxglove). Z3–9. This is an extremely tough foxglove with dark green, hairy leaves and 2'–3'-tall spires of greenish-yellow flowers veined with brown.

D. x mertonensis (strawberry foxglove). Z3–9. This clump-forming perennial grows 2'–4' tall with healthy-looking, toothed foliage and coppery pink spires. It generally will persist for several years in the garden and will self-sow.

D. purpurea (common foxglove). Z4–9. In spring, one-sided spikes of lavender flowers with purple and white interior spots appear on this plant's 3'–6' stems. They will flower for about a month, after which the plants can be removed or left to set seed. 'Foxy' is an especially welcome hybrid in that it will bloom the first spring from seed sown the previous fall; its colors include red, pink, pale yellow, white, and purple.

DOLICHOS lablab (Hyacinth bean vine). Annual. This is one of those annual vines that are worth making room for in the garden. All summer long, this 10' twiner is clothed in large (3"–6" long), dark-plum-colored, ovate leaves. In late summer, clusters of long-stemmed lavender and white flowers appear. The most wonderful aspect of this plant, however, is the fall fruit: bright purple bean pods that look like something out of a Dr. Seuss story. Plant the seed directly in the ground in a sunny spot after the frost-free date. Keep the vine watered during dry spells. In the southernmost parts of the coastal South this vine will overwinter.

DRACAENA australis. *See* CORDYLINE *australis*.

DRYOPTERIS (wood fern). This genus boasts well over a thousand species and hybrids, some of which do very well in the coastal South. They ask only for rich, moist soil in a shady spot where they will increase in size and beauty as the years go by.

D. affinis (scaly male fern, golden male fern). Z6–8. The highly dissected fronds of this semievergreen fern start out a light chartreuse green and darken as they mature. The midrib is golden brown and scaly. Scaly male ferns grow 1'–4' tall.

D. erythrosora (autumn fern). Z5–9. One of the very best ferns to grow in our gardens, the autumn fern remains evergreen in winter. Its unfurling copper-colored crosiers are a delight to behold. Plant it in full shade to part sun.

D. cycadina (shaggy shield fern). Z8–10. This is a tough, deciduous fern that can stand drought conditions. It sends up erect, lance-shaped fronds. Also known as *D. atrata*.

D. filix-mas (male fern). Z4–9. There are many varieties of *D. filix-mas* that stay fresh looking all summer and don't mind being dry from time to time. 'Undulata robusta' is an especially handsome, vigorous cultivar.

D. ludoviciana (Southern shield fern). Z6–10. This is a native evergreen fern with shiny green foliage that deals well with our heat and humidity.

ECHINACEA purpurea (purple coneflower). Z3–9. The foliage of this simple native wildflower is coarse and dark green. Pink, slightly recurved, daisy-like flowers with dark brown centers are borne on stems 2'–5'-tall, depending on the cultivar. Coneflowers need full sun, excellent drainage, and neutral to slightly alkaline soil. Wet feet in winter will kill them. Coneflowers tolerate heat, drought, and poor soil admirably and are good for beach plantings. They are beloved of butterflies. Birds and bees will come by too. Don't divide these coneflowers. Instead let them self-seed. Cultivars: 'Bravado'—large, rosy red flowers on 2'-tall plants; 'Bright Star'—excellent rose-colored flower with thick healthy foliage; 'Leuchstern'—rosy purple flowers with down-turned petals on 2' stems; 'Magnus'—one of the best, most drought-tolerant coneflowers for our area, 'Magnus' bears striking, crimson-purple flowers (7" across) on 3' stems for a long time in midsummer; 'White Swan'—creamy white flowers on 2' stems. Note: White coneflowers tend not to be as long-lived as their pink coneflower sisters.

ENDYMION hispanicus. *See* **HYACINTHOIDES** *hispanica.*

ENSETE ventricosum 'Maurelii' (red Abyssinian banana). Z8–10. Each leaf on this dramatic subtropical can reach 10' long. New foliage is a deep red. Culture same as *Musa*.

ERIGERON karvinskianus (Mexican daisy). Z8–10. This is a spreading, woody perennial with hairy, gray-green leaves and a lax habit. It bears small, pinkish-white, double-petaled daisies on 1'–2'-high stems all summer and into fall. Plant Mexican daisy in full to part sun in well-drained, sandy soil. This plant is good between paving stones, in a rock garden, or in containers and will naturalize where it's happy. Give it a thick winter mulch in cooler areas.

ERYNGIUM (sea holly). These drought-resistant, spiny-leaved plants do well in ordinary garden soil as well as in poor, sandy soil. They thrive in full sun and are good for beach gardens, in part

because of their long taproots. Their thistle-like, lilac-colored flowers are composed of bristly, spiny bracts with upright blue cones in the center. The leaves of sea holly are gray-green and usually spiny. We don't get the bluish tint in the foliage that our northern friends do because our summer nights are too warm. Sea hollies make great dried flowers.

E. amethystinum (amethyst sea holly). Z2–9. This 2'-tall evergreen sea holly has steely blue flowers in summer.

E. foetidum (wild coriander, Mexican coriander). Z8–11. This herb grows wild in many hot parts of the world and is used widely in cooking the same way as coriander (*Coriandrum sativum*). Known variously as "recao," "culantro," "herbe à fer," and "chadon benée," it is a tough plant that tolerates heat and humidity admirably. The edges of the whorled, dark green, basal leaves have small spines —not nearly as fierce as those of other *Eryngiums*. Flowers are greenish-white.

E. planum (flat sea holly). Z5–9. Silver-blue flower heads appear in summer on these 3'-tall plants. This species is especially tolerant of our heat and humidity.

E. yuccifolium (rattlesnake master). Z4–9. These 3'–6'-tall, multibranched natives have narrow, spiny, yucca-like basal leaves topped with greenish-white button flowers in summer.

ERYTHRINA (coral tree). These perennials are well suited to the coastal South. They are valued for their eye-catching, bright red flowers and the attractive red beans that appear when the seedpods split open in fall. Note that the beans are highly poisonous.

E. x bidwillii (hybrid coral bean). Z7b–10. This 6'-tall, deciduous, thorny shrub can grow to a 20' tree in the warmest parts of the coastal South. Prized for its spectacular display of erect, dark red flower racemes, which grow 1'–2' long, it blooms throughout the summer. This easygoing perennial loves a hot, sunny, dry location. Cut back branches after flowering. Give it a dry, protected spot and a good winter mulch above Zone 9.

E. crista-galli (crybaby tree). Z8–10. A southeastern coastal classic, this woody perennial grows to 5' tall, but will become a 20' tree in the warmest zones. From spring through fall its spiny branches are decorated with racemes of waxy, orange-red flowers, which "cry" drops of nectar. Cut back branches after each flowering. Give your crybaby tree a poor, dry spot in full sun.

E. herbacea (coral bean plant, mamou). Z8–10. This southeastern native is a deciduous woody shrub or small tree. It can be kept pruned back to

3' tall or allowed to grow as high as 15'. In summer it produces showy scarlet spikes that shoot up as much as a foot above the leaves. Coral bean does well all along the coastal South. Plant in full sun to light shade in fertile, moist, but well-drained soil. It is drought tolerant once established.

EUCOMUS COMOSA (pineapple lily). Z7–10. *Eucomus* is a tropical-looking plant with long, strappy leaves and unique pineapple-like flowers on 18" stems in summer. The blooms last on the plant for a long time. These bulbs want to be planted in full sun and given adequate watering. They can stand clay or sand. *E. bicolor* (also known as *E. comosa* 'Purpurea') has a slightly taller flower stalk and is tinged with purple in the flowers and foliage.

EUONYMUS fortunei (wintercreeper). Z5–9. This is a tough, trailing, evergreen groundcover (spreading out 15' long). It grows about a foot high in sun or shade. It can even stand dry shade and a little foot traffic. As its name suggests, it grows during cool weather and rests in the summer. Its tiny, tough leaves may be marked with cream, gold, or pink, depending on the variety. 'Emerald 'n' Gold' is an excellent groundcover with bright yellow leaf margins.

EUPATORIUM (Joe Pye weed). These hardy natives are important additions to the late summer and fall garden for their reliability and for the architectural effect they have. They do just as well in the garden as they do in neglected ditches by the side of the road. Most of them like full to part sun and moist soil, although they can tolerate drought. They can stand to be whacked back several times during the summer to make them bushier and to increase the flower production in the fall. Stop your whacking by the end of July though. All the Joe Pye weeds attract butterflies.

E. coelestinum (mistflower, hardy ageratum). Z6–10. This almost too-easy rhizomatous plant will spread around your garden in no time. Bright blue, densely packed corymbs appear atop 2'–3'-tall plants in late summer and early fall, brightening up the entire garden. Because they have a tendency to look lanky and weedy, the best bet is to shear your hardy ageratum a few times during summer to get them more bushy and presentable for their fall coming-out party. They even bloom in part shade. Definite no-brainers. Recommended varieties: 'Cori'—a bright blue hybrid; 'Wayside Form'—a shorter (15"-tall) blue hybrid.

E. fistulosum (giant Joe Pye weed). Z4–9. If you obtain the true *fistulosum* species, you will be growing a giant with bamboo-like stalks that progress upward to 12', taking people's breath away. In midsummer, huge lavender blooms appear, making the butterflies delirious.

E. maculatum (spotted Joe Pye weed). Z5–9. This 6'-tall species is known for the purple spots on its stems. Blooms are pink, purple, or white.

E. purpureum (sweet Joe Pye weed). Z3–9. This common native is underused in our gardens. In late summer you will enjoy clouds of rosy purple, which appear on sturdy stems 6'–9' tall. This plant likes full sun and plenty of water. Butterflies flock to it.

E. hyssopifolium (hyssop-leaf Joe Pye weed). Z5–9. This native may be our answer to baby's breath, with its airy white blooms that appear on 4' stems in late August. The really good news is that it takes a dry, shady location.

Note: *E. rugosum* is not recommended for our climate, because it requires cooler nighttime temperatures than we can give it.

EUPHORBIA (spurge). This genus covers an enormous variety of plants, some of which don't do particularly well for us and some that are useful but short-lived. The three described below are all groundcovers. Euphorbs like full sun, good drainage, and water in periods of drought. Don't let them sit in a wet spot during the winter.

E. characias (Mediterranean spurge). Z7–10. This woolly-stemmed subshrub or groundcover with blue-gray foliage grows about 1' tall and looks best during the cooler weather. It is clothed with chartreuse inflorescences in early spring. It is not long-lived in our area, but it tends to self-sow.

E. cyparissias (cypress spurge). Z4–9. This low-growing (4"–16" tall), finely textured, blue-green cypress look-alike spreads by stolons. Sulfur yellow inflorescences appear in summer. It prefers poor, dry soil and baking sun.

E. myrsinites (myrtle euphorbia, myrtle spurge). Z5–9. This low-growing, trailing, blue-green groundcover with succulent spiraling leaves tolerates our hot summers well. However, it will probably be short-lived. In spring it is clothed in sulphur yellow inflorescences that contrast well with the foliage.

EURYOPS pectinatus 'Viridis' (green-leaved bush daisy). Z8–10. This woody subshrub grows 2'–4' tall with an equal spread and is covered during the cooler months of spring and fall with bright yellow daisies. The dark green, deeply divided foliage is attractive year-round. The flowering will slow down or stop altogether during our hot summer weather. The plant needs full sun and impeccable drainage. It is excellent grown in containers and withstands beach conditions. Give your bush daisy extra protection from cold spells by covering it with burlap or a cotton sheet topped with pine straw. Reputedly, this green-leaved bush daisy performs better for us in the coastal South than its gray-leaved relatives.

FATSIA japonica (fatsia). Z8–10. An excellent evergreen shrub for full or part shade, fatsia is grown primarily for its dramatic, dark green, leathery foliage. The many-lobed, palmate leaves are very large (1'–1½' across) and keep their attractive appearance throughout winter. In fall and winter, fatsias produce striking umbels of greenish-white, spherical flower clusters followed by black berries. A great architectural plant, fatsia grows 5'–12' tall.

FICUS pumila (creeping fig). Z8–10. Creeping fig is used to great advantage all along the coastal South to give a soft, romantic appearance to walls, steps, and arches. It is a handsome plant with tiny, evergreen, ovate juvenile leaves. It climbs 10'–15' by sending out roots or holdfasts from its stems into whatever surface it is covering—stone, brick, masonry, or wood. (In the latter case it may foster wet rot.) Creeping fig adds a dimension of old-worldliness to whatever it clothes. There are also varieties available with gold or white variegation. Give *Ficus* full to part sun. Clip it back periodically to keep it neat, to prevent it from covering windows and chimneys, and to forestall the formation of thicker, fruit-bearing branches and larger, coarser leaves. Also known as *F. repens*.

FOENICULUM vulgare (fennel). Z6–9. The filigreed foliage of this herb adds variety to the perennial bed. If you want, you can dig up the young shoots and eat them. Use the foliage in salads and other dishes or collect the seeds for anise-flavored seasoning. Fennel likes full sun, good soil, and regular watering and normally grows 4'–6' tall. The foliage of 'Purpureum' (bronze fennel) is a bronzy dark-purple color that mixes well with almost anything in the garden. Swallowtail butterflies use it as breeding ground, so don't be surprised to see a host of bright green caterpillars in summer.

***FRAGARIA* 'Pink Panda'** (ornamental strawberry). Z5–9. The ornamental strawberry plant is often used for its handsome, serrated, shiny, dark green foliage. It works as an edging plant or ground-cover, producing pink flowers in spring and from time to time thereafter—sometimes even in winter. Don't expect much in the way of fruit, however. Give your strawberry plants full sun to

light shade in good soil with excellent drainage. They are also good for container planting.

GAILLARDIA (blanket flower). Blanket flowers are colorful, drought-tolerant perennials that withstand our climate well and are also prized for their long period of bloom. Flowers are the classic daisy form with striped petals and darker central disks.

G. x grandiflora (blanket flower). Z2–9. Generally the petals of this blanket flower are yellow with maroon at the base and the disks are burgundy. There are numerous variations on this theme. The foliage is gray-green and coarsely toothed. These 2'–3'-tall hybrids tend to be short-lived but self-sow with gusto. Recommended varieties: 'Burgundy'—deep wine-red central disk and petals; 'Goblin'—scarlet petals with a yellow rim on dwarf plants 9"–12" tall.

G. pulchella (blanket flower, firewheel). Annual. This native wildflower is an excellent candidate for beach plantings all along the coastal South. It withstands salt, sandy soil, and baking sun. Foliage is gray-green and the flowers may be all red, all yellow, or bicolored. It grows 1'–2' tall. There are hybrids with double flower heads as well.

GALPHIMIA glauca (shower of gold, thryallis). Z8b–10. This 4'–6'-tall semievergreen shrub is well suited to our climate. As its common name suggests, it is clothed in abundant branched clusters of golden-yellow flowers in summer and early fall. The foliage is blue-green. It can be trained up a trellis as a small vine or pruned as a shrub. Give it a position in full sun or part shade in well-drained, fertile soil and fertilize it on a regular schedule in the summer. This butterfly attractant may be tender in Zone 8a and north. Also known as *Thryallis glauca*.

GALTONIA candicans (summer hyacinth). Z6–10. In the summer, 2'–4'-long scapes rise up with large racemes of fragrant, white, dangling, bell-shaped flowers. The foliage is long and strappy. Plant summer hyacinths in full sun in rich soil, and give them plenty of water during the growing season. Deadhead for rebloom. Give the leaves a chance to turn yellow before cleaning up their somewhat bedraggled appearance. Make sure this bulb does not stay wet in winter.

GAURA lindheimeri (gaura, whirling butterflies). Z5–8. This 3'-tall native is a truly excellent plant for the coastal South. It blooms prolifically and for an extremely long period of time, from late spring through fall. The plant has an open airy feeling to it, with its wand-like stems topped with delicate panicles of white flowers that become pale pink as they age. Gaura prefers full sun, good drainage, and even moisture in somewhat poor soil. It is very drought tolerant once established and doesn't blink at our hot, humid summers. Louisiana gardeners also report that gaura survives in thick, wet gumbo soil. Red freckles on the leaves are normal and not cause for concern. Cultivars: 'Corrie's Gold'—leaves marked with cream and gold on 18"–24"-tall plant; 'Dauphin'—5'-tall variety with buds opening hot pink and finishing white; 'Pink Cloud'—an upright, 30"-tall variety with bright pink flowers all summer and through to frost; 'Siskiyou Pink'—mottled foliage and shocking-pink blossoms on a 24"-tall plant; 'Whirling Butterflies'—dwarf (2'-tall), extremely floriferous version with white flowers.

GAZANIA (gazania). Annual. This short-lived perennial is used as an annual for its ability to thrive in hot, baking conditions. Plants may be mound-forming or trailing, depending on the cultivars. Leaves are dark green or woolly gray, topped with 4"-wide, solitary, daisy flowers in bright sunny shades of orange, red, yellow, gold, bronze, pink, and white, often with a dark central eye. Some gazanias have petals banded or tipped in contrasting colors. Flowers often close on cloudy days. Give gazanias full sun and sandy, perfectly drained soil. Fertilize regularly and deadhead for more blooms.

GELSEMIUM (jessamine). Z7–9. Classic southern favorites, these evergreen vines are among the first plants to bloom in spring, adding a brilliant yellow color to roadside and garden alike. They can also be used as groundcovers. To maximize flowering, plant jessamine in full sun in moist, well-drained soil. They will tolerate a shady position, but the blooms will be sparser.

G. rankii (Swamp jessamine). Swamp jessamine is very similar to Carolina jessamine in appearance and habit, with the added advantage of blooming once again in the fall.

G. sempervirens (Carolina jessamine). This shrubby, evergreen, native vine twines to 20'. Its small, light green leaves are complemented by bright yellow, tubular flowers in late winter and early spring. 'Pride of Augusta' is a long-blooming cultivar with double yellow flowers.

GERBERA jamesonii (Gerber daisies, Transvaal daisy). Z6–10. These clump-forming perennials have lobed or toothed basal leaves from which spring erect, 1'–2'-long stems, each topped with a solitary, single or double daisy flower 4"–6" in diameter. Gerber hybrid colors include white,

cream, yellows, corals, oranges, pinks, purples, and reds. Give your Gerbers good soil, absolutely perfect drainage, and full to part sun. Don't plant the crowns too deeply. They prefer shallow planting on raised beds, and, as the saying goes, they highly resent being disturbed—so don't move them. If left alone, they will develop deep roots.

GLADIOLUS (gladiolus). We are all familiar with the annual hybrid gladioli, which have been bred for the large size and bright colors of their flowers. They will often overwinter for us, as long as the ground does not get soggy. There are some less dramatic but quite charming species that work for us as well. Give gladioli a position in full sun in rich, moist, well-drained soil.

G. byzantinus (Byzantine gladiolus, corn lily). Z5–9. These magenta-colored flowers are southern classics. Flowers rise up in loose racemes on 2'-tall spikes in the summer. They make excellent cut flowers.

G. callianthus (Abyssinian gladiolus). Z7–10. In late summer, sword-like foliage is topped with loose spikes of white, star-shaped flowers with maroon eyes. They are slow to emerge and benefit from being lifted and divided on a yearly basis to encourage flowering. They thrive in rich, wet or moist soil.

G. natalensis (parrot gladiolus, Natal lily). Z7–10. This glad sends up 3'–4'-tall spires of hooded orange and yellow flowers in late spring and early summer. Plant the corms 4" deep in full sun to part shade in good soil, and water them well. Where happy, they will naturalize well, spreading by underground runners. Also known as *G. dalenii*.

GLOBBA wintii (dancing girls ginger). Z8–10. This rhizomatous member of the ginger clan prefers a moist, fertile soil in part shade with excellent winter drainage. It is somewhat tender and would benefit from a winter mulch. Dancing girls, which grows 3' tall, has lanceolate/heart-shaped leaves with long petioles. It gets its common name from the unique inflorescences, which appear from late summer through fall. A combination of reflexed, mauve-pink bracts and extremely slender, long, yellow, tubular flowers, these whimsical apparitions appear to cascade down the plant in ribbons—unlike any other flowers you are likely to see.

GLORIOSA superba 'Rothschildiana' (gloriosa lily, glory lily, climbing lily). Z8b–10. This wonderful southern classic, growing 3'–6' tall, is a lily with tendrils at the end of its glossy green leaves. It will cling to whatever nearby support you give it and will spread where it is happy. The flower of the gloriosa lily is one of the most elegant blooms in the flower world. Curvy yellow lily tepals tipped in bright red bend back in Turk's cap fashion to expose prominent green reproductive organs. The flowers look like they are parachuting down the plant. Large, marble-like seedpods appear in the fall. Plant the rhizomes in full sun to light shade in rich soil with plenty of summer moisture. In Zones 8a and northward, lift the tubers and store them inside over winter. If you live in Zones 9 or 10, you may leave them in the ground, but gloriosas abhor winter wetness, so be advised. 'Citrina' has yellow flowers marked with reddish-purple stripes.

GYNURA *aurantiaca* **'Purple Passion'** (purple velvet plant, purple passion plant). Z8–10. This woody subshrub trails along the ground or twines up a nearby support as it grows larger. It gets its name from the reddish-purple hairs that clothe its lance-shaped, pale green leaves. It thrives in part shade in fertile, moist, well-drained soil and can grow from 3'–10' in length. Also known as *G. sarmentosa*.

HABRANTHUS (rain lily). Z7b–10. These underused little bulbs work well for us, producing delicate, funnel- or star-shaped flowers in a range of colors in the summer months. With the exception of the copper lily, which likes poor soil and dry, baking conditions, *Habranthus* enjoy rich, moist garden soil. They all like full sun and will rot if allowed to sit in wet soil during the winter. Raised beds work well.

H. *martinezii.* This species produces creamy white, funnel-shaped flowers on 8"–10"-tall stems.

H. *robustus* (pink rain lily). These bulbs produce gray-green, strappy leaves with mauve-pink, funnel-shaped flowers on 10" stems. This hard-to-kill species blooms in summer, especially after rains. 'Russell Manning' is a large pink cultivar.

H. *tubispathus* **var.** *texensis* (copper lily). After a summer rain, these Texas natives send up yellow-orange flowers with brown interiors and veined exteriors on 8"-tall stems. Poor dry soil preferred, but both moist and dry will work.

HAKONECHLOA *macra* **'Aureola'** (golden satin grass, Hakone grass). Z5–9. This is a low-growing, weeping grass with striped cream-and-green foliage. It grows to about 1' high, with narrow, sword-shaped leaves. Plant Hakone grass in light shade in a rich, moist soil. Once established, it will tolerate drought.

HAMELIA *patens* (Mexican firebush, scarlet bush,

firecracker shrub). Z8–10. This evergreen shrub can grow to 9' tall in the warmest parts of the coastal South but will be smaller (3'–4') farther north. The foliage is gray-green with red stems. It is covered with clusters of red-orange flowers from spring through frost and dark berries afterward. It prefers a spot in full sun with fertile, moist soil with perfect drainage. This is a good beach plant because it tolerates salt spray.

HEDERA (ivy). Ivy is an evergreen groundcover or vine that grows in part sun, part shade, or full shade and under almost any conditions, including neglect. It spreads by putting down roots where stems touch the ground and climbs almost any surface by holdfasts that burrow into the material. Trim it back regularly to keep it within bounds. Ivy also works in mixed container plantings—especially the smaller-leaved or variegated varieties. As ivy matures, it takes on a tree form with thicker stems, flowers, and berries, and the leaves change from lobed to entire.

H. *helix* (English ivy). Z5–10. There are hundreds of named cultivars of this classic ivy. The leaf shape may be rounded, heart-shaped, pentagonal, or lobed. Some have very finely toothed or elongated lobes; some have ruffled edges. There are yellow, white, black, and green English ivies as well as dozens of variegated forms.

H. *canariensis* (Algerian ivy). Z6–10. The large (3"–8"-wide) leaves are glossy green and heart-shaped or three-lobed. This dramatic-looking ivy tends to grow faster than English ivy. Variegated forms are available.

HEDYCHIUM (hardy ginger lily, butterfly ginger). Z7–10. These old southern classics are grown for their foliage and their fragrant flowers, which appear from late summer through fall. The rhizomes thrive in full sun to partial shade in rich, moist soil. They also work well as cut flowers.

H. *coccineum* **'Aurantiacum'.** Growing to 8' tall, this giant clump-former is covered with dark peachy flowers in late summer.

H. *coronarium* (white butterfly ginger). Pinecone-like buds appear in late summer on 5'-tall stalks, followed by very fragrant white, butterfly-shaped flowers.

H. x **'C. P. Raffle'.** This bright orange, bottlebrush-type ginger blooms from July through November on 6'-tall, stiff, upright stalks.

H. *gardnerianum* (Kahili ginger). This species boasts dense, fragrant yellow flowers on 6' stems.

H. *greenei* (orange delta ginger). This ginger produces brilliant orange, deep pink, to red flowers on a 6'-tall plant.

HELIANTHUS (sunflower). The annual sunflower is joined by a number of perennial relatives that perform well in our gardens. They need plenty of space and full sun but are not picky about soil. They flower in late summer and fall and may be propagated by division after flowering. It's a good idea to cut them back several times during the summer to encourage bushier growth and more flower production.

H. angustifolius (swamp sunflower). Z6–9. These bright-yellow-flowered beauties are terrific in the late summer garden where they light up the whole place. They appreciate rich soil and constant moisture, however, strangely enough, they are also drought tolerant. They can grow 6'–10' tall and they multiply rapidly. This sunflower does well in sun or part shade. Also known as *H. simulans*.

H. debilis (beach sunflower, dune sunflower, cucumber-leaved sunflower). Z8b–11. This terrific perennial or self-seeding annual grows in profusion along the Gulf coast. Its bright yellow, daisy flowers have a dark brown central disk, similar to black-eyed Susans. Beach sunflower will bloom all summer long in a baking hot location. It can grow to 3' tall but is generally used as a low groundcover, spreading by underground runners to form a dense mat. It is a perfect beach plant, often used for dune stabilization. 'Vanilla Ice' has creamy yellow flowers with dark central disks.

H. giganteus (giant sunflower). Z5–9. This striking plant grows 6'–10' tall with panicles of yellow daisy-like flowers in late summer to fall.

H. x 'Lemon Queen'. This 8'–10' clumper likes to bake in a hot, dry location. It produces butter yellow flowers in late summer.

H. maximiliani (Maximillian sunflower). Z4–9. A favorite of Lady Bird Johnson, who made use of it in her Texas beautification plantings, this erect sunflower grows 4'–6' tall. The large (3" across) flowers have yellow ray petals with central brown disks in late summer and fall. This one is a rapid spreader.

H. salicifolius (willow-leaf sunflower). Z5–9. This sunflower is more drought tolerant than the swamp sunflower. It grows 9'–12' tall, with narrow, willow-like leaves and bright yellow flowers that bloom in late summer. It also multiplies as soon as you turn your back.

HELIOPSIS *helianthoides* (false sunflower, heliopsis). Z3–9. These natives resemble the sunflowers but are somewhat shorter in stature, bloom slightly earlier in the summer, and are short-lived unless you lift and divide them every two years. They grow 4'–5' tall, producing pale yellow daisies with brown eyes. They like to bake in a hot, sunny spot in moist or dry soil.

H. helianthoides subsp. *scabra* **'Summer Sun'**. This 2'–4'-tall heliopsis is one of the best ones for us because it tolerates heat well. The flowers are bright yellow with a dark gold center. It blooms for many weeks in a row and keeps going when many others have quit. Also known as 'Sommersonne'.

HELLEBORUS *orientalis* (Lenten rose). Z4–9. These wonderful harbingers of spring add an irreplaceable presence to the late winter garden. Their lobed or fully divided, leathery, serrated, evergreen leaves are handsome in their own right, and the delicately colored flower cups suspended above and below the foliage appear like hidden treasures in late January, persisting for almost three months. The flowers can be anywhere from pale green to pink, creamy white or smoky-plum-colored, often with freckles inside. Lenten roses like rich, moist soil in light to deep shade and are extremely easy to grow. They will set out seedlings underneath once they're well established, and these seedlings can be lifted to start new plants. Some people like to remove the older hellebore leaves as soon as the flowers appear in order to better show off the flowers. This is perfectly okay. One other note: deer don't care for hellebores.

HEMEROCALLIS (daylily). Z3–9. These fibrous-rooted perennials belong in every garden. We are so spoiled now, with over 20,000 hybrid cultivars, to choose from that we can't imagine living without them. Any time from late spring through fall, depending on what cultivars you've planted, you will have a daylily flowering for you. Each bloom lasts only one day, but is followed by a succession of blooms from the same flower scape. There are cultivars available in just about every color but blue—from the palest creamy-white to the most vibrant red-orange. In between there are pinks, corals, yellows, greens, coppers, browns, and purples. Daylilies also come in a variety of blooming times and heights. Some have contrasting "eyes" in the center of the lily flower; some have ruffled petals. There are miniatures only 10" tall and giants on 6' scapes. Look for the new repeat bloomers (that bloom twice a season) and those that are being bred to bloom for 30–50 days at a stretch.

Daylilies are very easy to grow in full to part sun in good, well-drained soil, where the size of the clumps will increase steadily. Give them an annual topdressing of compost and/or a handful of balanced fertilizer. Although they are fairly drought tolerant, they do best with attention to watering. To increase your supply, lift and divide the clumps in the fall or early spring. Daylilies are generally disease-free. If you get aphids or spider mites, treat them with insecticidal soap. The foliage of some daylilies remains evergreen all winter. Others are herbaceous, meaning that the foliage goes dormant in cold weather. Daylilies also work in containers, as edging plants, and as a blooming groundcover—especially the smaller evergreen varieties. Daylily foliage is excellent for disguising the yellowing leaves of daffodils and other spring bulbs.

H. citrina (night-blooming daylily). This herbaceous species sends up nocturnal, pale yellow, fragrant, star-shaped flowers on 4' scapes in summer.

H. fulva (tawny daylily). This fast-spreading, common daylily has made itself at home all over the coastal South with absolutely no assistance. It sends up tiger-orange, recurved, trumpet-shaped flowers on 3'–6' scapes in summer.

H. lilio-asphodelus (lemon daylily). This is a long-blooming, semievergreen daylily, which sends up beautiful, pale yellow, star-shaped blooms on 3' scapes in early summer. Also known as *H. flava*.

Recommended *Hemerocallis* hybrids (a few arbitrary picks out of the 20,000 choices, arranged by color): Near whites—'Gentle Shepherd', 'Iron Gate Glacier', 'Joan Senior', 'White Temptation'; pink—'Fairy Tale Pink', 'Corryton Pink', 'Gauguin', 'Mae Graham', 'Persian Market'; pale peach—'Silver Ice'; dark plum—'Midnight Magic'; deep red—'Beryl Stone', 'Big Apple', 'Bryan Paul', 'Charles Johnston'; classic, clear yellow—'Hyperion'; pale lavender—'Catherine Woodbury'; bright orange—'Orange Vols', 'Brigade'; purple—'Super Purple', 'Siloam Plum Tree', 'Wayside King Royale'; repeat-blooming clear yellows—'Happy Returns' and 'Bitsy' (easier yellows to work with than the orangy-gold repeat bloomer 'Stella de Oro'); repeat-blooming strawberry red—'Little Business'.

HEUCHERA (alumroot and coral bells). These low-growing evergreen natives are generally admired for their subtle foliage. While not overwhelming, they provide a certain gentle beauty in lightly shaded parts of the garden. The more showy coral bells are more difficult to grow in the coastal South than the alumroots.

H. americana (American alumroot). Z4–9. The lobed, evergreen, heart-shaped leaves are a mottled purple when they first emerge. They are particularly attractive during the cooler months of spring, fall, and winter. Grow them in part to

full shade in rich, moist soil. There are dozens of hybrids to choose from.

H. sanguinea (coral bells). Z3–8. Coral bells have much showier flowers than alumroot but are trickier to grow. Because they don't like acid soil and require beyond-perfect drainage you may have to add sand and agricultural lime to the soil. Plant them in light shade. The delicate reddish-coral bells appear in spring on 12"–20"-long stems and last for several weeks. There are a large number of *Heuchera* hybrids with flower colors covering the spectrum of coral, white, pink, chartreuse, scarlet, and burgundy.

H. villosa (hairy alumroot). Z6–9. These southeastern natives are more reliable than coral bells for our hot, humid summers. The circular, lobed leaves are hairy, as are the flower stems. Unprepossessing sprays of whitish flowers appear in summer or fall on delicate 1'–3'-long stems. 'Purpurea' is a purple-leaved variety.

HIBISCUS (hibiscus). This is a genus for which we should get down on our knees and give thanks. It gives us flower power from summer through fall in a large variety of colors, shapes, and sizes. Many hibiscus are native to the Southeast, which explains why they do so well here. All hibiscus like a spot in full sun with wet feet and rich, organic soil, but they will tolerate a normal garden bed if it is kept well watered during the summer months.

H. coccineus (scarlet rose mallow, swamp hibiscus). Z6–10. Huge (6" across), bright red, semi-cruciform flowers clothe this 6'–10'-tall, skinny hibiscus from summer through fall. The foliage, which is also beautiful, resembles that of the marijuana plant. Ornamental seedpods persist in winter. This plant thrives in full sun with wet feet, so if you are not planting it in a bog, keep it well watered. It is late to break dormancy, so be patient. In Texas this plant is fondly referred to as the Texas star.

H. dasycalyx (Nacogdoches River mallow). Z7–10. This endangered, 4'-tall native is easy to grow in full to part sun. Soil can be boggy or dry. The attractive, thread-like foliage is complemented by dramatic, 4'-wide, white mallow flowers with dark maroon centers.

H. grandiflorus (great rose mallow, velvet mallow). Z7–9. Long, velvety, gray leaves clothe this 6'–7'-tall native. Large pink or lavender flowers with crimson centers are borne in late summer. Give it full to part sun with rich, moist soil like that of its original marshy habitat. Butterflies and humming-birds love it.

H. lasiocarpus (woolly rose-mallow). Z5–9. This 6'-tall native perennial grows in wet, clay soils in sun or part shade. From late spring through summer it produces large (6") white or pale pink flowers with purple or red centers. Foliage is gray-green and furry. This is a favorite of butterflies and hummingbirds. It is a great beach plant, which can even stand salt water.

H. moscheutos (common rose mallow). Z5–10. These sturdy, multistemmed plants grow about 3'–4' tall, blooming all summer. The flowers are saucer-sized beauties in shades of red, white, and pink. Plant them in full sun in moist soil. Unfortunately, they are beloved of Japanese beetles and many other chewing pests and can look badly eaten by midsummer.

H. mutabilis **'Flora Plena'** (Confederate rose, cotton rose). Z7–10. These fall-blooming plants can grow to the size of small trees, 8'–10' tall. Their leaves resemble maple leaves and the double flowers look something like peonies or camellias. On one plant you will see many shades, from light pink to almost red, as the flowers ripen. Confederate rose likes full sun and plenty of moisture. It is also late to break dormancy. Although there is a striking, pure red form, 'Rubrum', it is hard to come by.

H. rosa-sinensis (florist's hibiscus). This is the variety grown in the greenhouse, with shiny, dark green leaves and lusciously vibrant-colored single or double flowers that bloom nonstop in between the two frost-free dates. This is worth growing if you have somewhere indoors to overwinter it. It is unbeatable for the length and drama of its flower display—especially in containers.

H. syriacus (rose of Sharon). Z5–9. These tough, multibranched shrubs can grow 6'–12' high but can be kept pruned to a smaller size. They bloom from summer through fall, producing single or double crepey flowers of white, lilac-blue, pink, or red with a dark red or purple throat. Rose of Sharon tolerates some drought and likes a hot, sunny position. 'Diana' is a very long-blooming shrub with handsome, dark green foliage and pale pink, almost white flowers. It self-cleans nicely.

HIPPEASTRUM (amaryllis). These bulbs do well for us, sending up healthy, strappy green leaves in spring with sturdy 1'–2' scapes crowned with impressive outward-facing flower trumpets. Colors range from the palest pastels and white to the most vibrant reds and oranges. Dwarf varieties are also available. Give amaryllis a sunny, well-drained spot in rich soil, and they will increase for you over the years.

H. x **'Appleblossom'.** Z7–10. This is a beautiful amaryllis with creamy white trumpets tinged pastel pink at the petal margins.

H. x johnsonii (amaryllis, St. Joseph's lily). Z8–10. This old southern garden classic sends up clusters of bright red trumpet-shaped flowers with white stripes on multiple 2' stems.

H. x **'Nymph'.** Z7–10. One of the new peony-flowered varieties, this gem is creamy white with blush-pink highlights.

H. reginae (Mexican lily). Z8–10. Drooping umbels of bright red flowers with white stars in their throats appear in summer on 1'-long stems.

HOSTA (plantain lily, hosta). Z3–9. These may be the best-known perennials for the shade, grown principally for their foliage, although they also produce elegant wands of purple or white flowers in early summer. There are hundreds of varieties available now, with shiny, dull, pleated, ruffled, and/or quilted foliage. Leaf size ranges from petite (1") to substantial (20"). Foliage color can be green, chartreuse, gold, blue-green, or variegated. Hostas can be used as groundcovers, edging plants, general all-purpose mixers, or as specimen plants if they are especially large and interesting-looking. They prefer rich, well-drained soil with ample moisture. Hostas grow in light to deep shade and tolerate a small amount of sun. Some can stand more sun than others. Where happy, they will grow into large, impressive clumps. They are easily propagated by division in spring or fall. In the hot, humid coastal South, hostas may experience viridescence, in which the variegated leaves revert to solid green until the weather cools back down in fall. Be prepared for slugs, voles, and deer. If you're looking for out-of-the-ordinary hostas, Tony Avent at Plant Delights Nursery outside of Raleigh, North Carolina, has a scary number to choose from (see "Internet Sources" for the URL). A few suggestions: golden foliage—'Gold Standard', 'Sun Power', 'Zounds'; chartreuse foliage—'Piedmont Gold', 'Sum and Substance'; white and green variegation—'Delta Dawn', 'Fire and Ice', 'Patriot', 'Pilgrim'; yellow and green variegation—'Great Expectations', 'June'; quilted or corrugated leaves—'Royal Standard', 'Sunshine Glory', 'Tokudama Aureonebulosa'; blue-green foliage—'Halcyon', *H. sieboldiana* 'Elegans', 'Love Pat'; small-leaved, shorter varieties—'Green Eyes', 'Lemon Lime', 'Kabitan', 'Little Aurora', 'Masquerade', and 'Pandora's Box'.

HOUTTUYNIA *cordata* **'Chameleon'** (chameleon plant). Z3–8. The heart-shaped leaves of this spreading groundcover are splashed with pink, white, red, and light green. Although in some people's opinion the leaves smell disgusting, others use them in cooking in place of fresh coriander. There is no dispute, however, that this plant can take over where it's happy—in moist soil in sun to part shade. It has been known to revert to plain green in our hot summers.

HUMULUS japonicus 'Variegatus' (variegated hop vine). Z4–9. This herbaceous perennial vine, often grown as an annual, climbs very quickly to 20'–30', covering everything in its path. The large (6"-long), dark green leaves are streaked with white, and deeply lobed. Ovoid, green flower spikes appear in midsummer. Plant hops in full sun to part shade in fertile, moist, well-drained soil.

HYACINTHOIDES hispanica (Spanish bluebell, Spanish squill). Z4–9. Clusters of nodding, wisteria-blue, bell-shaped flowers hang from foothigh stems in spring. Plant bulbs 4" deep in rich, moist soil in part sun or light shade where they will naturalize. Give them spring moisture and a not-too-wet winter. (These bulbs are also sold as *Scilla campanulata*, *S. hispanica*, and *Endymion hispanicus* and are available variously in shades of violet, pink, and white.)

HYACINTHUS orientalis var. albulus (white French Roman hyacinths). Z7–9. This bulbous perennial is better suited to the coastal South than its Dutch relatives so readily available in the trade. It produces racemes of green-tinged white flowers in early spring on foot-high plants, but it may be hard to find in the trade. Grow it in sun or part shade.

HYMENOCALLIS (spider lily). Spider lilies are one reason we should feel grateful to be gardening in the coastal South. These somewhat odd, beautiful flowers do very well for us with little attention. From early spring until frost, depending on the species, *Hymenocallis* produce fragrant, whitish-green tubular flowers with whisker-like endings above strappy, dark green foliage. These bulbous natives range in size from miniature to impressive. Spider lilies like full sun to part shade and water during the blooming season. Make sure your spider lilies have excellent drainage in the winter months.

H. caroliniana (swamp spider lily). Z7–10. This vigorous native has umbels of large, fragrant, white flowers atop 2'-high scapes in spring and summer. Although they love ponds and bogs, they will do fine in rich garden soil if kept evenly moist. They can stand clay and even well-watered sandy soil. These increase quickly where they are happy.

H. festalis (Peruvian lily). Z8–10. Wonderful, white, spidery flowers are borne from late spring through early summer on 2'–3'-high stalks. The attractive, dark green, strappy foliage is semierect and arching.

H. imperialis (big fatty). Z8–10. The broad, spearshaped leaves have a grayish tint. The large white flowers bloom in spring.

H. x 'Advance' (Peruvian daffodil). Z8–9. Clusters of large (4"–6"-wide), fragrant, white, spider-like flowers with yellow-striped throats appear in late spring on a 2'–3'-tall plant.

H. narcissiflora (Peruvian daffodil). Z8–9. Umbels of scented white flowers striped with green are borne in summer atop 2' stems. Leaves are strappy. Also known as *Ismene calathina*.

H. x 'Sulfur Queen'. Z8–10. This cultivar sends up 2'-tall stems topped with umbels of fragrant, sulfur yellow flowers with green-striped throats. The leaves are long, strap-shaped, and semierect.

HYPERICUM (St. John's wort, St. Andrew's cross, hypericum). The *Hypericum* genus contains over 400 species. Some of the more commonly known St. John's worts will make do in the coastal South but without much of a flower display. The following two species, however, are terrific for our climate. Give these hypericums a position in sun or part shade with rich, moist, well-drained soil.

H. hypericoides (St. Andrew's cross, St. John's wort). Z7–9. This native evergreen subshrub grows about 2'–3' tall and produces lots of bright yellow flowers all summer long. It takes full sun or part shade and can survive in dry or moist ground. It is a spreading, groundcover-type shrub that doesn't like to be cut back severely. St. Andrew's cross is a good beach plant.

H. reductum (beach hypericum, St. John's wort). Z6–9. This 20"-tall, evergreen groundcover grows fairly vigorously in our climate, forming a kind of semiwoody subshrub or groundcover. For many weeks in summer it produces golden yellow, many-stamened flowers. It thrives in wet or dry soils and even prospers at the beach. Whack it back to keep it in shape.

IBERIS sempervirens (candytuft). Z3–8. This fine-leaved, mat-forming, evergreen perennial is covered with tiny white flowers in spring. It performs reliably only in the cooler parts of our region. Give candytuft full, baking sun in a perfectly drained location and shear it back to prevent it from becoming leggy. If you select a variety for its ability to rebloom in the fall, it will need more attention in the summer—maybe a little extra watering and fertilization to prepare it for its repeat performance.

IPHEION uniflorum (spring starflower). Z5–9. These little gems should be in every garden in the coastal South. They send up neat clumps of narrow, dark green leaves in late fall which stay decorative all winter. In late winter or early spring, tiny, milky blue, star-shaped flowers appear on 6" stems. The effect when hundreds of them are planted is very lovely. They work well with pansies and other early bulbs and naturalize easily in lawns. *Ipheion* asks only for full to part sun and a not too soggy winter soil. There are varieties available that are bright blue ('Rolf Fiedler'), lilac-blue ('Wisley Blue'), or bright white ('Album') and even a dark violet ('Froyle Mill'), but the off-blue-white of the species is mighty nice just as it is. Plant these by the hundreds and enjoy.

IPOMOEA (morning glory, quamoclit). The vines in this genus require well-drained soil and full sun. They do not need particularly rich soil and are among the best summer vines for our area. Note: When you're starting an *Ipomoea* vine from seed, it's a good idea to either soak the seed in warm water for two hours or notch the seed covering with a knife to help it to germinate.

I. alba (moonflower, moon vine). Annual. This fast-growing vine will rapidly climb to 20'–30' high by twining tendrils to cover fences and arbors. Leaves are heart-shaped. The 6"-wide, fragrant, white flowers open in late afternoon and evening and close back up the next morning. Flowering continues all summer long.

I. batatas (sweet potato vine). Annual. These terrific tuberous vines give us dramatic foliage color to mix and match as a groundcover in the garden or spilling out of a container. The deeply lobed, palmate leaves are plum-black in 'Blackie', vibrant chartreuse in 'Marguerite', a rich mid-green in 'Lady Fingers', and a variegated pink, cream, and light green in 'Tricolor'.

I. coccinea (star quamoclit). Annual. The star quamoclit vine is a coastal southern classic, boasting bright red, flared, tubular flowers all summer long. The dark green foliage is highly incised, giving it a delicate, lacy appearance. It will twine its way up to 6'–12' high. Dearly beloved of hummingbirds. Also known as *Quamoclit coccinea*.

I. nil (annual morning glory). Annual. These easy annual vines bear 2"-wide, funnel-shaped flowers in shades of blue, purple, red, and chocolate brown with white throats all summer long. The vines climb to 15' by twining.

I. pes-caprae (railroad vine, beach morning glory). Z8–10. This somewhat rampant native vine tolerates beach conditions, including salt spray. It is used as a groundcover to control erosion on sand dunes. A trailing vine with fleshy leaves, it puts out roots at the leaf nodes and can trail the length of two football fields, if allowed. Large (2"-wide), pink flowers appear all summer long.

I. purpurea (common morning glory). Annual. This vigorous, easy vine blooms within a short time from seed sown in the spring. Large (3"-wide), trumpet flowers bloom all summer in shades of white, pink, blue, magenta, and purple with white throats. To perform at its best, *I. purpurea* prefers poor soil kept on the dry side. This 6'–10'-tall vine is a reliable reseeder. Also known as *Convolvulus purpurea*.

I. quamoclit (cypress vine, cardinal climber). Annual. This is another classic vine for the Southern Atlantic and Gulf Coasts. It resembles star quamoclit somewhat, except that the foliage is so delicate that it is thread-like and the red, tubular flowers are prolific but tiny. It grows 6'–20' tall and prefers full to part sun. Although it is annual, it self-sows profusely. Hummingbirds love cypress vine. Also known as *Quamoclit pennata* and *Q. ipomoea*.

I. sagittata (salt-marsh morning glory). Z5–9. This 8'–10'-long, native trailing vine can be used as a semievergreen groundcover or allowed to twine up fences, arbors, and trellises. Leaves are arrowhead-shaped, and the large (2"–3"-wide), lavender or pink, funnel-shaped flowers bloom from mid-summer into the fall. It can take dry or wet soil in full sun.

I. tricolor (annual morning glory). Annual. Another annual morning glory that blooms easily from seed, this vine twines to 15'. In summer it bears large (4"–5"-wide), open, funnel-shaped flowers in shades of white, red, purple, pink, and violet. It requires a spot in full sun with regular watering. Flowers open in the early morning and close around midday.

IRIS (iris). This genus, comprising many species and many more hundreds of cultivars, was named for the goddess Iris, who walked from heaven to earth across a rainbow bridge, leaving a different colored iris flower everywhere her foot touched down. The French fleur-de-lis is actually a stylized iris. Orris root is the dried rhizome of iris, used for medicinal purposes and for scenting linen chests. We have to be somewhat choosy in deciding which irises will do best for us, but we do have a large selection. The most well-known irises are the bearded hybrids, so we will start there.

Bearded Irises

In our climate the modern hybrid bearded irises are not particularly good bets. The rhizomes suffer fungal rot due to our high humidity. However, the good news is that there are some wonderful old-fashioned bearded irises that have been around for a very long time and have proved their ability to give us predictable blooms. They will probably outlive us all. If you can get your hands on them, use them instead of the newer varieties. Plant bearded irises very shallowly, with the top surface of the rhizome showing above the soil. Give them a position in full sun with enriched, sandy, well-drained soil, slightly on the alkaline side. Keep them away from the automatic watering system if possible.

I. albicans (white flag iris). Z6–9. One of the most historical southern bearded irises, this species originated in the Persian Gulf and came to us by way of Europe. In early spring, white flowers with yellow beards appear above gray-green, sword-shaped leaves. White flags have been planted over many generations in graveyards, especially near the graves of young men killed in battle. White flags grow 1'–2' tall, blooming best if the clumps are left undisturbed. A tough, reliable survivor — one of the very best beardeds for the coastal South.

I. germanica **'Nepalensis'** (purple flag iris, purple German bearded iris). Z5–8. At the peak of spring in many old southern gardens, these 3'–4'-tall bearded irises bear lovely, fragrant, royal-purple flowers. They are reliable, sterile mules that will increase steadily over the years.

I. kochii (Italian iris). Z6–9. These deeply colored, reddish-purple irises are of an ancient European lineage. They thrive in our humid, hot climate, blooming in early spring and mixing well with other spring perennials. They may rebloom in fall or even in winter where they are happy. Their habit is compact and fairly short (1'–2' tall).

I. pallida (Dalmation iris). Z5–9. In late spring, pale amethyst blooms with yellow beards appear on 3'–4'-tall, branched stems. The foliage is blue-gray. This excellent, ancient bearded iris tolerates some shade. 'Variegata' has green-and-yellow-striped foliage.

I. plicata **'Madame Chereau'**. Z5–9. The color of this antique bearded iris is pale lavender-white with deeper lavender edging. Growing 2'–3' tall, it blooms reliably for us in spring.

Beardless Irises

The bearded iris described above are named for the noticeable small hairs (the beard) on the crest of their lowermost petal (the fall). The beardless iris, below, are each quite different from one another but have in common smooth, beardless falls.

I. cristata (crested iris). Z3–9. In our climate, crested irises prefer part shade in well-drained rich soil and ample watering. They will form clumps if they are happy. Their light blue blooms appear in spring on 6"–12" stems. They spread by creeping rootstocks.

Dutch iris. Z7–9. These are the common iris bulbs sold in mass distribution catalogs and garden centers all over the country. They can be used as short-lived perennials in our area and look best when planted in fairly abundant groupings. They flower from mid-May through June in an assortment of colors. Plant the bulbs 6" deep in good soil. They don't mind a wet spring and dry summer. Excellent as cut flowers — grown extensively for the florist trade.

I. ensata (Japanese iris). Z4–9. These large-flowered irises thrive in bog conditions in full to part sun. The best bet is to plant them in pots half submerged in water, lift the pots in late fall and stick them, pot and all, in the ground until the following spring. However, if you don't want to do this just plant them in rich, organic soil that is kept thoroughly watered. These are beautiful summer-blooming flowers, often with markings in more than one shade. Look for some of the new repeat bloomers.

I. foetidissima (stinking Gladwin). Z6–9. If you are patient, this evergreen iris will develop into a sizable clump that will produce fall seedpods that split open to reveal bright red seeds. These remain attractive all fall and winter. Removing the tattered leaves in spring is a good idea. The summer flower is not much to look at. These are quite shade-tolerant irises. If you don't want the stink, don't crush the leaves.

Louisiana iris. Z4–9. These beautiful irises used to grow in wild profusion in New Orleans before many of the swamps were drained to make way for new construction. They love the hot, humid summers of the coastal Gulf and Southern Atlantic, and they don't mind wet feet in winter. This, alone, makes them the most suitable irises for the coastal South.

But, in addition, they bloom in a huge variety of colors and sizes. Bloom time is about two weeks after bearded iris, in late spring or early summer. They require full to part sun and must have constant moisture to thrive. A pond or bog is best. If you don't have a bog, you can create one by lining an excavated, sunny site with sheet plastic and punching a few holes in it. Don't fertilize with bone meal or any other alkaline fertilizer. They appreciate rotted manure or acidic azalea-camellia fertilizer. The following three species of Louisiana irises are classics: *I. brevicaulis* (zigzag-stemmed iris)—dwarf (16'–20"-tall) Louisiana iris that comes in shades of bright violet-blue or white and prefers drier conditions than the others; *I. fulva* (copper iris)—bearing large, coppery-red flowers, it takes full to part sun, prefers wet feet, and blooms during the heat of summer; and *I. giganticaerulea* (giant blue iris)—has flowers of purple, blue, or white on plants that can reach 4' tall.

There are hundreds of hybrid Louisiana irises that do equally well in our climate. The following is a subjective and arbitrary list of beauties by color: white with tinges of pale yellow—'Sun Dream', 'C'est Magnifique', 'Clara Goula'; deep, wine red with touches of saffron orange—'Khan'; royal purple with a splash of yellow—'Hurricane Party'; golden yellow—'Green Elf'; violet-blue—'La Perouse'; midnight purple—'Black Gamecock'.

I. pseudocorus (water iris, yellow flag iris). Z5–9. This spring-blooming beauty can grow to 4' tall if it is submerged in water, its preferred habitat. But it can also be planted in regular garden soil if it is watered during droughts. In such a situation it will be of shorter stature. Yellow flag likes full sun but will tolerate filtered shade.

I. siberica (Siberian iris). Z3–9. These elegant beauties bloom from late spring to early summer on 2'–3'-high stalks. Healthy, narrow, sword-shaped leaves are attractive in the garden all summer and remain until heavy frost. Grow this clump-forming iris in full sun to part shade in rich, moist, well-drained soil. Siberian iris are much less susceptible to iris borer and leaf blight disease than the modern bearded hybrids. Only the well-established clumps bloom really heavily, so don't divide too soon. Recommended varieties: 'Caesar's Brother'—a deep, rich purple, widely used and reliable; 'Ewen'—a pinkish-violet color; 'Lavender Bounty'—a very easy, early-blooming, lavender color; 'Butter and Sugar'—subtle white and yellow coloring; 'Sky Wings'—a

beautiful sky blue; 'Pink Haze'—a lovely, mauve pink.

I. virginica (southern blue flag iris). Z6–9. The blue flag iris likes conditions similar to the yellow flag. Its blue or white blooms are highlighted by yellow patches on the petals. This is a vigorous, 3'-tall native, well suited to the coastal South. 'Contraband Girl' forms handsome clumps with large lavender flowers.

JACOBINIA. *See JUSTICIA.*

JASMINUM (jasmine). The following jasmines are evergreen twiners, unless otherwise indicated. Jasmines are fairly undemanding plants, which thrive in full sun or part shade in moderately fertile, moist, well-drained soil. In the colder reaches of the coastal South they may be semi-evergreen or even tender and will benefit from a protected position and a heavy mulch. Some gardeners grow them as sprawling shrubs. Some prune them severely (and regularly) to create blooming evergreen hedges. Some let them behave in a twining, vining fashion.

J. angulare (South African jasmine). Z8–11. Fragrant, pale pink flower clusters appear in summer on a 20', glossy-leaved vine.

J. grandiflorum (Spanish jasmine). Z8–11. Attractive, glossy-green leaves clothe a 10'–15' plant with pink-tinged white, fragrant flowers appearing all summer long. This is a semievergreen or deciduous jasmine.

J. humile (Italian jasmine). Z7–10. This arching, 8'-tall, semievergreen shrub or vine has willow-like leaves. It produces clusters of bright yellow, salverform flowers in summer. Works well as a clipped hedge.

J. mesnyi (primrose jasmine). Z8–10. This is a good weeping jasmine to use to cascade over walls, pergolas, or banks, where its 6'–10'-long stems will have something to support them. The flowers are single or double, bright yellow, and salverform. They are produced in late winter and spring and sporadically thereafter.

J. multiflorum (downy jasmine, star jasmine). Z8–10. This late-winter/early-spring bloomer has gray-green, woolly foliage and starry white blooms. It can be trained as a shrub or allowed to grow into a 20'-high vine.

J. nudiflorum (winter jasmine). Z6–9. This deciduous plant can reach 15' tall if trained as a vine; otherwise, it is used as a weeping 4'-tall shrub with a width of 7'. Solitary, bright yellow, salverform flowers appear in late winter before the plant leafs out. The bright green stems of winter jasmine are attractive in the winter landscape. Although it tolerates light shade, winter jasmine needs full sun to bloom well.

J. officinale (common white jasmine, poet's jasmine). Z8–10. This vigorous, fast-growing, semievergreen woody vine can twine its way up 40'. In early summer it produces clusters of highly fragrant, white, salverform flowers. Bloom continues on and off until frost. 'Aureovariegatum' has handsome, yellow-edged foliage.

J. polyanthum (pink jasmine, Chinese jasmine). Z8–10. This robust vine climbs quickly to 20' with finely divided, evergreen foliage. In late spring it bears cymes of fragrant white flowers. It can be pruned as a weeping shrub.

J. sambac (Arabian jasmine). Z8–10. This jasmine grows as a 5'-tall, shrubby evergreen with glossy green foliage. In summer it bears clusters of fragrant white flowers. 'Grand Duke of Tuscany' is an old southern favorite, producing double, gardenia-like, white flowers.

JUSTICIA (justicia, plume flower). These plants are classics for the coastal South. They thrive in our hot, humid summers and, more importantly, give us late summer and fall blooms in the shadiest parts of the garden. Give your justicias rich, moist, well-drained soil. Fertilizing a few times during the summer will increase the fall blooms.

J. aurea (Brazilian plume). Z8b–11. From late summer to frost, this 3'–6'-tall shrub sends up showy yellow flower panicles.

J. brandegeana (shrimp plant). Z8–10. This 3'-tall, semievergreen shrub has arching, pendent plumes of shrimp-colored bracts with tubular white flowers emerging from them. When it blooms in summer, it is quite a conversation piece. Shrimp plant has the best bloom color in part shade. Give it fertile soil and good drainage. Keep it pinched back to encourage a bushier shape.

J. carnea (Brazilian plume flower). Z8–10. Plume-like spikes of dark pink flowers are borne on this 3'–6'-tall plant from midsummer to fall. Give it part to full shade with rich, moist soil. Pinch it back and deadhead it to keep it bushy and to promote bloom. It will die back to the ground except in the warmest parts of the coastal South. Also known as *Jacobinia carnea*.

KAEMPFERIA (peacock ginger). Z8–10. These beautiful, heat-loving shade plants are part of the reason we feel privileged to garden in the coastal South. They are grown principally for their subtly variegated, stemless foliage. Plant peacock gingers in rich, well-drained soil in part to full shade and keep them well watered during the growing season, dry in winter. Delicate, orchid-like flowers appear in late spring or summer. Peacock ginger can be used as a groundcover in place of the less heat-tolerant hostas. These rhizomatous or tuberous plants multiply rapidly where they are happy. They grow 6"–18" tall, depending on the species.

K. gilbertii (variegated peacock lily). This 4"-tall species has narrow, white-margined, green leaves with silver undersides and purple and white, orchid-like flowers in late spring.

K. pulchra (bronze peacock ginger). A sturdy, 6"-tall plant with bronzy, dark green, broadly elliptical leaves veined with silver in a feathery pattern. The late summer blooms are rosy-lilac-colored. This will spread to make a handsome groundcover. 'Silverspot' has rounded, green leaves splotched with maroon and silver.

K. rotunda (resurrection lily, Asian crocus). The narrow leaves of this tuberous peacock ginger grow more upright than some of the others. Altogether the plant is about 18"–24" tall. The leaves have silver variegation on top with purple underneath. Lavender and white orchid-like flowers appear at ground level in spring before the leaves emerge.

KALIMERIS *pinnatifida* (Oxford orphanage plant, Genghis Khan aster, false aster, Japanese aster). Z4–9. For a plant with so many common names, this is really a very simple little thing. It has tiny, white, aster-like blooms on 1'–2'-high slender stems with fine, pinnately lobed leaves. It is the sort of unremarkable remarkable plant that doesn't look much like anything, but once it gets to spreading itself around and making a nice crowd of itself (which it does very readily), it is terrific! It blends and melds and complements and pokes out between things or makes large drifts if you want it to. It blooms nonstop from early summer through frost, needing only an occasional whacking back to recharge its batteries. It grows in full to part sun and even tolerates a little shade. Moist soil, dry soil, poor soil, good soil. Also known as *Asteromoea mongolica*.

KNIPHOFIA *uvaria* (red hot poker, torch lily). Z5–8. Torch lilies are clump-forming, rhizomatous perennials with arching, grassy leaves. They are available in the well-known red-and-orange varieties and in pure red, yellow, green, bronze, cream, white, tangerine, coral, and bicolor variations. They range in height from dwarf (18") to a majestic 8' tall. Blooming in early summer, their tubular flowers cluster together in a torch formation. Torch lily flowers mature upward and change color as they do so. While the top buds on the spike may be opening red, the bottom half may be ripening to yellow green. Remove the flower stems after blooming to promote continued flowering. Give torch lilies full or partial sun and perfect drainage. They especially hate to have their feet wet in winter. They also prefer not to be disturbed once they've gotten established. 'Primrose Beauty' is a handsome, 2'-tall, butter yellow color. There are coral, tangerine, green, and creamy-white cultivars as well.

KOSTELETZKYA *virginica* (marsh mallow, seashore mallow). Z6–11. Although you can't roast these marshmallows over an open fire, you do need to have one in your garden. These 4'–5'-tall native subshrubs thrive in our climate. They take full to part sun and wet conditions but will also grow in ordinary garden soil. The leaves are light green, toothed, and hairy. Hibiscus-like pink flowers with bright yellow stamens cover the bush from midsummer through early fall. This is one of those fail-safe plants you wish you'd known about earlier in your gardening life. 'Immaculate' is a white-flowered version.

LAGERSTROEMIA *indica* (crape myrtle). Z7–9. Crape myrtles are tried and true classics for the coastal South. You can see them in bloom in the summer from Northern Virginia down through Florida and across the Gulf Coast to Texas. Growing 7'–40' tall, depending on the cultivar, these deciduous woody shrubs and trees bloom for many months in the summer. Colors include white, pink, red, lavender, and purple. Give crape myrtle a position in full sun with well-drained soil. Prune back in winter or early spring. Flowers bloom on new wood.

LANTANA (hardy lantana). These long-flowering, colorful summer bloomers are used as annuals farther north, but we can leave them in the ground over winter provided we plant them in spring or early summer so they have time to establish a good root system. Lantanas are available in a myriad of colors, from pale pastels to vibrant reds and oranges. They produce multiple flat corymbs of flowers from early summer through frost. Give lantanas full sun in any garden soil. They will tolerate wet feet as well as dry conditions, but they bloom better in well-drained soil. Butterflies love lantana. They do well at the beach and work well in containers. Don't cut lantana back in the fall or winter; wait for spring.

L. *camara* (hardy lantana, bushy lantana). Z7b–10. This bushy, woody lantana can grow anywhere from 2' to 6' tall, depending on the variety. Leaves are rough, toothed, and hairy. Foliage may be solid or variegated. Dozens of cultivars are available with multicolored flowers in shades of pink, yellow, red, orange, and white.

L. *montevidensis* (weeping lantana). Z7b–10. This is a low-growing, mounding or trailing variety of lantana that spreads 3'–6' wide. The dark green leaves are ovate and finely toothed. Flowers are multicolored or solid in shades of lilac, pink, white, or violet blue.

L. 'Tangerine' (orange lantana). Z7b–10. This vigorous, shrubby lantana can grow 3'–6' tall. From spring through fall it is constantly covered with clusters of orange-and-yellow flowers.

LATHYRUS (sweet pea). Gardeners in the coastal South can grow both the annual and the perennial versions of this old-fashioned, cottage garden classic.

L. *latifolius* (perennial sweet pea). Z5–9. We are lucky to be able to grow a sweet pea vine that comes back year after year. The foliage of this sweet pea is blue-green, and the flowers bloom pink, reddish-purple, or white in spring and early summer. Give it full sun or part shade and well-drained soil. It is quite drought tolerant once established. This vine will twine up to about 9' high with clasping tendrils.

L. *odoratus* (annual sweet pea). Annual. Plant these cool-weather annuals in the fall and enjoy the flowers in spring as the vines twine up a trellis or other support. Soak the seeds overnight before planting them in rich soil, well amended with rotted manure. Full sun or light shade.

LAURENTIA *fluviatalis* (bluestar). Z7–10. Tiny, sky blue, star-shaped flowers cover this small-leaved groundcover in spring. It prefers part sun to light shade in rich, moist soil. This semievergreen mat former works well between stepping-stones. It grows 1" tall with a spread of 12"–18" the first year.

LEONITIS *leonurus* (lion's ear). Z8b–11. This 4'–6' semievergreen subshrub, beloved of hummingbirds, has square stems and hairy, lance-shaped leaves. From late summer through fall it produces wonderful tiers of velvety orange-red, tubular flowers. It is somewhat tender in the cooler parts of the coastal South. Give it a protected position in full sun to light shade and a good winter mulch. The soil should be fertile and well drained. Cut it back after it finishes blooming. Also known as *L. menthaefolia*.

LEUCANTHEMUM *maximum*. *See* LEUCANTHEMUM *superbum*.

LEUCANTHEMUM. This genus includes a large number of annual and perennial daisy flowers.

L. superbum (Shasta daisy). Z4–9. Although these clump-forming perennials are popular, they tend to be quite short-lived for us. They like rich, moist, well-drained soil and dry feet in winter. They don't especially enjoy our wet winters. For this reason, some gardeners divide and replant their Shastas each year. Shastas grow 2'–3' tall in full sun or light shade. The following are the two best bets: 'Becky' stays healthy looking all summer and produces white daisies for many weeks in late summer; the foliage is leathery and stems are sturdy. 'Thomas Killian' produces large white daisies with a yellow center and does especially well at the beach. Also known as *L. maximum*, *Chrysanthemum superbum*, and *C. maximum*.

L. vulgare (ox-eye daisy, common daisy). Z3–9. This is the classic, yellow-centered white daisy that blooms from spring through fall. Grow in full sun in moderately fertile, well-drained soil. This 2'–3'-tall daisy is reputed to grow better for us than the Shasta. In some areas it spreads so rapidly that it qualifies as a weed.

LEUCOJUM aestivum (summer snowflake). Z4–9. Why this bulb is named summer snowflake is a complete mystery, in light of the fact that it blooms from late winter to midspring. Don't be deterred by the name. This is one of the very best spring bulbs for us. The flowers are lovely, white scalloped bells dotted with green that nod on 12"–18" stems for several weeks at a time. Give them a few years and they will form sizable, floriferous clumps. The foliage is a handsome dark green and narrowly strappy. Plant *Leucojum* in sun to part shade. Although they enjoy ample moisture, they can tolerate a fairly dry site once established. Note: You will also occasionally see *Leucojum vernum* (spring snowflake) offered. First of all, this is often really *Leucojum aestivum* in disguise. Secondly, the true *L. vernum* is reputed to do poorly in our area.

LEYCESTERIA formosa (Himalayan honeysuckle). Z8–10. This upright, deciduous shrub grows 4'–6' tall, eventually spreading to form a thicket. Juvenile shoots are blue-green and resemble bamboo. From late summer through fall it is covered with drooping spikes of white bellflowers with attractive, plum-colored bracts. Purple berries follow. This honeysuckle bush likes full sun to part shade in well-drained soil.

LIATRIS spicata (blazing star, gayfeather). Z3–9. In the summer 3'–4'-tall mauve spikes appear on this familiar tuberous native. It is excellent as a cut flower. Plant *Liatris* in full sun and perfectly drained soil. Cultivars are available in white, pink, and dark purple as well. Make sure *Liatris* has dry feet in winter. Kansas gayfeather (*L. pycnostachya*) is reputed to do even better for us than *L. spicata*. It sends up dense spikes of lavender flowers in summer.

LIGULARIA tussilaginea (leopard plant, ligularia). Z7b–10. These shade-loving ligularia survive our heat and humidity much better than the more commonly known leopard plant species. They like rich, organically amended soil that stays well-drained both summer and winter. Leopard plants are grown primarily for their handsome, kidney-shaped foliage, which is held above the stems in an umbrella-like fashion. In late summer, small, yellow daisy flowers appear on 2'–3' stalks above the foliage. Plant ligularia in part to full shade. 'Argenteum' has beautiful, creamy-white variegation. 'Aureomculata' is spotted bright yellow. 'Crispata' has ruffled leaf edges. Also known as *Farfugium tussilaginea*.

LILIUM (lily). This genus is blessed with almost a hundred species and hundreds of hybrids from which to choose. Learning the fine details that distinguish one from another is ultimately a time-consuming process and is not necessary to your enjoyment of lilies. In the coastal South we probably have better luck with the Asiatic hybrid lilies than the Orientals. In addition, there are many species lilies that do well for us. Lilies are not particular about soil requirements. They prefer full to part sun with excellent air circulation and rich, well-drained soil, although they will tolerate average soil. Because the bulbs have no outer sheath to protect them from drying out, you need to plant them immediately upon getting them.

Asiatic hybrid lilies. Z4–9. These are probably the easiest to grow in our area. They flourish in a well-drained soil with a little fertilization in the spring. Give them full sun or very light shade. They grow 1'–3' tall, displaying trumpets that generally, but not always, face upward. They are the first lilies to bloom, usually in early to midsummer and are available in a huge variety of colors. The Columbia-Platte strain has some interesting shades and shapes, but there are hundreds of other hybrids to choose from.

L. candidum (Madonna lily). Z4–9. Large, funnel-shaped, dazzling white lilies are borne on fairly short (2'–4') stems in summer. These lilies mix well with other perennials. Plant the bulbs of this particular lily very shallowly—1" below the surface.

L. formosanum (Formosa lily, Philippine lily). Z5–9. This 5'–7'-tall, fragrant giant blooms in late summer or fall with large white trumpets striped with purple, on purplish stems. It doesn't mind our hot summers. Give it well-drained, humusy soil.

L. lancifolium (tiger lily). Z3–9. This well-known native bears bright orange, recurved flowers with dark purple spotting. Because it seems to grow under just about any conditions you can give it, including dry shade, it can be a wee bit invasive.

L. longiformium (Easter lily). Z7b–10. We all know the large, white trumpets of the Easter lily. It can be planted outdoors in full to part sun in good, well-drained soil and will perennialize for us.

L. martagon (Turk's cap lily). Z3–10. These 3'–4'-tall plants tolerate more shade than other lilies and prefer a somewhat alkaline soil. If your soil is very acidic, add a little agricultural lime. They are recognizable by the reflexed petals of their pendent flowers, which are often spotted in the center. Nice, sturdy stems. This lily may take a bit more water than others.

Oriental hybrid lilies. Z4–8. Oriental hybrids are generally taller and have larger blooms than the Asiatics. They are among the last of the hybrid lilies to bloom, usually in mid- to late summer. Give them full sun to light shade in moist, acidic soil, and mulch well. Again, there are hundreds of cultivars to choose from. They are not as reliable as Asiatics for the coastal South.

L. regale (regal lily). Z3–10. These fragrant lilies, reaching 6' high, are truly regal and should be given a place in the garden where they can show off alone during their early summer bloom. Regals generally have wine-and-cream trumpets with yellow shading inside. Plant in full sun to part shade and do not disturb the planting. It will increase over the years.

LIMONIUM latifolium (sea lavender). Z4–9. Sea lavender is recognizable for its basal rosette of dark green leaves surmounted by thin, branching stems and delicate, papery, lavender-blue flowers. It grows 2'–3' tall in full sun in sandy, perfectly drained soil and blooms in late summer. Sea lavender tolerates beach conditions.

LIPPIA graveolens (Mexican oregano). Z8–11. This somewhat tender perennial herb is one of the most flavorful of the oreganos. It grows easily and rapidly into a 5'-tall shrub in full sun or light shade. Give it fertile, moist, well-drained soil, slightly on the alkaline side. In summer it bears tiny, creamy white flowers. Use the leaves in cooking as you would use oregano.

LIRIOPE muscari (lily turf, liriope). Z6–9. Without too much exaggeration, liriope and its look-alike, monkey grass (*Ophiopogon japonicus*), might claim to be the toughest characters in the whole neighborhood. They are both very hard to destroy. Liriope grows in part sun to deep, dark shade. It is not particular about soil. In fact, it will grow in the dry, root-clogged soil under large trees. It tolerates drought, heat, and humidity as though it were a part of the hardscape. In late summer the narrow, grass-like, evergreen leaves are topped with spikes of lavender flowers followed by dark berries. Use liriope as an edging, to mix in containers, as a groundcover, or in place of grass. The variegated forms, with cream-and-green-striped leaves, are especially attractive plants for lighting up a shady area. If you want a neater appearance, cut back the ratty-looking foliage in late winter.

If you're confused about the difference between liriope and monkey grass, so are many other people. For the record: liriope leaves are slightly thicker and more substantial, and its flowers are held up higher above the foliage.

LOBELIA (lobelia). These summer-blooming perennials prefer very moist garden conditions in filtered sunlight or part shade. Give lobelias good, rich soil and do not mulch in winter. Humming-birds and butterflies love the brightly colored, tubular flowers.

L. cardinalis (cardinal flower). Z2–9. Bright, cardinal-red flower spikes, 2'–4' tall, appear in late summer. This native tends to be short-lived in our area.

L. x 'Rose Beacon'. Z3–9. Bright pink flowers are borne on 2'–3'-tall plants. This hybrid will grow in a bog and tends to do very well in our area.

L. siphilitica (great blue lobelia). Z4–8. Probably the best, most reliable lobelia for the coastal South, this moisture lover sends up its blue spires somewhat later than the cardinal flower. The stalks grow 2'–3' tall.

LONICERA (honeysuckle). Honeysuckle has the ability to bring us back to our childhood with its summer scent and its familiar clusters of tubular flowers, each enclosing one drop of honey nectar. The Japanese honeysuckle that is most prevalent in our country (sold as 'Hall's Purple') can get out of control and become a menace. There are many other varieties, however, in a range of flower colors that are better adapted to the garden. Honeysuckle takes full sun to full shade in average soil. You will get many more blooms in full sun. Once-a-year fertilization will encourage blooming.

L. fragrantissima (winter honeysuckle). Z5–9. From late winter through early spring this 8'–12'-tall shrub produces highly fragrant, tiny white flowers touched with pink on the reverse. Foliage is blue-green.

L. heckrottii (gold flame honeysuckle). Z6–9. This semievergreen twiner is clothed in blue-green foliage and spring-to-frost flowers that are pink on the outside and orangy-yellow on the inside. It will climb to a height of 15'. Red berries often follow the flowers.

L. nitida 'Baggensen's Gold'. Z7–9. This honeysuckle makes a compact 3'×3' bush with boxwood-like, golden leaves. The gold color is excellent in the garden year-round. Plant this one in sun to light shade.

L. sempervirens (coral honeysuckle, trumpet honeysuckle). Z3–9. Fans of slender, red-orange tubular flowers are borne profusely in early summer and intermittently thereafter through winter. This semievergreen vine also gives us small, translucent red berries in winter. Hummingbirds love it, and it is drought resistant once established. Recommended varieties: 'Magnifica' —deep scarlet flowers; 'Sulphurea'—sulfur yellow flowers that bloom later than the species but for a longer period of time.

LOROPETALUM chinense 'Rubrum' (Chinese fringe, loropetalum). Z7–9. This woody, evergreen shrub mixes well with perennials. Growing 6'–15' tall, its juvenile foliage is reddish-purple, a good contrast or color echo in the garden. In winter and early spring the shrub is covered with small, shocking-pink, tassel-shaped flowers. Give it full to part sun, rich, acidic soil, and water it during periods of drought. Can be pruned into a small tree.

LUNARIA annua (honesty, money plant). Z4–8. These spring-flowering plants are prized not only for their purple flower clusters, which are borne on 2'–3' stems, but also for the silver-colored, flat, round, paper-thin seedpods that are often used in dried arrangements. Honesty is a biennial that self-seeds readily. The white-flowered honesty (var. *alba*) is equally common and easy to grow. For best results, plant honesty in full sun to part shade in poor soil. 'Variegata' is a particularly handsome variety, with its toothed, white-margined leaves and magenta flowers.

LYCHNIS coronaria (rose campion). Biennial. This cottage garden favorite is a southern classic that reseeds fairly readily. It grows 1'–3' tall with gray, woolly leaves. The branching stems produce salverform, magenta-to-crimson flowers from spring through summer. Seeds sown in the fall

will produce basal leaves the following spring and flowers the spring after that. Grow *Lychnis* in full to part sun in fertile, well-drained soil. 'Angel Blush' has flowers that start out white and turn pale pink.

LYCORIS (resurrection flower). These bulbs have the interesting habit of going dormant all summer and sending up their naked flower stalks in late summer or early fall before the new leaves have appeared. Plant them in well-drained soil in full to part sun. Don't let them stay wet in winter.

L. aurea (golden lycoris). Z7–10. Yellow-gold, funnel-shaped flowers appear in summer on 1'–2' stems. Plant these bulbs barely below the surface.

L. radiata (spider lily). Z7–10. This bright red lycoris prefers full sun. Its spidery flowers appear for two weeks in late summer or early fall on 12"–18"-long stems.

L. squamigera (naked ladies, autumn lycoris). Z5–9. This bulb increases rapidly, giving us rosy-pink, spidery flowers on 2'-long stems in mid- to late summer. The leaves are a healthy green all winter, but tend to become unattractive as they go dormant in spring.

LYGODIUM japonicum (Japanese climbing fern, trailing maidenhair). Z7–10. The chartreuse green, lacy fronds of this semievergreen southern classic can be found twining their way up trees or other supports to a height of 15'. It has naturalized in many parts of the coastal South. Give it rich, moist soil and full to part shade. Prune it back in spring. Some gardeners find Japanese climbing fern invasive and have banished it from their gardens.

LYSIMACHIA (loosestrife, moneywort). Some of the moneyworts are wonderful groundcovers for us and work well with spring bulbs and summer perennials. Others are invasive weeds, so watch out which ones you grow. (Avoid *L. clethroides* (gooseneck loosestrife), a particularly noxious. invasive species.) *Lysimachia* enjoys rich, moist soil with some shade, so keep it well watered.

L. congestifolia 'Outback Sunset' (golden money-wort, golden globes loosestrife). Z7–9. This is a mottled groundcover with touches of yellow, cream, rust, and light green. Yellow flowers bloom off and on in summer. Grow this *Lysimachia* in full sun to part shade. Rich, moist soil will give best results. It makes a terrific groundcover for spring bulbs, especially the smaller *Narcissi*.

L. nummularia 'Aurea' (golden creeping jenny, golden moneywort). Z3–9. This is a terrific little groundcover with bright golden-yellow, rounded leaves that creeps at a good pace by sending roots down from its trailing stems. Small yellow flowers are borne in summer, but it is grown primarily for its semievergold foliage. Plant in part sun to part shade. Use this plant as an underplanting or to form a golden pool where the eye needs a resting spot in the garden. It also looks great spilling over the edge of a container. 'Sunset Yellow' is a good cultivar that stays attractive all winter.

L. japonica 'Minuitissima'. Z6–9. This is a mat-forming groundcover (2" tall) with tiny, yellow-green leaves. It also works well between stepping-stones or in a rock garden. Yellow starflowers appear in summer. Give it ample moisture.

L. punctata (yellow loosestrife). Z5–9. Primrose yellow flowers are borne in whorls atop 18" stems in summer on this old-timey plant. It will grow in full sun or light shade and is not particular about soil. But pay attention, because this is one of those plants that can get away from you and make itself at home *all* over your garden.

MACFADYENA unguis-cati (cat's claw vine). Z8–10. This is a vigorous, semievergreen vine that can grow to 30' by twining upward with its claw-like tendrils and attaching its holdfasts to masonry, wood, and cement. It is clothed in glossy, green, ovate leaflets and produces large (2"–4" across), bright yellow, tubular flowers in spring. The flowers are followed by bean-like seedpods. Grow cat's claw in full to part sun in well-drained soil. This vine will take over large areas by sending down roots where its stems touch the ground. It also seeds itself freely and develops very deep, tuberous roots that may be hard to remove. Because it has so many successful ways of making itself at home, it is considered invasive by some coastal gardeners.

MALVAVISCUS arboreus drummondii (Turk's cap, wax mallow, sleeping hibiscus). Z7b–10. Turk's cap is a great plant for the coastal South. This fascinating native shrub grows 3'–8' tall, bearing strange, twisted, red flowers that never fully open. Plant in part sun in moist, well-drained soil and prune in spring, because flowering occurs on new wood. Turk's cap will continue blooming from mid-June through late September. This somewhat floppy shrub is beloved of hummingbirds. In most parts of the coastal South it will die back to the ground in winter. A white-flowered version, 'Alba', is also available.

MANDEVILLA laxa (mandevilla, Chilean jasmine). Z9–10. This vine is not hardy in all of the coastal South and will have to be brought indoors at the first frost. However, it is such a spectacular, reliable bloomer all summer and fall that it should be grown even north of Zone 9. It tolerates our heat and humidity, doesn't suffer particularly from pests or disease, and has handsome, dark green foliage to complement the profusion of large (2" across), tubular, flared blooms. *Mandevilla* cultivars are available in pink, white, and yellow. Plant in full sun in rich, well-drained soil and keep it watered during periods of drought. It grows to 15' on arbors, trellises, and any other available support.

MASCAGNIA lilacina (butterfly vine, lavender orchid vine). Z8–10. This 15'–20' deciduous vine resembles honeysuckle in its foliage. Lilac-blue, orchid-like flowers appear in summer, followed by winged seedpods that look something like butterflies, hence its other common name. Grow this vine in full sun with rich, moist soil. It can withstand some drought.

MAZUS reptans (mazus). Z3–8. This diminutive, creeping groundcover works well between paving stones in part sun to part shade, producing tiny blue or white flowers in late spring or early summer. The foliage is bright green and toothed. It needs to be kept moist but not wet in order to thrive. In mild winters it will be evergreen. This is a very tough groundcover.

MELAMPODIUM paludosum 'Million Gold' (butter daisy, melampodium). Annual. This is one of the best annuals for the hot summer months in the coastal South. It thrives in our heat and humidity and is very drought tolerant. The oval, toothed, evergreen leaves remain remarkably healthy-looking, and the yellow daisy flowers (with yellow central disks) bloom nonstop. The plants grow about 3' tall and will form a bushy clump if planted in full sun with rich, well-drained soil and some slow-release fertilizer. Melampodiums don't require deadheading or any other ministrations. Also known as *Leucanthemum paludosum*.

MELISSA officinalis (lemon balm). Z4–9. This semievergreen, stoloniferous relative of the mints grows well in full sun to full shade. The lemon-flavored leaves can be added to teas and many other kitchen creations. The cultivars 'Allgold' and 'Aurea' give us, respectively, bright yellow and variegated yellow-and-green foliage, which are especially useful in the winter garden. Small flower spikes are borne on and off in summer.

MENTHA (mint). There are lots of flavors of mint, including spearmint (*M. spicata*, Z3–9), pepper-mint (*M. x piperita*, Z3–9), lemon mint (*M. x piperata citrata*, Z3–9), apple mint (*M. suaveolens*, Z6–9), and pineapple mint (*M. suaveolens* 'Variegata', Z6–9), among others. This easy-to-grow herb flourishes almost too well under conditions ranging from full sun to full shade and can, in fact, take over rather quickly. Some people grow mint in containers for this reason. Not just for flavoring ice tea and mint juleps, mint is also used in cooking the main course in many parts of the world. Note: Corsican mint (*M. requienii*)—a tiny, creeping, mat-forming mint that is used as a groundcover between paving stones in part shade and moist, perfectly drained soil—is fairly averse to our hot, humid summers and is not recommended.

MILLETIA reticulata (evergreen wisteria). Z7–9. This vigorous, semievergreen wisteria produces erect racemes of wine-colored flowers in late summer, followed by attractive seedpods in late fall. This vine likes our climate, especially if you plant it in full sun to light shade in moist, rich, well-drained soil. It will grow to 20' or higher and twice as wide, twining on fences, arbors, or other structures. It can get out of control and clamber up into trees if you're not careful.

MIRABILIS jalapa (four o'clocks). Z8–10. The flowers of this old southern standby open in the late evening, usually well past four o'clock, from midsummer through fall. They are borne in clusters of fragrant white tubes atop a strong, shrubby, 3'–4'-high plant. There are also yellow and red forms and some with variations in between. Plant four o'clocks in full sun in well-drained soil. This tuberous-rooted perennial will die back to the ground except in the warmest parts of the coastal South. Four o'clock reseeds readily.

MISCANTHUS sinensis (maiden grass, eulalia grass). Z6–9. This ornamental grass is a great addition to the garden, growing in full sun to part shade and even tolerating drought and salt spray. *Miscanthus* cultivars are available in heights from 3' to 7' tall, which gives you a wide choice, depending on your needs and the space available. The attractive fall flower plumes remain on the plant through winter, adding variety to the winter landscape. Recommended varieties: 'Adagio'—gray-green foliage on a 2'–4'-tall plant, with pink plumes that age to white; 'Cosmopolitan'—6'-tall, with wide leaves with creamy striped margins, works well as a specimen plant; 'Gracillimus'—4'–5'-tall, narrow-leaved with a white midrib, excellent bronze color in the fall; 'Morning Light'—compact, 4'–5' tall, with narrow, white-margined leaves and plumes that emerge reddish and mature to tan; 'Rotsilber'—the leaves on this 4'-tall plant have a silver midrib, its autumn feathers are silvery red; 'Silver Feather'—an 8'-tall plant bearing silvery or pinkish-brown plumes; 'Variegatus'—6'-tall plant with creamy white and pale green bands running the length of the foliage; 'Zebrinus'—5'–7'-tall plant with horizontal golden striping and silver plumes. Note: *M. sinensis* 'Purpurescens' is not recommended for our area because it doesn't achieve the deep purple-red coloration in the fall that it does elsewhere. Here it just gets ugly.

MONARDA (bee balm, bergamot). These herbaceous perennials are known for their attractive, whorled flowers and colorful flower bracts. Bloom time is from midsummer onward. Wild bee balm and spotted bee balm are the two best choices for our area.

M. didyma (bee balm). Z3–8. Although this is the most commonly known bee balm, it is not the best for the coastal South. After the first year it may not bloom reliably, and it is prone to powdery mildew. The spidery flowers are surrounded by colorful bracts on 2'–4' stems. This species likes part shade to full sun in very moist soil in an area with good air circulation. Cultivars are available in purple, pink, white, red, and many in-between shades. Cultivars: 'Jacob Kline'—dark red flowers on 2'–3' tall, mildew-resistant plants; 'Marshall's Delight'—clear pink flowers on mildew-resistant plants; 'Petite Delight'—lavender-pink flowers on 15"-tall, mildew-resistant plants.

M. fistulosa (wild bee balm, wild bergamot). Z4–9. Much more heat tolerant and resistant to mildew than *M. didyama* and its hybrids, this species is somewhat less showy. The whorled flowers are lavender to whitish and its purple bracts are borne on 2'–5'-long stems. One of the best bee balms for the South, it is a clump former that will grow bushy over time.

M. punctata (spotted bee balm, spotted horsemint). Z4–9. This native bee balm performs well for us in sun or part sun and well-drained soil. The flower corollas are creamy yellow with maroon markings. Attractive, lavender-colored flower bracts add interest. This is a good beach plant.

MUHLENBERGIA (muhly grass). These terrific, drought- and heat-tolerant native grasses should be used more widely in the coastal South. They have thin, whip-like foliage and an attractive weeping habit. Plant them in full to part sun in dry or moist soil. Muhly grows at the beach too.

M. capillaris (hairy awn muhly grass, sweet grass, purple muhly, Gulf muhly). Z6–9. This 18"–30"-tall, very showy muhly bursts forth with clouds of purplish-pink flowers on 4'–5' stems in late summer and fall, stealing the show. Also known as *M. filipes*.

M. dumosa (bamboo muhly grass). Z8–9. This grass has a clumping, bamboo-like habit and makes a graceful, fountain shape. It grows 4'–6' tall.

M. lindheimeri (Lindheimer's muhly). Z6–9. This 3'-tall, clump-forming blue grass boasts dramatic, 5'-tall, grayish-purple plumes in the fall.

M. rigens. Z8–9. This whip-like grass grows 3'–4' tall and produces impressive, 6'-tall, silvery seed spikes in the fall. Plant it in full sun to light shade. It tolerates both dry and moist locations.

MUSA (banana). These large-leaved, tropical-looking plants add a touch of drama to any garden. There are numerous species and cultivars with variations of size and foliage color. Generally, the actual banana that you eat with your cornflakes will appear only in the warmest regions of the coastal South, but you never know. Plant your bananas in full sun to part shade in very rich, moist soil with excellent drainage. Don't allow the banana plant to have wet feet in the winter.

M. acuminata (giant sweet edible banana). Z8–11. This tropical-looking monster can grow to 20'-high with 9'-long, dark green, shiny leaves. There are dwarf varieties that grow 5'–6' tall and some with attractive red foliage.

M. basjoo (hardy banana). Z7–11. Probably the hardiest of the *Musas*, this giant grows to 15' tall with huge, 8'-long leaf blades. Creamy yellow flowers appear in summer.

M. ornata (rose banana). Z9–11. This tender, ornamental banana is a favorite in New Orleans gardens. Growing to 9' tall, it has waxy, blue-green leaf blades that grow 4'–6' long. The bird-like, purplish-pink and yellow inflorescences are held high atop erect, "false" stems.

M. velutina (pink banana). Z7–11. This 4'–8'-tall banana has showy orange flowers surrounded by pink bracts in summer.

M. zebrina (bloodleaf banana). Z8–11. This striking banana has huge green leaves splotched with wine red. It grows 6'–8' tall, producing many offshoots, which can be removed and planted.

MYRRHIS odorata (sweet cicely). Z7–10. This herb produces umbels of white flowers in early summer on 3'–4' stems. The foliage resembles parsley and can be cut often to rejuvenate the plant and to use in garnishes and salads. The root and seeds are also used in cooking and baking. The flavor lies somewhere between celery and anise. Grow sweet cicely in rich, well-drained soil in part shade.

MYRTUS communis (Greek myrtle). Z7–10. This dwarf evergreen shrub, which was sacred to the Greeks and Romans, will grow 3'–5' tall but can be kept clipped if you want. It is excellent for topiaries and knot gardens in the coastal South. Greek myrtle takes full to part sun in somewhat sandy soil and perfect drainage. The aromatic branches may be tossed on the grill, the leaves can be used in marinades and vinegars, and the berries can be used like juniper berries.

NARCISSUS (daffodil, jonquil). Spring wouldn't be spring without daffodils. This large genus offers us many, many wonderful species and hybrids to choose from. Just keep in mind that not all daffodils thrive in our climate. Those that are well adapted will give you years and years of pleasure. As with many bulbs, *Narcissus* likes a sunny position in good, well-drained soil and benefits greatly from an annual spring application of bulb booster. For best performance, plant the biggest bulbs you can get your hands on and always let the leaves senesce (turn yellow) before you remove them; otherwise, you are stealing their mechanism for producing food and a good show of blooms the following year.

There are *Narcissi* that begin blooming in January, there are some that bloom in the late spring, and many choices in between. Although the trumpet-shaped and the large- and small-cupped daffodils are perhaps better known and more common in the trade, the following wonderful species and cultivars do very well in the coastal South. The trumpet part of the daffodil is called the corona, the petals surrounding it are called the perianth.

N. bulbicodium (hoop petticoat daffodil). Z7–9. These tiny wild daffodils have 4"-tall, grass-like winter foliage that is almost tubular in appearance. The corona is a bright yellow, flaring funnel with tiny, narrow, star-like perianth segments at its base. Hoop petticoats bloom from midwinter to spring and are among the most prolific bloomers of all *Narcissi* in our area.

N. cyclameneus (reflexed jonquils). Z6–9. These small (4"–6"-tall), early-blooming gems need perfect drainage in sandy soil. They are characterized by a recurved perianth and a long, narrow corona. They bloom in February and early March before the heat sets in, which gives them a leg up in terms of survival. The hybrids best suited to our climate include 'February Gold', 'March Sunrise', and 'Peeping Tom'. The miniatures— 'Beryl', 'Jack Snipe', 'Jetfire', and 'Tête à Tête'— should be given a leafy soil, part shade, and plenty of water during the growing season.

N. jonquilla (jonquil). Z4–9. These early-spring daffodils perform very well for us, tolerating damp winters and baking hot summers. The species is a diminutive plant with slender, rush-like foliage and clusters of tiny, fragrant, yellow flowers. Jonquils grow 6"–10" tall and can tolerate standing water and heavy clay. Among the early and midseason *jonquilla* hybrids, some of the best for us are 'Autumn Gold', 'Baby Moon', 'Bell Song', 'Bunting', 'Curlew', 'Divertimento', 'Golden Dawn', 'Key Lime', 'Orange Queen', 'Pink Angel', 'Pipit', 'Pueblo', 'Quail', 'Suzy', and 'Trevithian'.

N. x *odorus* Linnaeus **'Campernelli'** (the campernelle). Z4–9. This may be one of the oldest and most commonly occurring daffodil species in the South. It is a very considerate bulb in that its foliage withers discreetly, unlike some of its hybrid cousins. Like jonquils, campernelles tolerate our damp winters and hot summers. Clusters of fragrant, long-lasting, golden yellow blooms appear atop 12"–15" stems in very early spring. Some people consider the *jonquilla* hybrid 'Trevithian' to be the modern equivalent of the wild campernelle.

N. pseudonarcissus **'Telemoneus Plenus'** (Lent lily). Z3–9. Widely naturalized in southeastern meadows and roadsides, this 6"–8"-tall, pale-yellow-and-deep-yellow species daffodil is the earliest of the daffodils to bloom, a little later than the paperwhites. This is really a wildflower in disguise—small, informal, and unprepossessing.

N. tazetta (bunch-flowering narcissus or paper-whites). *Tazettas* do very well in our area. Recognizable by their very shallow, almost flat coronas, these fragrant *Narcissi* generally grow 12"–15" tall. The following are some of the best *tazetta* hybrids and varieties.

  N. tazetta **'Avalanche'**. Z6–9. Similar to the old southern garden favorite known as 'Seventeen Sisters', 'Avalanche' blooms in early spring, producing a white perianth and lemon yellow corona on strong, 18"-long stems.

  N. tazetta **'Erlicheer'**. Z6–9. This Dutch-bred strain has become something of a substitute for 'Grand Primo', with clusters of double white flowers in early spring. It may take several years to get established.

  N. tazetta **'Grand Primo'**. Z7–9. This southern classic is a survivor. It is not picky about soil, being able to withstand both wet and dry conditions. Its apparently snowy white blooms are actually a subtle combination of very pale yellow and cream. They are borne in bountiful clusters in early spring after the paperwhites have finished. This may be the most vigorous *Narcissus* we can grow in the coastal South.

  N. tazetta var. *orientalis* (Chinese sacred lily). Z8b–10. A somewhat tender, winter-blooming tazetta with highly fragrant, sizable flower umbels. A yellowish-orange corona is surrounded by a creamy white perianth. This excellent bulb is also known as 'Grand Emperor'.

  N. tazetta var. *papyraceus* (paperwhites). Z8b–10. Clusters of highly fragrant, bright white flowers are borne on 14"-tall stalks in late winter. Every few years, lift your paperwhites and replant them to a depth of 6". They have a tendency to rise up in the ground and to split into small, non-flowering-sized bulbs, which is against their own and the gardener's best interest. 'Galilee' and 'Ziva' are among the newer bulbs bred in Israel for increased flower size.

N. triandrus (angel's tears). Z4–9. Triandrus are recognizable by the clusters of drooping flowers each made up of a globular corona and a reflexed perianth, looking together quite tear-like. They bloom later in the spring than the jonquils and campernelles, and their blooms tend to be long lasting. Not only are they not particular about soil conditions, they will even bloom in light shade. They grow to about 9"–12". Good bets are 'Hawera', 'Ice Wings', 'Petrel', 'Thalia', and 'Tuesday's Child'.

NEOMARICA *gracilis* (walking iris). Z8–10. This rhizomatous perennial has erect, sword-shaped leaves arranged in basal fans. The white iris flowers with blue markings in the center are borne on 2'-high, leaf-like stalks in summer. Give walking iris a spot in part shade in fertile, moist, well-drained soil. The plant will "walk" by setting down roots wherever the stalk touches the soil. This is a somewhat tender perennial, so give it a protected spot and mulch it well in winter. It is a southern classic.

NEPETA (catnip, catmint). Both of the common names for this perennial herb have been earned over the centuries as untold numbers of cats have sprawled, wallowed, and rolled deliriously in its aromatic foliage. Leaves are woolly and gray-green. Lavender flower spikes appear in late spring and summer. These plants are members of the mint family, which means they spread rapidly and easily. Some gardeners find that catmint does better in containers than in the ground. In a container the stems will hang down and form themselves into a J shape. Plant catmint in part sun to shade and well-drained soil.

N. cataria (catnip, catmint). Z3–9. This is a tough, 3'-tall perennial with lavender-spotted, white flowers. 'Citriodora' has lemon-scented foliage reputed to be distasteful to felines.

N. x *faassenii* 'Souvenir d'André Chaudron' (catnip, catmint). Z5–9. This cultivar, which is probably the best one for the coastal South, grows 3' tall with lavender-blue flowers.

NEPHROLEPIS *cordifolia* (Southern sword fern). Z8b–11. This is a tender fern that thrives in the warmest parts of the coastal South, where it will spread itself around a partially sunny or shady spot. It can be used in poor soil and neglected areas and makes a good shady groundcover. Its erect, sword-shaped fronds rise up 1'–3'. Wait until spring to cut off the ratty-looking fronds. Give this fern a heavy mulch of pine straw where there is danger of heavy frost.

NICOTIANA *sylvestris* (flowering tobacco). Annual. Flowering tobacco has been used as a summer annual for many generations in the South. The fragrant, white flowers are borne atop branched, 3'–5'-tall stems. The flowers are narrow, flared tubes and often open in the evening. Flowering tobacco needs a spot in full sun to light shade in fertile, moist, well-drained soil. Add a slow-release fertilizer at planting time. In mild winters the plants may die back to the ground and reappear the following summer.

NIPPONATHEMUM *nipponicum* (Montauk daisy, Nippon daisy). Z5–9. This bushy, 2'–3'-tall, leather-leaved, white daisy works very well for us, blooming from early fall through frost. It is good for the beach because it tolerates drought and salt spray. Give it a position in full sun with fertile, perfectly drained soil and consider disguising its leggy stems behind something else. Montauk daisy abhors wet feet, especially in winter. Cut it back drastically when it stops blooming in the fall.

ODONTONEMA *strictum* (firespike). Z9–11. This somewhat tender, clumping shrub has 4"–6"-long, glossy-green, wavy-edged leaves and a tendency to sprawl. It grows 3'–6' tall in full sun or part shade. In summer it produces spikes of bright red tubular flowers. Give firespike fertile, moist, well-drained soil. It is a favorite of hummingbirds.

OENANTHE *javanica* 'Flamingo' (creeping celery, flamingo plant). Z8–11. These delicately foliaged plants work well as a groundcover in a partially sunny spot, growing to about 8" tall. The variegation in the leaves includes pale pink, white, and light green, and is quite lovely. Creeping celery enjoys moisture and can stand to grow in a bog, but it will also grow in regular garden soil. In Asia this plant is used as a vegetable.

OENOTHERA (evening primrose, sundrops). Many of the native *Oenothera* do well for us, some so

well that people throw them out of their garden. The evening primroses are so-called because of their habit of opening their blooms in the late afternoon and early morning only. Sundrops, on the other hand, bloom all day long. *Oenothera* prefer full sun and good drainage.

O. *fruticosa* (common sundrops). Z4–8. Clusters of bright yellow flowers are borne on 18"–24"-long red stems in summer.

O. *drummondii* (beach evening primrose). Z8–10. Gray-green, hairy leaves are topped with pale yellow flowers on this native, spreading plant. This tough perennial prefers a poor, sandy soil and baking sun. It tolerates salt spray and is a good one for the beach.

O. *perennis* (nodding sundrops). Z3–8. Lance-like green leaves are topped by 1'–2'-high stems that bear loose racemes of open yellow flowers. They like full sun and well-drained soil.

O. *speciosa* (showy evening primrose). Z5–8. This native has naturalized in the South as elsewhere, even in the most neglected vacant lots. Some people consider it weedy. Others find it incredibly beautiful, with its shell-pink, almost white, delicate flowers and finely pinnate leaves. It blooms in late spring and early summer and will colonize by stolons where it is happy. Give it full sun and just about any kind of soil.

OPHIOPOGON (monkey grass, mondo grass). Z5–10. Like *Liriope*, with which it is often confused, monkey grass is everywhere in the South. It is so easy to grow that a few fleshy root divisions will make a thick clump in no time. Use this 6"–8"-tall, evergreen, rhizomatous perennial as an edging or as a groundcover in those spots where nothing else will grow. Monkey grass grows in just about any soil from full sun to full shade, spreading rapidly by stolons and tuberous roots. It is happiest in a shady moist spot. The leaf blades are narrower and shorter generally than those of *Liriope*. It produces small lavender flower spikes in summer followed by glossy purple berries in fall.

O. *japonicus* (mondo grass). Z6–9. This is the most commonly grown monkey grass, which has dark green, 15"-long leaves. 'Nana' (dwarf monkey grass) grows only 3" tall and can be used to make a fake lawn where regular grass won't grow. It looks nice in a checkerboard pattern between brick or cement pavers too.

O. *planiscapus* 'Nigrescens' (black mondo grass). Z6–9. This interesting 6"-tall mondo grass has black foliage and pink lily-of-the-valley-type flowers in summer. It needs good drainage and even moisture in a shady position. It is somewhat slower to mature than the dark green varieties but is worth the wait. A terrific accent plant for containers.

ORIGANUM (oregano, wild marjoram). Z3–8, except as noted. This classic culinary herb takes full to part sun and well-drained soil. Don't make the soil overly rich. Some oreganos and marjorams are more decorative than flavorful. It pays to select carefully if you are growing the herbs for your kitchen. Mexican oregano (*Lippia graveolens*) is another excellent choice for strong oregano flavor.

O. laevigatum (oregano). This 2'-tall, woody subshrub performs well in the coastal South, producing wiry-stemmed, lavender flowers in late summer and dying back each winter. The stems root at the joints on this somewhat sprawling plant. Used as a groundcover and for erosion control.

O. majorana (sweet marjoram). Annual. Trim this 1'–2'-tall annual or tender perennial to maintain a bushy shape, and cut off the pinkish-white flower clusters. The flavorful, small, gray-green leaves are used in cooking.

O. vulgare (common oregano). This rhizomatous, woody perennial forms a subshrub 1'–3' tall. Although this is the most commonly sold oregano (especially in seed packets), it is not particularly flavorful. Some of the cultivars are attractive for mixing with other herbs and perennials. Recommended varieties: 'Aureum'—this 1'-tall, slow-spreading plant with golden leaves is especially good for making a river of gold, as it keeps its bright yellow foliage all winter long; 'Compactum'—compact and low-growing (6" tall), this variety spreads well and can be used as a groundcover; 'Humile'—growing only 2" tall, this creeping perennial does well in rock gardens and has a good marjoram flavor; 'True Greek'—a favorite among cooks for its excellent flavor.

O. vulgare* subsp. *hirtum (Greek oregano). Z3–8. This is one of the most flavorful of all the oreganos, with a strong, sharp taste—an excellent choice for cooking. Also known as *O. heracleoticum* and *O. hirtum*.

ORNITHOGALUM (ornithogalum). Good spring bulbs for the coastal South. Plant in full sun to light shade in fertile, well-drained soil. Once established, they will tolerate drought. The clumps will increase over the years if conditions are to their liking.

O. dubium. Z8–10. This tulip look-alike boasts long-blooming clusters of yellow-orange, tulip-shaped flowers on 10"–20"-long stems, beginning in spring.

O. narbonense (virgin's spray). Z6–10. This excellent little bulb does well for us, sending up graceful, 15"–24"-tall, pyramidal racemes of white star-flowers in late spring and early summer above attractive, gray-green basal foliage.

O. umbellatum (star of Bethlehem). Z4–10. Clusters of white, star-shaped flowers appear on 9"-long stems in spring. The foliage is grassy.

OSMUNDA. Two of the best native, deciduous ferns for the coastal South are in this genus. These rhizomatous ferns normally grow in part to full shade, but they can tolerate sun if their feet are kept wet. They need rich, organically amended soil, slightly on the acid side. Keep them moist to wet!

O. cinnamomea (cinnamon fern). Z3–9. This native fern grows 2'–3' tall, producing stiff, fertile fronds in spring, which turn to a cinnamon color before they die back. The sterile fronds appear first as fiddleheads, emerging from the aboveground roots, and then grow into arching fronds with brown, woolly fibers at the base. The fronds turn bronze before they die back in late fall.

O. regalis (royal fern). Z4–9. Like cinnamon fern, the stately royal fern can be grown successfully here if it is given rich, moist soil. Royal fern ranges in height from 3' to a dramatic 6', depending on how thoroughly its requirements are being met. Emerging fronds are bronzy red and turn green as they mature. Fertile fronds are tipped with tasseled, rust brown spore cases. The fibrous, matted roots are used in orchid culture.

OSTEOSPERMUM *jucundum* (African daisy). Z8–10. This is the hardiest of the *Osteospermums*, a genus of subshrubby perennials with attractive daisy-like flowers. The flowers of this species have magenta ray florets and purple central disks. They bloom all summer long on 4"–20"-tall stalks. This clump former needs full to part sun, fertile soil, and good drainage. Other *Osteospermums* seen more frequently in the trade (such as *O.* 'Cannington Roy', *O. ecklonis*, and *O. caulescens*) have mauve-tinged, white ray florets with blue-purple central disks. These are not reliably hardy but may be used as annuals and overwintered indoors.

OXALIS (wood sorrel, four-leaf clover, shamrock). Not the common, noxious, yellow-flowered weed, these cultivars of *Oxalis* are an excellent addition to the garden. These little bulbs will often bloom in late winter and spring and repeat the show on and off in summer and fall. They appreciate shade but will also survive in a partially sunny spot. Give them organically rich, moist soil. They form attractive clumps where they are happy. *Oxalis* generally reach 2"–4" in height.

O. deppei. Z6–9. These *Oxalis* have soft green, clover-like foliage and sprays of small pink flowers. The green leaflets of the cultivar 'Iron Cross' have purple markings that form a cross shape. Also known as *O. tetraphylla.*

O. depressa. Z5–9. The yellow-throated pink flowers of this *Oxalis* form swirling, pinwheel-like patterns as the lips of the flower funnels fan out.

O. enneaphylla. Z6–9. Attractive, blue-green foliage and open, funnel-shaped, pink and white flowers.

O. obtusa. Z8–9. The pink, red, or yellow of the large, wide-open, funnel-shaped flowers of this mat former are set off dramatically against gray-green foliage.

O. purpurea. Z8–10. This species has larger leaves and larger flowers than many other *Oxalis.* The flowers, usually rosy red, are also available in shades of pink, white, and lavender.

O. regnelli. Z6–8. These *Oxalis* have burgundy- to plum-colored leaves and flowers of pink or white. They make an excellent, small, color highlight when mixed among other perennials.

O. versicolor 'Candy Cane'. Z8–10. True to its name, this cultivar has solitary white flowers with red striping. The buds are striped red also.

PACHYSTASIS lutea (yellow shrimp plant, lollipop plant). Z8–11. A good semievergreen shrub for the coastal South, shrimp plant grows 3'–6' tall with 6"-long, narrow, dark green leaves. In full sun or light shade, it bears showy spikes of bright yellow inflorescences, each one made up of a cone-like formation of overlapping, yellow bracts with protruding, tubular, white flowers. Flowering begins in late spring and continues through summer. Give this plant fertile, moist, well-drained soil. To encourage a more bushy shape, cut it back in late winter and keep it pruned during the growing season.

PANCRATIUM maritimum (sea daffodil). Z8–11. These summer-blooming bulbs grow 12"–18" high and resemble spider lilies with their white, whiskery flowers. Their leaves are blue-green, strap-like, and semievergreen. Sea daffodils, as their name suggests, do well at the beach because they like sandy soil and hot, baking sun in summer. Don't let them sit in boggy soil.

PANDOREA jasminoides (bower vine). Z8–11. This somewhat tender, fast-growing, evergreen climber reaches 20'–30', producing clusters of large, white, trumpet-shaped flowers with dramatic, deep-pink throats in summer. There are pure white and pure pink cultivars as well. Bower vine appreciates a spot in light shade in average

soil. Also known as *Bignonia jasminoides* and *Tecoma jasminoides.*

PANICUM virgatum (switchgrass, panic grass). These native ornamental grasses make tight upright clumps of narrow-leaved foliage in full to part sun. They tolerate drought but appreciate some watering. Cultivars: 'Heavy Metal' (Z5–9)—a very rigid, upright plant with metallic blue leaves that turn to yellow in the fall and reddish-brown, upright plumes that add to its attraction in late summer and fall; 'Cloud Nine' (Z2–9)—this sturdy switchgrass grows 6'–9' tall with blue foliage and rusty-colored plumes in fall; 'Warrior' (Z5–9)—fall color is deep red on this 4'–5'-tall plant.

PARTHENOCISSUS quinquifolia (Virginia creeper). Z3–9. This native vine is vigorous and reliable. Growing in sun or shade, it climbs to 50' via twining tendrils and also attaches itself to wood, masonry, or other structures with disk-like suckers. It can be used to cover fences and walls, as a trailing groundcover, and for erosion control on banks. It is a fast tree-climber. The palmate leaves have five separate, sharply toothed leaflets. The reddish fall color is not as dramatic in the coastal South as it is in cooler areas.

PASSIFLORA incarnata (passionflower vine, maypop). Z6–10. This deciduous, 8'–10' vine produces stunning white or pale lavender flowers with purple- or pink-colored, wavy corona filaments and large white stamens in the center. Plant passionflower vine in full to part sun in rich, moist soil. Pollinated flowers will produce egg-shaped, yellow-green fruits. There are other passionflower species, as well as a number of hybrids available in pure white, pink, red, and combinations or gradations in between. Some are not reliably winter hardy above Zone 9. 'Byron Beauty' is a particularly beautiful, floriferous cultivar, bearing stunning, fragrant, white-and-blue flowers with purple centers.

PATRINIA (patrinia). Z5–9. These heat- and humidity-tolerant perennials work well for us. They mix nicely with just about everything else in the garden, sending up yellow or white, flat-topped flower corymbs for weeks at a time. Plant patrinia in full to part sun in a good, well-drained soil, and water it during dry spells. Patrinia develops a taproot, so don't disturb it.

P. scabiosifolia. This excellent 5'–6'-tall plant is topped with umbels of mustard yellow flowers for several weeks in summer. The Japanese form, 'Nagoya', is very similar but shorter, reaching a height of about 3'.

P. villosa. This 2'–3'-tall, somewhat sprawling patrinia is a fast-growing clump-former. Small white flower heads appear in late summer and fall.

PAVONIA (pavonia). These hibiscus relatives produce beautiful mallow flowers all summer long. They prefer full to part sun in moist, fertile soil with excellent drainage. They tolerate our heat, humidity, and occasional drought very well. Pavonias attract butterflies.

P. brasiliensis (South American mallow). Z8–10. A 4'-tall bush covered in summer with pale pink, cup-shaped blossoms with red centers.

P. hastata (Brazilian pavonia). Z8b–10. This woody, 4'-tall subshrub produces pale pink mallow flowers with dark pink eyes all summer long. It also seeds itself about quite readily.

P. lasiopetala (pavonia, rock rose). Z7b–10. This 3' × 3' native subshrub is covered with pink, cup-shaped flowers from summer through fall. Keep it pruned to increase bushiness.

PENNISETUM (fountain grass). Z5–9, except as noted. This popular ornamental grass gets its common name from its beautiful weeping habit. It is easy to grow in full to part sun in any well-drained location. It is salt tolerant and does very well at the beach.

P. alopecuroides (perennial fountain grass). The showy plumes of this 2'–3'-tall species range from copper to plum-colored and resemble a bushy tail. 'Moudry' (black fountain grass) is a 30"-tall cultivar that boasts black flower plumes in the fall but tends to seed itself around a little too readily.

P. villosum (feathertop grass). This 18"-tall species is surmounted by white feathery plumes in spring and summer.

P. setaceum 'Rubrum' or 'Purpureum' (red or purple fountain grass). Z9–11. This 3'-tall *Pennisetum* is not reliably hardy north of Zone 9, but its deep purple foliage and wonderful furry purple-and-beige cattails are so attractive in a mixed perennial border that it's worth growing as an annual. Just bring a couple of divisions inside for the winter and plant them back out after the frost-free date in spring. The cultivar 'Burgundy Giant' grows to 5' tall and sports rich, wine red foliage and dramatic plumed panicles. *P. setaceum* 'Rubrum' is also known as *P. rueppellii*.

PENSTEMON (penstemon, beardtongue). Penstemons bloom for two weeks or more in late spring and early summer. Bell-shaped flowers clothe erect spikes that look somewhat like foxgloves. Penstemons demand a well-drained location in full sun to part shade. Deadhead them to encourage

reblooming. There are many hybrid penstemon available in shades of purple, red, pink, and white. They tend to be short-lived in our area. The best bet is probably Gulf Coast penstemon (*P. tenuis*).

P. cobaea (wild foxglove). Z6–10. This is one of the best penstemons for our area because it tolerates drought, heat, and humidity very well. It can stand wet, clayey gumbo soil as well as dry soil. The showy flowers are white or lavender streaked with purple inside. This 18"–30"-tall perennial is a favorite of hummingbirds.

P. digitalis (smooth white penstemon). Z3–9. This 2'–3'-tall native can stand a moist spot better than the other penstemons. The pinkish-white flowers are borne in panicles in early summer. The species is reputedly more reliable than most of its hybrid offspring.

P. 'Garnet'. Z7–10. 'Garnet' is a terrific penstemon for the coastal South, growing into a bushy, 2'–3'-tall plant. It bears deep red tubular flowers from midsummer until fall.

P. gloxinoides 'Midnight'. Z6–9. This 18"-tall cultivar is a bushy, purple-flowered variety that reputedly does well for us. Its main season of bloom is spring, but it repeats on and off through summer.

P. smallii (showy beardtongue, Small's penstemon). Z6–9. This semievergreen native grows to 2' tall, producing mauve and white flowers in late spring. It prefers poor soil and excellent drainage. It doesn't mind a little shade.

P. tenuis (Gulf Coast penstemon). Z6–9. This 18"–36"-tall native of Texas and Louisiana is an excellent choice for the coastal South. It tolerates wet or dry conditions, full sun or filtered shade. Its loose panicles of rosy-purple flowers bloom for many weeks in spring and early summer. Hummingbirds love it.

PENTAS lanceolata (pentas). Annual. Pentas is a candidate for best hot-weather annual for the coastal South. Showy, 4"-wide flower corymbs of pink, red, lilac, or white starflowers appear atop bushy 2'–3'-tall plants. Flowers keep coming nonstop all summer long. The foliage remains a healthy, bright green. Plant pentas in rich, well-drained soil in full sun to light shade, and add some slow-release fertilizer at planting time. Deadheading encourages more blooms. Fail-safe and wonderful.

PETROSELINUM crispum (parsley). Biennial. Parsley may be the easiest of all the herbs to grow. It sprouts reliably from seed sown any time of year and forms attractive, healthy clumps. Use it as an edging for the herb garden, to mix in containers or in the perennial bed, or just grow it by itself. Parsley is very undemanding if given sun, good soil, and some attention to watering. Parsley plants overwinter in the coastal South for several years in a row. Italian parsley (*P. crispum* var. *neapolitanum*) has the strongest flavor.

PETUNIA *integrifolia* (hardy petunia). Z8–9. Perhaps not the most reliable perennial, this petunia is worth giving a try. Plant it in full sun with perfect drainage and wait until spring to do any kind of trimming and cleaning up. With luck, it may bloom for you from spring through frost. Colors are deep pink or white; however, the white is not as hardy as the pink. Some coastal gardeners find that our summers are too hot for this petunia and its annual relative.

PHLOX (phlox). Perhaps one of the best known and most widely used garden perennials in the country, phlox are available in a large variety of habits, colors, and attributes. If you take the path of least resistance and buy (or start from seed) any old phlox, you may end up with the phlox of least resistance. In our area, phlox can suffer from pests, fungus, root rot, and general all-around failure to tolerate the heat and humidity. Better to research the latest cultivars to find ones that are suited for our climate. The following is a brief overview.

P. bifida (sand phlox). Z4–8. Those in the upper reaches of the coastal South can plant this low-growing phlox in poor, sandy soil in full sun and let it enjoy the neglect. Pale violet blooms appear in spring. This is a drought-tolerant plant.

P. carolina 'Magnificence' (wedding phlox). Z7–9. This phlox gives us loose panicles of large pink flowers in spring. If you place it in full sun with perfect drainage, it will reward you by saying no to mildew. It actually likes the heat.

P. divaricata (wild blue phlox, Louisiana phlox). Z3–9. This low-growing phlox prefers a semishady spot with good moisture and perfect drainage where it will spread by stolons. Panicles of sky blue flowers are borne on 12" stems in spring. It does fairly well for us. 'Blue Dreams' is an excellent lilac blue color; 'Fuller's White' is covered in white blooms for several weeks in spring.

P. glabberima (smooth phlox). Z4–9. An excellent, spreading native with lavender-pink flowers that bloom on 2'–3'-tall stems in late spring. Tolerates our heat and humidity nicely. 'Triflorum' is an excellent 8"–12"-tall variety.

P. maculata (spotted phlox). Z3–8. This phlox looks a lot like *P. paniculata* but is more resistant to mildew. The stems are often spotted red, hence the name. It flowers in early summer. Cultivars: 'Miss

Lingard'—a pure white phlox that does well for us; 'Natascha',—pink and white flowers on a 2'-tall plant with good disease resistance; 'Rosalinde'—large, dark pink flowers that are long-lasting and do well in our climate.

P. nivalis (trailing phlox). Z6–8. This phlox is similar to *P. subulata* in that it is a mat-forming ground-cover that blooms in spring in shades of purple, pink, or white. Grow it in full sun with excellent drainage and it will stand up stoically to the heat and humidity.

P. paniculata (garden phlox, summer phlox). Z4–9. This native species phlox is more mildew resistant than the modern hybrids. Magenta flower clusters bloom on 2'–4'-tall stalks for many weeks in summer. For best results, plant summer phlox in moist, rich, well-drained soil in full sun or part shade, although it will tolerate drought and baking conditions. It will spread by forming a clump and by reseeding. Dig out the center of old clumps every few years.

P. paniculata hybrids (hybrid garden phlox). Z4–8. Many of the hybrids sold today suffer from our heat and may become susceptible not only to powdery mildew but also to root rot. Plant garden phlox in full sun with plenty of air circulation and good drainage. It may not be possible to grow these very attractive perennials without heavy use of fungicides. One choice is to grow other types instead. When healthy, phlox will send up beautiful thick panicles of pink, lavender, red, or white flowers and many shades in between. Cultivars: 'David'—reputedly a highly disease-resistant white variety that grows to 3' tall; 'Katherine'—a 2'–3'-tall, lavender-colored phlox with some mildew resistance; 'Lavender'—probably really the *P. paniculata* species in disguise and, as such, tough and totally mildew resistant, though its flowers aren't quite as showy as those of the hybrids; 'Norah Leigh'—its best attribute is its variegated green-and-cream-edged foliage, joined in late summer by light pink flowers with dark eyes; 'Robert Poore'—a mildew-resistant variety with deep purple flowers that is very popular in the coastal South.

P. pilosa (prairie phlox). Z5–9. This phlox produces small pink flowers on 1'–2'-tall stems in early summer. It takes full to part sun and tolerates our heat and drought. Deadhead it for possible rebloom. It spreads fairly rapidly by stolons.

P. stolonifera (creeping phlox). Z2–8. This creeping native produces lavender blooms in spring on an evergreen, spreading plant. Creeping phlox likes partial shade, rich soil, and moisture to do its best.

Cultivars are available in white, purple, and pink also.

P. subulata (moss phlox, mosspink). Z2–10. If you give this well-loved evergreen native full, baking sun, and poor, well-drained soil, you will be rewarded with a carpet of 6"–8"-tall, brightly colored blooms in late February. Moss phlox, which spreads easily, is the flower you suddenly see everywhere one early spring weekend—especially in bright pink along the roadside. Cultivars are available in white, lavender, and red as well. Foliage is dark green and needle-like.

PHORMIUM tenax (New Zealand flax, flax lily, phormium). Z7b–10. Phormiums are striking, architectural foliage plants. Most of them suffer in our hot, humid summers and wet winters, however *P. tenax* does better than the rest. Sending up erect, sword-shaped leaves, it grows about 6' tall. Once established, it will send dull red, erect flowers shooting up a full 15' into the air. 'Atropurpureum' is one of the only hardy, purple-leaved plants of its kind for our area. 'Rubrum' is a shorter purple-leaved version with narrower leaves. Give phormiums full to part sun, and rich, moist, well-drained soil.

PHYGELIUS (Cape fuchsia). These somewhat sprawling, woody subshrubs may remain evergreen in the warmer parts of the coastal South. Over a long period of time in late summer and fall they produce erect spikes of loosely clustered, tubular flowers in shades of yellow, orange, red, or deep pink. Plant *Phygelius* in fertile, moist, well-drained soil in full to part sun. Tidy up the shrubs with pruning shears in early spring. *Phygelius* spreads by suckering and by branches that root where they touch the ground.

P. aequalis. Z7–9. This upright, 3'-tall shrub with dark green, ovate leaves sends up stalks clustered with pendent, rosy pink, tubular flowers with yellow throats. 'Yellow Trumpet' has butter-yellow, slightly flared trumpet flowers and light green leaves.

P. x rectus. Z7–9. This is an upright, 5'-tall hybrid with dark green foliage. Red flower panicles appear in summer. 'African Queen' bears red-orange flowers; 'Devil's Tears', hot pink flowers with yellow throats; 'Moonraker', creamy yellow; 'Salmon Leap', salmon red.

P. capensis. Z7–9. This upright shrub with dark green leaves can grow to 5' tall. In summer it produces dramatic, 2'-high flower spikes of orangy-red tubular flowers with yellow throats.

PHYSOSTEGIA (obedient plant). These easy, rhizomatous perennials are graced with showy spikes of white, pink, or lavender flowers that somewhat resemble snapdragons. Leaves are shiny, dark green, and toothed. They grow in full sun to part shade in rich, moist, well-drained soil. They spread extremely rapidly, within a couple of years.

P. angustifolia (early obedient plant). Z6–9. This native obedient plant grows 3'–4' tall. In late spring and early summer it produces showy, mauve flower spikes.

P. virginiana (obedient plant). Z2–9. Lilac-pink flowers are borne on somewhat sprawling 3'–4'-tall stems from late summer through fall. White and variegated varieties are also available.

PLANTAGO major 'Rubrifolia' (red-leaved plantain). Z4–9. This 2'–3'-tall plantain is grown mostly for its wide, ovate, purplish-bronze basal foliage. Plant it in full sun in moist to wet soil.

PLATYCODON grandiflorus (balloon flower, Chinese bellflower). Z3–8. This old-fashioned cottage garden perennial takes its name from the inflated buds, which look quite globular until they open into five-petaled, deep blue flowers in summer. Give it a spot in part sun with rich, moist soil and good drainage. Make sure it is protected from the brutal afternoon sun. Mark the spot carefully, because balloon flower is late to emerge in spring. The more commonly planted, better-known varieties may not do as well for us as the following two highly recommended cultivars. 'Komachi' is a 1'–2'-tall balloon flower with deep blue summer flowers that keep their balloon shape, never opening completely; very long-lived in the coastal South, 'Komachi' tolerates our heat and humidity wonderfully. 'Sentimental Blue' is a dwarf variety that is an excellent selection for the coastal South; with large (3" across), blue flowers on 6"–8"-tall plants that stay more upright than others of the species, this is a long-lived, heat-tolerant plant that will not need dividing.

PLUMBAGO auriculata (Cape leadwort, Cape plumbago). Z8–10. This weeping shrub or climbing woody plant is smothered in sky blue flowers all summer long in the warmer areas of the coastal South, practically blanketing downtown Charleston with its blossoms. There is also a white variety. In more northerly parts of the coast it won't get going until late summer and fall, but it's lovely nonetheless. Plumbago grows 3'–6' tall and likes full to part sun in moist, well-drained soil. If trained to climb up a wall or other structure, it may reach 10'–20'. Cape plumbago tolerates beach conditions. It may take a few years to get thoroughly established, but then it will be a tough survivor. North of Zone 9 it would benefit from a winter mulch. Also known as *P. capensis*.

PODOPHYLLUM peltatum (May apple, wild mandrake). Z4–9. This native rhizomatous perennial is a lover of deep, shady woodlands but withstands our heat and humidity remarkably well. Each handsome, glossy green leaf rises up on a long leaf stalk like a folded umbrella. The umbrella opens to reveal a deeply lobed, toothed, palmate leaf that remains green during the cooler months. Foliage goes dormant in summer. In spring, delicate, waxy, white flowers appear beneath the leaves. Give May apple a good, rich, leaf mold to grow in. It requires full to part shade. Even though it would prefer moist soil, it is reliably drought tolerant. It will slowly spread by underground rhizomes to make an attractive shady groundcover.

POLIANTHES tuberosa (tuberose). Z7–10. These tall, white, waxy-looking flowers are known for their extremely fragrant natures. They bloom in late summer and fall on 3'-tall plants. Plant the tubers in full sun once all danger of frost has passed and give them a protective winter mulch. Above Zone 8 lift them for the winter. The best tuberose for our area is the variety 'Mexican Single'.

POLYGONATUM (Solomon's seal). These shade-loving, rhizomatous perennials enjoy moist, fertile, well-drained soil. They will bloom even in deep shade. The pendent, tubular flowers appear in spring along the leaf axils of the arching, laddered stems.

P. biflorum (Solomon's seal). Z3–9. Pendent, greenish-white flowers are borne along the leaf axils of the arching stems of this native, 3'-tall Solomon's seal from late spring to midsummer. Blue-black berries follow. The foliage goes dormant in summer.

P. odoratum (fragrant Solomon's seal). Z3–9. In late spring tiny, green-tipped, white flowers appear at the leaf axils of this 18"–36"-high woodlander. The scented flowers are followed by black fruits. 'Variegatum' bears cream-colored bellflowers and leaves edged in creamy white.

POLYSTICHUM polyblepharum (tassel fern). Z6–9. A dense, lacy evergreen fern with spiny-toothed margins on the pinnae. The unfurling fronds grow 2' tall and are covered with golden hairs. Give tassel fern rich, moist, well-drained soil in full to part shade. Tassel fern can tolerate some sun if its feet are kept moist.

PONCIRUS trifoliata (hardy orange). Z5–9. This unusual-looking rounded shrub or small tree, its bright green branches covered with sharp spines, is popular from Charleston to Florida and across the Gulf Coast. Fragrant, white, saucer-shaped flowers appear in spring and summer, followed by attractive, inedible, orange-like fruits. Hardy orange, which grows to about 15' tall, is deciduous. The dwarf 'Flying Dragon' is popular for its interesting twisted branches. Give hardy orange a position in full sun with fertile soil and perfect drainage. Water during dry spells.

PORTULACCA oleracera (purslane). Annual. Purslane looks almost identical to the better-known annual, portulacca (*P. grandiflora*), but it performs much better in our heat and humidity. Both grow only about 2" tall, with trailing stems and needle-like, fleshy leaves. The brightly colored flowers are cup-shaped. Purslane's stems and leaves are chubbier. The species (*P. oleracera*) is unexceptional and weedy, but terrific hybrids are available in white, yellow, pink, red, lavender, orange, coral, and mixed colors. Purslane (*P. oleracera*) will keep going long after the other portulaccas have hit the wall. Give it a spot in full sun with good drainage; it is not particular about soil and withstands drought. Use it as an annual groundcover, in containers, or in a rock garden.

PRUNELLA (self-heal). Self-heal was used for medicinal purposes in the past. It is grown now as a flowering shade plant.

P. grandiflora (self-heal). Z5–8. With dark green, oak-like leaves and short purple flowers in summer, this is a good, mat-forming groundcover for partial shade or filtered sunlight. It needs rich, moist, well-drained soil to do well. Deadhead the spent flower stalks to keep it neat looking. It spreads moderately fast.

P. vulgaris. Z8b–10. Native self-heal grows 1'–2' tall and bears dense spikes of lavender, pink, or white flowers in late spring and early summer. It grows wild along the Southern Atlantic and Gulf Coasts and thrives in our climate. It is not particular about soil.

PSEUDERANTHEMUM alatum (chocolate plant). Annual. The chocolate plant is used along the coast for its chocolate brown foliage splotched with silver on top. It grows 12'–18" tall in sun to light shade in moist, rich soil. Although it is tender, it will often return the next year after having died back during the winter. Racemes of small lavender blossoms appear in summer.

PYRACANTHA (firethorn, pyracantha). Z6–9. These thorny, evergreen vines and shrubs are valued primarily for their dramatic late summer and fall berries, which may persist through winter. Berry colors include shades of red, orange, and yellow.

The leaves are glossy green. Depending on the cultivar, pyracantha can grow 3'–20' high. The vines are often espaliered up a trellis or wall for dramatic effect. Pyracantha can also be used as a shrub or groundcover. This is an easy, vigorous, and fast-growing plant. Give it full sun and excellent drainage. For best results, select disease-resistant varieties.

PYRETHRUM marginatum. See AJANIA *pacifica.*

QUAMOCLIT coccinea. See IPOMOEA *coccinea.*
QUAMOCLIT ipomea. See IPOMOEA *quamoclit.*
QUAMOCLIT pennata. See IPOMOEA *quamoclit.*

RANUNCULUS repens 'Pleniflorus' (creeping buttercup). Z3–9. The shiny green, deeply cut leaves of this low-growing perennial quickly fill in to form a spreading mat in sun or shade. Bright yellow, button-shaped flowers appear in spring. It may spread too fast for your taste, so beware. 'Buttered Popcorn' is a variegated cultivar with well-incised leaves of green, gold, and chartreuse, which shows the most color in a sunny location.

RATIBIDA columnifera (ratibida, Mexican hat plant, yellow coneflower). Z3–8. This 2'–3'-tall native is distinguished by the long, chestnut brown, almost maroon-colored cone that protrudes up from a drooping fan of yellow, lobed ray petals. Plant ratibida in full sun or light shade in well-drained soil. Whack it back after its first summer bloom to induce further flowering. The variety 'Pulcherima' has reddish-brown ray petals.

REHMANNIA elata (Chinese foxglove). Z7–10. Large, bright mauve, foxglove-like flowers appear on this 1'–2'-tall perennial in spring and often repeat in summer. The foliage is hairy and evergreen. Plant in full sun to part shade in sandy, well-drained soil. *Rehmannia* will colonize rapidly where it is happy.

RHAPIDOPHYLLUM hystrix (needle palm, porcupine palm). Z6–10. Needle palm is a hardy native palm found naturally all along the Southern Atlantic and Gulf Coasts. It grows very slowly to 5'–6' tall with beautiful blue-green, fan-shaped, deeply cut foliage. Each leaf is about 3' long. The fans appear to emerge directly from the ground without assistance of a trunk or stems. Needle palms are highly flexible, thriving in full sun and part shade, in poor or fertile soil. It is illegal to cull them from the wild.

RHAPIS excelsa (broadleaf lady palm). Z8–10. Often grown as an indoor plant, broadleaf lady palm can survive winters in all but the upper reaches of the coastal South. Long-stalked, dark green, deeply cut fans spread out dramatically atop bamboo-like stems. Broadleaf lady palm grows very slowly, eventually reaching 5'–15' tall. It is adaptable to full sun or shade, dry or moist conditions, and poor soil. If you plant it in rich, moist soil in filtered light, it will be even happier. There are also variegated forms. Also known as *R. flabelliformis.*

RHODODENDRON (azalea). One of the easiest and most reliable of all the flowering shrubs for the coastal South, azaleas (except for the later-flowering Satsukis described below) put on a spectacular spring show around the same time as the dogwoods, redbuds, and flowering fruit trees. They are emblematic of spring in our area. We are able to grow some of the more unusual and dramatic varieties that don't survive northern winters.

Azaleas grow best in filtered shade, although some cultivars can take full sun. They will live and bloom in deep, dark shade, but not brilliantly. They need rich, well-drained, moist, acidic soil in order to do well. If your soil is alkaline or full of clay, plant them in raised beds with lots of organic material added. The well-developed surface roots of azaleas are essential for their survival. Therefore, they need to be planted shallowly with the root ball slightly above the soil line. Fertilize annually in early spring and mulch with pine bark or pine straw.

Pruning is not necessary except to remove dead, damaged, or diseased branches. If you want to prune your azaleas to a certain size or shape, do so soon after flowering stops. If you delay too long, you will be cutting off next year's (hidden) flower buds. This doesn't damage the shrub, just the aesthetic pleasure in spring.

The evergreen Southern Indica hybrids have very large, showy blossoms and are vigorous, fast growers. 'Formosa' (magenta), 'Mrs. G. G. Gerbing' (white), and 'George Lindley Taber' (pale pink) are three well-known cultivars.

The Satsuki hybrids include the low-growing, evergreen Gumpos and Macranthas, which come in shades of white, pink, red, magenta, and coral. Their advantages include their compact, neat shape (good for small gardens) and the fact that they bloom in early summer when the other azaleas have long since finished.

Kurume hybrids are perhaps the most widely used. They form fairly compact, evergreen shrubs sized between the larger Indicas and smaller Satsukis. There are dozens of hybrids in shades of pink, red, lavender, coral, and white.

Deciduous azaleas in beautiful shades of gold,

tangerine, and bright orange generally prefer the cooler, mountain regions. However, breeders in Alabama and Mississippi have come up with some heat-tolerant varieties that do well for us. Look for the Dodd and Dodd hybrids or the Aromi hybrids. The 10'-tall Florida flame azalea (*Rhododendron austrinum*) is a deciduous azalea that tolerates heat and humidity well. It grows in full sun, putting forth ruffled, tubular orange, red, cream, pink, or yellow flowers on bare stems in early spring. A similar sized, native deciduous azalea, the honeysuckle azalea (*R. canescens*), has fragrant, pale pink or white flowers in spring and grows in sun or shade. It spreads by suckering.

RHODOPHIALA *bifida* (oxblood lily, schoolhouse lily). Z7–10. This classic southern bulb blooms in fall at the same time as *Lycoris*. It looks something like a miniature amaryllis with deep red, funnel-form flowers on 1' stalks. This is a very easy plant that will spread in almost any kind of soil. Give it full sun or light shade.

RICINUS *communis* (castor bean plant). Z9–10. This tender perennial can be grown from seed as an annual and will put on 6'–15' of growth in a season. It is used for the dramatic effect of its giant, large-lobed, dark green leaves, which spread 1'–3' across. There are a number of bronze-red or purplish-red cultivars that add excellent color to the garden, among them 'Carmencita', 'Impala', 'Red Spire', and 'Sanguineus'. Plant castor bean in full sun and keep it watered regularly. Note: The seeds of this plant are highly poisonous. Do not plant it if there are children around.

ROHDEA *japonica* (sacred lily). Z5–9. These tough evergreen perennials can be used in dry shade where nothing else will grow. They somewhat resemble hostas, generally growing 12"–18" tall, and are used in similar fashion. They prefer moist, rich soil, but they can stand dry soil. The small white blooms are insignificant. These tend to be collectors' plants with very expensive price tags.

ROSMARINUS *officinalis* (rosemary). Z6–10. This gray-leaved, evergreen herb will form a 4'–6'-tall woody subshrub if you plant it in full sun in dead dry conditions and let it bake its heart out. The needle-like foliage and silver color are terrific additions to the sunny garden and look handsome in a stand-alone container. Even though the sky blue, white, or pink flowers are tiny, they are a pleasant sight in the dead of winter. Use it as a low hedge for your knot garden or use creeping rosemary as a trailing plant for container gardening. This is a very easy herb to grow if it is given conditions to its liking. Rosemary leaves are used

in grilling, baking, and seasoning of all sorts of dishes as well as in potpourris and bath scents. Recommended varieties: 'Arp'—a particularly good rosemary for the South, this fine, gray-leaved variety grows 3' tall and as much as 10' across where it's happy, its dark blue flowers blooming from fall through spring; 'Athens Blue'—a floriferous, upright form; 'Irene'—a creeping rosemary that grows only 12"–18" high, bears deep blue flowers, and spreads vigorously in hot, dry locations. 'Salem' is a 3'-tall, dark green variety that works well for topiary purposes. 'Tuscan Blue', a fast-growing rosemary that bears blue flowers on narrow, erect, 6'-tall branches, is held by some gardeners to be the best variety for the coastal South.

R. *prostratus* (creeping rosemary). This gray-leaved rosemary grows 2' high and will spread to make a trailing, twisting groundcover. It looks best spilling over a wall, in a rock garden, or hanging over the side of a large container. Flowers are lavender-colored. It does well in the coastal South.

RUBUS *calycinoides* (creeping raspberry). Z6–8. This prickly evergreen groundcover is extremely heat and drought tolerant and will grow in full sun to full shade. The leaves, resembling those of true raspberries, are green in spring and summer, turning reddish in the fall and winter. This is a tough, if not particularly showy, all-purpose groundcover. It grows about 4" tall and spreads as far as it is allowed to. Also known as *R. pentalobus*.

RUDBECKIA (coneflower, black-eyed Susan). It's hard to imagine a perennial garden, especially one in the coastal South, without some sort of *Rudbeckia* growing in it. There are *Rudbeckias* for sun, part sun, and light shade. They require nothing and, in return, bloom reliably, multiply, and often hold their place in winter with evergreen basal tufts.

R. x 'Autumn Sun'. Z3–9. This handsome, clump-forming, rhizomatous perennial grows 5'–6' tall with branching stems and glossy, mid-green leaves. It blooms from midsummer to early fall. The flowers have a protruding green central disk and long, drooping, sulfur yellow ray petals. It may need staking. Cut it back for possible rebloom. This variety is also sold as *R.* 'Herbstsonne'.

R. *fulgida* (orange coneflower, black-eyed Susan). Z3–9. These rhizomatous plants grow about 2' tall, producing a large number of orangy-yellow, daisy-like flowers with dark centers in mid- to late summer. The classic in this species is the 2'-tall *R. fulgida* var. *sullivantii* 'Goldsturm', which tends to bloom the longest of all the *Rudbeckias*, beginning in late July. Plant *R. fulgida* in full to part sun in good soil. Both 'Goldsturm' and the variety *R. fulgida deamii* are particularly heat and drought tolerant.

R. grandiflora (tall coneflower). Z7–10. This 3'-tall native coneflower blooms all summer long in full sun. Yellow ray petals droop around a gray-green central disk. Butterflies love this plant.

R. hirta (gloriosa daisy, black-eyed Susan). Z3–10. These long-blooming *Rudbeckias* are short-lived perennials sometimes grown as annuals. They start blooming in early summer and keep on through fall. Many of them have markings similar to those of a gloriosa lily: pinwheels of gold with red bands at the lower portion of each petal and a reddish-brown central cone. Others have pale yellow ray flowers and brownish-purple central disk flowers. Their branching stems are stiff and erect. Plant in full sun or shade. Although they prefer a moist spot, they will tolerate dry conditions. Most of them grow a little over a foot tall. Also known as *R. gloriosa*, these plants often self-seed. Recommended varieties: 'Indian Summer', a 3'-tall gloriosa with golden yellow flowers; 'Irish Eyes'—2' tall, with bright yellow ray petals and a green central disk, this plant is also known as 'Green Eyes'.

R. lanciniata (green-headed coneflower, cutleaf coneflower). Z3–9. These long-lived natives thrive in moist soil in full sun to part shade. Drooping, yellow ray flowers surround green disks on 2'–4'-tall stems in mid- to late summer. The leaves are light green and deeply cut. These are the best *Rudbeckias* for lighting up a partially shaded area. Deadhead them for repeat bloom from summer through fall. This heat-tolerant species is beloved of butterflies. 'Gold Drop' is a 2'–4'-tall, clump-forming variety that sports double, yellow flowers that resemble mop heads in September and October. 'Gold Drops' are very easy to grow in full to part sun, though in full sun the stems will be stronger and the plant will stand up better. 'Hortensia' (golden glow) is a southern classic that reaches a stately 6'–8' tall and will need staking if you don't want to look at a sprawling mess. It produces bright, golden yellow, pom-pom-type flowers in summer and spreads rapidly by underground stolons.

R. maxima (giant black-eyed Susan). Z4–9. These *Rudbeckias* are favored by garden designers because of their large, blue-green basal leaves. The stems rise 6'–7' into the air, topped in summer by flowers with yellow ray petals and dramatically protruding brown cones. This giant enjoys a dry

position in full, baking sun but can also tolerate wet feet.

R. nitida. Z3–9. This autumn-blooming species boasts dissected foliage and large, green-centered, yellow coneflowers on 4'–6'-tall stems.

R. triloba (three-lobed coneflower). Z3–10. Another *Rudbeckia* that does well in partial shade, this 2'–3'-tall, clump-forming biennial has orangy-yellow ray flowers with brownish-purple centers. The stems are erect and multibranched. It seeds itself readily and is a great addition to the garden. It is reputedly even more floriferous than 'Goldsturm', blooming from summer through early autumn.

RUELLIA (wild petunia, Mexican petunia, ruellia). These are excellent, long-blooming perennials for the coastal South. The profuse flowers are lovely, showy, pendent trumpets, 1½" across. Fail-safe. Wonderful.

R. brittoniana (Mexican petunia). Z7b–10. This excellent escapee from Mexico has made itself at home in the Southeast. It sends up a shrub-like colony of erect, narrow-leaved stems 2'–3' high. From midsummer to fall, purple funnel-shaped flowers appear and fall to the ground neatly when they've finished blooming. *Ruellia* takes full to part sun and doesn't seem to care about much else. It is drought tolerant, can stand wet feet, and attracts butterflies. In the lower parts of the coastal South it is considered by some gardeners to be too well suited—that is, invasive. The dwarf cultivars are less invasive. Recommended cultivars: 'Chi Chi'—a bright pink version, just as reliable as the purple; 'Colobe Pink'—a pink dwarf (8" tall); 'Katie'—a 6"-tall, purple, clump-forming dwarf with attractive, narrow foliage; 'Strawberries and Cream'—a 6"-tall dwarf with creamy variegated foliage and purple flowers; 'White Katie'—an 8"-tall, clump-forming dwarf with attractive, narrow foliage and bright white flowers.

R. caroliniensis (wild petunia, Carolina ruellia). Z8–10. This is the bushy, native ruellia that produces lavender-colored, trumpet-shaped blooms from summer through early fall. It grows 2' tall and self-seeds. Give it full sun to part shade and rich, well-drained soil.

R. malacosperma 'Alba' (white wild petunia). Z6–11. This 2'–3'-tall native has wider, shorter leaves than *R. brittoniana*. Pure white flowers are produced from midsummer to frost. Extremely adaptable, this plant takes full sun to full shade and wet or dry soil.

RUSSELIA equisetiformis (firecracker plant, fountain plant, coral fountain). Z8–10. This wonderful fountain of a plant is loaded with red tubular flowers on rush-like stems throughout summer and fall. It grows 3' tall in full sun or light shade and can withstand drought. It appreciates application of a balanced fertilizer periodically. An excellent plant for the coastal South.

RUTA *graveolens* (rue). Z4–9. This herb is used primarily for its decorative, blue-green, delicately incised foliage, not for the yellow flowers it produces in summer. This woody subshrub will grow 1'–3' tall in full, baking sun. It needs perfect drainage or it will disappear.

SABATIA *kennedyiana* (swamp pink gentian). Z2–8. This branching, 2'-tall native is topped with large, pink, yellow-eyed daisies in May. It prefers to be grown in full sun in sandy, well-drained soil.

SABAL (palmetto, cabbage palm). These hardy palms are easy and useful additions to the south-ern coastal garden. They are tolerant of heat, humidity, and seashore conditions, including salt spray. The fan-shaped, palmate leaves are deeply divided, handsome, and dramatic. Give them full sun to light shade. They grow very slowly.

S. *blackburniana* (Hispaniola palmetto). Z8–11. This giant will grow up to 80' tall with fans 9' across.

S. *mexicana* (Texas palmetto). Z8–11. A giant that grows up to 50' tall, this palmetto does not transplant well.

S. *minor* (dwarf palmetto, scrub palmetto, Louisiana palmetto). Z7–11. This 3'–6'-tall dwarf palmetto is one of the most ubiquitous palms in the coastal South. The long-stalked, deeply divided, blue-green fans grow to about 3' long. The plant normally appears trunkless. Erect, 10'-tall flower stalks bear panicles of cream-colored flowers in summer. It is adaptable to sun or shade, wet or dry conditions. Dwarf palmetto tends to resent being transplanted. Native Americans and early French settlers used the fans to make baskets, brooms, and chair bottoms.

S. *palmetto* (cabbage palm). Z8–11. Another easy, tough character, the cabbage palm is found in communities all along the Gulf and South Atlantic Coasts. Growing slowly to 90' tall, this is a great palm for the beach as it can grow in sand and tolerates drought, salt spray, and high winds. Clumps of 5'–6'-long, fan-shaped, deeply divided leaves appear at the top of a long, narrow trunk. Long-stalked, white flower clusters appear in summer, followed by black berries. Unlike some of the other palmettos, this one is very easy to transplant.

SACCHARUM *arundinaceum* (hardy sugar cane). Z6–10. This giant (10'-tall by 10' wide), clump-forming ornamental grass adds a stately blue-green presence to an area with enough room to accommodate it. In fall it is topped by showy, reddish-purple flower plumes. Give it full to part sun and well-drained soil.

SALVIA (sage). Gardening in the coastal South is made possible, in part, by the generosity of the sage family. There are hundreds and hundreds of species, but getting to know just a few of them will definitely be worth your while. Their square stems identify them as members of the mint family. Except as noted below, plant *Salvias* in full to part sun in good, well-drained, moist soil and stand back. They will get bigger or more populous, as the case may be, in no time. Many of them are beloved of butterflies and hummingbirds.

S. 'Anthony Parker'. Z8–10. From late summer through fall 3'-tall, dark purple flower spikes are borne in profusion on this compact, clump-forming perennial.

S. *azurea* (azure sage). Z4–9. Dense, azure blue spikes appear on this 3'–4'-tall southeastern native in the late summer and fall. The variety 'Grandiflora' has paler blue blooms. Azure sage eats up our heat and humidity, has attractive silvery leaves, and will rebloom if cut back. A very good choice for the coastal South.

S. *blepharophylla* (painted lady, eyelash sage). Z8–11. The foliage on this 2'-tall evergreen salvia is shiny, and the coral-red bloom is somewhat furry. Eyelash sage appreciates a lightly shaded or partially sun position. It attracts butterflies all summer.

S. *buchannii*. Z8–11. Loose racemes of magenta flowers with purplish-brown calyces are produced on 2'-tall stems from midsummer through fall.

S. 'Cherry Queen' (cherry queen autumn sage). Z7b–11. This long-lived, cherry pink hybrid blooms from early summer until frost and is an excellent choice for our climate. Growing to about 18" tall, its habit is semiprostrate.

S. *coccinea* (Texas sage, scarlet sage). Z8b–11. This is an excellent sage for the Southeastern Atlantic and Gulf Coasts. It grows 2'–4' tall in a bush shape with cherry red, white, or coral-pink flower spikes from spring through fall. This *Salvia* will bloom in light shade as well as full sun. It is adaptable to a variety of soils. It reseeds readily and benefits from being whacked back now and then to keep it flowering and bushy. This is a favorite of hummingbirds and butterflies. Cultivars: 'Alba'—a white form; 'Coral Nymph'—coral-colored bloom;

'Lady in Red'—compact, 2'-tall scarlet sage; 'Orange Sunset'—4'-tall plants with creamy orange blossoms.

S. confertifolia. Z8b–11. This heat- and drought-tolerant sage grows 6' tall and puts forth 2'-long, velvety red flower spikes in late summer and fall. Its habit is similar to that of *S. leucantha*. Plant it in full sun or light shade in well-drained soil and cut it back after it blooms to encourage another flowering. Give it a winter mulch. Good butterfly attractant.

S. discolor (Peruvian sage). Z8b–11. The dark purple, almost black blooms contrast nicely with the silver leaves on this 1'–2'-tall, somewhat sprawling plant. This sage is not as hardy as others, so give it a protected spot and a winter mulch.

S. elegans (pineapple sage). Z8b–11. The leaves smell like pineapple and the spires of small, bright red flowers are just what you need to perk up your fall garden. Pineapple sage looks terrific with the other fall-blooming sages and with goldenrod and swamp sunflower. It grows about 2'–4' tall and loves rich, moist, well-drained soil in full or part sun. 'Freida Dixon' is a pink cultivar.

S. farinacea (mealycup sage). Z8–11. A terrific, native sage that sends up rich violet-blue spikes all summer long on bushy, 2'–3'-tall plants. Foliage is gray-green on white, mealy stems. 'Victoria' is a 1½'-tall bushy dwarf. Give this sage a well-drained, slightly sandy soil.

S. gregii (autumn sage). Z7b–11. These are deciduous subshrubs, which need a dry position in sun to part sun to do well. Many gardeners in the coastal South consider our climate too humid for these particular sages. Generally the flowers are two-lipped and borne in swirls along the stems. Colors include red, pink, white, yellow, and violet. Give autumn sage full sun, rich soil, and perfect drainage. Prune the old wood back in spring. If the plant gets unruly, it can be sheared back after the first flush of bloom. 'Desert Blaze', a 1'–2'-tall plant, has variegated green-and-white foliage that is evergreen and has red flowers that appear in spring and fall. 'Faye Chappell' is a recommended red variety, as is 'Furman's Red', a 3'-tall red variety. 'Pink Preference' is a 3'-tall pink variety.

S. guaranitica (blue anise sage). Z7–11. This butterfly magnet grows 3'–5' tall and flowers from early summer until frost. The long, two-lipped flowers are a lively deep blue. The entire plant has an airy, see-through feeling to it. Grow it in full sun to light shade and give it good drainage. It spreads rapidly by runners, so you will have plenty to give away to friends or to plant in other parts of the garden. Cut it back during the season if you want a bushier plant. This is a good, easy, wonderful plant! Butterflies and hummingbirds agree. 'Argentine Skies' is a paler blue version. 'Black and Blue', a large, fuzzy-leaved subshrub reaching up to 6' tall, has dark blue flowers with near-black calyxes, hence the name (also known as *S. caerulea*). The giant 'Costa Rica Blue' grows 7' tall and sports huge purple-blue flowers.

S. 'Indigo Spires'. Z7b–11. This vigorous, 3'–5'-tall, somewhat arching sage makes a big splash in the garden, flowering summer through frost. The twisting columns of furry blue flowers turn a deep indigo color as the weather gets cooler. Don't cut this to the ground until spring, at which time you can also fertilize lightly. This is another very easy, wonderful *Salvia* that gives you a great bang for your buck. Butterflies, bees, and hummingbirds flock to 'Indigo Spires'.

S. involucrata 'Bethelii' (rosebud sage). Z8–11. Similar to *S. leucantha* in its attention-getting presence, this 4'–6'-tall, fall-blooming sage has fuzzy, fuchsia-pink flowers.

S. koyamae (Japanese yellow sage). Z5–11. This sage is grown for its shade tolerance. If given good soil, part shade, and adequate moisture, it will spread in groundcover fashion, producing soft yellow flower spikes above large, fuzzy foliage from late summer to frost. It grows to about 2' tall.

S. leucantha (Mexican bush sage). Z7b–11. Everyone who sees this gorgeous plant in bloom in the late summer and fall wants one for their own garden. If you have to choose only one fall-flowering plant, this should be the one. *S. leucantha* forms a 4'-tall, bushy, gray-leaved subshrub that is clothed in spectacular spikes of furry purple and pale lavender flowers all fall up until frost. Give your Mexican bush sage a protected spot in full to part sun and mulch it well in the winter. In the upper reaches of the coastal South it occasionally fails to survive the winter. Butterflies and hummingbirds are big fans of Mexican bush sage, too. Solid-color purple versions of *S. leucantha* include 'Blue on Blue', 'Midnight', 'Purple and Purple', and 'All Purple'. The dwarf 'Santa Barbara' produces two-toned purple flower spikes on a 2'-tall plant.

S. lyrata (lyre-leaf sage). Z6–9. The leaves of this native sage are shaped like lyres and remain attractive even when the plant is not in bloom. From early spring until May it produces beautiful, 1'–2'-tall, lavender-blue flower spikes. Keep this sage as dry as possible. It is quite adaptable to sun or shade and readily self-sows.

S. madrensis (forsythia sage). Z7b–11. Starting in the fall, this 6'–7'-tall sage produces lovely, butter-yellow flower spikes that bloom until a hard frost, when little else is in bloom. Give it full to part sun. It takes dry or moist conditions. In the lower regions of the coastal South this sage has been known to reach 16' tall with a vigorous spread. Some gardeners have found it to be invasive. 'Dunham' is a particularly hardy, showy cultivar.

S. 'Maraschino' (cherry sage). Z6–11. This cherry-red-flowered subshrub takes full to part sun and blooms all summer long.

S. mexicana (Mexican sage). Z8–11. This shrubby, 5'×5' sage produces showy purple flowers in late summer and fall in full to part sun. It attracts hummingbirds and butterflies. 'Blue' has showy, bright blue flowers on 1½'-tall, chartreuse flower spikes. 'Limelight' has beautiful blue flowers offset by lime-green calyxes.

S. microphylla (little leaf sage). Z7–11. This semievergreen sage takes full to part sun and produces bright pink flowers in spring and fall with some blooms in between. It grows to 2' tall and can be pruned two or three times during the summer to keep it bushy. The leaves are tangerine scented. 'San Carlos Festival' is a long-blooming, compact plant with magenta flowers that bloom all summer long. 'Wild Watermelon' produces large, bright pink flowers in spring and fall.

S. officinalis 'Berggarten' (culinary sage). Z5–9. This 1'–2'-tall cultivar may be the best variety of *S. officinalis* for our area, although in general the culinary sages prefer cooler summers. This perennial, many-branched subshrub has wide, gray-green leaves and blue flowers in summer. To thrive, it requires full, baking sun, perfect drainage, and excellent air circulation. Try growing it in a container.

S. oresbia (Galena red sage). Z7–11. In late summer and fall this 2'–3'-tall, spreading *Salvia* produces showy, foot-high, red flower spikes. Give this sage full to part sun and well-drained, dry soil. It is very drought tolerant.

S. puberula. Z7–11. Magenta spires appear in fall on 4'-tall plants.

S. prunelloides. Z8–11. This low-growing, glossy-foliaged perennial is used as a spreading ground-cover in full to part sun. In late summer and fall it produces short, dark blue flower spikes.

S. 'Purple Majesty'. Z7b–10. This hybrid bears rich, deep purple flowers from summer through frost on 5'-tall stems. It forms a 3'-wide clump where it is happy. Plant it in light shade in well-drained soil. Butterflies and hummingbirds love it.

S. 'Raspberry Royale'. Z7–9. This 3'-tall hybrid makes a sizable, dense bush and is covered with magenta flowers in summer and fall.

S. regla (royal sage). Z7–11. Bright reddish-orange, tubular flowers appear on this woody, 3'–4'-tall sage in late summer and fall. The leaves resemble mint leaves. It does very well for us in the coastal South in a moist, partially shady position. Don't prune it back until spring.

S. sinaloensis (purple-leaf sage, sapphire sage). Z8–11. This low-growing (6"–12" high), semi-evergreen sage is used as a spreading groundcover in part sun to light shade. It bears deep blue flower spikes above purple-tinged leaves in early summer and again in the fall.

S. uliginosa (bog sage). Z6–11. Masses of bright blue flowers bloom from early summer to frost on 4'–6'-tall plants. Bog sage, of course, loves boggy soil, but it will thrive in average garden soil in full sun to light shade. This is a stoloniferous spreader, visited by hummingbirds and butterflies.

S. vanhouttii (wine sage). Z9–11. This shrubby, 3'–4'-tall *Salvia* loves a partially shady spot. Masses of rich, deep wine-red blooms are borne all summer. The color combines surprisingly well with many other colors in the garden. As it is more tender than some of the other sages, give it a protected position and a good, dry winter mulch.

SANTOLINA (lavender cotton, santolina). This plant is used a great deal in the coastal South, especially at the beach, even though it isn't supposed to tolerate our humid summers.

S. incana (lavender cotton). Z6–9. These woody, silvery-white, fine-foliaged subshrubs do well in a bright, sunny area with perfect drainage. They won't tolerate wet feet and actually prefer poor, sandy soil, so they are excellent for a beach setting. Cut them back severely after blooming to keep them from getting leggy. Lavender cotton is grown mostly for its furry, gray-white foliage. It grows 1'–2' tall and is very aromatic. Opinion is divided as to whether the yellow disk flowers are attractive or not. Santolina may rot in our high humidity, but give it a try. Also known as *S. chamecyparissus*.

S. virens (green santolina). Z6–9. This less fragrant lavender cotton has leaves that resemble rosemary and are green rather than the usual gray. Small yellow flowers are borne on 2'-tall stems in summer.

SAPONARIA officinalis (soapwort, bouncing Bet). Z3–9. Grow this tough plant in full sun with average watering and it will produce dense flower cymes all summer long in shades of pink, red, or white. Soapwort grows 2' tall and can spread rapidly by underground rhizomes if the soil is especially moist and rich. Poor soil and neglect, however, won't deter it.

SARRACENIA (pitcher plant). Z6–10. These native insectivores are grown for their interesting pitcher-shaped foliage, which is often colorful, and for their habit of eating whatever insects they can attract. The plant is named for the conical, vase-shaped, upright leaves or "pitchers" that flare out or end in hooded lids (something like periscopes). Foliage may be green, yellow, red, white, orange, or shades in between. It is often strikingly veined, splotched, netted, or mottled. In spring, nodding, cup-shaped flowers appear on stalks that rise above the foliage. Pitcher plants must have full to part sun and boggy, acidic soil. (They do not want to be fed table scraps.) Don't overfertilize your pitcher plants or you will kill them.

SATUREJA *montana* (winter savory). Z5–9. This semievergreen, woody subshrub is prized for its long summer of bloom, its drought tolerance, and its aromatic foliage. As an herb, its strong flavor is used to season game, pâté, and other foods. Blooms are lavender-pink to purple on low-growing (6"–15"-tall) plants. There is a white cultivar as well. Winter savory can be clipped back as an edging plant or allowed to grow bushy. Plant in full sun to part shade in well-drained, slightly alkaline soil. Don't let it stay wet in winter. Cut back old stems in early spring. *S. montana* 'Prostrate White' is a creeping, white-flowered variety that can be used as a spreading ground-cover. *S. georgiana* is an evergreen southeastern native with a habit similar to the *S. montana*. It blooms from late summer through the winter.

SAUROMATUM *venosum* (voodoo lily). Z8–10. This rhizomatous perennial is one of those strange plants with a spathe and spadix arrangement. In spring and early summer it sends up a strappy, purple-spotted, greenish-white spathe (this is the outside leaf/sheath part of the plant) and a foul-smelling greenish-purple spadix (the erect, inner part of the plant that protrudes out of the spathe). The whole kit and caboodle reaches 12"–14" high. Give your voodoo lily humus-rich, well-drained soil in part shade.

SAXIFRAGA *stolonifera* (strawberry begonia, strawberry geranium, mother of thousands). Z7–9. This may be the only member of the saxifrage family that can even think about growing in our hot climate. This semievergreen groundcover grows 1'–2' tall and prefers rich, moist soil in full to part shade, but it also requires perfect winter drainage to survive. The attractive,

rounded leaves have dark purple coloring underneath and gray veining on top. In summer the plant is topped with loose panicles of five-petaled white flowers. Where it is happy, it will spread to form large colonies by way of thin, ground-level stolons.

SCABIOSA (pincushion flower). Pincushion flowers may die out unless they are planted in a lightly shaded or partially sunny spot. Give them rich soil, moisture, and good drainage. *Scabiosas* bloom for us in the cooler months of late fall, winter, and early spring. *Scabiosa* looks best planted in groups of three or five. Deadhead for rebloom.

S. *caucasica*. Z4–9. This gray-green-leaved pincushion flower has pinnatifid leaves and pale blue, lavender, or white flowers. It grows about 2' tall.

S. *columbaria*. Z3–8. The leaves are hairy and finely divided. Lilac-blue flower heads are borne on 1'–2'-tall stems for months at a time. 'Butterfly Blue' is especially heat and drought tolerant. 'Pink Mist' is a good pink variety for our area.

SCHIZOPHRAGMA *hydrangeoides* (Japanese climbing hydrangea). Z6–9. This woody, deciduous vine climbs to 40', attaching itself to nearby structures by aerial roots. The leaves are 3"–5" long, ovate, and sharply toothed. In summer it bears cymes of greenish-white flowers with showy, creamy white sepals. Grow this climbing hydrangea in part shade in fertile, moist, well-drained soil. The 'Moonlight' cultivar has blue-green foliage, veined dark green.

SCHIZOSTYLIS *coccinea* (kaffir lily). Z7–9. This clump-forming, rhizomatous perennial sends up spikes of red, white, pink, or salmon-colored flowers on 2' stems in the fall. The leaves are erect and sword-shaped. Plant kaffir lily in full sun in rich, moist, well-drained soil.

SCILLA (squill). Although there are members of the squill clan who don't like us, the following species are good bets.

S. *campanulata*. See HYACINTHOIDES *hispanica*.

S. *hispanica*. See HYACINTHOIDES *hispanica*.

S. *peruviana* (Cuban lily, Peruvian lily). Z6–10. Other than Spanish bluebells (*Hyacinthoides hispanica*), the former squill now turned hyacinth, the Cuban lily is probably the best squill for the coastal South. It has wide, evergreen, semierect leaves and produces sizable, ball-shaped clusters of 50–100 purple, star-shaped flowers in late spring. The ball rises up as the flower scape grows to about 10" tall. Plant these large bulbs shallowly (up to their necks) in an area with full to part sun, perfect drainage, and somewhat poor, gritty soil and you will be rewarded with many squill offspring in future years. 'Alba' is a white variety.

S. scilloides (Chinese scilla). Z6–8. Dense racemes of mauve-pink flowers bloom in late summer and fall on 6"–8"-tall stalks. Foliage is grass-like. This scilla is better suited to the cooler parts of the coastal South.

SCUTELLARIA (skullcap). Z5–9. Skullcap enjoys a well-drained, somewhat sandy, slightly alkaline soil.

S. incana. This excellent native puts on a show of blue flowers in summer on a 4'-tall plant that grows well in sun or part shade. A very good skullcap for the coastal South, it attracts butterflies.

S. formosiana 'Royal Purple'. An excellent plant for the coastal South, this 12"–15"-tall spreading groundcover bears deep purple and white flower spikes from spring through frost. This drought-tolerant skullcap takes full sun and perfect drainage.

S. suffrutescens 'Texas Rose'. This low-growing (1'-tall), spreading skullcap bears hot pink, snapdragon-like flowers. Unfortunately, it suffers from our humidity. For best results, give it a spot in full sun and clip it back lightly in the fall.

SEDUM (stonecrop, sedum). Species number in the hundreds. They are fleshy-leaved plants—some with very tiny, mat-forming foliage and some that are larger, upright varieties. In the coastal South, sedums prefer protection from the full, baking sun. Give them fertile, somewhat sandy, well-drained soil. They don't like wet feet, especially in winter. Once established, sedums are relatively drought-tolerant, easygoing plants. If you put down a mulch in the fall, be careful not to cover the basal rosettes or they may rot away from too much moisture retention. Sedums are easy to propagate by breaking off a piece of the plant and planting it in a new location where it will form roots. Use the small sedums in containers, in rock gardens, and to form attractive pools of color in the garden. The larger varieties mix well with other perennials.

S. acre (goldmoss stonecrop). Z3–9. This easy-to-grow creeping sedum has tiny, needle-like, fleshy leaves that form dense mats of bright green. In late spring, tiny, sulfur yellow flowers cover the plant. In the winter garden it provides an attractive, bright green groundcover.

S. albaroseum 'Medio-variegatum'. Z3–9. The attraction of this 2'-tall sedum is the fleshy foliage, which is variegated in tones of cream, yellow, and green. The plant retains a handsome appearance from spring through fall. Greenish-white flower clusters are produced in late summer.

S. 'Autumn Joy'. Z3–9. Because this plant has been so popular, problems have arisen with supply and demand, shortcuts have been taken, and now some 'Autumn Joy' plants may not be exactly what they're supposed to be. If yours doesn't bloom in late summer or fall, you may have an impostor, but it will still probably be a pretty good plant. 'Autumn Joy' has succulent, bluish-green leaves, which start as basal rosettes in spring and grow up to 1'–2' tall. In midsummer, flower clusters form in flat corymbs on top of the stems. The flowers start out pale green, move through a reddish-pink stage, and end up brick red. 'Autumn Joy' is enjoyable in all of its stages. Its colors work well with reds, browns, and plum colors. It is often listed as a hybrid of S. spectabile (see below).

S. 'Frosty Morn'. Z3–9. The fleshy leaves of this 1'–2'-tall sedum have creamy white margins. The late summer flowers are pale pink. Similar in habit to 'Autumn Joy'.

S. kamtschaticum 'Variegatum' (variegated kamtschatka stonecrop). Z3–9. The leaves of this low-growing, 6"-tall groundcover are pale green outlined with cream. The small flowers that cover the plant in summer are yellowish-orange.

S. lineare. Z7–10. This fast-spreading, evergreen sedum grows only 6" tall, with small, star-shaped rosettes and yellow flowers. There is also a variegated type.

S. 'Matrona'. Z3–9. This 2'-tall sedum has dark purple stems with grayish-purple, succulent foliage and pale pink flower heads in late summer.

S. 'Neon'. Z4–9. This 1'–2'-tall sedum has a habit similar to that of 'Autumn Joy'. The summer flowers are a bright, cerise-pink.

S. palmeri (nan plant). Z7–10. Glaucous blue leaves and a sprawling habit distinguish this creeping, evergreen sedum. Deep orange flowers in summer also make it one of the more unusual species.

S. reflexum. Z7–10. This is another mat-forming, evergreen sedum that grows about 10" tall and sports yellow flowers in early summer.

S. sieboldii. Z3–9. The glaucous blue color of the succulent leaves is particularly attractive on this creeping sedum. Leaves at the tips of the stems are margined in pinkish-red. The rosettes of leaves are rounded and compact.

S. spectabile 'Brilliant' (showy stonecrop). Z3–9. This is similar in habit to 'Autumn Joy', with attractive chartreuse foliage and lavender-pink flower heads. It also has a similar pattern of growth and bloom as 'Autumn Joy'. The color of 'Brilliant' mixes well with pink and pastel tones. ('Autumn Joy' works with reds, browns, and plum colors.)

S. spurium (two-row stonecrop). Z3–8. This low-grower does best in the cooler parts of the coastal South. Purple- and red-leaved forms, such as 'Dragon's Blood' and 'Red Carpet', perform better in the cooler weather of spring and fall. During the hot, humid summer, they may revert to green, or they may disappear completely.

S. stoloniferum. Z7–10. An evergreen, mat-forming groundcover with pink flowers, this sedum survives well in the coastal South.

SELAGINELLA (club moss). It's nice to walk through the garden and realize that you've got something growing there that an observant triceratops might recognize. Give these prehistoric fern relatives a partially sunny or shady spot with rich, moist soil and they will provide an attractive evergreen presence. They work in rock gardens or as a groundcover.

S. braunii (arborvitae fern, Chinese lace fern, dwarf cedar fern, moss fern). Z7b–10. This 10"-tall, rhizomatous, creeping evergreen looks ferny but isn't technically a fern. It has dark green, lacy foliage resembling that of an arborvitae or cedar that takes on something of a burgundy cast in winter. Also known as *S. pallescens*.

S. kraussiana 'Aurea' (spreading golden clubmoss, golden Irish moss, trailing spikemoss). Z8–10. This low-growing, mat-forming groundcover retains its bright golden color year-round. Foliage looks like miniature branches of a fir tree.

S. uncinata (peacock moss). Z6–10. This 6"-tall, evergreen, metallic blue-green groundcover spreads via trailing, rooting stems. The color is at its peak in spring.

SEMPERVIVUM tectorum (hen and chicks). Z4–9. This mat-forming, succulent, evergreen perennial is a southern classic for rock gardens, containers, and raised beds. However, it is not necessarily easy to grow. With full sun and perfect drainage, its tight, gray-green, basal rosettes tinged with red (hens) will send out small offset clusters (chicks). In summer, reddish flower clusters are borne on 2'-high stalks. The hens die away after sending up blooms, but the chicks carry on. There are many named cultivars. Also known as *Echeveria secunda*.

SENECIO (senecio)—With many hundreds of species spread all over the world, this genus includes the very well known, lacy-leaved dusty miller (*S. cineraria*), a silvery-white plant that mingles well. In mild winters dusty miller may be perennial here. All senecios can get quite ratty looking by the end of the summer and benefit from being pinched back now and then to keep them bushy. The following senecios need dead-dry (perfectly drained) spots in full sun and poor soil to do their best. For this reason, they make good beach plants.

S. leucostachys (sea ragwort). Z8–10. This 2'–4'-tall senecio has especially attractive, deeply incised, whitish-gray foliage. Also known as *S. vira-vira*.

S. tomentosus. Z3–9. This 2'–3'-tall plant has grayish-white, woolly leaves and stems. Yellow flowers with orange centers appear in summer.

SETCRESEA pallida 'Purple Heart'. *See* **TRADESCANTIA** *pallida 'Purpurea'.*

SILENE regia (royal catchfly). Z5–9. This is a southeastern native that does very well for us, sending up many vibrant, reddish-orange flowers on 2'–4'-tall stalks in late summer. Plant in full to part sun in a dry spot.

SOLANUM (potato vine, Jerusalem cherry). Potatoes and eggplant are two recognizable members of this plant genus. There are some ornamental relatives as well.

S. crispum 'Glasnevin' (Chilean potato vine). Z9–10. This woody vine grows 20' high. In late summer it is clothed with lovely, dark blue flowers with prominent yellow stamens.

S. jasminoides (potato vine). Z8–10. This semi-evergreen vine grows 15'–30' high. It prefers a position in full sun to part shade and rich, well-drained soil. Clusters of white, star-shaped flowers with prominent yellow stamens appear in spring and summer.

S. seaforthianum (St. Vincent lilac). Z9–10. This semievergreen vine grows to 20' with handsome, dark green foliage. In summer it bears pendent flower panicles of sky blue starflowers followed by red berries. It is somewhat tender and should be given a protected spot and a heavy winter mulch. There are pink and white varieties as well.

S. pseudocapsicum (Jerusalem cherry, Christmas cherry). Z8–10. This bushy evergreen subshrub (1'–1½'-tall) is valued for its neat habit, glossy green foliage, and decorative rounded fruits. The fruits, which follow the white, star-shaped summer flowers, remain on the plant through fall and winter. Fruit colors may be yellow, red, or reddish-orange. The variegated kind even has variegated berries! Jerusalem cherry makes an excellent border or edging plant. It prefers full to part sun and fertile, moist, well-drained soil. Note: The fruits cause severe discomfort if ingested.

SOLIDAGO (goldenrod). Before you turn up your nose, you need to know that this much maligned plant does not cause hay fever. Ragweed, which hides in and around goldenrod, is the true culprit. Goldenrod uses the whole summer to grow taller and taller before it puts on its fall flower display. Sometimes by this point it has become floppy, but it makes a nice splash of color at a time when color is appreciated. Plant goldenrod in full sun to light shade with ample moisture and good drainage. Don't give it rich soil or you may get more leaf than flower.

S. odora (sweet goldenrod, scented goldenrod). Z3–9. The foliage of this 3'–4'-tall goldenrod smells like anise. It can be used as a substitute for tarragon. Showy yellow flowers are borne in panicles in late summer.

S. rugosa 'Fireworks' (rough-leaf goldenrod). Z5–9. This native goldenrod is particularly useful because it grows only 3' tall and begins blooming in July, with arching sprays of bright yellow for up to six weeks in a row. This butterfly attractant seems to stay healthier than some of its relatives. It spreads by rhizomes to form good-sized clumps where it is happy, but it is not invasive.

S. sempervirens (seaside goldenrod). Z6–9. As its common name suggests, this goldenrod tolerates sandy soil and salt spray. The dense yellow flower racemes appear on 4'–6'-tall stalks in the fall.

S. sphaecelata 'Golden Fleece'. Z4–9. This popular dwarf goldenrod grows to little over a foot high and produces drooping, warm-yellow-colored panicles in late summer and fall.

SPIGELIA marilandica (Indian pink). Z5–10. This 1'–2'-tall southeastern native produces lovely, tubular red flowers with pale yellow throats in the late spring and early summer. The leaves are broad and spear-shaped. It prefers part shade and a rich, moist, well-drained soil.

STACHYS byzantina 'Countess Helen von Stein' or **'Big Ears'** (lamb's ears). Z4–10. Although this variety of lamb's ears is not as silvery gray as the species, it has the advantage of tolerating our hot, humid summers better. As the common name suggests, its foliage is larger than that of the species. It grows 8"–10" tall, forming a dense mat with the same woolly haired texture as the species. Grown primarily for its foliage, it doesn't produce many flowers. Plant in full sun in slightly sandy soil with absolutely perfect drainage.

STACHYTARPHETA jamaicensis (porterweed). Z9–11. This tender perennial can be used as an annual in cooler parts of the coastal South, where it will reseed itself freely. It grows 2'–3' tall with dark green, wrinkled, toothed leaves. In summer and fall it produces thin, wavy spikes of rich, deep blue flowers. Give it a spot in part sun or light shade. Some gardeners consider this plant an invasive, weedy pest, not suited to the perennial garden; others like it. In any case, butterflies appreciate it.

STEMODIA tomentosa (woolly stemodia). Z8–10. This woolly, grayish-white-leaved, perennial groundcover is extremely heat and drought tolerant. Growing only about 4" high, it will spread rapidly in a sunny, dry spot. Small blue flowers appear in late summer and fall. This is a great beach plant.

STERNBERGIA lutea (autumn daffodil). Z7–9. The small, bright yellow flowers of this bulbous perennial grow atop 6" stems. They don't actually resemble daffodils, but rather crocuses. These may be the "lilies of the field" referred to in the Bible. Grow these bulbs in full sun and fertile, perfectly drained soil. They will form large colonies where happy.

STIGMAPHYLLON ciliatum (orchid vine, butterfly vine, fringed Amazon vine). Z8–10. This semi-evergreen, twining vine grows 20'–30' tall in full sun or part shade and rich, acidic soil. The heart-shaped, toothed leaves are complemented by clusters of bright yellow, orchid-like flowers in late summer and fall. The seedpods that follow are shaped like butterflies, hence the common name. Give this vine a protected spot and a good winter mulch.

STIPA (feather grass, needle grass). These grasses are appreciated for the way they move in the wind and for the needle-like "awns" at the base of each flower that give the flower stalks an airy, wand-like feeling. For best results, plant feather grass in full sun and well-drained soil.

S. gigantea (giant needle grass, giant feather grass). Z7–10. The panicles of golden brown flowers appear on 6' stems in June. This *Stipa* forms a fountain of long, fine, blue-gray leaves at the base. A great see-through plant

S. tenuissima (Mexican feather grass). Z7–10. This lower growing (to 18" tall) needle grass has extremely fine, bright green foliage that moves with the breezes. In early summer chartreuse flowers appear with the distinctive awns that sparkle when they catch the sunlight. This grass self-sows with some abandon.

STOKESIA laevis (Stokes' aster). Z5–9. This native wildflower has been hybridized into many good garden varieties. It grows 1'–2' tall, producing lacy blue flowers for several weeks in early summer. *Stokesia* does well here in part sun in very well drained soil, where it will form goodly clumps.

It also lasts a long time as a cut flower. Cultivars: 'Alba'—15"-high with white flowers; 'Blue Danube'—18"-high evergreen with lavender-blue flowers; 'Mary Gregory'—1'-tall, butter yellow native that blooms throughout the summer; 'Purple Parasols'—dark purple flowers on a 15"-tall plant

STROBILANTHES dyerianus (Persian shield). Z8–10. This shade-loving perennial is grown for the electric-purple-and-silver cast of its foliage—a very dramatic addition to a dark, shady spot. It can reach 4' in height and become somewhat bush-like. Give it fertile, well-drained soil and keep it moist. Direct sunshine will make this plant wilt badly.

TAGETES (perennial marigold). In addition to the ubiquitous annual marigold, we can grow two perennial species. Give them full, baking sun or very light shade and perfect drainage.

T. lemonnii (shrub marigold, citrus marigold). Z8–10. This prolific bloomer takes full sun and well-drained soil. The foliage is lemon-scented, hence the name. The orange flowers appear in late fall and may continue through the winter and into spring if the weather is not too severe. You may want to keep this plant clipped back so it doesn't get out of hand. It normally grows 4' tall by 4' wide.

T. lucida (Mexican mint marigold, Mexican tarragon). Z7–10. This low-growing, 2'-tall perennial is often used as a substitute for French tarragon, which doesn't do particularly well in our climate. Mexican tarragon loves our heat and humidity and produces orangy-yellow flowers in the fall. 'Sweetie' grows 15" high with a stronger tarragon flavor than the species.

TANACETUM parthenium (feverfew). Z4–9. This 1'–2'-tall woody perennial is covered with white daisies in summer. It demands a position in full sun with somewhat sandy soil. Drainage must be perfect, as it abhors wet feet. The chartreuse-leaved cultivar 'Aureum' produces pale yellow daisies. A number of cultivars bear white or yellow pom-pom flowers. Feverfew self-sows readily.

TECOMA jasminoides. *See* PANDOREA *jasminoides.*

TECOMARIA capensis (Cape honeysuckle). Z8b–10. This somewhat tender evergreen perennial is a good choice for the warmer parts of the coastal South, including seashore locations. It can either be cut back and used as a 6'-round shrub or allowed to grow into a 25'-tall vine. In late summer and fall it is smothered with clusters of bright orange-red tubular flowers that attract hummingbirds. Give Cape honeysuckle a position in full sun or light shade. It can tolerate wet or dry conditions.

TETRAPANEX papyriferus (rice paper plant). Z8–10. This southern classic is used as an accent plant in a spot where its large, dramatic foliage and imposing silhouette can best be appreciated. In frost-free areas it will grow to 15' and remain evergreen, but in Zone 8 it is deciduous and grows only to about 6'. It is not fussy. It will grow in sun or part shade, in moist or regular soil. The deeply lobed leaves are gray-green on top and felted white underneath. In late fall and early winter, creamy white flower spikes appear. The pith is used in Asia to make rice paper. Rice paper plant spreads a great distance by suckering.

TEUCRIUM fruticans (silver germander, shrubby germander). Z8–10. This woody subshrub has tiny, whitish, woolly new shoots and aromatic, evergray leaves clothed in white fuzz on the undersides. Although its main bloom season is summer and fall, this germander often gives us the welcome gift of tiny, lavender-blue flowers in the dead of winter when not much else is going on. It grows to about 2' tall and can be clipped in the spring if it gets out of shape. Plant it in full sun with perfect drainage.

THALICTRUM aquilegifolium (meadow rue). Z5–9. The glaucous blue foliage of this plant resembles columbine foliage so closely that it's hard to tell them apart if you're just looking at the basal leaves. It grows 3'–5' tall, producing wands of lavender flower panicles in late spring. Give it part shade and sandy, well-drained soil. It will spread by self-sowing.

THELYPTERIS kunthii (Southern shield fern). Z7–9. Arguably the best fern for the coastal South, the Southern shield fern sends up stately, light green, arching, triangular fronds 3'–5' in length, which set off the darker greens of the shady garden very well. Southern shield fern spreads rapidly by underground stolons to form handsome colonies. The entire effect is airy and graceful.

THERMOPSIS caroliniana (Carolina lupine, Southern lupine). Z6–9. This native perennial is not a lupine but is close enough in terms of what it adds to the garden. In April, *Thermopsis* bears erect racemes of pale yellow, lupinesque flowers on 3'–4'-tall plants. This clump former will become more floriferous each year in full to part sun in well-drained soil. Cut the foliage back a month after flowering. It dislikes being moved.

THRYALLIS glauca. *See* GALPHIMIA *glauca.*

THUNBERGIA. These tender, twining vines or trailing groundcovers need a position in full sun to very light shade with rich, moist, well-drained soil. The flowers are wonderful and interesting. In the lower coastal South they can be grown as perennials.

T. alata (black-eyed Susan vine, clock vine). Annual. This vine is a treat from midsummer through fall, when it is covered with black-eyed Susan flowers—flared tubes of pale yellow, gold, or white with dark eyes. It is easy to grow from seed sown in spring and may live through mild winters or reseed itself. It grows about 6' tall and can be used in containers.

T. grandiflora (sky vine, Bengal trumpet vine). Z9b–10. From late summer through fall this spectacular vine is clothed with 2'-long pendent clusters of glorious, sky blue, flared trumpet flowers with yellow throats, each individual bloom 3" across. It grows 10'–20' tall and prefers rich soil with ample moisture all summer long. In the warmest parts of the coastal South it will be perennial. Elsewhere, gardeners can try growing it as an annual but may not have success. (It normally flowers only after the second year.)

THYMUS (thyme). This herb has been grown for hundreds of years as a seasoning and a medicinal remedy. Unfortunately it doesn't do as well in our heat and humidity as it does farther north, but that doesn't stop people from growing it. It requires full sun and perfect drainage and even given these conditions may disappear in midsummer. The woody stems are prostrate and covered with tiny leaves. Creeping thyme is often used between paving stones and benefits from being cut back on a regular basis. There are lemon thymes (*T. citriodorus*), woolly thymes (*T. pseudolanuginosus*), and a number of wild thymes (*T. serphyllum*). Look for gold-, silver-, and cream-edged foliage. Flowers can be violet-blue, pink, or white.

TIBOUCHINA urvilleana (princess flower). Z8b–10. This somewhat tender perennial shrub with hairy, ovate leaves bears dramatic panicles of dark purple, saucer-shaped flowers in late summer and fall. It can grow up to 10' tall in the warmest parts of the coastal South but will be considerably smaller farther north. Give it full sun, moist fertile soil, and regular fertilization. Protect in winter with a heavy mulch. The cultivar 'Athens Blue' is an improved version that blooms earlier and longer than the species. The species *T. grandifolia* is grown for the large size of its velvety leaves. *T. urvilleana* is also known as *T. semidecandra*.

TITHONIA rotundifolia (tithonia, Mexican sunflower). Annual. Orange or orangy-red daisy flowers appear on 3'–6'-tall stems from midsummer through fall. The shorter, 4'-tall cultivar 'Torch' has near-red flowers. The smallest, most compact cultivars are 'Sundance' and 'Goldfinger'. Grow tithonia in full sun and well-drained, poor soil. When using tithonia as a cut flower, sear the stem first. Tithonia is a good butterfly and hummingbird attractant. It tolerates drought well and self-sows readily.

TOVARA virginiana 'Painter's Palette' (tovara). Z4–8. This fast-spreading groundcover is valued for its showy foliage. The cream-colored, ovate leaves are splotched with light green and pink and have a reddish-black chevron near the base. Spikes of tiny electric-red flowers appear in late summer and fall. Give tovara a shady spot in moist or regular soil. It grows about 18" tall. This plant can easily become invasive, so keep a careful watch on it. Also known as *Polygonum virginianum*.

TRACHELOSPERMUM (jasmine). Two *Trachelospermum* vines grow very well in the coastal South and can be counted on for a reliable, evergreen presence. People sometimes confuse these jasmines with Carolina jessamine (*Gelsemium sempervirens*), an excellent spring-blooming vine. There are also jasmines in the genus *Jasminum*. Plant *Trachelospermum* in full sun to part shade in well-drained soil.

T. asiaticum (Asiatic jasmine). Z8–10. This glossy-leaved, woody evergreen perennial can be used as a groundcover or a climbing vine, but it will bloom only when climbing. The leaves are small and handsome, and the summer flowers are creamy white, aging to yellow. The variegated type has attractive cream-and-pale-green leaves.

T. jasminoides (Confederate jasmine). Z8–10. This much beloved, woody evergreen vine has glossy foliage slightly larger than that of the Asiatic jasmine and is smothered in fragrant, white, star-shaped flowers in early summer.

TRACHYCARPUS fortunei (windmill palm). Z8–11. This palm, growing on a single 30'–40'-tall trunk makes a good specimen or accent plant. The long-stalked, fan-shaped, deeply divided leaves are borne in a cluster at the top of the narrow trunk. Fans are 1'–3' across. In early summer, pendent clusters of yellow flowers emerge, followed by small, blue-black fruits. The windmill palm will grow in full sun or part shade in rich, well-drained soil.

TRADESCANTIA (spiderwort). This is one of the easiest of all perennials to grow. The flowers are not particularly dramatic, but they make a nice addition to a sunny or partially sunny border.

T. pallida 'Purpurea' (purple heart). Z7b–10. Either you like how this plant looks or you don't. One thing we could probably all agree on is that its location should be carefully chosen, to place it where its very intense, wine-red foliage will complement and not fight with the coloration around it. If you need a vibrant, red-plum colored, sprawling groundcover about 6"–12" tall, this will do the trick. Small lavender flowers appear in early summer. Although this plant is technically herbaceous, it will often persist all year round in our climate. Plant in full to part sun in well-drained soil. Also known as *Setcresea pallida* 'Purple Heart'.

T. virginiana (spiderwort). Z4–9. This native is a simple but useful perennial for the mixed border. It is an easy, clump-forming plant, which can be divided every few years. The somewhat lax, branching stems grow 1'–2' tall, bearing terminal cymes of small, three-petaled flowers for several weeks beginning in early summer. There are cultivars available in shades of lavender, dark purple, pink, red, and white. Plant spiderwort in full to part sun in moist, fertile soil. Cut the plants back for a possible rebloom in fall. Also known as *T.* 'Andersonia Group'.

TRICYRTIS (toad lily). Toad lilies are recognizable for their arching stems with alternate, lanceolate leaves and their orchid-like flowers in late summer and early autumn. These rhizomatous or stoloniferous perennials prefer rich, moist, well-drained soil and bloom best in partial shade.

T. formosana (Formosa toad lily). Z4–9. Funnel-shaped, pinkish-white flowers spotted red on the inside appear on these 1'–2'-tall plants from late summer until frost. Where they are happy, plants will form a large colony by spreading stoloniferous roots. Pure white and lavender cultivars are also available.

T. hirta (common toad lily). Z4–9. This hairy-leaved toad lily grows 2'–3' tall with arching stems. The pale purple flowers are splotched dark purple and appear in early fall.

TRILLIUM (trillium, wakerobin, wood lily). Trilliums are not naturally suited to the coastal South, preferring cooler winters. However, the following species may work for us. Give them rich, moist, well-drained soil in part shade. Trilliums are deeply attached to the number three: three whorled leaves, three petals, and three sepals.

T. catesbaei (rosy wakerobin). Z7–9. This is a southeastern native with wavy-edged leaves and

pale-to-deep-pink-colored flowers that hide under the leaves in spring and summer. The flower petals and sepals are reflexed.

T. cernuum (nodding trillium). Z6–9. Pale pink, recurved flowers with prominent purple stamens and red ovaries appear on 2'-long stalks beneath diamond-shaped green leaves in spring.

T. cuneatum (whippoorwill flower). Z6–9. In spring, stalkless, dark maroon flowers sit atop rounded green leaves speckled with silver.

T. erectum (purple trillium). Z4–9. Deep purple-red flowers are borne on erect 20"-tall stalks in spring. Flowers are occasionally white or yellow.

T. underwoodii (underwoods trillium). Z5–10. This is another southeastern native trillium. The foliage bears an unusual checkerboard pattern in various shades of green. The dark purple flowers are borne on 8"-tall stems in spring.

TULBAGHIA violacea (society garlic). Z8–10. Despite their common name, these rhizomatous plants are not really any kind of garlic. They got their name because of the smell of their foliage when crushed. The narrow, strappy, blue-green foliage stays presentable all year round. Lilac-colored umbels appear atop 15" stems from summer through fall, blending well with other plants. Plant society garlic in full to part sun in well-drained soil. These bulbous plants will form sizable clumps where they are happy. 'Variegata' has cream-striped leaves that lend an evergray presence to the winter garden.

VERBENA (vervain, verbena). This genus gives us many good species for our gardens. All verbena asks is impeccable drainage and full, baking sun. Water it during periods of drought.

V. bonariensis (tall verbena). Z6–10. This 3'–5'-tall verbena bears tiny purple flower panicles all summer long and into fall. It grows taller in rich soil and may be cut back to form a more bushy plant. If left to grow tall, it makes a nice see-through addition to the garden—especially if several are planted together. The bad news is that it almost always develops an unsightly mildew, which affects its appearance but not its vigor.

V. canadensis (rose verbena). Z8–10. If you can't think of anything else to plant in a dry sunny location, by all means try 'Homestead Purple' for a foolproof plant that will flower all-summer long. Many of the other cultivars are good too. The species rose verbena is a native clump-former that roots where the procumbent stems meet the ground. Flowers appear profusely all summer long on short, dense spikes. Colors include purple, violet, red, pink, white, and bicolor combinations. Recommended varieties: 'Abbeville'—a vigorous cultivar with lavender-colored flowers that bloom best in spring; 'Homestead Purple'—perhaps the easiest and most vigorous of all the cultivars, it spreads out where it's happy, its deep electric-purple flowers blooming nonstop from late spring through fall; 'Lavender Lace'—a pale lavender cultivar that stands up well to the heat.

V. rigida (tuber vervain). Z7–10. Here is a heat- and humidity-tolerant verbena for the coastal South that flowers nonstop from early summer until frost. The deep mauve flowers are borne on 2'-tall stems, giving it an appearance similar to *V. bonariensis* only shorter. 'Flame' is a vigorous, red-flowered dwarf variety that grows only 6" tall. 'Polaris' is a clump former that bears silvery-blue flower corymbs atop 2'-tall plants.

V. tenuisecta (moss verbena, cutleaf verbena). Z7–10. This lacy-foliaged verbena grows 8"–12" tall and is covered with spikes of tiny lilac-colored flowers from late spring until frost. Deadhead to keep the flowers coming on this drought- and heat-tolerant profuse bloomer. The cutleaf verbenas are hybrids of *V. tenuisecta* and are available in shades of lavender, purple, pink, red-purple, and white. These plants are generally evergreen in mild winters.

VERNONIA (ironweed). These are back-of-the-border plants that add color to the fall garden. Grow them in sun or part shade in moist or wet, fertile soil. Ironweed will become drought tolerant once established.

V. altissima (giant ironweed). Z5–9. As its name suggests, this native ironweed grows very tall—8'–10' if given its druthers. From late summer through fall the plant produces 1'-wide, purple-blue flower heads on top of rigid stems.

V. noveboracensis (New York ironweed). Z5–9. This drought-tolerant native grows to about 5' tall, producing large, loose cymes of tubular, red-purple flowers in late summer and fall. It can be cut back repeatedly during the summer to make it more bushy.

VERONICA spicata (spike speedwell). Z3–8. Probably the very best veronica for the coastal South, spike speedwell is a mat former that roots where the stems touch the ground. From early to late summer, dense, triangular racemes of starry, bright blue flowers rise 1' high. There are white, pink, and purple cultivars available as well. Some cultivars have furry silver foliage that contrasts well with the flowers. In general, veronicas don't tolerate heat and humidity well, so they will fare better in the cooler parts of the coastal South. Give them full to part sun, fertile, moist soil, and perfect drainage.

VINCA (periwinkle, vinca). We are lucky to be able to grow variegated *Vinca major* as a year-round evergreen while in other parts of the country it is used primarily to fill in among annuals in summer containers. It makes a nice groundcover in a shady area and softens winter containers with its graceful cascades of creamy-margined leaves. Plant all vincas in part sun to full shade in rich, moist soil. They are carefree plants that need only trimming or yanking up now and then to keep them from wandering where you don't want them.

V. major (large periwinkle). Z7–11. This popular plant sets down roots where its stem touches the ground and can cover a sizable area easily. In winter and spring, lovely, funnel-shaped lilac-colored flowers complement the foliage. The best-known variegated form is *V. variegata*, but there are others with interesting coloration as well.

V. minor (common periwinkle). Z4–9. This is similar in almost every way to *V. major* except that leaves and flowers are on a smaller scale. Another tough plant.

V. rosea. See **CATHARANTHUS *roseus*.**

VIOLA (pansy, violet). Some of the true perennial violets will persist and establish colonies even in the face of our hot summers. They need a shady spot in rich, well-drained soil where they will colonize slowly to make a groundcover. They dislike wet feet in winter. Pansies and Johnny-jump-ups prefer a position in full to part sun.

V. cornuta (horned violet, tufted violet, viola). Z7–9. These 6"–8"-tall rhizomatous perennials are reputed to be able to stand our hot summers. They bloom in the winter and early spring. If you cut them back, you may also get a fall bloom. The little spurred violet flowers bloom in just that color. White, pink, and yellow forms are also available. The variety *V. cornuta* var. *lilacina* is especially good for our area.

V. cucullata (marsh blue violet). Z8–9. These rhizomatous natives are known self-seeders. The solitary, violet-colored, spurred flowers are held above the foliage on 3"–6"-long stems. White and pink varieties are available. Many gardeners consider this violet to be an invasive weed. Also known as *V. obliqua*.

V. hederacea (Australian violet, ivy-leaved violet). Z8–9. This 4"-tall, mat-forming, stoloniferous violet bears up well in the coastal South. The long-blooming flowers may be white, pale violet-blue, deep violet, or white splotched with purple. It works well as an edging plant, a shady ground-cover, or in containers.

V. odorata (sweet violet). Z6–9. These 8"-tall rhizomatous perennials are the violets grown by the perfume industry for their scent. They have a long and distinguished history as prized flowers of powerful men and women. They bloom in fall through the winter and early spring and spread by runners. They may be dark purple, violet-blue, or white.

V. tricolor (Johnny-jump-ups). Annual. These lovely, delicate cousins of the pansies are grown as cool-weather annuals in the coastal South. As the species name suggests, the flowers of most Johnny-jump-ups have three distinct colors. Often the uppermost petals are a dark royal purple. The other petals may be pale blue, white, or yellow. 'Bowles Black' and 'Molly Sanderson' are two beautiful, solid-black varieties. Plant Johnny-jump-ups in the fall in full to part sun in rich, well-amended soil. Add some slow-release fertilizer at planting time to help flower production. Keep them regularly watered. Some gardeners report that Johnny-jump-ups self-sow; others say not so.

V. wittrockiana (pansy). Annual. Pansies add invaluable color to the winter and spring garden in the coastal South. Growing about 6"–9" high, these annuals are available in a variety of colors, including white, orange, black, yellow, violet-blue, royal purple, copper, pink and red shades, pastels and bicolors. Some have dark, central eyes or bicolored "faces." Pansies work well in the perennial garden or in containers. Plant them in the fall in rich, well-drained soil with some slow-release fertilizer. They need sun or part sun to bloom well. Keep them watered during dry spells.

WASHINGTONIA (fan palm, thread palm, Washington palm, washingtonia). Z8–11. Washingtonias are some of the most reliable, hardy native palms, and they are gigantically tall. Widely planted in the coastal South—especially along streets and boulevards—for their large, dramatic silhouettes, they require full sun, fertile soil, and good drainage.

W. filifera (desert fan palm, Northern washingtonia). This gigantic palm grows 60'–80' tall with long-stalked, fan-shaped, gray-green leaves (5'–10' long) at the top of a thick, columnar trunk. The leaves arch or fan out attractively. As the leaves die, they form an apron of thatch around the trunk. In summer the palm bears 15'-long panicles of creamy white flowers.

W. robusta (thread palm, Mexican Washington palm). With a tapering trunk that is thinner than the trunk of the desert fan palm, the thread palm grows 80'–100' tall. This fast-growing palm produces bright green, deeply divided, fan-shaped leaves that arch out from the top of the trunk. The thatch skirt is similar to that of the desert fan palm. Thread palms make great beach plants.

WEDELIA trilobata (ground daisy). Z8b–10. This trailing groundcover with bright yellow, daisy-like flowers blooms from spring through fall. It roots wherever the stems touch the ground. In the northern reaches of its hardiness, it will die back in winter. It tolerates high heat and humidity and is a good candidate for seashore planting. Give *Wedelia* full sun or light shade and excellent drainage. The cultivar 'Outenreath Gold' has become popular for the gold variegation of its foliage.

WISTERIA (wisteria). Z5–9. There are only a couple of things to keep in mind when growing this well-loved, spring-flowering vine. First, plant only cutting-grown, budded, or grafted plants; those grown from seed may not bloom for years. Secondly, keep your pruning shears handy so that you can keep the plant within a chosen size and shape. Wisterias, especially the Asian varieties, need an extremely strong structure to climb on. They can easily pull down drainpipes, trellises, and other lightweight structures. The Chinese wisteria (*W. sinensis*) is generally the one running loose in the woods. Japanese wisteria (*W. floribunda*), which has been bred into white and pink cultivars as well as the traditional lavender, is another footloose species. The best behaved are Kentucky wisteria (*W. macrostachya*), which comes in shades of violet blue and purple, and American wisteria (*W. frutescens*) in pale lilac or white. Wisteria prefers a position in full sun to part shade with fertile, moist, well-drained soil.

WOODWARDIA (chain fern). *Woodwardia* are very good ferns for the coastal South, tolerating our hot summers well. Their arching, feathery, pinnate fronds are deeply lobed. Give chain ferns a position in full to part shade with rich, organic, moist soil.

W. orientalis (mother fern). Z8–9. This 3'-tall evergreen fern has large, dark green fronds that form a cascading mound. Emerging crosiers are a reddish-bronze color. Mother fern prefers a sandy, well-drained loam. It doesn't like constantly wet feet. Give it a protected spot in full or part shade and a good winter mulch.

W. virginica (Virginia chain fern). Z4–9. This 1'–2'-tall, deciduous native fern can grow in part sun with wet feet or in moist to wet shade. Bronze crosiers unfurl into bright green, deeply cut, arching fronds. Virginia chain fern is rhizomatous and will spread rapidly if given the right conditions.

XANTHOSOMA *sagittifolium* 'Albomarginatum Monstrosum' (Mickey Mouse elephant ear). Z8–10. The trunk of this elephant ear grows 3' tall. From there, 3'-wide, glaucous, creamy-margined, arrow-shaped leaves extend on 3'-long petioles. The name "Mickey Mouse" comes from the end of the leaf, which has an unusual pocket formation and a pointy tip or "tail." Giant spathes and spadixes are produced intermittently, beginning in the summer. Grow in humus-rich, well-drained soil in partial shade. Another striking elephant ear, *X. violaceum*, grows to 8' tall with purple veining on the undersides of the leaves.

YUCCA *filimentosa* (yucca, Adam's needle). Z5–9. This yucca and the many other species that are now becoming available in specialty nurseries are used in the garden mainly for what they add in the way of architecture. The indestructible, upright, sharply pointed leaves add a sense of drama and verticality. In summer, stalks bearing clusters of large white flowers can rise as tall as 10'. Yuccas demand full sun and perfect drainage and do well under beach conditions. There are also some interesting variegated forms with cream-colored or yellow stripes or edging. Yellow-margined 'Bright Edge' and the yellow-centered 'Golden Sword' and 'Garland Gold' are both striking. *Y. aloifolia* (Spanish bayonet) is another southern classic, which grows slowly to 10' with especially spiny leaf tips.

ZEPHYRANTHES (zephyr lily, rain lily, fairy lily). One of the many reasons to be glad we garden in the coastal South is that we can grow these wonderful little bulbous perennials. They are easy and rewarding. A handful of bulbs will produce lovely, flared, funnel-shaped flowers, and each year the colony will increase. The foliage is narrow and grass-like, making these bulbs very unobtrusive minglers. There are zephyr lilies for three out of the four seasons—spring, summer, and fall. Plant them in full sun to light shade in fertile, moist soil with good drainage. (If a particular species tolerates drought, wet feet, or poor soil, it is noted below.)

Z. atamasco (wild Easter lily, Atamasco lily). Z7–10. The Atamasco lily actually prefers boggy soil, but it also grows in woodlands and prairies. It is early blooming, often in April, at the same time as the azaleas. Its 3"-across, white flowers bloom on 10" stems.

Z. candida (white rain lily). Z7–10. These small, silvery white flowers grow in such profusion in Argentina that the country was named after the effect they created. Growing on 8"–12"-tall stems, these flowers have yellowish-orange stamens and rush-like leaves. They bloom prolifically from late summer until frost. They tolerate wet or dry conditions, but not too dry, and perform very well in our climate.

Z. citrina (yellow rain lily). Z8–10. This bright gold rain lily is good for areas of drought and poor soil. It blooms from early summer through fall with the biggest period of bloom in fall. It reseeds itself if left to naturalize.

Z. grandiflora (pink rain lily). Z8–10. Bright pink flowers 3" in diameter appear on 10" stems after it rains in the summer, making these lilies especially endearing. These clump formers enjoy rich soil and appreciate an annual fertilization.

Z. '**Labuffarosea**' (rain lily). Z7–9. This very easy, prolific bloomer sends up large pink or white flowers (2"–3" across) on 6" stems from midsummer to fall.

Z. refugiensis (yellow rain lily). Z7–10. These 10"-tall, bright yellow rain lilies bloom from late summer through fall. Found in ditches all along the Gulf Coast, they survive well in our climate. Clumps will increase over the years.

Z. reginae (Valles yellow rain lily). Z7–10. Bright, golden yellow flowers bloom on 6" stems from summer through frost. These rain lilies multiply quickly in moist, filtered shade.

ZINGIBER (ginger). These dramatic subtropicals are great plants for the coastal South. Give them a spot in part shade with rich, organically amended soil and keep them moist during the growing season, dry in winter. Plant the rhizomes fairly shallowly.

Z. mioga (Japanese ginger). Z8–10. This ginger grows 3' tall and produces pinecone-shaped inflorescences that are a combination of greenish-white bracts and yellow-lipped white flowers. There is also a handsome variegated *Z. mioga*.

Z. rubens (red-spotted ginger). Z8–10. This herbaceous subtropical bears red-spotted, white flowers at ground level, followed by bright red fruit studded with white seeds. A dramatic and interesting plant.

Z. zerumbet (pinecone ginger). Z8–10. This tropical-looking ginger reaches about 6' tall with large, dark green leaves. Cone-like inflorescences appear on short stalks in late summer. The cones start out green and turn bright red and yellow. There is also a variegated species. Pinecone ginger makes a good cut flower.

ZINNIA angustifolia (narrow-leaf zinnia). Annual. These zinnias have narrower leaves and smaller flower heads than other annual zinnias, but they withstand our heat and humidity and periods of drought *much* better. The daisy-like flowers are bright orange, bright yellow, or white. Plant them out after danger of frost. Give them a spot in full sun with rich soil and some slow-release fertilizer. They don't require deadheading. Butterflies will visit them. Also known as *Z. linearis*.

Recommended Reading

*A bee visiting a Mexican sunflower (*Tithonia rotundifolia*).*

Armitage, Allan. *Herbaceous Perennial Plants.* 2d ed. Champaign, Ill.: Stipes, 1997.

Beckett, Kenneth, David Carr, and David Stevens. *The Contained Garden.* New York: Viking Penguin, 1993.

Bender, Steve, ed. *The Southern Living Garden Book.* Birmingham, Ala.: Oxmoor House, 1998.

Bender, Steve, and Felder Rushing. *Passalong Plants.* Chapel Hill: University of North Carolina Press, 1993.

Brickell, Christopher, and Judith D. Zuk, eds. *American Horticultural Society A–Z Encyclopedia of Garden Plants.* New York: DK, 1996.

Brookes, John. *The Complete Gardener.* New York: Random House, 1994.

The Brooklyn Botanic Garden Gardener's Desk Reference. Edited by Janet Martinelli. New York: Henry Holt, 1998.

Cathey, Dr. H. Marc. *Heat-Zone Gardening: How to Choose Plants That Thrive in Your Region's Warmest Weather.* New York: Time-Life Books, 1998.

Clark, Ethne. *Gardening with Foliage Plants.* New York: Abbeville, 1999.

Dirr, Michael. *Manual of Woody Landscape Plants.* 4th ed. Champaign, Ill.: Stipes, 1990.

Druitt, Liz, and Michael Shoup. *Landscaping with Antique Roses.* Newtown, Conn.: Taunton, 1992.

Durse, Ken. *The Collector's Garden.* New York: Clarkson Potter, 1996.

Duncan, Wilbur H., and Marion B. Duncan. *Seaside Plants of the Gulf and Atlantic Coasts.* Washington, D.C.: Smithsonian Institution Press, 1987.

Eck, Joe. *Elements of Garden Design.* New York: Henry Holt, 1996.

Foote, Leonard E., and Samuel B. Jones Jr. *Native Shrubs and Woody Vines of the Southeast.* Portland, Oreg.: Timber, 1989.

Harper, Pamela, and Frederick McGourty. *Perennials.* Tucson, N.Mex.: H. P. Books, 1985.

Heath, Brent, and Becky Heath. *Daffodils for American Gardens.* Washington, D.C.: Elliott & Clark, 1995.

Hill, Madalene. *Southern Herb Growing.* Fredericksburg, Tex.: Shearer, 1987.

Huber, Kathy. *The Texas Flowerscaper.* Salt Lake City: Gibbs & Smith, 1995.

King, Michael, and Piet Oudolf. *Gardening with Grasses.* Portland, Oreg.: Timber, 1998.

Kowalchik, Claire, and William Hylton, eds. *Rodale's Illustrated Encyclopedia of Herbs.* Emmaus, Penn.: Rodale, 1987.

Lacy, Allen. *Gardening with Groundcovers and Vines.* New York: Harper Collins, 1993.

Lawrence, Elizabeth. *A Southern Garden.* Chapel Hill: University of North Carolina Press, 1991.

Ogden, Scott. *Garden Bulbs for the South.* Dallas: Taylor, 1994.

Proctor, Rob, and David Macke. *Herbs in the Garden.* Loveland, Colo.: Interweave, 1997.

Rehder, Henry. *Growing a Beautiful Garden.* Wilmington, N.C.: Banks Channel, 1997.

River Oaks Garden Club. *A Garden Book for Houston.* 4th ed. Houston: Gulf, 1989.

Rose, Graham. *The Romantic Garden.* New York: Penguin, 1988.

Seidenberg, Charlotte. *The New Orleans Garden.* Jackson: University Press of Mississippi, 1990.

Staff of the L. H. Bailey Hortorium, Cornell University. *Hortus Third.* Rev. ed. New York: Macmillan, 1976.

Stuckey, Irene, and Lisa Lofland Gould. *Coastal Plants.* Chapel Hill: University of North Carolina Press, 2000.

Taylor's Guide to Annuals. Boston: Houghton Mifflin, 1986.

Taylor's Guide to Garden Design. Boston: Houghton Mifflin, 1961.

Taylor's Guide to Perennials. Boston: Houghton Mifflin, 1986.

Taylor's Guide to Roses. Boston: Houghton Mifflin, 1995.

Trustees' Garden Club. *Garden Guide to the Lower South.* Savannah, Ga.: Trustees' Garden Club, 1991.

Walker, Jacqueline, *The Subtropical Garden*, Portland, Oreg.: Timber, 1996.

Wasowski, Sally, and Andy Wasowski. *Gardening with Native Plants of the South.* Dallas: Taylor, 1994.

Welch, William. *Antique Roses for the South.* Dallas: Taylor, 1990.

———. *Perennial Garden Color.* Dallas: Taylor, 1989.

Welch, William, and Greg Grant. *The Southern Heirloom Garden.* Dallas: Taylor, 1995.

Wilson, James W. *Landscaping with Herbs.* Boston: Houghton Mifflin, 1995.

Whaley, Emily. *Mrs. Whaley and Her Charleston Garden.* New York: Simon & Schuster, 1997.

Internet Sources for Information & Ordering Plants

Beach sunflower (Helianthus debilis) *blooms along a white picket fence in Seaside, Florida.*

PLANT INFORMATION

American Azalea Society <www.azaleas.org>
American Camellia Society <www.camellias-acs.com>
American Hemerocallis Society <www.daylilies.org>
American Hibiscus Society <www.americanhibiscus.org>
Association of Florida Native Nurseries <www.afnn.org>
Crosby Arboretum <www.msstate.edu/dept/cred/camain>
Florida Native Plant Society <www.fnps.org>
Georgia Native Plant Society <www.gnps.org>
Louisiana Native Plant Society <www.lnps.org>
Mercer Arboretum <www.cp4.hctx.net/mercer>
Native Plant Society of Texas <www.npsot.org>
Society for Louisiana Irises <www.louisianas.org>
South Carolina Native Plant Society <www.clemson.edu/scnativeplants>
Southern Gardening <www.Southerngardening.com>
Southern Living <www.Southern-living.com>
Southern States Online Gardening Information <www.gardenSouth.com>
Virginia Native Plant Society <www.vnps.org>

SOURCES FOR ORDERING PLANTS, SEEDS, BULBS, AND GARDEN ITEMS

The Antique Rose Emporium <www.antiqueroseemporium.com>
Association of Florida Native Nurseries <www.afnn.org>
Brent and Becky's Bulbs <www.brentandbeckysbulbs.com>
Burpee <www.burpee.com>
The Cook's Garden <www.cooksgarden.com>
Dodd & Dodd Native Plant Nursery <www.doddnatives.com>
Fancy Fronds <www.fancyfronds.com>
Gardens Alive! <www.gardensalive.com>
The Gourd Place <www.gourdplace.com>
Heronswood Nursery Ltd. <www.heronswood.com>
The Iris City Gardens <www.iriscitygardens.com>
Lilypons Water Gardens <www.lilypons.com>
Louisiana Nursery <www.durionursery.com>
Niche Gardens <www.nichegdn.com>
Park Seed <www.parkseed.com>
Plant Delights Nursery <www.plantdelights.com>
Sandy Mush Herb Nursery <www.brwm.org/sandymushherbs>
Shepherd's Garden Seeds <www.shepherdseeds.com>
Stokes Tropicals <www.stokestropicals.com>
Thompson & Morgan <www.thompsonmorgan.com>
Wayside Gardens <www.waysidegardens.com>
Woodlanders, Inc. <www.woodlanders.net>
Yucca-Do Nursery <www.yuccado.com>

Index

*The breathtaking white bloom of the Southern magnolia (*Magnolia grandiflora*).*

Note: Boldface page numbers indicate location of color plates.

Salvia, annual (*Salvia splendens*), 62, 85, 155

Salvia azurea, 72, 241

Salvia blepharophylla, 37, 241

Salvia coccinea, 68, 92, 241

Salvia confertifolia, 242

Salvia elegans, 72, 92, 148, 242

Salvia farinacea, 36, **92**, 242

Salvia gregii, 37, 242

Salvia guaranitica, **37**, 68, **81**, 92, **148**, 242

Salvia 'Indigo Spires', 36, **37**, 68, 92, 242

Salvia involucrata 'Bethelii', 72, 242

Salvia koyame, 37, 92, 115, 242

Salvia leucantha, **7**, **71**, **81**, 82, 92, **169**, **172**, 242

Salvia lyrata, 242

Salvia madrensis, 72, 243

Salvia mexicana, 243

Salvia microphylla, 37, 243

Salvia officinalis 'Berggarten', 243

Salvia prunelloides, 243

Salvia puberula, 72, 243

Salvia regla, 72, 243

Salvia sinaloensis, 343

Salvia uliginosa, 37, 68, 92, 243

Salvia vanhouttii, **vi**, 37, **81**, 243

Sanguisorba minor, 148

Santolina spp., 102, 147, 148, 243

Sanvitalia procumbens, 104

Sarracenia spp., 46, 244

Sasanqua (*Camellia sasanqua*), 65, **111**, 112, 201

Satureja montana, 244

Sauromatum venosum, 244

Savory, winter (*Satureja montana*), 244

Saxifraga stolonifera, 113, 244

Scabiosa spp., 15, 244

Scaevola aemula, 156

Scarlet rose mallow. *See* Texas star mallow

Schizophragma hydrangeoides, 58, 131, 244

Schizostylus coccinea, 79, 127, 244

Scilla spp., 26, 110, 244–45

Scuttelaria spp., 45, 245

Sea daffodil (*Panacritum maritimum*), 128, 233

Sea holly (*Eryngium* spp.), 103, 210

Sea lavender (*Limonium latifolium*), 104, 225

Sea oats (*Uniola paniculata*), **140**

Seashore mallow (*Kosteletzkya virginica*), 33, 89, 223

Seaside goldenrod (*Solidago sempervirens*), 104, 247

Sedge (*Carex* spp.), 113, **114**, 142, 202

Sedge, broom (*Andropogon virginicus*), 142, 195

Sedum spp., 14, **31**, 79, **92**, 113, 139, 173, 245–46

Seed, propagation from, 188–89

Selaginella spp., 12, 112, 144, **145**, 246

Self-heal (*Prunella grandiflora*), 113, 139, 237

Sempervivum tectorum, 103, 246

Senecio spp., 102, 246

Senna (*Cassia* spp.), 65–66, **66**, **81**, 85, **172**, 202

Setcresea pallida. *See Tradescantia pallida*

Shade, gardening in, 109–15

Shamrock. *See* Wood sorrel

Shasta daisy (*Chrysanthemum* x *superbum*; *Leucanthemum superbum*), 42, 104, 224

Shower of gold (*Galphimia glauca*), 112, 212

Shrimp plant (*Justicia brandegeana*), 35, 90, 112, 222

Shrimp plant, yellow (*Pachystasis lutea*), 112, 117, **118**, 120, 233

Silene regia, 68, 246

Silk flower (*Abelmoschus* spp.), 62, 105, 191

Silver and gold (*Ajania pacifica*), 193

Skullcap (*Scuttelaria* spp.), 45, 245

Sky vine (*Thunbergia grandiflora*), **76**, 132, 249

Snapdragon (*Antirrhinum majus*), 158

Soapwort (*Saponaria* spp.), 243

Society garlic (*Tulbaghia violacea*), **54**, 69, 93, 128, 250

Soil, 177–79

Soil, gumbo, 178

Soil polymer, 181

Solanum crispum 'Glasnevin', 58, 75, 246

Solanum jasminoides, 58, 75, **132**, 246

Solanum pseudocapiscum, 246

Solanum seaforthianum, 58, 75, 132, 246

Solidago spp., **70**, **85**, 104, 246–47

Solomon's seal (*Polygonatum* spp.), 22, **114**, 115, 237

Southern maidenhair fern (*Adiantum capillus-veneris*), 145, 193

Southern shield fern (*Thelypteris kunthii*), 145, 248

Southern sword fern (*Nephrolepis cordifolia*), 145, 231

Spanish bayonet (*Yucca filamentosa*), **1**, 12, **103**, 116, 253

Spanish bluebell (*Hyacinthoides hispanica*), **21**, 22, 26, 110, 127, 218

Speedwell (*Veronica* spp.), 44, 138, 251

Spider flower (*Cleome hasslerana*), 63, 156

Spider lily, pink (*Lycoris squamigera*), 77, 127, 226

Spider lily, red (*Lycoris radiata*), **77**, 127, 226

Spider lily, yellow (*Lycoris aurea*), 77, 127, 226

Spider lily (*Hymenocallis* spp.), **53**, 89, 110, 128, 218

Spiderwort (*Tradescantia* spp.), 27, 115, 249–50

Spigelia marilandica, 29, 114, 247

Spikemoss, golden trailing (*Selaginella kraussiana* 'Aurea'), 144, **145**, 246

Spiral ginger (*Costus* spp.), 78, 87, 127, 206

Spirea, 107

Spring starflower (*Ipheion uniflorum*), 16, 21, **89**, **125**, **126**, 127, 173, 219

Squill (*Scilla* spp.), 26, 110, 244–45

Stachys byzantina, 14, 69, **102**, 247

Stachytarpheta jamaicensis, 105, 153, 247

Starflower, spring. *See* Spring starflower

Star jasmine (*Solanum jasminoides*), 58, 75, **132**, 246

Star of Bethlehem (*Ornithogalum umbellatum*), 110, 232

Star quamoclit (*Ipomoea coccinea*), 59, 75, 132, 219

Stemodia, woolly (*Stemodia tomentosa*), 103, 247

Stigmaphyllon ciliatum, 75, 132, 247

Stipa spp., 142, 247

Stock (*Mattihola incana*), 19, 158

Stokes' aster (*Stokesia laevis*), **44**, 247–48

Stokesia laevis, **44**, 247–48

Stonecrop (*Sedum* spp.), 14, 31, 79, **92**, 113, 139, 173, 245–46

Strawberry begonia. *See* Strawberry geranium

Strawberry geranium (*Saxifraga stolonifera*), 113, 244

Strawberry, ornamental (*Fragaria* 'Pink Panda'), **15**, 21, 138, 212

Strobilanthes dyeranus, 113, **115**, 248

Subtropical plants, 116–20. *See also* individual plant names

Sugar cane, hardy (*Saccharum arundinaceum*), 142, 241

Summer hyacinth (*Galtonia candicans*), 128

Summer snowflake (*Leucojum aestivum*), **16**, 21, 90, 127, 224

Sundrops (*Oenothera* spp.), 231

Sunflower, annual (*Helianthus annuus*), **101**, **155**, 156

Sunflower, beach (*Helianthus debilis*), **88**, **257**

Sunflower, dune (*Sanvitalia procumbens*), 104

Sunflower, false (*Heliopsis* spp.), 215

Sunflower, Mexican (*Tithonia rotundifolia*), 61, 105, 153, 249, **255**

Sunflower, perennial (*Helianthus* spp.), 71, 88, 104, 215

Sunflower, swamp (*Helianthus angustifolius*), **71**, 215

Swamp gentian (*Sabatia kennedyiana*), 28, 241

Swamp hibiscus. *See* Texas star hibiscus

Swamp jessamine (*Gelsemium rankii*), 130, 213

Swamp spider lily (*Hymenocallis caroliniana*), 218

Swedish ivy (*Plectranthus* spp.), **154**

Sweet cicely (*Myrrhis odorata*), 229

Sweet flag, dwarf golden (*Acorus gramineus* 'Ogon'), 137, 142, 193

Sweet pea, annual (*Lathyrus odoratus*), 19, 158, 223

Sweet pea, perennial (*Lathyrus latifolius*), 132, 223

Sweet pepperbush (*Clethra alnifolia*), 106